# Rights in Security

Legal Topics for Business Studies

# Rights in Security

Legal Topics for Business Studies

L A Sheridan
University College, Cardiff

Collins London and Glasgow

first published 1974
© L A Sheridan
printed in Great Britain
Collins clear-type press
ISBN 0 00 460109

# contents

v

# table of statutes

xviii

xxi

xxiii

## Acts of The Northern Ireland Parliament

# table of cases

xxvii

xliii

l

li

# foreword

A feature of the age in which we live is that the law now touches upon the lives of so many people, at so many points, that it is understandable that a wider interest should be taken in it and that it should no longer be an area of interest exclusively for those who practise, or intend to practise, the law. One important result is that the courses of legal studies, which have for many years been a part of the preparation for many careers in business, in industry, and in the professions, apart from the law itself, have widened and proliferated, as can be seen in the many and varied courses, mainly, though not exclusively, concerned with the commercial aspects of the law, which are now available at centres of higher education of all kinds.

With the provision of such courses arises the need for students' textbooks, designed to supply, primarily, the need of the business student whose studies may be closely confined to isolated branches of the law and who does not have the opportunity to relate those studies to the other aspects of law which are demanded of a student reading for a degree in law, or preparing himself to practise it. These textbooks should seek to impart their instruction in as direct and non-technical a form as possible and should each be self-contained. While they may thus be described as elementary textbooks, each in its chosen field, they should not, by over-simplification, mask the situations of real difficulty which the law has to regulate.

The challenge presented to the authors is thus a formidable one and in this series they are met with the added challenge of presenting to the reader both the English and the Scottish law. That is thought to be a feature of some value for those for whose use the books have been written and it is possible, since the law in regard to commercial matters achieves the closest *rapprochement* between the two systems. Even so, these two legal systems are divergent in places and every effort has been made to direct attention to differences, where they are of moment.

It is hoped that the aim of this series, to give the reader some insight into the working of the Commercial law throughout the United Kingdom as a whole, will be achieved and that it will prove to be both useful and stimulating.

It is gratifying to introduce Professor Sheridan's book on Rights in Security as the first of the Legal Topics series. He has produced a clear and readable account of an extremely technical and exacting subject, but one which is at the same time of great importance in the management of commercial affairs. *JBM*

# preface

This book on security for obligations takes the whole of the United Kingdom as its territorial scope. For the reader interested in only one jurisdiction, it is hoped that sub-headings and similar devices make clear whether any particular proposition relates to the law of England and Wales, of Northern Ireland, of Scotland or of two or all three.

I have been acutely aware of the dangers of writing about selected parts of the law of Scotland without the background of a general training in Scots law. Such blemishes on the finished product as can be put down to that deficiency – or to any other cause – are naturally my responsibility. They would have been more numerous but for the advice and criticism of Professor Bennett Miller and Professor John Halliday, both of the University of Glasgow Faculty of Law. Professor Miller, the general editor of the series to which this book belongs, made many improvements (by no means confined to the law of Scotland). Professor Halliday read the chapters on land and, with meticulous care, emended the treatment of heritable securities in many ways. I am very grateful for their revisions and for the urbane indulgence with which they reacted to what was put before them. *L A Sheridan*

# 1 introduction

Security relates to the obligation to pay money – usually either to repay a loan or to pay a sum due under a contract, such as the price of goods supplied on short-term credit. A creditor seeks security when, for some reason, he is not satisfied that the mere obligation of the debtor to pay him will give him a good enough chance of receiving all the money due to him. The giving of security is the making of an arrangement under which the creditor is to have some rights over and above the right to sue the debtor for the money if it is not duly paid. One very common type of security is to set aside some specific property of the debtor's as an asset the creditor can sell, if the debt is not otherwise paid, satisfying himself out of the proceeds.

**Reasons for Seeking Security**  By far the most usual reason for a creditor wanting security is to avoid the full consequences of his debtor's insolvency. It may well occur to a financier that his debtor, or someone to whom he is contemplating making a loan or granting credit, may at some future material time be unable to pay all his debts. Such an insolvent debtor, if an individual, may be adjudicated bankrupt or, if a limited liability company, may go into liquidation and be wound up. When a person goes bankrupt in England and Wales or Northern Ireland, nearly all the property of which he could have disposed immediately before the bankruptcy vests in an official receiver (or, possibly, later, a trustee in bankruptcy) for the purpose of paying the bankrupt's debts. In Scotland, when a person's estates are sequestrated in bankruptcy, his property is vested in a trustee for that purpose. Since by hypothesis the amount of the debts is greater than the value of the assets that pass into the hands of the official receiver or trustee, creditors who are relying on this distribution (i.e., unsecured creditors) will not usually be paid in full. They may get nothing: the bankrupt may have had no assets. They may get something: if assets have been realised by the official receiver or by the trustee, the proceeds will be divided among the unsecured creditors – generally in proportion to the amounts owed to them, though some classes of creditors, such as the tax authorities, are entitled to payment before ordinary creditors get anything. In bankruptcy, unsecured creditors will get paid in full only in the rare eventuality of the bankrupt later acquiring sufficient property for that purpose. But if some property has been appropriated by the debtor to a particular creditor as security, that property does not become available for paying unsecured creditors on the debtor's bankruptcy except to the extent that its value exceeds the amount of the debt it secures. The liquidation of an insolvent company is similar to the bankruptcy of an individual.

Three examples will illustrate the way these rules work in practice.

**Example 1**  Albert borrows £1,000 from Bernard to buy a car, £17,000 from Cecil to buy a shop and £300 from Donald to pay tradesmen's bills. Albert has also run up an overdraft of £600 at the Eastern Bank, and has spent the £600 on general living expenses. None of Albert's creditors is secured when he goes bankrupt. The trustee in bankruptcy sells the car for £400 and the shop for £12,000. There are no other realisable assets. Creditors to the total value of £18,900 must share £12,400. Bernard will get $\frac{10}{189}$ of this sum, Cecil $\frac{170}{189}$, Donald $\frac{3}{189}$ and the Eastern Bank $\frac{6}{189}$.

**Example 2**  Francis borrows £1,000 from George to buy a caravan, £7,000 from Henry to buy a bungalow and £1,000 from Ian to buy shares in a company. Francis has also run up an overdraft of £600 at the Judicial Bank, and has given the bank security in the form of a mortgage of the shares he bought. When Francis has gone bankrupt, the trustee in bankruptcy sells the caravan for £400 and the bungalow for £7,200. He cannot sell the shares, for they are appropriated to the bank. The Judicial Bank sells the shares for £800. They keep £615 (being their debt of £600 plus the cost of realising their security) and pay £185 to Francis's trustee in bankruptcy. The unsecured creditors to the value of £9,000 must thus share in a fund of £7,785, of which George will get $\frac{1}{9}$, Henry $\frac{7}{9}$ and Ian $\frac{1}{9}$.

**Example 3**  Kenneth borrows £2,000 from Leonard to buy a boat and £10,000 from Michael to buy a house. Kenneth also owes £600 to various shops. The £10,000 owed to Michael is secured by a mortgage on the house bought with that money. When Kenneth goes bankrupt, the trustee in bankruptcy sells the boat for £1,000. He cannot sell the house, as that is appropriated as security for Michael. Michael sells the house for £9,250 and incurs costs of £250 in doing so. Michael keeps the proceeds, which pay his costs and $\frac{9}{10}$ of his debt. He is still owed £1,000 as to which he is unsecured. The trustee in bankruptcy has only £1,000 which must be shared by Leonard ($\frac{5}{9}$), Michael ($\frac{5}{18}$) and the shops ($\frac{1}{6}$ between them).

The secured creditor in examples 2 and 3 has done better than the unsecured creditors because some property, having been appropriated by the debtor as security for one creditor, does not become available for the unsecured creditors. That property is available to the secured creditor to pay himself to the full value of the debt he is owed, or to the full value of the property used as security, whichever is less. If the property used as security is worth more than the debt, the balance goes to the other creditors; if the security is worth less than the debt, the creditor becomes an unsecured creditor as to the deficit.

A second reason for a creditor wanting security is to save himself trouble with an unsatisfactory debtor. The creditor may not doubt his debtor's capacity to pay, but may doubt his willingness. A solvent but refractory debtor may have to be sued by an unsecured creditor, thus causing the latter trouble, expense (which he will mostly get back when awarded costs, but will have to lay out, at least in part, first), nervous tension and delay in receiving payment. The secured but unpaid creditor, on the other hand, to whom some property of the debtor's has been appropriated by way of security (e.g., by mortgage) can generally sell the security himself or by order of the court. In that way he either avoids litigation altogether or, at worst, has a lawsuit for sale of the security, which is much less troublesome than an action to recover an unsecured debt.

Sometimes security is required by law and the lender takes it not because he is worried about his borrower's capacity or readiness to repay, but because the loan could not otherwise be lawfully made. For example, a trustee is not allowed to lend money to individuals without security, unless specifically authorised to do so by the instrument creating the trust; but he is allowed to invest trust money, provided he has obtained and considered proper advice, in mortgages of land in England and Wales or Northern Ireland and in loans on heritable security in Scotland (see the Trustee Investments Act 1961).

**Types of Security**   When a debtor uses some of his property as security for his creditor, the object from the creditor's point of view is that he (the creditor) should be able to use that property to pay himself, which means he must be able to sell it, keep it in lieu of or until payment, or be able to use or let it out so as to produce an income that will pay him off. As a corollary, the debtor must be prevented from using or disposing of that property in any way that will interfere with the creditor's security. There are all kinds of legal mechanism that can be employed for this purpose.

(1)   The whole ownership can be transferred to the creditor with a condition attached. Probably the earliest form of mortgage of land in medieval English law was the conveyance of the title to the land to the mortgagee, subject to a condition *precedent* that the debt be not repaid on the due date. Later practice was to transfer the title to the creditor subject to a condition *subsequent*, i.e., that if the debt was paid on the due date, the land must be reconveyed to the mortgagor. With either of these types of condition, if the debtor (mortgagor) did not repay the debt on the date on which repayment was due, the full ownership of the land passed, free from any condition, to the creditor (mortgagee). These methods of mortgaging land went out of fashion in favour of more sophisticated transactions, and are not permitted in England and Wales since the Law of Property Act 1925 came into force. They can be used for giving security over chattels personal (moveable property) or over incorporeal property such as debts or shares, but that is not the practice. Analogous to that is the Scottish bond and disposition in security, though that was usually redeemable on a fixed period of notice rather than on a specified date. No new securities of this kind can be created in land since the Conveyancing and Feudal Reform (Scotland) Act 1970 came into operation, but this type of transaction can still be used for moveable property.

(2)   The creditor can be given a right of ownership less than that of the debtor. This is technically possible only in the case of land. A freehold owner could give his creditor a lease for, say, 500 years,

4

the lease to be surrendered if the debt was repaid. That was also done in medieval England, but in turn gave way to improved kinds of security and was fairly rare in England and Wales after the fifteenth century, until it became one of the two permissible modes of granting a legal mortgage of land under the Law of Property Act 1925. The mortgage of land by demise or subdemise is not known in Scotland.

(3) The whole ownership can be transferred to the creditor under a contract that he will transfer it back to the debtor if the debt is paid on the due date. This is the basic form of the modern English mortgage of land. Initially, this device suffered from the disadvantage that if the debtor paid his debt and the creditor did not reconvey the land, the debtor's only remedy in a common law court was the recovery of damages for breach of contract. Later, by the fifteenth century, the Court of Chancery would order specific performance of such contracts, i.e., order the creditor to reconvey the land when the debt was paid. Later still, the Court of Chancery would order reconveyance of the land if the debt was paid even *after* the date on which it was due. This type of mortgage developed considerably over the centuries, but is not permitted in England and Wales under the Law of Property Act 1925. It can be used for giving security over chattels personal (moveable property) or over incorporeal property such as debts or shares, but there are also other ways of doing it. The Scottish security by *ex facie* absolute disposition is of this type (except that redemption is usually on notice, not a fixed date). It, too, is confined to moveable subjects now, by virtue of the Conveyancing and Feudal Reform (Scotland) Act 1970, but there will remain in existence for some time securities of this kind created in respect of heritable subjects before the 1970 Act came into force.

(4) The creditor may be given merely possession, not ownership, of the asset by way of security. It stops the owner using or disposing of the thing, and that is an inducement to him to redeem it, but such a pledge or lien does not otherwise assist the pledgee or lienee in enforcing payment, unless he also has the right to keep or sell the article if he is not paid. In English law, the pledge is most commonly used to pawn fairly small moveable articles to a pawnbroker, who has a right of sale if he is not repaid within a certain time.

(5) Documents of title, without which the property cannot, or cannot normally, be dealt with, may be deposited with a creditor by way of security. This is done with title deeds to land, stock and share certificates, bills of lading of goods and similar documents.

5

As with the pledge, this arrangement gives the debtor an incentive to redeem in that he cannot deal with his property, in general, until he gets his documents back, but the better to secure payment the creditor in England and Wales and Northern Ireland is given additional rights. The debtor may expressly give him a power to sell the property when payment is overdue; if not, the creditor may apply to the court for an order of sale.

(6)   The creditor may be given no rights of ownership, no possession, no documents of title, but merely a standing to apply to the court for orders (generally for sale) as to the property if the debt is not otherwise paid. Such a transaction is known as *a charge or lien or hypothec*. The problem with this type of security is that, as the creditor is in possession of neither the property nor documents of title, some way has to be found of preventing the debtor from dealing with the property as if the charge did not exist. In the case of an equitable charge by way of mortgage of land in England and Wales before 1926, the charge was lost if the debtor sold the legal estate in his land to a bona fide purchaser for value without notice of the charge. Hence, the chargee would try to ensure that relevant people would get notice of his interest, by obtaining a deposit of the title deeds, or, if these had already been deposited with another secured creditor, by serving notice on that prior creditor to pass the title deeds on to the later chargee when the earlier debt was paid. The equitable charge was the only type of charge the parties could create by way of security over land in England and Wales before 1926, and it is still possible to use it. But now, under the Law of Property Act 1925 and the Land Charges Act 1972, registration has replaced notice. If the charge is registered in the register of land charges, it binds everybody; while if it is neither so registered nor accompanied by a deposit of title deeds, it binds no one but the debtor. There are no equitable charges in Scotland.

The 1925 legislation also introduced a legal charge by way of mortgage of land, but that gives a chargee all the rights of possession, management and foreclosure, available to any legal mortgagee and is not merely a charge in the sense of a right to apply to the court on non-payment. Similar in effect to that charge by way of legal mortgage are the registered charge over registered land in England and Wales and Northern Ireland and the standard security in respect of heritable subjects in Scotland.

It is usual to call the equitable security a *charge* if it is created expressly by way of security; and to call it a *lien* if it arises by operation of law. An example of the latter type of right is the unpaid vendor's lien: the right of a vendor who has sold land, and transferred it, to apply to the court for appropriate orders if he is not otherwise paid the purchase-money. Equitable charges and liens do not exist in Scotland, but there are legal charges and liens throughout the United Kingdom.

Charges may be created otherwise than as security for a debt owed by the chargor to the chargee. For example, an annuity may be charged on land for the support of a widow while the land itself is left by will to a son.

A charge may be placed on any property, moveable or immoveable, including incorporeal property. When a ship or its cargo is charged, the transaction is sometimes called *hypothecation*. (*Hypotheca* was the term of Roman law, which has passed into the usage of civil-law countries. Shipping law in England and Wales was influenced by Roman law because of the former admiralty jurisdiction of the ecclesiastical courts.) In Scotland, *hypothec* is the term applied to a landlord's security for rent over his tenant's goods.

(7) A floating charge is a special type of security which can be created only by a limited liability company, registered friendly society or (except in Scotland) a farmer. Such an association or farmer can give other types of security, e.g., by mortgaging premises, plant or goodwill. But if it wants to raise money on the security of stock-in-trade, a trading company cannot mortgage or pledge these goods without ceasing to trade in them. The device which allows the creation of security without impeding business is the floating charge. It is a charge on the assets for the time being. As stock is sold in the ordinary course of business, the customer takes items free from the charge; as stock is bought or made, so it becomes subject to the charge. The charge ceases to float and becomes a fixed charge if certain events occur: at that moment, the goods then in stock and other assets (as specified in the charge) become specifically charged in favour of the creditor, whose rights over them to realise his security cannot be over-reached by the company selling them.

**Other Proprietary Rights of Creditors** All the types of security outlined so far share the characteristic of being purposely created by act of the parties. Security for a debt may also arise by operation of law. The most obvious illustration of this is the lien. *A legal lien is the right to retain possession of goods until payment of a debt due in respect of them.* An unpaid repairer of a motor car, for example, has a legal right to detain the car in his custody until the repair bill is paid. Similarly, the unpaid seller of goods who has not yet delivered them has a statutory right under the Sale of Goods Act 1893 to hold on to them until he receives the purchase price. An equitable lien gives no right to possession of the property over which the lien exists, but empowers the lienee to apply to the court for equitable remedies (usually an order for sale or for the appointment of a receiver). Examples of equitable liens (which do not exist in Scotland) are those relating to the purchase-price on sale of property other than goods. An unpaid vendor has a lien over land he has sold; and a purchaser who has paid for land not yet conveyed to him also has a lien.

There are various rights of creditors which serve the same purpose as security, but which do not, strictly speaking, fall into the category of security, and are not dealt with in this book. The following are examples of frequent occurrence.

(1) **Distress** This is the right to seize goods of a wrongdoer and to retain them until, or, in certain instances, in the last resort, to sell them for, payment of a debt. A landlord in England and Wales may distrain for rent overdue, i.e., he may enter on the land and seize chattels belonging to his tenant. (Distress for rent has been replaced in Northern Ireland by a new procedure under the Judgments (Enforcement) Act 1969, while in Scotland sequestration for rent under the landlord's hypothec fulfils an analogous function.)

(2) **Right of entry** or **right of re-entry** An obligation to pay money may be charged on land for any reason. Freehold land may be sold subject to the payment of a perpetual rent to the vendor and his successors. Such a rent is called a *fee farm* rent. It is rare in England and Wales, except in certain areas of south-west and north-west England, but is common in Northern Ireland. The grant may reserve a right of entry to the grantor, on non-payment of rent, and in that event, the grantor may then forfeit the land and retake the freehold estate. Or a right of re-entry may be reserved, which means that the grantor may enter upon the land, not forfeiting the estate but occupying the land and taking the income of it until the arrears of rent have been paid off. In England, a fee farm rent is a rentcharge (though in Northern Ireland it is usually a rent-service i.e., a rent due to a landlord). Another type of rentcharge is that created by a family settlement under which the right to occupy the land goes to a son and the land is charged with an annuity in favour of his widowed mother. (Rights of entry may be reserved in respect

8

of terms of years as well as freehold estates; and for breach of obligations other than obligations to pay money.)

(3) **Hire-purchase: the right to retake goods**  Under a hire-purchase agreement, the title in the goods does not pass to the 'purchaser,' who is in law a hirer, until the last instalment of money has been paid and the hirer has opted to buy the goods. The agreement is usually, in form, one for hire of goods while weekly or monthly payments are made for a stipulated period, with an option given to the hirer to buy the goods for a small sum when he has paid the last instalment. If the hirer defaults in payment of instalments, the owner of the goods may, subject to statutory safeguards and limitations, repossess them. (Similar rights may be reserved under credit-sale and conditional sale agreements.)

**Personal Security**  So far, security has been referred to exclusively in terms of property, and that is its usual meaning. There are other means by which a creditor may seek to render his position more secure than it would be if he had merely the contractual obligation of the debtor to rely on. He may enter into an arrangement by virtue of which, if the debtor does not do so, someone else is liable to pay the debt. This is usually done by guarantee, and a person who guarantees another person's debt is called a surety or guarantor or, in Scotland, a cautioner. A guarantor may be sought not only for repayment of a loan, but also for future possible debts. It is a condition of entry into some trades, businesses or professions (e.g., to become an underwriting member of Lloyd's), that proprietary security, or sureties, or both, be provided for the satisfaction of liabilities that may thereafter be incurred. The idea of suretyship is that, if the principal debtor does not pay, the creditor can sue the surety. Sometimes, for example when a married woman borrows money from a building society to buy a house, the lender requires both real security (in this example, a mortgage of the house) and a guarantor (in this case, if he is in suitable employment, probably the borrower's husband).

There are other ways of providing alternative recourse for a debt besides suretyship. For example, a borrower may get a friend or relative to give the lender a postdated cheque, to be cashed if the borrower does not repay the loan himself. Or a borrower may himself give the lender a postdated bill of exchange; if that is accepted by the third party on whom it is drawn, the third party is liable on it.

**Additional Recourse Against the Debtor** Proprietary and personal security is distinguishable from ancillary obligations undertaken by the debtor. A person under a duty to pay or repay money may do all sorts of things in favour of his creditor which do not amount to security. He may execute a bond for payment, or give an I.O.U. or a promissory note. These devices may make it easier for the creditor to sue the debtor, or provide the creditor with additional means of doing so, but they do not create any rights besides personal recourse against the debtor's general funds. Hence, if the debtor goes bankrupt the creditor must prove as an ordinary creditor and is liable to receive only a dividend: a proportion of what is owed to him.

Even if a debtor assigns property to trustees on trust to pay his debts, the creditors have no proprietary rights. It would be different if the trust were for the payment of a specified amount to a specified person, but a trust for the payment of debts generally passes no beneficial interest in the property to any creditor, and therefore (as the equitable proprietary interest is still in the debtor), the debtor can revoke the trust and claim back any property his trustees have not already distributed to creditors.

The payment of *earnest* falls into the category of transactions that make the payer more likely to perform his obligations but do not alter the creditor's status from that of an ordinary unsecured creditor. It is usual for the purchaser to make such a payment when contracting to buy a house (commonly a deposit of 10% of the purchase price), which does provide some comfort to the vendor in showing the purchaser's seriousness and, usually, in providing a sum in hand which the vendor can retain as compensation if the purchaser, in breach of contract, does not go ahead with the transaction.

**Obligations for Which Security is Usually Given** A person who owes or borrows money does not necessarily give security. Many loans are domestic or between friends, but even commercially money is lent without security, as is the case with large commercial concerns, whose credit is good, when they issue unsecured debenture stock. Many contracts, e.g., contracts of employment, are entered into without security for the financial obligations.

**Borrowing** Probably the most widely experienced occasion for individual borrowing is that of buying a house. The vast majority of people who buy houses do so by borrowing a large proportion of the price from a building society, securing the loan by a mortgage to the society of the house itself. Relief from income tax is granted in respect of the interest on the loan. Sometimes, additional tax advantages may be obtained by mortgaging to the building society a life insurance policy as well, for there is income tax relief in respect of the premiums. The contents of the house, if not paid for in full out of cash resources, are usually acquired by hire-purchase, credit-sale or conditional sale rather than by borrowing.

Secondly, having secured an undertaking from a building society (or bank, employer or other lender) to lend most of the price (commonly four-fifths in the case of a modern house), the purchaser may need to borrow the rest of the price. He may have a temporary need, for example because he is waiting to be paid for another house he is selling, in which case he may get a bridging loan from his bank. Such a loan may be unsecured, or may be secured on other assets, such as investments. Alternatively, the purchaser may need a long-term loan of what he cannot get from a building society, in which case he may be able to persuade his employer or some other lender, such as a finance company, to advance it, perhaps on a second mortgage of the house.

Borrowing may also be necessary or convenient for the purpose of improving a house. Assuming the improvements to enhance the value of it more or less permanently, the money can be borrowed in the same way as the purchase-price, and income tax relief will again be allowed on the interest. Apart from house purchase and improvement, interest on loans for private or domestic purposes does not generally attract relief from income tax, except for interest above £35 a year.

In the commercial world, business premises may be acquired by borrowing, as may working capital, e.g., for the purchase of plant, stock or goodwill. Such a borrowing is likely to be from a merchant bank or joint stock bank or, in the case of a public limited liability company, from the general public. Premises, plant and goodwill are quite likely to be mortgaged to secure the loan. Stock would not be mortgaged, but stock of a limited liability company can be used as security by way of a floating charge. When a limited company borrows money, whether with or without security, it usually issues debentures, or debenture stock, to the lenders or to trustees for the lenders. The raising of working capital by the issue of debentures is different from raising it by a new issue of shares. The former is borrowing; the latter is increasing the nominal capital (i.e., the joint stock owned by the shareholders) of the company and is normally not repayable unless the company is wound up and there are assets available after all debts have been paid. Interest on money employed in a business is deducted from gross profits in the accounts so as to compute the net profit liable to income tax (in the case of a privately-owned business) or corporation tax (in the case of a company). Dividends on shares are paid out of net profits *after* payment of corporation tax.

Just as a trading company may borrow to provide stock and other items necessary for the conduct of its business, so may companies engaged in plying vehicles for hire borrow to buy their vehicles. Purchases of ships are usually financed by borrowing (secured by mortgage of the ship), while aeroplanes are, equally usually, bought out of borrowed money with repayment secured by charge on, or mortgage of, the aircraft. Cars, lorries and taxis are more commonly bought on hire-purchase.

Investments may sometimes be bought out of borrowed money. For that to be worth while for the private investor, he must expect to make more out of dividends (less income tax) or out of capital growth (less capital gains tax), or from a combination of the two, than he will have to pay in interest. That is not likely nowadays, when there is no relief from income tax in respect of the first £35 of annual interest. Consequently, borrowing for private investment is much rarer than it was when there was such tax relief and when there was no capital gains tax. It may happen more frequently again if interest rates come down or if tax relief is restored, and it may occasionally be worth while today if big capital gains are anticipated, especially if the investment can be linked, as it can in the case of some unit trusts, with life insurance (thus attracting tax relief on the premiums). Even now, it is worth while for certain types of professional investor, such as investment trusts, who may mortgage stocks on which they expect capital appreciation so as to borrow money to buy higher yield investments with a fixed income, such as government stocks, or mortgage gilt-edged stocks to buy equities, in either case combining present income and future capital gain. They pay corporation tax on their net profits after deduction of mortgage interest.

Borrowing for general living expenses, or to pay for holidays, may be backed by the giving of security, e.g., by a mortgage of shares. The source of such loans, if not arranged privately, is usually a bank or a moneylender. Both will lend with or without security. Banks will usually allow reliable customers moderate overdrafts without security, but they ask for security when that seems prudent. Interest rates of moneylenders are much higher than those of banks, even when security is provided.

Finally, a debtor may borrow in order to pay off an existing debt. A mortgagor, for example, may redeem one mortgage by borrowing on security of another mortgage of the same property when the first has become repayable or when he can secure a new mortgage on more favourable terms than those of the existing mortgage. Related to this is the common case of a householder who moves, pays off the mortgage on the house he is selling out of the purchase-money, and finances the buying of his new house by mortgaging that.

**Buying on credit**   Buying something on credit is very like borrowing – borrowing from the vendor. In the case of a loan, cash or something representing cash (such as a cheque) changes hands, whereas in a sale on credit that does not occur: the buyer enters into a contract to pay, not to repay.

The sale of goods on credit does not usually involve giving security, at least when it is a retail sale, though in order to open an account at a store, say for monthly settlement, the customer may be required to furnish a guarantor. The acquisition of goods for domestic purposes otherwise than for immediate cash settlement is usually by hire-purchase or on a sale on credit without security. In the case of commercial goods, security will commonly be given. The manufacturer who acquires machinery on credit may well mortgage it, or something else, such as his premises or book debts, to the vendor. The wholesale company may well give the vendor a floating charge. The purchaser of a ship may mortgage it to the vendor. More usually, in these cases, the vendor requires cash, and the purchaser borrows on security from a third party, such as a bank, rather than receiving credit from the vendor. Similarly, the purchaser of land will usually borrow on security from a third party, such as a building society, rather than receive credit from the vendor. However, it may be agreed that the purchase-price, or a proportion of it, is to remain owing, secured by a mortgage to the vendor of the land bought. That is most likely to happen when the land is sold by trustees, the leaving of the price on mortgage being an authorised trustee investment.

**Other contractual money obligations**   It is very unusual to give security for the performance of contractual obligations to pay wages or charges for services (though a lien may arise by operation of law over goods, in respect of which services have been rendered, still in the custody of the creditor) or other obligations to pay. However, any duty to pay may be secured on property, or be the subject of a guarantee. Agents or servants who handle money on behalf of their principals or employers are sometimes required to give security for their duty to account for the money, or to provide sureties.

**Security for non-money obligations**   There is no reason to believe that security is legally confined to the support of a primary obligation to pay money. Since, however, the main remedy in respect of a security is to enforce it by getting money (e.g., by sale of mortgaged property or suing sureties), security for any non-money obligation must be viewed as security for compensation for the non-performance of that other obligation. In practice, one does not come across security for non-money obligations outside the realms of the judicial process. Courts and other authorities, may, for example, require sureties for the release on bail of a person charged with a crime, but the failure of the accused to surrender himself to the court is visited with money penalties. So also, when sureties are required for good behaviour of a person bound over by the court, the failure of that person to keep out of trouble results in financial sanctions on the sureties.

Once a civil obligation of another kind has been converted into a judgment debt, e.g., by the award of damages for breach of contract, the court may make an order charging the defendant's land or shares with the payment of the amount due under the judgment. Such an order by way of enforcement of a judgment has much the same effect, in English law, as an equitable charge created by the defendant in favour of the plaintiff.

**Property Available for Use as Security**   In general, any property may be used to give security. From this must be excluded (if it be properly described as property at all) any right or thing that cannot be disposed of by the owner. So also must money be excluded: that should be used to pay the debt, not to secure it. Moreover, some property which could legally be used as security is unsuitable in fact, for example because there is no ready market for it, because it is of small value, or because (usually in the case of land), the debtor's title is not acceptable to the creditor by reason of incumbrances upon it.

The types of property most usually offered by way of security are:

(*a*) freehold or leasehold estates in land;

(*b*) equitable interests in land under trusts or contracts;

(*c*) rights over somebody else's land such as rent charges, profits à prendre (e.g., mining rights), or mortgages (a mortgage of a mortgage is a sub-mortgage);

(*d*) moveable or personal property, such as jewellery, machinery, stock-in-trade, ships or aircraft and their cargoes;

(*e*) stocks and shares;

(*f*) life insurance policies;

(*g*) 'choses in action,' as they are called in England and Wales and Northern Ireland, or incorporeal moveable property, as it is called in Scotland, i.e., debts and rights to receive sums of money under a contract or an equitable obligation such as a trust;

(*h*) commercial incorporeal property such as goodwill, copyrights and patents.

# 2 land: forms of legal and equitable mortgages and heritable securities

### Legal Mechanisms

**Mortgages in English Common Law**  In England and Wales, before statutory intervention in the nineteenth and twentieth centuries, three main types of transaction had developed by way of mortgaging a freehold or leasehold estate, viz.:

i. conveyance of the estate to the mortgagee subject to a proviso for reconveyance to the mortgagor on redemption, i.e., on the debt being paid off;

ii. the grant of a long or medium-term lease to the mortgagee of a freehold estate, or of a sub-lease to the mortgagee of a leasehold estate, subject to a proviso for cesser of the mortgage term on redemption;

iii. conveyance of the estate on trust for sale, the debt to be paid off out of the proceeds, but no sale actually to take place if the mortgagor redeemed.

Only the first of these was popular and of frequent occurrence.

The proviso for redemption related to the obligation of the mortgagor to repay the loan on a stipulated date. At common law, if he did not repay on that date, the mortgagor ceased to have any right of redemption and the legal estate became the beneficial property of the mortgagee. The Court of Chancery intervened to bring about a different result. By early in the seventeenth century, it was settled Chancery doctrine that, from the moment the legal estate was transferred to the mortgagee, the mortgagor had a corresponding equitable estate called the *equity of redemption*. There were many facets of this equitable estate, one of the most valuable being an *equitable right to redeem* the legal estate after the legal date for redemption had passed. This equitable right to redeem would continue indefinitely, until it was ended by the mortgagee foreclosing or exercising his power of sale or until it was ended by adverse possession or by the legal estate coming into the hands of a bona fide purchaser for value without notice of the existence of the equity of redemption. The evolution of the equity of redemption, embracing the equitable right to redeem, is but one aspect of Chancery intervention in mortgages, but it is the basic one[1] and explains why so much of modern English mortgage law consists either of rules of equity or of statutory adoption of rules of equity.

One of the consequences of the mortgagor conveying his legal estate to the mortgagee was the impossibility of raising further money on mortgaged land by granting another legal mortgage. Since the mortgagor's estate was merely equitable, any subsequent mortgage, too, had to be merely equitable.

**Legal Mortgages in England and Wales Today**  By virtue of the Law of Property Act 1925, sections 85 and 86, the common law form of mortgage by transfer of title to the mortgagee was prohibited and now the only two possible transactions by way of legal mortgage of unregistered land are:

   i.  (*a*) in the case of freehold land, the grant of a lease (usually for 3,000 years) to the mortgagee, subject to a provision for cesser on redemption, or

      (*b*) in the case of leasehold land, the grant of a sub-lease (at least one day shorter than the mortgagor's lease) to the mortgagee, subject to a provision for cesser on redemption;

  ii.  in the case of freehold or leasehold land, a charge by deed expressed to be by way of legal mortgage.

These methods may also be used for registered land, but an alternative is the registered charge in accordance with the Land Registration Act 1925, section 25. This is a charge by deed which becomes effective at law when registered. If a registered owner uses one of the forms of legal mortgage appropriate for unregistered land, the mortgagee may protect himself by caution[2] in a specially prescribed form and in no other way.[3] The mortgage is equitable,

1. See, further, Keeton and Sheridan, *Equity*, pp. 166–71.
2. The registrar may not register any dealing, contrary to a caution lodged with him, without serving notice upon the cautioner, who then has an opportunity to take appropriate steps: Land Registration Act 1925, s. 55.
3. See *Barclays Bank Ltd.* v. *Taylor* [1973] Ch. 63; Jackson (1972) 88 *Law Quarterly Review* 476.

and liable to be over-reached as a minor interest, until the caution is entered. After entering a caution, the mortgagee can have his mortgage registered as a charge with the same priority as the caution. Unless he does, he cannot deal with the land by registered disposition (Land Registration Act 1925, section 106).

In the case of the mortgage by demise or sub-demise, the mortgagee has a legal estate, while the holder of a charge by way of mortgage has not. That makes no difference. By the Law of Property Act 1925, section 87, a chargee by way of legal mortgage has the same protection, powers and remedies as if the mortgage had been by lease or sub-lease, as the case may be. Every first legal mortgagee of unregistered land is entitled to the same documents of title as if the mortgagor's estate had been transferred to him. The position of the registered chargee of registered land is similar. He has all the protection, powers and remedies of a legal mortgagee of unregistered land. He is issued with a charge certificate and the proprietor must surrender his land certificate for retention at the Land Registry until the charge is paid off (Land Registration Act 1925, section 65).

There is no advantage in using the demise or sub-demise rather than the charge. There are advantages in the charge: it is shorter, more realistic, and can be used to mortgage freehold and leasehold land and registered and unregistered land in the same deed.

One consequence of the change of system is that there can be several co-existing legal mortgages of the same land. So long as he can find a lender, the mortgagor can go on creating charges or leases (each longer than the last) by way of mortgage. If he is a lease-holder mortgaging by sub-demise, he must remember to make his first mortgage several days shorter than his own lease if he wants to make further mortgages by sub-demise; otherwise later legal mortgages will have to be by charge.

Any attempt to mortgage land by transferring the title, to the mortgagee or on trust for sale, operates as follows:
  i. in the case of freehold land:
    (a) if a first mortgage, as a grant of a term of 3,000 years;
    (b) if a subsequent mortgage, as a grant of a term one day longer than that of the immediately prior mortgagee;
  ii. in the case of leasehold land:
    (a) if a first mortgage, as a grant of a sub-lease ten days shorter than the mortgagor's lease;
    (b) if a subsequent mortgage, as a grant of a sub-lease one

day longer than that of the immediately prior mortgagee or, if the latter has a sub-lease only one day shorter than the mortgagor's lease, then as a sub-lease the same length as that of the immediately prior mortgagee.

There may be difficulty in recognising whether a transaction by the owner of a legal estate is a mortgage or not. The documents should reflect clearly the intentions of the parties and if they do, all will be well. But sometimes there is a misunderstanding and sometimes there are deliberate attempts to gain an improper advantage. The question generally arises where the transaction is in form an outright transfer of a freehold estate and the transferor tries to redeem, i.e., he claims that the money he got was a loan and that he can get his land back by repaying with interest, while the transferee claims that the money was paid as the purchase-price and he can keep the land. If the deed of transfer is silent, the question is whether there is an equitable right to redeem and the principle of equity is that effect must be given to the true nature of the transaction regardless of its form.

**Example 1**   Arthur is the fee-simple owner of Blackacre, which is worth £8,700. He executes a deed of conveyance of Blackacre to Cyril in fee simple in consideration of a payment of £5,800, and Cyril goes into possession. For five years, Arthur pays Cyril interest at 8% per annum on the £5,800 and then tenders £5,800 to Cyril and asks for Blackacre back. On reading the conveyance to Cyril you would think he had bought Blackacre, and he now relies on the deed for a claim to keep the property. Arthur proves that it was agreed orally between him and Cyril that the transaction was to be a mortgage. The court will hold: (*a*) the conveyance is a mortgage; (*b*) Cyril's claim to keep Blackacre, when he knows that is not the intention, is fraudulent, and therefore the mortgage agreement can be enforced notwithstanding that there was no written evidence as required by the Law of Property Act 1925, section 40; (*c*) the conveyance operates to give Cyril not a fee simple estate but a mortgage term of 3,000 years by virtue of section 85(2) of that Act; (*d*) Arthur can redeem the mortgage, thus putting an end to Cyril's lease.[4]

**Example 2**   Daniel contracts with Edward to buy Greenacre for £8,700, but finds he cannot raise sufficient money to carry out his agreement. Daniel resells Greenacre to Frank, who pays the

---

4. See *Lincoln* v. *Wright* (1859) 4 De G. & J. 16; *Grangeside Properties Ltd.* v. *Collingwoods Securities Ltd.* [1964] 1 W.L.R. 139.

£8,700 to Edward. Greenacre is conveyed to Frank in fee simple by Edward. Daniel goes into possession of Greenacre and pays for its upkeep. Three years later, Daniel offers Frank £8,700 and asks for a conveyance of Greenacre. Frank is willing to convey Greenacre to Daniel but only if he is paid £9,900 and given a right of way over the land. This example differs from the previous one in the following respects: (a) there was no agreement between Daniel and Frank that the arrangement was to be a mortgage rather than a transfer of Daniel's equitable interest under the contract with Edward; (b) the transaction does not look like a loan because the payment by Frank was of the full amount of the purchase price and Daniel paid Frank no interest. The court will hold that the documents are to be given their face value and that Frank was a purchaser, not a mortgagee, from Daniel. Accordingly, Daniel has nothing he can redeem and cannot get Greenacre from Frank unless they can agree on a new contract.[5]

**Legal Mortgages in Northern Ireland Today**   There has been no legislation as to the form of legal mortgage of unregistered land. Such land is therefore usually mortgaged by transferring the legal title of the mortgagor to the mortgagee, subject to a proviso for reconveyance or redemption, as was the case in England before 1926. The long lease is sometimes used for the purpose of mortgaging freehold land held subject to a fee farm rent, a form of landholding which is common in Northern Ireland, and leasehold land is occasionally mortgaged by granting the mortgagee a sub-lease. Registered land is mortgaged by registered charge in accordance with the Land Registration Act 1970, section 41 and schedule 7. The Land Law Working Party[6] recommended the replacement of all other forms of legal mortgage of unregistered land by a simple charge similar to that used for registered land.

**Heritable Securities in Scotland**   The creation of heritable security now depends entirely on the Conveyancing and Feudal Reform (Scotland) Act 1970, as amended by the Redemption of Standard Securities (Scotland) Act 1971. Section 9(1) of the Act of 1970 introduced a new form of heritable security known as a *standard security*, while section 9(3) prohibits the creation of any other form of heritable security. However, section 31 provides for

5. See *Beattie* v. *Jenkinson* [1971] 1 W.L.R. 1419.
6. *Survey of the Land Law of Northern Ireland* (H.M.S.O., 1971), p. 79, para 204.

heritable securities duly recorded in the Register of Sasines before 29th November 1970 to continue to be as valid as they were before, capable of being enforced and dealt with. It will therefore not be until the last of these has been redeemed, or realised, that security over land in Scotland will be confined to the new standard form.

*Old forms of heritable security.* There were three main types of heritable security as follows:

(1) The commonest, known in the case of land held on feudal tenure as a *bond and disposition in security*, was a transfer by the borrower to the lender of the title to the land, the deed of transfer giving the borrower a right of redemption on three months notice (usually to expire on Whitsunday or Martinmas). When leasehold land was given in security in this way, the transaction was known as a *bond and assignation in security*.[7] Such a security (over feudal or leasehold land) could originally be given only by a proprietor who was infeft (i.e., whose title was recorded in the Register of Sasines), but it was later enacted[8] that, provided the lender's grant had been duly recorded, a grant of security by one uninfeft was to become valid as from the subsequent record of the grantor's title. The bond and disposition or assignation in security could make the land stand as security only for an existing debt, or a debt then incurred, specified in the bond.[9]

(2) A variant for securing overdrafts was introduced by statute and is now governed by the Debts Securities (Scotland) Act 1856, section 7. It is in form the same as the bond and disposition or assignation in security, differing only in that it was given to secure an overdraft of fluctuating amount, up to a specified maximum. This type of transaction is known as a *bond of cash credit and disposition* (or *assignation*) *in security*.

(3) The *ex facie absolute* disposition by the debtor to the creditor, there being frequently (but not necessarily) an undertaking, in a separate document (a *back letter* or *back bond*), by the creditor to reconvey the land to the debtor on payment of the debt. This kind

7. See the Registration of Leases (Scotland) Act 1857, s. 4. Security over leases at common law had to be completed by the assignee going into possession: see *Mess* v. *Hay (Sime's Trustee)* (1898) 1 F. (H.L.) 22. See also *Benton* v. *Craig* (1864) 2 M. 1365; *Clark* v. *Liquidators of the West Calder Oil Co.* (1882) 9 R. 1017. Cf. *D. MacPhail & Son* v. *Maclean's Trustees* (1887) 15 R. 47; *Moncrieffe* v. *Ferguson* (1896) 24 R. 47. But under the 1857 Act, a recorded security over a lease for 31 years or more became complete without possession.
8. Conveyancing (Scotland) Act 1924, s. 3, as extended by the Conveyancing Amendment (Scotland) Act 1938, s. 1; as to leasehold land, see also s. 24 of the 1924 Act.
9. See the Bankruptcy Act 1696; *National Bank of Scotland* v. *Forbes* (1858) 21 D. 79, a case of a bond and assignation in security of a life insurance policy.

of heritable security would support not only sums owed at its creation but also future debts incurred by the grantor to the grantee,[10] unless otherwise provided by the contract of the parties.[11]

*The standard security.* This is available for feudal land and lease-hold land and other interests in land, such as a ground annual, as were the old forms of heritable security. The standard security is created by one of the two forms of deed set out in schedule 2 to the Conveyancing and Feudal Reform (Scotland) Act 1970. Form A is for cases where the personal obligation to pay the debt is created by the deed of security and Form B for cases where the personal obligation is separately created. Both forms consist of an attested deed indicating that the land in question is being constituted security for a specified sum, or up to a specified maximum, or for all debts due or later to become due from the grantor to the grantee. The security takes effect when recorded in the Register of Sasines.[12]

By section 11(1) of the Act of 1970:

Where a standard security is duly recorded, it shall operate to vest the interest over which it is granted in the grantee as a security for the performance of the contract to which the security relates.

The grantee is entitled to the title deeds, including all searches and all conveyances not duly recorded, or to get them after some prior incumbrancer ceases to be entitled to them.[13]

Certain other effects are attributed to deeds of security by section 10 of the Act, and section 11(2) imports into the relations between the parties a set of standard conditions set out in schedule 3. These relate to the duties and powers of the parties, including the grantor's right of redemption and the grantee's enforcement of his security. Any condition may be deleted or varied, and other conditions may be added, except that there may be no variation of the standard conditions relating to procedure on redemption, to the power of sale or its exercise or to the power of foreclosure or its exercise.[14]

Section 32 of the 1970 Act makes the legislation governing a bond and disposition or assignation in security applicable to a standard security, except for (i) enactments inconsistent with the 1970 Act and (ii) certain statutes listed in schedule 8. Among the enactments applicable are the provisions for validation of security given by an

10. See *Colquhoun's Trustee* v. *Diack* (1901) 4 F. 358.
11. See *Anderson's Trustee* v. *John Somerville & Co. Ltd.* (1899) 36 S.L.R. 833, where the back letter stated that the land was disposed as security up to £700, the debtor later borrowed to a higher total, and the security was held to extend only to £700.
12. 1970 Act, s. 9(2), (6).    13. 1970 Act, s. 10(4).
14. 1970 Act, s. 11(3) (as amended by the Redemption of Standard Securities (Scotland) Act 1971, s. 1(a)) and s. 11(4).

uninfeft proprietor of land.[15] Further provision is made by section 12 of the 1970 Act for a standard security to be valid even if granted by a proprietor who is uninfeft, and even if the grantor's title is not subsequently recorded, if in the deed creating the standard security the grantor deduces his title from the person who appears in the Register of Sasines as having the last recorded title to the land. Since the deed of standard security is itself recorded, there is an indirect record of the grantor's title. Such a security is effective 'for the purposes of the rights and obligations between the grantor and the grantee thereof and those deriving title from them, but for no other purpose . . .'

## Equitable Mechanisms

### Evolution of Chancery Doctrines in England and Wales and Northern Ireland
If a borrower has only an equitable interest in his land, not a legal estate, all his dealings with the land must be equitable, not legal. Hence, he can grant equitable mortgages, not legal mortgages. It may be that what the borrower has is an equitable life interest under a trust of the land. He can mortgage that. Chancery doctrine has always been that any transaction intended to be a mortgage will be given effect as a mortgage. Since, however, his status is merely equitable, the mortgagee will not have any legal rights such as the right to take possession of the land. The rights and remedies he has will depend in the first instance on the terms of the mortgage instrument, which must be in writing[16] but need not be by deed.

A tenant for life wishing to grant a mortgage of his equitable life interest would be likely to use one of two forms. First, he might assign his life interest to the mortgagee subject to a provision for assignment back to him on redemption. The mortgagee would thus acquire an equitable interest pur autre vie. Secondly, he might execute a document charging his interest with repayment of the loan. In the case of mortgage by assignment, the mortgagee, to realise his security if the mortgagor defaulted in repayment, could: (*a*) apply to the court for an order to sell the life interest free from the equity of redemption; (*b*) so sell without an order of the court if authorised by the mortgage instrument, or if the mortgage was by deed; (*c*) sell the life interest subject to the equity of redemption;

15. S. 3 of the 1924 Act and s. 1 of the 1938 Act, footnote 8, p. 21 *ante*.
16. Law of Property Act 1925, section 53 (1) (*c*), in England and Wales at present.

(*d*) apply to the court for the appointment of a receiver, or appoint one out of court if so authorised by the mortgage instrument or if the mortgage was by deed; (*e*) bring foreclosure proceedings. In the case of a charge, the mortgagee could: (*a*) proceed as in (*a*) above; (*b*) proceed as in (*b*) above; (*c*) sell his charge; (*d*) proceed as in (*d*) above.

Prior to 1926 in England and Wales, when a legal mortgage had been granted of a legal estate in land by transfer of the estate to the mortgagee, any subsequent mortgage of the same land while the first mortgage stood unredeemed would have to be equitable. The legal estate was vested in the legal mortgagee and the mortgagor consequently had only an equitable interest in the land, the equity of redemption, which he could mortgage. Since 1925, when a legal mortgage has been granted by demise, sub-demise or charge, the mortgagor still has the fee simple absolute in possession or term of years absolute, as the case may be, and so can grant further legal mortgages by demise, sub-demise or charge.

Both before 1926 and after 1925 it was and is possible for the owner of a legal estate in land to grant an equitable mortgage, either in preference to the grant of a legal mortgage or because effect is given in equity to some varieties of abortive attempt to create a legal mortgage. The three methods of creating an equitable mortgage of a legal estate are: (*a*) giving an equitable charge (known since the seventeenth century); (*b*) deposit of title deeds of unregistered land (known since the eighteenth century) or, in the case of registered land, deposit of the land certificate; (*c*) making an agreement to grant a legal mortgage (a doctrine developed during the nineteenth century).

**Equitable Charge: England and Wales**  An equitable mortgage by way of charge is simply carried out by way of a document charging the land in equity with the payment of the specified sum. A document is required (except in cases where it would be fraudulent to plead the absence of writing) by virtue of the Law of Property Act 1925, section 53(1) (*a*). For the charge to be valid, the document need not be under seal, but if a deed is used the mortgagee has certain statutory powers (e.g., to sell the mortgagor's legal estate without an order of the court) under section 101 of the Law of Property Act 1925. If the mortgage is not by deed, the powers and remedies of the chargee depend in the first instance on the instrument of charge. Apart from the terms of that document, if it is unsealed, and apart from any powers conferred on him by the mortgagor by any other document, the chargee has no powers to deal with the legal estate without an order of the court. He may apply to the court for an order for the sale of that estate free from any right to redeem.[17] He may apply to the court to appoint a receiver. He may sell his charge. But he may not foreclose.[18]

An equitable charge may also be held to exist when the owner of a legal estate makes an unsuccessful attempt to create a legal mortgage. That will be so where all the substantive elements of a legal mortgage are present, but where some formality has not been observed, e.g., the mortgage instrument is unsealed.

If an equitable charge is given over registered land, it may be protected by caution (if not by deed) or by caution in a specially prescribed form (if by deed). It can subsequently be converted into a legal charge if it was by a deed envisaging that (see the Land Registration Act 1925, section 106).

**Equitable Charge: Northern Ireland**   The law is the same as that of England and Wales, except that there is no legislation equivalent to the Law of Property act 1925, section 90. Writing is required for the creation of an equitable charge over land by the Statute of Frauds (Ireland) 1695, section 4. If it is by deed, the mortgagee has the statutory powers set out in the Conveyancing Acts 1881, section 19, and 1911, section 4.

**Scotland**   There are no equitable charges in Scotland. However, a landowner who granted a heritable security in one of the old forms could grant further securities in the same forms. Even when a mortgage had been granted by way of an ex facie absolute disposition, the mortgagor could create subsequent such securities during the subsistence of the first. (The mortgagor in this case had the alternatives of: (a) conveying his radical right in the land, excepting the prior ex facie absolute disposition from the warrandice; or (b) conveying simply his reversionary right in the land. Each alternative involved disadvantages, which made such subsequent securities rare in practice.) Later securities were not characterised as equitable, the mortgagor's right to redeem not being itself so regarded. Nowadays, any number of successive standard securities may be created in respect of the same land.

17. The inherent power of the court to make an order for sale is augmented by the Law of Property Act 1925, s. 90.   18. See, further, Keeton and Sheridan, *Equity*, p. 186.

**Deposit of Title Deeds or Land Certificate: England and Wales** An equitable mortgage may be made simply by depositing the title deeds of the mortgagor's estate, if it is unregistered land, with the mortgagee by way of security. Notwithstanding the Law of Property Act 1925, section 53(1) (*a*), no document is necessary.[19] Title deeds may be deposited by the owner with someone else for a variety of reasons besides security for a debt, of which the commonest are deposit with a bank for safe-keeping and deposit with a solicitor while arrangements are going through for the sale of the land. If the deposit is intended as security, an equitable mortgage is created. If there is no document, the intention can be inferred from other evidence, such as the loan.[20]

So long as the mortgagee holds on to the deeds (or, at least, parts with them to no one but his own agent or someone who agrees to hold them on his behalf), he is secure because the owner of the legal estate will find it hard to deal with the land without the title deeds. If the mortgagor tries to sell the land, the prospective purchaser will ask for the deeds so that he can investigate the title. The mortgagor then has a choice of three courses: (*a*) decline to produce the deeds or to say where they are: the prospective purchaser will then deal with him no further; (*b*) tell the prospective purchaser where he can see the deeds: the mortgage will then come to the purchaser's notice and will bind him unless the vendor redeems it; (*c*) tell lies to the prospective purchaser about the deeds: now, if the purchaser goes ahead with the deal, he will take free from the mortgage only if the mortgagor's story is credible and is believed by the purchaser and if the purchaser acted reasonably in taking a conveyance without seeing the title deeds. Such a train of events is unlikely; the mortgagor has in any case rendered himself liable to civil and criminal proceedings for fraud. It is about as likely as his stealing the deeds from the mortgagee or burgling the land registry and altering the register. One cannot guard against everything.

Sometimes there will be a written contract accompanying the deposit of the deeds. This will be so if special terms of agreement are desired, for example, if the mortgagor is to be placed under a restrictive covenant, or if additional powers of realising his security are to be conferred on the mortgagee. In the absence of agreement, the mortgagee cannot enforce his security out of court: his remedies

---

19. *Russel* v. *Russel* (1783) 1 Bro. C.C. 269, decided when the law as to documentary evidence was contained in the Statute of Frauds, 1677.
20. See further, Keeton and Sheridan, *Equity*, pp. 181-4.

are actions claiming (*a*) to be put in possession of the land; (*b*) appointment of a receiver; (*c*) sale of the land; or (*d*) foreclosure. A contract may empower him to do any of these things out of court, except foreclose. Sometimes there may be an agreement to grant the depositee a legal mortgage on request. Sometimes the depositee is given a power of attorney to sell the legal estate or to vest a legal mortgage in himself. It is less usual for a mortgagee by deposit to have to realise his security than it is for other mortgagees because mortgage by deposit is commonly used for short-term loans quickly repaid, such as a temporary overdraft accorded by a bank.

Such a mortgage may, like any other, be a first or subsequent mortgage, but it will probably be a first mortgage because any prior mortgagee would probably have taken custody of the title deeds himself.

The title deeds are chattels and controversy has occurred as to whether a depositee has a pledge of or lien over these chattels at law as well as a mortgage of the land in equity. It usually does not matter, because the mortgage is better security than such a lien, but it was an important question in *Re Molton Finance Ltd.*[21] Stockbrokers lent £15,000 to Molton Finance Ltd. The company, who were legal chargees of land, deposited the title deeds to that land by way of sub-mortgage, i.e., to mortgage their mortgage. The equitable sub-mortgage was void because it was not registered as required by the Companies Act 1948, section 95(1). The stockbrokers then claimed that they had a lien over the deeds. The Court of Appeal held that there was no lien separate from the mortgage, so the stockbrokers had no security. This decision has been examined by Sunnucks,[22] who considers it limited in its application. In any case, one could pledge deeds separately from mortgaging the land.

In the case of registered land, the equivalent of a deposit of title deeds is a mortgage by deposit of the land certificate (or, in the case of a sub-mortgage by the owner of a registered charge, deposit of the charge certificate). That creates an equitable mortgage by virtue of the Land Registration Act 1925, section 66, which says that what the deposit does is 'create a lien . . .'

21. [1968] Ch. 325. See also *Re Wallis & Simmonds (Builders) Ltd.* [1974] 1 All E.R. 561.
22. ' "Lord Thurlow's Equity" or "A Cuckoo in the Legal Nest"?' (1970) 33 *Modern Law Review* 131.

### Deposit of Title Deeds or Land Certificate: Northern Ireland

The law as to deposit of title deeds is the same as that of England.[23] If, however, the transaction is in writing, or accompanied by a written memorandum of terms, the document will have to be registered in accordance with the Registration of Deeds Act (Northern Ireland) 1970, in order to protect the mortgagee against subsequent registered incumbrances and against prior unregistered ones.[24]

Equitable mortgages of registered land by deposit of the land certificate, and sub-mortgages by deposit of a charge certificate, are governed by the Land Registration Act (Northern Ireland) 1970, section 50.

### Scotland

**Scotland** There are no securities by deposit of title deeds to land.[25] Nor is there registered title. The recording of deeds in the Register of Sasines has important effects in the process of creating a real right to the subjects conveyed – i.e., infeftment – but it has not the effect of constituting a registered title to the subjects.

### Agreement for a Legal Mortgage: England and Wales and Northern Ireland

**Agreement for a Legal Mortgage: England and Wales and Northern Ireland** If there is a debt actually incurred, an agreement to give the creditor a legal mortgage over land owned by the debtor constitutes an equitable mortgage, provided the agreement is an enforceable contract. Of course, if the agreement is performed by the creation of a legal mortgage, the anterior equitable mortgage will lose almost all its significance. Not quite all, because the equitable mortgage may have priority to the legal mortgage. But the main importance of holding that an enforceable contract to grant a legal mortgage is itself an equitable mortgage, and not merely a contract, is in cases where the landowner goes bankrupt or into liquidation after making the contract and before performing it. Had there been a mere contract the creditor would rank with the other unsecured creditors, but because there is equitable security the creditor can satisfy himself out of the land.

The requirement that there be a debt actually incurred does not mean that the debt must exist at the time of the agreement to mortgage. But if there is an agreement to borrow and to grant a

---

23. Despite the absence of writing, otherwise required by the Statute of Frauds (Ireland) 1695, s. 4.
24. See, further, Keeton and Sheridan, *Equity*, p. 182, n. 70.
25. See *Christie* v. *Ruxton* (1862) 24 D. 1182.

legal mortgage in the future, no equitable mortgage will arise until the money is lent because until there is an obligation to repay there cannot be security for that obligation.

The requirement that there be an enforceable contract means that there must be evidence in writing, in accordance with the statutory provisions, or part performance. It does not mean that the contract must be specifically enforceable. Indeed, in the typical case it is not, at least at its inception.

**Example** Patricia contracts to buy the fee simple absolute in possession in Blackacre from Veronica for £15,000. Patricia borrows £1,500 from the Offshore Bank Ltd. in order to pay the deposit on Blackacre and contracts to grant the bank a charge by deed expressed to be by way of legal mortgage over Blackacre, to secure the £1,500. Patricia then goes bankrupt. The bank will be held to have an equitable mortgage over Blackacre. At this stage, the fee simple is still vested in Veronica, so that Patricia's interest is equitable, so the contract to grant the bank a legal mortgage cannot be specifically enforced as Patricia has no legal estate over which a legal mortgage could be created. (If Veronica later conveyed the fee simple to Patricia and Patricia went bankrupt without having granted a legal mortgage to the Offshore Bank Ltd., the bank's equitable mortgage would bind Patricia's legal estate.)[26]

**Scotland** A contract to grant a legal mortgage has no more than contractual force, and therefore is no security for the creditor.

---

26. See further, Keeton and Sheridan, *Equity*, pp. 184–6.

# 3 land: common terms in mortgage deeds

**Introduction** Certain terms must obviously appear in every mortgage deed: the identification of the parties and of the premises to be mortgaged, specification of the type of mortgage being granted[1] (whether legal or equitable, whether by charge or demise if legal, etc.), the amount of money to be secured (if the mortgage is for a definite amount or maximum), the date on which it must be paid (in England and Wales and Northern Ireland), and the rate of interest (if any).

There are other terms which are implied. In England[2] and Northern Ireland[3] these are covenants for title, e.g., a covenant by someone granting a mortgage as beneficial owner that he has the right to make the mortgage, and a covenant that, apart from any stated exceptions, the land is free from incumbrances. In Scotland, a similar result is achieved by the deed of standard security including the words: 'And I grant warrandice' or 'And, subject as aforesaid, I grant warrandice.'[4]

There are other terms which, being neither implied nor essential, are almost certain to appear. These include obligations on the mortgagor to maintain and repair the premises[5] and to insure them[6] and also, in relation to all land in Scotland and where the mortgagor

---

1. Not in Scotland, where only a standard security can be granted.
2. Law of Property Act 1925, s. 76 and sch. 2.     3. Conveyancing Act 1881, s. 7.
4. Conveyancing and Feudal Reform (Scotland) Act 1970, ss. 9 and 10 and sch. 2.
5. As to the standard security in Scotland, see the Conveyancing and Feudal Reform (Scotland) Act 1970, s. 11 and sch. 3, standard condition 1.
6. Scotland: see standard condition 5.

is a tenant or rentchargor in England and Wales or Northern Ireland, to perform obligations in respect of the land like paying the rent.[7] Another such term is one allowing the mortgagee to carry out the mortgagor's obligations if the mortgagor does not do so, at the expense of the mortgagor, and adding the cost to the debt for which the land is security.[8]

**Date of payment** In England and Wales and Northern Ireland it is usual to specify a short period for the loan, even if it is not intended that it shall be repaid so quickly. The mortgagor commonly covenants to repay six months after the date of the mortgage deed. The purpose is to make the loan repayable on or after that date, if the mortgagor gives due notice demanding repayment. The position is not that the mortgagor must pay on the date mentioned, or cannot redeem thereafter, but that he cannot redeem before that date and the mortgagee cannot recall the money before that date.

In the case of a building society mortgage, where repayment is to be by instalments, the repayment date for the whole sum will still be stated to be a short period after the loan, but the deed will also provide that the loan will not be called in as long as the instalments are paid punctually. The effect is to enable the mortgagee to make the outstanding amount of the loan repayable in a lump sum if there is default in paying instalments after the repayment date in the deed.

The standard security in Scotland does not incorporate a date for repayment. The amount secured is payable to the creditor when he calls it up in accordance with the terms of the deed or, in the absence of express contract, in accordance with the statutory provisions.[9]

**Interest** Normally interest is payable. The rate will vary with, or rather a little after, variations in national monetary circumstances, and also with the type of lender, the amount and duration of the loan and other relevant factors. Since bank and related interest rates alter during the currency of any but the shortest mortgages, a deed will usually contain a term providing for the mortgage interest to vary correspondingly. In the case of building society mortgages where payment is by instalments, the usual rearrangement is by increasing or decreasing the period for which instalments have to

---

7. Scotland: see standard condition 3.     8. Scotland: see standard condition 7.
9. See the Conveyancing and Feudal Reform (Scotland) Act 1970, s. 11 and sch. 3, standard condition 8, and s. 19 and sch. 6, Form A.

be paid rather than by increasing or decreasing the amount of each instalment. One type of provision for varying interest rates which the English courts have held void is the penalty for late payment. It is not permissible to have a term that, if interest is not paid on time, it is to be paid at a higher rate. On the other hand, the courts have upheld terms allowing a lower rate of interest as a reward for punctual payment.[10] The law of Scotland is the same.[11]

**Insurance**  Arrangements may be agreed between the parties. Building societies frequently want a term entitling them to insure at the borrower's expense or as the borrower's agent. That is because they get commission for introducing the business to the insurance company. In the absence of express terms in the mortgage contract, in England and Wales, the Law of Property Act 1925, section 101(1)(ii), gives a mortgagee whose mortgage is made by deed a power to insure the mortgaged property against fire and to add the premiums to his secured debt.[12] The law of Northern Ireland is the same under the Conveyancing Act 1881, section 19(1)(ii).[13] In Scotland, standard condition 5 obliges the debtor to insure or, at the creditor's option, to permit the creditor to insure the mortgaged property, to the extent of its market value, against fire and such other risks as the creditor may reasonably require.

**Building society rules**  In addition to the terms of the mortgage deed itself, taking a building society mortgage makes the mortgagor a member of the society and hence subject to its rules.

**Other terms**  Other stipulations appear with varying degrees of frequency in certain types of mortgage. They call for further discussion in the remainder of this chapter.

**Further Advances**  A mortgage deed may provide that the land is to be security not only for a debt then due but also for future loans which the creditor may agree to make to the debtor, or which the contract obliges him to make at the request of the debtor, either up to a stated maximum or not. A typical arrangement of this type is a mortgage to secure an overdraft at a bank. A problem may arise, if the debtor makes a second mortgage of the same land, as to the

---

10. See further, Keeton and Sheridan, *Equity*, pp. 178, 206.
11. See *Gatty* v. *Maclaine* 1921 S.C. (H.L.) 1, upholding a term for interest at 5%, reduced to 4% for punctual payment.
12. See also s. 108, limiting the insurance to two-thirds of the cost of reinstatement in the event of total destruction, unless otherwise agreed.
13. See also s. 23. *The Survey of the Land Law of Northern Ireland* (1971), paras. 224 and 230, recommends statutory authority for cover against flood, storm and tempest, and a statutory limit of the maximum amount due to the mortgagee.

priority of the competing claims of the two mortgagees, should the security be inadequate to pay them both in full, supposing the first mortgagee to have made further loans after the granting of the second mortgage.

In England and Wales, the position is now governed, except as to registered charges over registered land, by the Law of Property Act 1925, section 94, whose first two subsections provide:

(1)  ... a prior mortgagee shall have a right to make further advances to rank in priority to subsequent mortgages (whether legal or equitable)—

(a)  if an arrangement has been made to that effect with the subsequent mortgagees; or

(b)  if he had no notice of such subsequent mortgages at the time when the further advance was made by him; or

(c)  whether or not he had such notice as aforesaid, where the mortgage imposes an obligation on him to make such further advances.

This subsection applies whether or not the prior mortgage was expressly made for securing further advances.

(2)  In relation to the making of further advances ... a mortgagee shall not be deemed to have notice of a mortgage merely by reason that it was registered as a land charge ..., if it was not so registered at the date of the original advance or when the last search (if any) by or on behalf of the mortgagee was made, whichever last happened.

This subsection applies only where the prior mortgage was made expressly for securing a current account or other further advances.

If the first mortgagee is obliged to make further advances after the second mortgage is made, he is entitled to be repaid them before the second mortgagee gets anything (section 94(1) (c)). A person proposing to become a second mortgagee will discover that when inspecting the title deeds; if he does not like it, he does not lend. The same applies to cases of arrangement with the second mortgage (section 94(1) (a)): if he does not like it, the second mortgagee does not agree to the arrangement. In other cases, the first mortgagee takes priority for his further advances only if he makes them without notice of the existence of the second mortgage (section 94(1) (b)). Where the prior mortgage is not expressed to secure further advances, the second mortgagee may give notice to the first either expressly or by registering his mortgage under the Land Charges

Act 1972.[14] Where the prior mortgage is expressed to secure further advances, registration of the second mortgage under the Land Charges Act is not notice to the first mortgagee, unless he searches the register, so the second should serve express notice on the first. This is to save a bank which has granted a secured overdraft from having to inspect the register of land charges every time it pays a cheque drawn on the account.

The holder of a registered charge in England and Wales is not so favourably treated by statute. If the charge is not expressed to secure further advances, it cannot do so. If it is so expressed, the chargee can add further loans only if he makes them before receiving notice in the post from the registrar of a subsequent charge, or if he is under an obligation, noted on the register, to make a further advance.[15] Hence, to secure an overdraft on registered land, a mortgage otherwise than by way of registered charge should be used.

With regard to Northern Ireland, unregistered land is not regulated by statute in this respect,[16] and hence is governed by the same law as pertained in England prior to 1926. If the first mortgage is not expressed to secure further advances, they cannot be made so as to rank for repayment in priority to a second mortgage already in existence when the further loans are made (unless the second mortgagee agrees to that). If the first mortgage is expressed to secure further advances, these further loans are added to the security of the first mortgage unless, at the time of making the further loans, the first mortgagee has notice of a second mortgage.[17] The idea is that, on receiving such notice, if the first mortgagee does not like to be postponed to a second mortgagee, he need not make further advances. The case of a mortgagee obliged by the contract to make further advances is dealt with by saying that receipt of notice of a second mortgage releases him from that obligation.[18] Registration of the second mortgage under the Registration of Deeds Act (Northern Ireland) 1970 is not notice to the first mortgagee,[19] so the second mortgagee should protect himself by serving express notice.[20]

14. Under s. 2(4), as a class C (i) land charge (legal mortgage not protected by deposit of title deeds), a class C (iii) land charge (mortgage by equitable charge) or a class C (iv) land charge (agreement to make a legal mortgage).
15. Land Registration Act 1925, s. 30, as amended by the Law of Property (Amendment) Act 1926, s. 5.
16. But see the proposal in the *Survey of the Land Law of Northern Ireland* (1971), para. 220, to assimilate unregistered land to registered land in this respect.
17. *Hopkinson* v. *Rolt* (1861) 9 H.L.C. 514.    18. *West* v. *Williams* [1899] 1 Ch. 132.
19. *Re O'Byrne's Estate* (1885) 15 L.R.Ir. 373.
20. See further, Keeton and Sheridan, *Equity*, pp. 175, 220-2.

Registered charges in Northern Ireland are governed in this respect by the Land Registration Act (Northern Ireland) 1970, section 43, which provides:

(1) Where a registered charge is expressed to be created on any land for the purpose of securing future advances (whether with or without present advances), the registered owner of the charge shall be entitled in priority to any subsequent charge to the payment of any sum due to him in respect of such future advances, except any advances which may have been made after the date of, and with express notice in writing of, the subsequent charge.

(2) In this section, 'further advances' includes sums from time to time due on an account current and all sums which by agreement or the course of business between the parties are considered to be advances on the security of the charge.

In Scotland, prior to the introduction of the standard security, this problem was dealt with in a manner similar to that of the English rule in *Hopkinson* v. *Rolt*.[21] In *Union Bank of Scotland Ltd.* v. *National Bank of Scotland Ltd.*[22] there occurred: (1) a mortgage of land to one bank by ex facie absolute disposition; (2) a second mortgage of the same land in the same form to a second bank; (3) intimation to the first bank of the existence of the second mortgage; (4) further advances to the mortgagor by both banks. It was held that the first bank's security was limited to the advances they made before receiving the intimation of the granting of the second security to the second bank. Now, by the Conveyancing and Feudal Reform (Scotland) Act 1970, section 13(1), it is provided:

Where the creditor in a standard security duly recorded has received notice of the creation of a subsequent security over the same interest in land or any part thereof, or of the subsequent assignation or conveyance of that interest in whole or in part, being a security, assignation or conveyance so recorded, the preference in ranking of the security of that creditor shall be restricted to security for his present advances and future advances which he may be required to make under the contract to which the security relates and interest present or future due thereon (including any such interest which has accrued or may accrue) and for any expenses or outlays (including interest thereon) which

21. (1861) 9 H.L.C. 514. See p. 34, *ante*.
22. (1886) 12 App. Cas. 53. See also *Campbell's Judicial Factor* v. *National Bank of Scotland Ltd.* 1944 S.C. 495.

may be, or may have been, reasonably incurred in the exercise of any power conferred on any creditor by the deed expressing the existing security.

The second mortgagee should protect himself by serving express notice on the first mortgagee because recording the second mortgage in the Register of Sasines is not notice.[23]

By section 42, it is provided that, in relation to the effect on the preference in ranking of any heritable security constituted by ex facie absolute disposition or assignation, section 13 is to apply as it applies to the preference in ranking of a standard security. The effect is to stop the addition to the security of any loans made after the creditor gets notice of a disposition or assignation of the rights of the debtor in the land.

**Reservation of Right to Consolidate Mortgages**  Consolidation is an equitable doctrine relating to the redemption of mortgages in England and Wales and Northern Ireland (there is no such doctrine in Scotland: possibly a lender could be given a right to consolidate securities by the contract with the borrower, but that is not the practice in Scotland). Before the Conveyancing Act 1881 came into force, the doctrine applied to all mortgages. Now it applies only if the parties so provide.

In its origin, it was a simple doctrine that a mortgagee who held two mortgages for two debts from the same mortgagor could consolidate them if the mortgagor sought to redeem only one of them, i.e., the mortgagee could insist on the mortgagee redeeming both or neither.[24] The need for the mortgagee to do this would arise when one of the properties had declined in value, so that it would be inadequate security for the debt secured on it, and the mortgagor wished to redeem only the other property. Many technicalities were added to the doctrine by nineteenth century decisions, resulting in some cases in injustice the very antithesis of the equitable objectives the doctrine was invented to achieve. For that reason, the Conveyancing Act 1881, section 17, abolished the doctrine except in cases where the parties stipulated that it should apply. Section 17 of the 1881 Act is still in force in Northern Ireland, but in England and Wales it has been replaced by the Law of Property Act 1925, section 93, of which subsections (1) and (3) provide:

23. 1970 Act, s. 13 (2) (*a*).
24. As to the early development of the doctrine, see Keeton and Sheridan, *Equity*, pp. 175–6.

(1) A mortgagor seeking to redeem any one mortgage is entitled to do so without paying any money due under any separate mortgage made by him, or by any person through whom he claims, solely on property other than that comprised in the mortgage which he seeks to redeem.

This subsection applies only if and as far as a contrary intention is not expressed in the mortgage deeds or one of them.

(3) Save as aforesaid, nothing in this Act, in reference to mortgages, affects any right of consolidation or renders inoperative a stipulation in relation to any mortgage . . . reserving a right to consolidate.

Absence of a right to consolidate proved less acceptable than a right subject to undesirable technicalities, so it became usual after 1881, and remains usual today, for mortgage deeds to express a contrary intention to subsection (1) and reserve a right to consolidate in accordance with subsection (3). Because that is usual, the proposal has been made[25] in Northern Ireland that the position should be reversed and that the right to consolidate should exist unless excluded by the parties.

For the doctrine to operate, the following conditions must be satisfied: (a) there must be at least two mortgages of two different properties,[26] redemption being sought of only one or some; (b) these mortgages must have been made by the same mortgagor; (c) these mortgages must be held by the same mortgagee; and (d) at least one of the mortgage deeds must reserve the right to consolidate. Each of these requirements needs some elaboration.

(a) Wherever there are two or more mortgages of any type, legal or equitable, of any kind of property, real or personal, consolidation is available to the mortgagee on the mortgagor seeking to redeem some or one. The doctrine applies only to mortgages, not to other types of security.

(b) The mortgages must have been made by the same owner, but it is not necessary that the equities of redemption be in the same hands at the time of consolidation. If the mortgagor has assigned one property and seeks to redeem the other, he can be made to redeem both or neither (if all the conditions for consolidation are satisfied).

---

25. *Survey of the Land Law of Northern Ireland* (1971), paras. 217-18, pp. 82-3.
26. The decision of Wright J. in *Re Salmon* [1903] 1 K.B. 147, that there could be consolidation of several mortgages on the same property, is probably wrong.

**Example** Arthur mortgages Blackacre to Clarence by a deed excluding section 93. Then Arthur mortgages shares to Clarence. Then Arthur sells Blackacre to David subject to the mortgage. If Arthur seeks to redeem the shares, Clarence can make him redeem Blackacre as well or redeem neither. If Arthur does redeem both, he becomes the absolute owner of the shares and the owner of the mortgage on Blackacre. Clarence could consolidate in the same way if it were David seeking to redeem Blackacre.[27]

(c) Only mortgages held by the same mortgagee can be consolidated, but they need not have been made originally to the one mortgagee.

**Example 1** Edward mortgages Blackacre to Felicity and Whiteacre to George, the mortgage of Whiteacre excluding section 93. Later, Edward sells Whiteacre to Harriet, subject to the mortgage. Later still, George buys Felicity's mortgage of Blackacre. Harriet seeks to redeem Whiteacre. George can insist on her redeeming Blackacre as well (or redeeming neither), notwithstanding that the mortgage of Blackacre did not come into George's hands until after Harriet bought Whiteacre from Edward.[28]

**Example 2** Edward mortgages Blackacre to Felicity by a deed excluding section 93. Then Edward sells Blackacre to Harriet, subject to the mortgage. Next, Edward mortgages Whiteacre to George. Finally, George buys Felicity's mortgage of Blackacre. Harriet seeks to redeem Blackacre. She is entitled to do so without redeeming Whiteacre because her equitable right to redeem Blackacre is a prior equity to George's equity to consolidate, as Edward had not yet mortgaged Whiteacre when Harriet bought Blackacre.[29]

(d) No equitable right to consolidate arises unless and until section 93 of the Law of Property Act 1925 (in England and Wales) or section 17 of the Conveyancing Act 1881 (in Northern Ireland) is excluded by one of the mortgage deeds.

**Example 1** Ian mortgages The Nook to Joan, The Nest to Katherine and Chez Nous to Leonard. Only the deed mortgaging Chez Nous excludes section 93. Leonard buys Joan's and Katherine's mortgages. Ian cannot redeem any of the properties without a right on Leonard's part to make him redeem all three.

---

27. See *Hughes* v. *Britannia Permanent Benefit Building Soc.* [1906] 2 Ch. 607.
28. See *Pledge* v. *White* [1896] A.C. 187.
29. See *Jennings* v. *Jordan* (1881) 6 App. Cas. 698.

**Example 2**  Ian mortgages The Nook to Joan and The Nest to Katherine. Then, Ian sells The Nest to Monica, subject to the mortgage. Next, Ian mortgages Chez Nous to Leonard. The only deed excluding section 93 is the mortgage of Chez Nous. Finally, Leonard buys Joan's and Katherine's mortgages. If Monica wants to redeem The Nest, she is entitled to do so without redeeming either of the other properties, because her equitable right to redeem The Nest is a prior equity to Leonard's equity to consolidate, as Ian had not yet made a mortgage excluding section 93 when Monica bought The Nest.[30]

**Exclusion of Leasing Powers: England and Wales and Northern Ireland**  In England and Wales and Northern Ireland, the powers of a mortgagor in possession and of a mortgagee in possession to grant leases of the mortgaged property were put on a statutory footing by the Conveyancing Act 1881, section 18. That enactment is still in force in Northern Ireland,[31] but has been replaced in England and Wales by the Law of Property Act 1925, section 99. Section 99 provides that, if the lease complies with the specifications laid down in the section, the mortgagor or mortgagee in possession may grant agricultural or occupation leases for a term not exceeding fifty years[32] and building leases for a term not exceeding nine hundred and ninety-nine years.[33] Such a lease, if granted by a mortgagor in possession, binds every incumbrancer, including the mortgagee; and, if granted by a mortgagee in possession, binds prior incumbrancers and the mortgagor.

By section 99(13)–(15) of the 1925 Act,[34] the leasing powers of the parties may be curtailed, extended or otherwise varied by the contract.[35] Most mortgage deeds do contain express provisions as to the powers of letting the land. The commonest clause is one providing that the powers of the mortgagor in possession are not to be exercised without the consent of the mortgagee. That is because the

30. See further, Keeton and Sheridan, *Equity*, pp. 197–202.
31. Together with the Conveyancing Act 1911, s. 3 (10), (11).
32. Twenty-one years under s. 18 (3) (i) of the 1881 Act.
33. Ninety-nine years under s. 18 (3) (ii) of the 1881 Act.
34. Northern Ireland: Conveyancing Act 1881, s. 18 (13)–(15).
35. Subs. (13), which authorises curtailment or exclusion by the deed of the statutory powers, does not apply to the power to grant leases under the statutory provisions relating to renewal of business tenancies: Landlord and Tenant Act 1954, s. 36(4) (England and Wales); Business Tenancies Act (Northern Ireland) 1964, s. 17(4), (5). Subs. (13) does not apply either to a mortgage executed after 1st March 1948 of agricultural land, in England and Wales, within the meaning of the Agriculture Act 1947: Agricultural Holdings Act 1948, s. 95 and sch. 7, para 2. There is no corresponding legislation relating to agricultural land in Northern Ireland.

mortgagee, should he have to realise his security, will probably want to sell the premises with vacant possession, so will not wish to be saddled with a mortgagor's tenant who cannot be evicted. Sometimes the statutory powers are acceptable, and sometimes the deed may even extend the mortgagor's powers, as, for example, where the mortgage is of a block of flats, where the whole value of the security depends on the mortgagor making lettings. But in mortgages of single dwellings, the clause eliminating the power of the mortgagor to grant leases without the consent of the mortgagee is so usual that the Northern Ireland Land Law Working Party recommended[36] the redrafting of the statutory power in such a way as to provide that leases granted by a mortgagor in possession would not bind a mortgagee who had not consented to the exercise of the power.

The effect of the mortgagor granting a lease contrary to the provisions of the mortgage deed is generally exactly the same as the effect of granting one which is authorised except that the lease will not bind the mortgagee.

**Example**   Tower Ltd., fee simple owners of a block of offices which they occupy for the purposes of their business, mortgage the premises to Loans Ltd. The mortgage deed contains a clause to the effect that 'the borrowers shall not except with the previous written consent of the mortgagees exercise the power of leasing conferred by the Law of Property Act 1925 on a mortgagor in possession'. Another clause in the deed provides that, if the mortgagors pay interest punctually and perform all their other obligations under the mortgage, the mortgagees will not require repayment for at least ten years. A year after the mortgage is created, Tower Ltd. find they have no need for one room in their office block, and they grant a lease of it for thirty years to Makeshift Ltd. The court will hold: (a) that the lease to Makeshift Ltd. was not made under the statutory powers; (b) that it was made under Tower Ltd.'s common law powers; (c) that it was therefore binding on Tower Ltd. but not on Loans Ltd.; (d) that therefore Loans Ltd., on exercising a right to possession against Tower Ltd., could also eject Makeshift Ltd. (unless the latter chose to redeem the mortgage); (e) that therefore the making of the lease was not a breach of covenant by Tower Ltd.; (f) that therefore Loans Ltd. could not call for repayment of the loan before the ten-year period was up; and (g) that the lease was given no additional

36. *Survey of the Land Law of Northern Ireland* (1971), para. 223, p. 84.

validity by the Law of Property Act 1925, section 152,[37] because it did not purport to be made under the statutory power.[38]

In the case of a mortgage of agricultural land in England and Wales, since the mortgagor's statutory powers of leasing cannot be excluded or curtailed by agreement, it seems that a general covenant by the mortgagor not to let the land without the mortgagor's written consent will be construed as a covenant not to exercise the mortgagor's common law powers, i.e., as a covenant not to grant a lease which is not binding on the mortgagee because it fails to comply in some particular with section 99 of the Law of Property Act 1925. That was the attitude of Goff J. in *Rhodes* v. *Dalby*.[39] However, in that case the learned judge held that there had been no letting of the land where the arrangement between the mortgagor and the person he allowed into posesssion of a bungalow on the premises was expressed to be 'a gentleman's agreement, with nothing in writing . . . for two years . . . at a rent of £2. 10s. per week.'

If the mortgagor's powers of leasing without the consent in writing of the mortgagee have been excluded, a lease granted by the mortgagor without the consent of the mortgagee has nevertheless been held binding on the latter where the mortgage deed said: '. . . but it shall not be necessary to express such consent in any such lease . . . nor shall any lessee be concerned to see that any such consent has been given';[40] and where the mortgagee has done acts adopting the tenancy, such as taking the rent and confirming the terms of the letting.[41] Mere failure by the mortgagee to evict the mortgagor's tenant is not adoption of the lease.[42]

### Exclusion of Leasing Powers: Scotland

Standard condition 6 of the standard security[43] runs:

It shall be an obligation on the debtor not to let, or agree to let, the security subjects, or any part thereof, without the prior

---

37. See p. 53, *post*.
38. See *Iron Trades Employers' Insurance Assoc.* v. *Union of House and Land Investors Ltd.* [1937] Ch. 313; *Dudley and District Benefit Building Soc.* v. *Emerson* [1949] Ch. 707; *Rust* v. *Goodale* [1957] Ch. 33; *Barclays Bank Ltd.* v. *Stasek* [1957] Ch. 28; *Taylor* v. *Ellis* [1960] Ch. 368; *Barclays Bank Ltd.* v. *Kiley* [1961] 1 W.L.R. 1050; *Bolton Building Soc.* v. *Cobb* [1966] 1 W.L.R. 1; Keeton and Sheridan, *Equity*, pp. 227-30.
39. [1971] 1 W.L.R. 1325.
40. *Lever Finance Ltd.* v. *Needleman's Trustee* [1956] Ch. 375.
41. See *Stroud Building Soc.* v. *Delamont* [1960] 1 W.L.R. 431; *Chatsworth Properties Ltd.* v *Effiom* [1971] 1 W.L.R. 144.
42. See *Parker* v. *Braithwaite* [1952] 2 All E.R. 837; *Taylor* v. *Ellis* [1960] Ch. 368. Ireland: *Re O'Rourke's Estate* (1889) 23 L.R.Ir. 497.
43. Conveyancing and Feudal Reform (Scotland) Act 1970, s. 11 and sch. 3.

consent in writing of the creditor, and 'to let' in this condition includes to sub-let.

The standard condition can be varied by the parties,[44] but an agreement to vary this condition is unlikely except by way of conferring power on the debtor to let the land without the consent of the creditor in cases where the security is over premises habitually let, e.g., a block of offices.

Under the old forms of heritable security, the powers of the borrower in possession to grant leases were not statutory, but in the absence of express terms in the security agreement it would seem that he could grant leases, provided he was infeft or had the authority of the heritable creditor, and provided the leases were not unfair to the creditor.

It seems from *Ritchie* v. *Scott*[45] that a person who is infeft, and who has disponed his estate to a creditor by ex facie absolute disposition by way of security, has, by virtue of his radical right, power to grant leases. A fortiori if the owner is authorised to grant leases by the back letter or by implication by being left in possession with management of the property. This authorisation expressly or by implication could also apply where the owner was not infeft. All these propositions derive from the opinion of Lord Kinnear,[46] but what was actually decided in *Ritchie* v. *Scott* was that a lease granted by an owner who was neither infeft, nor authorised by the heritable creditor to grant it, was not valid as against that creditor. Here the debtor, B, was not infeft because B bought the land from V, the vendor, by borrowing from C, the creditor; V conveyed the land to C, not to B, and C gave B a back letter. In *Abbott* v. *Mitchell*[47] an owner who had given security by ex facie absolute disposition, who was left in possession, was held to have the implied authority of the feudal owner (i.e., the creditor, who was infeft under an ex facie absolute disposition) to grant leases, which, consequently, were held binding on the trustee in the debtor's sequestration. The theory of the borrower's radical right is supported by *Edinburgh Entertainments Ltd.* v. *Stevenson*.[48] Once again, the security was by way of ex facie absolute disposition. A lease granted by the borrower was held binding on the heritable creditor. The borrower was infeft, and was also held to have an implied mandate from the lender to grant the

---

44. S. 11(3), (4), of the 1970 Act.    45. (1899) 1 F. 728.
46. 1 F. 734. Lord President Robertson and Lord Adam 'concurred *simpliciter* with Lord Kinnear, who, in effect, delivered the opinion of the court.' (*Per* Lord Justice Clerk Alness, *Edinburgh Entertainments Ltd.* v. *Stevenson* 1926 S.C. 363, 375.)
47. (1870) 8 M. 791.    48. 1926 S.C. 363.

lease. It also seems from that case that, if the borrower has power to grant leases, any lease is valid provided it does not depreciate the security. Generally, the borrower's powers of leasing without the authority of the lender have been excluded or specified by the disposition or back letter. *Reid* v. *M<sup>c</sup>Gill*[49] is a case where a lease by a borrower was held void as against the heritable creditor under a bond and disposition in security on the ground of unfairness to the creditor. It was a lease of minerals, in which various terms were regarded as unfair to the lender, for example, the length of the lease (fifty years, which was too long).

49. 1912, 2 S.L.T. 246.

# 4 land: invalid terms and terms of doubtful validity or usefulness in mortgage deeds

**Penalty for Default in Payment**   So far as the cases in England Wales go, there is an arbitrary distinction in relation to interest rates. If one interest rate on a mortgage debt is prescribed as the contractual rate, and a higher rate of interest is provided for in the event of interest at the contractual rate being overdue, the provision for higher interest is void as a penalty. On the other hand, there is no objection to reduction for prompt payment. This distinction puts the whole matter in the realm of drafting devices. In other words, if the deed stipulates for interest at 5%, but rising to 6% if interest gets into arrears, the stipulation for 6% is void; but if the deed states that interest is to be 6%, but going down to 5% if punctually paid, the agreement for 6% is valid.[1]

No such distinction has been drawn where the penalty is to make the loan repayable. It is quite common to provide in instalment mortgages that the capital sum shall be repayable in six months, but that the mortgagee will not call for the capital sum, or the balance of it outstanding, so long as the instalments are paid punctually. That is a valid provision, and so is the converse: contracting for repayment by instalments, with the qualification that, if there is default in payment of one instalment, the whole capital sum (or the unpaid balance of it) is to become repayable.[2] Similar remarks apply to all conditions for repayment on default. So long as the mortgagor is only being required to repay what he has borrowed,

1. See Keeton and Sheridan, *Equity*, p. 178. See also p. 32, *ante*.
2. See Keeton and Sheridan, *Equity*, p. 206.

the sum may be expressed to become due on breach of any term of the mortgage contract, e.g., letting a room without the mortgagee's consent, or failure to repair the premises.

**Premium**　If there is a mortgage to secure a loan, and the security is expressed to be for an obligation to pay more than was lent, that obligation can be enforced only if it is fair. It will not be fair if the premium is exorbitant and the security is adequate. It will be fair if the premium is instead of interest or the security is hazardous.

**Example 1**　Smith buys a house from Jones for £6,000. Smith pays Jones £1,200 out of his savings and £4,800 which he borrows from Robinson. Smith mortgages the house to Robinson to secure £6,960, payable by monthly instalments of £116 for five years. After paying Robinson promptly for one year, Smith defaults on the thirteenth instalment. Robinson claims £5,578 and interest on it from the date of the loan. The court will hold that a premium of £2,160 on a loan of £4,800 is too high because (a) looked at as being in lieu of interest, it would be in lieu of exorbitant interest; and (b) if the house was worth £6000, it was adequate security for a loan of £4,800, but not for an obligation to pay £6,960 and a charge for the latter amount would render Smith's interest in the property valueless. The court will allow Smith to redeem on paying Robinson £4,800 (the sum actually lent), plus reasonable interest, minus what has already been paid.[3]

**Example 2**　Smith, who owns a lease of a theatre, the lease having ten years to go, borrows £2,000 from Robinson to enable him to run the theatre. Smith covenants to repay Robinson by instalments for five years, and also to pay him one-third of the rents from underleases, and mortgages the lease to Robinson to secure both sums. The lease is worth more than these sums put together, although running a theatre is a hazardous enterprise. Smith seeks to redeem his lease without paying Robinson one-third of the rents paid by sub-lessees. The court will hold that he cannot do that, as the contract was fair and reasonable.[4]

**Clogs on the Equity of Redemption**　In England and Wales and Northern Ireland, the right to redeem must arise within a reasonable

3. See *Cityland and Property (Holdings) Ltd.* v. *Dabrah* [1968] Ch. 166, where interest was allowed at 7% per annum.
4. See *Santley* v. *Wilde* [1899] 2 Ch. 474; Keeton and Sheridan, *Equity*, pp. 206-7.

45

time and, once it has arisen, must continue until either it is exercised or statute-barred or the mortgagee takes the appropriate steps to realise his security.[5]

There is no rule of law specifying that a mortgaged property must become redeemable in six months in England and Wales and Northern Ireland, though that is the usual agreement, later and earlier dates being met in practice. Problems do arise when the date is made too far in the future. The principle of equity is that the specification of the date before which the mortgage cannot be redeemed is valid if the bargain is fair, but if the term is oppressive or unconscionable the mortgagor will be allowed to redeem earlier. Factors going to show oppression or unconscionableness include: (a) the mortgage being of a lease, the right to redeem being postponed until shortly before the lease is due to expire;[6] and (b) that during the period of irredeemability of the mortgage, the mortgagee is not precluded from calling for his money back.[7]

**Example** The Knightsbridge Estates Trust Ltd., owners and managers of shops, houses and a block of flats, borrowed £310,000, at $5\frac{1}{4}\%$ interest per annum, from an insurance company on security of the block of flats, eight shops and seventy-three houses. The mortgagors promised to repay by eighty equal half-yearly instalments (each instalment also including interest due). The right to redeem was to arise on payment of the last instalment. The mortgagors claimed to redeem after less than six years. The Court of Appeal held that the mortgagors could not redeem prematurely, because the forty year period was not oppressive or unconscionable: the parties were business concerns with expert advice; the mortgagors, who had proposed the terms, had been enabled to pay off a previous mortgage on less favourable terms; the sum was large; and the mortgagors had deliberately addressed themselves to a company seeking a long-term investment.[8]

In Scotland, the right to redeem is not generally specified to arise on any particular day, but on giving an agreed period of notice. In the case of the standard security, in the absence of an express term, two months' notice is required,[9] but the parties may stipulate longer or shorter notice or no notice at all.[10] In the case of the pre-1970

5. See Keeton and Sheridan, *Equity*, pp. 176-8.
6. *Fairclough* v. *Swan Brewery Co. Ltd.* [1912] A.C. 565.
7. *Morgan* v. *Jeffreys* [1901] 1 Ch. 620.
8. *Knightsbridge Estates Trust Ltd.* v. *Byrne* [1939] Ch. 441. See also Keeton and Sheridan, *Equity*, pp. 202-4. Scotland: see *Ashburton* v. *Escombe* (1892) 20 R. 187.
9. Conveyancing and Feudal Reform (Scotland) Act 1970, s. 18(1), as amended by the Redemption of Standard Securities (Scotland) Act 1971, s. 1(b).
10. 1970 Act, s. 18(1A), added by the 1971 Act, s. 1(c).

heritable securities, the length of notice required also depended on agreement and, in the case of a disposition ex facie absolute, solely on agreement. Under a bond and disposition in security, in the absence of agreement to the contrary – and agreement to the contrary was unusual – the statutory period of notice was three months.[11]

Similarly, throughout the United Kingdom, a term in a mortgage deed which will enable the mortgagee to make the property his own (otherwise than by realising his security) is void. In England and Wales and Northern Ireland, the equitable right to redeem after the legal date for redemption makes it impossible for the mortgagee to become owner by default of repayment when a very short period for the loan is specified. Scotland has an analogous doctrine. In *Smith* v. *Smith*,[12] A made an ex facie disposition by way of security to his brother, B, redemption to be within one year of the death of their mother. The court upheld A's attempt to redeem later, saying that a security could not cease to be a security and become the absolute property of the creditor 'without declarator of expiry of the legal,' i.e., without a declarator by the court of the extinction of the borrower's proprietary right.

An option given to the mortgagee to buy the mortgagor's interest in the property is void, if given in the mortgage deed,[13] or in a separate contract which is part of the same transaction,[14] whether or not there is oppression, for it is an insurmountable feature of mortgages that the borrower may get his property back on redemption. On the other hand, once he has made a mortgage, the mortgagor may sell his interest in the property, and, if he decides to do so, there is no reason why he should not sell to the mortgagee or grant him an option.[15] Similarly, there would be no objection to a mortgage deed giving the mortgagee a right of pre-emption, for it is then still up to the mortgagor to decide whether he wishes to sell or not.

**Contracts in Restraint of Trade**   Mortgages of retail business premises are sometimes made to secure loans granted by the suppliers of the goods retailed on those premises. When that occurs, a term will sometimes be found in the mortgage agreement restricting the right of the borrower to retail goods not supplied by the

11. See *Ashburton* v. *Escombe* (1892) 20 R. 187.   12. (1879) 6 R. 794.
13. *Samuel* v. *Jarrah Timber and Wood Paving Corp. Ltd.* [1904] A.C. 323.
14. *Lewis* v. *Frank Love Ltd.* [1961] 1 W.L.R. 261.
15. *Reeve* v. *Lisle* [1902] A.C. 461. Ireland: see *Maxwell* v. *Tipping* [1903] 1 I.R. 498.
See further, Keeton and Sheridan, *Equity*, pp. 177-8, 205-6.

lender. Questions then arise as to the validity of these terms. Some such restrictions are valid, but they are not allowed to go too far. Much of the case law of the late nineteenth and early twentieth centuries arose out of mortgages of public houses to brewers, while recently the courts have considered a number of disputes relating to mortgages of garages to oil companies.

So far as England and Wales and Northern Ireland are concerned, there are two lines of authority. One of these is the common-law doctrine that a contract in restraint of trade is void if it is unreasonable to the person restrained or to the public interest by going further than is necessary for the protection of the reasonable trade interests of the person favoured by the restraint. This doctrine was evolved in cases of restraints of competition by a former employee against his former employer and in cases of restraints imposed on a purchaser of a business in favour of the vendor. Only recently has the doctrine been applied to mortgages, in *Esso Petroleum Co. Ltd.* v. *Harper's Garage (Stourport) Ltd.*[16] There, H mortgaged a garage to E to secure a loan of £7,000 repayable by instalments over a period of twenty-one years. By a separate agreement, H covenanted to sell no motor fuel on the premises except fuel supplied by E for a period expiring three months before the last mortgage instalment was due. Two years later, H started selling other petrol at the garage and, a year after that, tried to redeem the mortgage. It was held that the restriction on H was void because a tie for twenty-one years was too long: the period exceeded that for which developments were foreseeable and there was no evidence that it gave E any advantage that would not be equally secured by a shorter period of restraint. The principles relating to the validity of contracts in restraint of trade are the same in Scotland. In *MacIntyre* v. *Cleveland Petroleum Co. Ltd.*,[17] on facts similar to those of the *Esso* case, they were applied so as to render void a condition in a back letter relative to an ex facie absolute disposition of heritable subjects.

The other line of authority in England and Wales and Northern Ireland (of which there is no Scottish equivalent) consists of the equitable doctrine against turning a security into something different. Exactly what the doctrine is cannot be said for certain because the House of Lords has adopted different approaches. It is probable that the correct doctrine is, in the words of Lord

16. [1968] A.C. 269. Ireland: see *Irish Shell and BP Ltd.* v. *Ryan* [1966] I.R. 75. See also *Texaco Ltd.* v. *Mulberry Filling Station Ltd.* [1972] 1 W.L.R. 814; Keeton and Sheridan, *Equity*, pp. 207–8.
17. 1967 S.L.T. 95.

Parker of Waddington in *Kreglinger* v. *New Patagonia Meat and Cold Storage Co. Ltd.*,[18] 'that there is now no rule in equity which precludes a mortgagee, whether the mortgage be made upon the occasion of a loan or otherwise, from stipulating for any collateral advantage, provided such collateral advantage is not either (1) unfair and unconscionable, or (2) in the nature of a penalty clogging the equity of redemption, or (3) inconsistent with or repugnant to the contractual and equitable right to redeem.' In that case the House of Lords upheld a term in a floating charge,[19] redeemable on one month's notice, by which the chargors promised not to sell their sheepskins to anyone except the chargees for five years, so long as the chargees were willing to purchase the skins at a price equal to the best price offered by anyone else. The charge was redeemed after three years, but it was held that the term in restraint of trade was binding for the whole five years. It did not come within one of the three objectionable categories mentioned by Lord Parker. Their lordships treated the principles applicable to a floating charge as being the same as those governing mortgages.

That is the latest English case. Earlier cases are reconcilable with it, but the process is sometimes difficult. In *Noakes and Co. Ltd.* v. *Rice* the mortgagor[20] was a publican who borrowed money from some brewers on the security of his twenty-six year lease of his public house. In the mortgage deed, the mortgagor promised that for the remainder of his lease, even if he redeemed the mortgage, he would sell no beer on the premises except beer supplied by the mortgagees. Six months later, the mortgagor tried to redeem, and the House of Lords held that the restrictive covenant became void on redemption. The restraint of trade was regarded as a clog on the equity of redemption because according to its terms it was to continue after redemption: the borrower, having mortgaged a free house, would be redeeming a tied house. The difficulty is that, in the *Kreglinger* case, where *Noakes* v. *Rice* was cited and binding, a restriction was held not oppressive despite the fact that it was to continue after redemption. Perhaps the true distinction is that in *Noakes* v. *Rice*, unlike the *Kreglinger* case, the restriction, if valid, would have continued throught the mortgagor's ownership of the public house. (The restraint of trade was valid and effective until the mortgage was redeemed.)[21]

---

18. [1914] A.C. 25, 60–1. See also Keeton and Sheridan, *Equity*, pp. 208–9.
19. See pp. 126–43, *post*.    20. [1902] A.C. 24.
21. *Biggs* v. *Hoddinott* [1898] 2 Ch. 307.

Another difficult case is *Bradley* v. *Carritt*.[22] It does not relate to land, but the principles are the same. The owner of shares in a tea-producing company mortgaged those shares to a tea broker and promised that, in his capacity of shareholder, he would use his best endeavours to secure that the mortgagee would always thereafter be the broker on the sale of the company's teas; he also promised to pay the mortgagee the commission the mortgagee would have earned as broker should the company employ another broker. The shares were redeemed, and subsequently the company employed a tea broker other than the ex-mortgagee, who now sued the ex-mortgagor on the promise to pay his commission. All five judges of the House of Lords thought it a clear case. The majority (Lords Macnaghten, Davey and Robertson) held that the action failed because the mortgagor's promise was void, at least after the mortgagor had redeemed his shares. It would appear that it was void either because it provided for a collateral advantage to the mortgagee after redemption and fettered the shareholder's freedom of voting, or because it made redemption illusory in that the shareholder would not be able to sell the shares for fear of losing influence to get the company to employ the former mortgagee as broker. Lords Shand and Lindley were for the plaintiff, being of the opinion that the mortgagor's promise was valid because it was not unconscionable, fraudulent or obtained by undue influence or extortion. They said that the shareholder, after redemption, was free to sell his shares, and, if the company employed another broker, to pay up what had been agreed.

**Attornment Clauses**    Sometimes a legal mortgage in England and Wales or Northern Ireland includes a clause which states that the mortgagor is to be the mortgagee's lessee: 'the mortgagor hereby attorns tenant to the mortgagee.' Such a clause, which creates the relation of landlord and tenant so far as consistent with the relationship of mortgagee and mortgagor, is of little practical value nowadays. It used to secure some benefits to the mortgagee, but changes in the law have, for the most part, made these benefits unattainable with an attornment clause or available without one.[23]

---

22. [1903] A.C. 253. Ireland: see *Browne* v. *Ryan* [1901] 2 I.R. 653.
23. As to the past and present value of the attornment clause, see Keeton and Sheridan, *Equity*, pp. 282–4.

# 5 land: mortgagor and mortgagee in possession

## Mortgagor in Possession

Legal mortgagees of land in England and Wales, and legal mortgagees of unregistered land in Northern Ireland have a right to possession. Normally, however, any mortgagee will leave the mortgagor in possession, at least until realising the security, for the intention is that the owner, the mortgagor, is to use the mortgaged property; and the mortgagee has made an investment, not a purchase, and does not intend to take on the trouble and responsibility of occupation and management. Equitable mortgagees of land in England and Wales and all mortgagees of registered land in Northern Ireland can take possession only by agreement with the mortgagor or under an order of the court. A mortgagor can be, but seldom is, granted security of tenure, or a right to notice before ejection, by the mortgage contract. While he is in possession, the mortgagor has general powers of managing the mortgaged land.

In Scotland, a heritable creditor's right to possession arises only on default by the debtor. Under the old forms of express security, the right to possession on default was conferred by the Registration of Leases (Scotland) Act 1857, section 6, and the Heritable Securities (Scotland) Act 1894, sections 3 and 5. Where the security was constituted by an ex facie absolute disposition, the creditor's right to possession, except on default, was excluded by the contract between the parties. In the case of the standard security, by virtue of the Conveyancing and Feudal Reform (Scotland) Act 1970, section 11 and schedule 3, standard condition 10(3), the creditor's right to possession again arises only on default.

**Management and Protection of the Land**  Generally speaking, the mortagor in possession can do anything that will not interfere with the mortgagee's security. He can cut timber or mine minerals, so long as the value of the land as security is not jeopardised.[1] Subject to stringent limitations, he can let the land.[2] If the land is let before or after the making of the mortgage, he can enforce the tenant's obligations.[3] He can sue to protect the land, e.g., from trespass or nuisance.[4]

In Scotland, it has been held[5] that where feus were granted by the owner of land subject to a bond and disposition in security, without the heritable creditor's authority, the feuars' property was subject to the mortgage, even if the feuars did not know of the bond and disposition in security. Here they did not know of it – though they could have found out by consulting the Register of Sasines – and they had built houses on their land: so the houses became part of the disponee's security.

**Leasing Powers**  The powers of a mortgagor in possession to grant leases have already been referred to in connection with clauses in mortgage deeds regulating or excluding such powers.[6]

In England and Wales, in the absence of express terms in the mortgage contract, the powers of the mortgagor in possession to grant leases are conferred and regulated by the Law of Property Act 1925, section 99. This section[7] sets out in detail the types of lease that can be granted and the terms upon which they can be granted, e.g., the best rent reasonably obtainable must be reserved.[8] In Northern Ireland,[9] the law is similar, except that the permitted lengths for different kinds of lease are shorter than in England and Wales.

1. See, further, as to England and Wales and Northern Ireland, Keeton and Sheridan, *Equity*, pp. 222–4.   2. See below.
3. England and Wales and Northern Ireland: *Fairclough* v. *Marshall* (1878) 4 Ex.D. 37. Additional powers are conferred on the mortgagor in England and Wales by the Law of Property Act 1925, s. 141(1), replacing the Conveyancing Act 1881, s. 10 (still in force in Northern Ireland), applied in *Turner* v. *Walsh* [1909] 2 K.B. 484.
4. England and Wales: Law of Property Act 1925, s. 98, replacing the Judicature Act 1873, s. 25(5). Northern Ireland: Judicature Act (Ireland) 1877, s. 28(5). Scotland: *M'Bride* v. *Caledonian Railway Co.* (1894) 21 R. 620, where, after an ex facie absolute disposition, the mortgagor in possession was held able to sue for damage caused to the property by the negligent construction of a sewer; *Scobie* v. *William Lind & Co. Ltd.* 1967 S.L.T. 9 (another case of a mortgage by ex facie absolute disposition). See also *Vincent* v. *Wood* (1899) 6 S L.T. 297.   5. *Soues* v. *Mill* (1903) 11 S.L.T. 98.
6. See pp. 39–43, *ante*.   7. See p. 39, *ante*; Keeton and Sheridan, *Equity*, pp. 224–9.
8. See also s. 100 of the 1925 Act, which authorises the mortgagor to accept a surrender of a lease for the purpose of granting one under s. 99.
9. See p. 39, *ante*. Power to grant leases: Conveyancing Acts 1881, s. 18, and 1911, s. 3(10), (11). Power to accept surrenders: 1911 Act, s. 3(1)–(7).

The effect of a lease by a mortgagor in possession in England and Wales or Northern Ireland, granted in accordance with the statutory powers, is that the mortgagee is bound by the lease. That means that the mortgagee cannot eject the tenant. If the mortgagee takes possession as against the mortgagor, that simply means that in future the tenant must pay his rent to the mortgagee instead of the mortgagor. If the lease granted by the mortgagor is outside his statutory powers, the lease binds him but does not bind the mortgagee. That means that the mortgagor cannot interfere with the tenant's rights under the lease, but if the mortgagee goes into possession as against the mortgagor he can, if he wishes, eject the tenant too. This was the result in *Hughes* v. *Waite*,[10] for example, where the leases were ultra vires because they were not granted at a rent but at premiums. If a mortgagor's tenant is liable to be ejected by the mortgagee, the only way he can protect himself is by redeeming the mortgage (in which case he will stand in the shoes of the mortgagee as against the mortgagor). To a very limited extent, invalidity may be cured by statute where the mortgagor intended to exercise his power of leasing and made the lease in good faith, and where the lessee has entered on the land. In such a case, the invalid lease takes effect as a contract to grant a valid lease on the terms of the invalid lease as varied so as to make them valid.[11] In *Pawson* v. *Revell*[12] this statutory provision was applied to save an oral letting which had not included a condition for re-entry for non-payment of rent.

In Scotland, the debtor who has given a standard security has no statutory power of leasing the land without the consent of the creditor. Such consent may be given in writing, under standard condition 6, to a particular lease, or by excluding or varying that condition when the standard security is created. Under the old forms of heritable security there were no statutory powers either, the rights of the debtor in possession, in the absence of express agreement, depending on his radical title or on the implied authority to manage the property given to him by the mortgagee leaving him in possession.[13]

---

10. [1957] 1 W.L.R. 713.
11. England and Wales: Law of Property Act 1925, s. 152, replacing the Leases Acts 1849 and 1850, which are still in force in Northern Ireland.
12. [1958] 2 Q.B. 360.   13. See pp. 41-3, *ante*.

## Mortgagee in Possession

### The Mortgagee's Right to Possession  *England and Wales.* A
legal mortgagee:

> ... may go into possession before the ink is dry on the mortgage
> unless there is something in the contract, express or by implication,
> whereby he has contracted himself out of that right. He has the
> right because he has a legal term of years in the property or its
> statutory equivalent. If there is an attornment clause, he must
> give notice. If there is a provision that, so long as certain payments
> are made, he will not go into possession, then he has contracted
> himself out of his rights. Apart from that, possession is a matter of
> course.[14]

The mortgagee asks the mortgagor to hand over possession of the
land; if the mortgagor agrees, the mortgagee goes in; if the mortgagor does not agree, the mortgagee has to bring an action for
possession. Apart from the considerations mentioned by Harman J.,
there would be no answer to the mortgagee's common law claim
except to redeem the mortgage. The courts exercise an inherent
jurisdiction to grant a short adjournment of the mortgagee's action
for possession if there is a reasonable prospect of the mortgagor
paying off the debt during the adjournment, but there is no discretion under the inherent jurisdiction to keep the mortgagor
waiting long or in any other circumstances.[15] The discretion has
been embodied in section 36 of the Administration of Justice Act
1970 where the mortgagee is applying (otherwise than in a foreclosure[16] action) for possession of premises which consist of or include
a dwelling-house. If it appears to the court that the mortgagor is
likely to be able, within a reasonable period, to pay what is due to
the mortgagee, or to remedy any other default than failure to pay
debts, the court may adjourn the action for possession, or make an
order for possession subject to a stay of execution or with a postponed
date for yielding up possession, or order a stay or postponement
after making an order for possession if the order has not yet been
executed. Any adjournment, stay or postponement will be for such

---

14. *Four-Maids Ltd.* v. *Dudley Marshall (Properties) Ltd.* [1957] Ch. 317, 320, *per* Harman J.
See also Keeton and Sheridan, *Equity*, pp. 230–2.
15. See *Birmingham Citizens Permanent Building Soc.* v. *Caunt* [1962] Ch. 883; *London Permanent Benefit Building Soc.* v. *de Baer* [1969] 1 Ch. 321; Ryder, 'The Legal Mortagee and His Right to Possession' (1969) 22 *Current Legal Problems* 129.
16. As to the application of the discretion in foreclosure actions, see the Administration of Justice Act 1973, s. 8(3).

period as the court thinks reasonable. It can be granted subject to conditions, e.g., as to payment, imposed on the mortgagor.[17] By the Administration of Justice Act 1973, section 8(1), the court is empowered to treat as due, under section 36 of the Act of 1970, only sums which would be due under the agreement if the mortgagor had not defaulted (thus empowering the court to give the mortgagor some relief from a contractual provision that the whole mortgage money, and not merely arrears of instalments or interest, is to become due on default in an obligation). Section 8(2) of the 1973 Act states that the power under section 36 of the Act of 1970 is not to be exercised, by virtue of section 8(1), unless the mortgagor is likely to be able to pay any additional sums becoming due during the reasonable period allowed for payment.

The equitable mortgagee, not having a legal estate in the land, is not entitled to possession. However, if he takes it with the consent of the mortgagor, he will be entitled to retain possession. Furthermore, he may claim a court order for possession. The difference between an action for possession by a legal mortgagee and such an action by an equitable mortgagee is that the latter is seeking an equitable remedy. Equitable remedies are discretionary, and may be granted on terms. However, if there is nothing inequitable in granting possession, he will get it as a matter of course.

**Example** A husband who owns the matrimonial home mortgages it by equitable charge in favour of a bank. The husband later deserts the wife, leaving her living in the house. She gets a court order, under section 17 of the Married Women's Property Act 1882, entitling her to go on living there. Later, the husband goes bankrupt and the bank apply to the court for an order giving them possession of the mortgaged house. The court will grant the application because the mortgagees have an equity which is prior to that of the wife.[18]

**Northern Ireland** The law is the same as that of England and Wales,[19] except with regard to legal mortgages of registered land. The owner of a registered charge over such land has, in general, all the rights of a legal mortgagee of unregistered land:[20] the exception

17. See also ss. 37–9; Samuels, 'Actions by Mortgagees for Possession' (1970), 34 *Conveyancer* 324; *Corbiere Properties Ltd.* v. *Taylor* (1971) 23 P. & C.R. 289; *Halifax Building Soc.* v. *Clark* [1973] 2 Ch. 307; *First Middlesbrough Trading & Mortgage Co. Ltd.* v. *Cunningham* (1974), *The Times* newspaper, 26th February.
18. See *Barclays Bank Ltd.* v. *Bird* [1954] Ch. 274.
19. The Administration of Justice Act 1970, ss. 36 and 39, applies to Northern Ireland: see s. 54(6); and so does s. 8(1), (2), of the Act of 1973.
20. Land Registration Act (Northern Ireland) 1970, s. 41 and sch. 7, para. 5(4).

is the right to take possession at will. The legislation[21] provides that he may apply to a county court for possession of the land, and that the court may grant possession only if: (a) the principal money secured by the mortgage has become due and the court thinks it proper to grant the application; or (b) the court is satisfied that there are urgent and special reasons for granting possession.

**Scotland** In respect of the standard security, the creditor may go into possession of the land when the debtor has defaulted in his obligations to him, either by agreement with the debtor or in accordance with a term of the security contract, but apart from such a term he has no right to take possession. Standard condition 10(3)[22] entitles the creditor to enter into possession of the security subjects and to receive or recover feu duties, ground annuals or, as the case may be, the rents of those subjects or any part thereof. Additional powers of entry for limited purposes are conferred by standard conditions 7(2) and 10(6).

A creditor secured by ex facie absolute disposition may go into possession of the land because he has the feudal title.[23] No action of maills and duties, no diligence of poinding the ground, is necessary – or, indeed, competent, for the creditor is not an incumbrancer, and an owner cannot poind his own ground. The holder of a bond and disposition or assignation in security (where the lease is not a short one where possession is necessary to complete the security), or of a bond of cash credit and disposition in security, has a statutory right, upon default by a debtor, to possession of the heritable subject.[24] On the debtor defaulting, becoming a notour bankrupt or granting a trust deed for his creditors, the mortgagee can go into possession by consent or by bringing an action of maills and duties against the debtor, giving notice of the action to any tenants there may be.[25]

### Reasons For and Against the Mortgagee Taking Possession

A mortgagee who goes into possession of the mortgaged land usually does so in conjunction with his exercise of the power of sale. He wants vacant possession so as to pass it on to the purchaser. If the

21. 1970 Act, sch. 7, para. 5(2), (3).
22. Conveyancing and Feudal Reform (Scotland) Act 1970, sch. 3.
23. *Scottish Heritable Security Co. (Ltd.)* v. *Allen, Campbell & Co.* (1876) 3 R. 333. See also *Rankin* v. *Russell* (1868) 7 M. 126. Cf. *Scottish Property Investment Co. Building Soc.* v. *Horne* (1881) 8 R. 737.
24. Heritable Securities (Scotland) Act 1894, s. 5. See also the Registration of Leases (Scotland) Act 1857, s. 6.
25. Conveyancing (Scotland) Act 1924, s. 25(1) (q). See also the Heritable Securities (Scotland) Act 1894, s. 3.

mortgagee sells without having gone into possession, the purchaser can get the mortgagor out; but it is easier to find a purchaser for a property with vacant possession than it is to sell a property with a right to obtain vacant possession.

The mortgagee may feel it necessary to go into possession in order to manage the property, e.g., in order to grant leases of it, because the mortgagor, by not managing the property properly, is not producing sufficient income to keep down the mortgage interest or is even diminishing its value as security for the principal debt. But if a mortgagee can avoid going into possession, except as a short-term measure, he will avoid doing so because, by entering into possession of the property, the mortgagee saddles himself with duties of good management and to account to the mortgagor for his stewardship.[26]

As a temporary expedient, the mortgagee may take possession of mortgaged premises to rectify something, e.g., to carry out repairs that should have been done by the mortgagor, but in that event the mortgagee will go out of possession again as soon as he has secured his objective. If the property is producing income, but the mortgagor is not paying his interest or instalments of repayment punctually. the mortgagee need not go into possession, but can appoint a receiver of the income.[27]

### Leasing Powers of the Mortgagee in Possession

**England and Wales and Northern Ireland** The statutory powers of the mortgagee in possession to grant leases of the mortgaged land are similar to those of the mortgagor in possession.[28] It is not usual for the mortgage contract to curtail those powers.

**Scotland** In the case of a standard security, the position of the creditor is governed by the following standard conditions:[29]

10(4) Where he has entered into possession . . . , he may let the security subjects or any part thereof.

10(5) Where he has entered into possession . . . , there shall be transferred to him all the rights of the debtor in relation to the granting of leases or rights of occupancy over the security subjects and to the management and maintenance of those subjects.

In the case of an ex facie absolute disposition, the disponee in possession can grant leases because he is the feudal owner. The

---

26. See pp. 58–9, *post.*    27. See pp. 67–9, *post.*
28. See pp. 52–3, *ante.*
29. Conveyancing and Feudal Reform (Scotland) Act 1970, sch. 3.

creditor in possession under one of the old express heritable securities has a statutory power to grant leases.[30]

A creditor in possession can bring an action against a tenant for sequestration for non-payment of rent, based upon his right of hypothec as landlord.[31] If he collects rents, the creditor in possession must pay feu duty thereout.

> **Example** Angus disponed his block of flats to Basil by bond and disposition in security. Later, Angus granted a second security over the same block of flats to Charles, by ex facie absolute disposition. Both securities were created before 1970. After 1970, Basil goes into possession of the block of flats, collects rents from tenants of individual flats, and uses the money he collects in partial payment to himself of arrears of interest due on the debt. Donald, the superior, collects feu duty from Charles, who is liable as feudal owner to pay it. The court will hold that Basil is liable to repay Charles the amount of the feu duty.[32]

## The Accountability of the Mortgagee in Possession

A mortgagee in possession who collects rents or other income from the land must account for it to the mortgagor. He may retain for himself only his costs of management of the property and what is due to him in respect of the mortgagor's arrears of interest or of instalments of repayment. Any balance must be handed over to the mortgagor or, where appropriate, to a later mortgagee to whom payments are due.

If the mortgagee in possession is guilty of wilful default in his management of the property, he must account not only for the money he actually receives but also for the higher amount he would have received if he had not so defaulted.

> **Example** Leonard owns a garage at which he sells petrol and oil supplied by various companies. In order to raise capital for expansion of his business, Leonard mortgages his garage to the Mollusc Oil Co. Ltd. When Leonard defaults in payment of interest, the mortgagee company take possession of the garage and grant a lease of it for ten years to Oliver at a rent of £1,500 a year. Oliver contracts that he will sell only petrol supplied by Mollusc. Mollusc make a profit of 4p a gallon on petrol supplied

30. Heritable Securities (Scotland) Act 1894, ss. 6 and 7; *Mackenzie* v. *Imlay's Trustees* 1912 S.C. 685; *Macrae* v. *Leith* 1913 S.C. 901.
31. *Robertson's Trustees* v. *Gardner* (1889) 16 R. 705. See also *Chambers' Judicial Factor* v. *Vertue* (1893) 20 R. 257.
32. See *Liquidators of the City of Glasgow Bank* v. *Nicolson's Trustees* (1882) 9 R. 689.

to Oliver. Had there been no restrictive covenant by the lessee, the market rent of the garage for a ten-year lease would have been £1,750 a year. The court will hold that the mortgagee (a) need not account for the profit on the petrol supplied to the lessee; (b) must account on the basis of a rent of £1,750 a year (i.e., hand to the mortgagor £1,750 a year less the mortgagees' expenses and less what is due to them in respect of the secured debt).[33]

The law is the same throughout the United Kingdom.

---

33. See *White* v. *City of London Brewery Co.* (1889) 42 Ch.D. 237. See further, Keeton and Sheridan, *Equity*, pp. 235–8.

# 6 land: redemption and enforcement of securities

## Redemption

**Date of Redemption** In England and Wales and Northern Ireland, the legal date for redeeming a mortgage is that specified in the contract of loan as being the date for repayment.[1] If the mortgage is not redeemed on that date, an equitable right to redeem it thereafter continues indefinitely. That right to redeem will end when the mortgagee realises his security[2] or extinguishes the right of redemption by adverse possession.[3] There is no right to redeem a mortgage before the date specified in the contract,[1] but the mortgagee may, of course, agree to accept payment early and discharge the security.

In Scotland, the right to redeem any security depends on the contract of the parties. Usually, no date is mentioned, but the debtor is empowered to redeem on giving a specified period of notice. In the absence of agreement to the contrary, in the case of the standard security, for example, the period of notice is two months or such shorter period as the debtor may persuade the creditor to accept.[4]

**Who May Redeem** Obviously the mortgagor may redeem if, and only if, he still owns the mortgaged property. If the mortgagor has parted with the property, his successor in title may redeem. There

---

1. As to clogs on the equity of redemption, see pp. 45–7, *ante.*
2. See pp. 69–81, *post.*     3. See pp. 65-6, *post.*
4. Conveyancing and Feudal Reform (Scotland) Act 1970, s. 18(1), as amended by the Redemption of Standard Securities (Scotland) Act 1971, s. 1(*b*); s. 18(1A) of the 1970 Act, added by s. 1(*c*) of the 1971 Act; and standard condition 11(1), (2), in sch. 3 of the 1970 Act, as amended by s. 1(*g*) of the Act of 1971.

may also be redemption by a person with a current limited interest in the mortgaged property, derived from the mortgagor or his successor in title, being an interest which would be overridden by the mortgagee's enforcement of his security. These persons would usually be: (a) a subsequent mortgagee; (b) a lessee under a lease not binding on the mortgagee,[5] or, in Scotland, a feuar or other grantee in such a position; (c) a tenant for life under a trust of the mortgaged property;[6] (d) a person who has contracted to buy the equity of redemption.[7]

Subject to agreement to the contrary,[8] the right to redeem a standard security in Scotland is described[9] as belonging to the debtor, or, where the debtor is not the proprietor, to the proprietor of the security subjects. This presumably includes a limited proprietor. In respect of the older types of heritable security, it was held in *Cunningham's Trustees* v. *Hutton*[10] that, if a prior mortgagee is selling the security subjects, a subsequent mortgagee cannot stop him and insist on redeeming the prior mortgage if the subsequent mortgagee's debt would be paid off in full out of the proceeds of the prior mortgagee's sale.

In general, a person with no current interest in the mortgaged property cannot redeem. He may persuade the mortgagee to accept payment and transfer or discharge the mortgage, but that is not redemption. Redemption is payment and discharge without the mortgagee having the option of not complying. In England, it has been held that no right to redeem can be exercised by, for example: (i) a subsequent mortgagee whose rights against the mortgagor were statute-barred;[11] and (ii) a person claiming an interest in proceeds of sale of land held on trust for sale: an interest in such proceeds is not an interest in land for this purpose.[12] In England and Wales and Northern Ireland, a person with no interest in the mortgaged property can redeem if sued for the debt or part of it. Such would be the position of a mortgagor who had sold his land subject to the mortgage[13] or who had been foreclosed[14] or whose land had been

---

5. See *Tarn* v. *Turner* (1888) 39 Ch.D. 456.
6. See, further, Keeton and Sheridan, *Equity*, pp. 187, 189–90.
7. Cf. *Duke* v. *Robson* [1973] 1 W.L.R. 267.
8. Conveyancing and Feudal Reform (Scotland) Act 1970, s. 18(1), (1A); Redemption of Standard Securities (Scotland) Act 1971, s. 1(b), (c).
9. Conveyancing and Feudal Reform (Scotland) Act 1970, s. 18(1).
10. (1847) 10 D. 307.
11. *Cotterell* v. *Price* [1960] 1 W.L.R. 1097.
12. *Irani Finance Ltd.* v. *Singh* [1971] Ch. 59.
13. *Kinnaird* v. *Trollope* (1888) 39 Ch. D. 636.
14. *Mexborough U.D.C.* v. *Harrison* [1964] 1 W.L.R. 733.

sold to the mortgagee in a foreclosure action,[15] and who, in each case, was subsequently sued for the debt or part of it under his personal contract to pay.

In Scotland, too, a person who is not a proprietor of any interest in the mortgaged propery is generally not entitled to redeem.[16]

**The Process of Redemption**  The person redeeming a mortgage must pay the mortgagee everything that is due to him – the principal debt or the unpaid balance of it, arrears of interest, if any, and reimbursement of proper costs the mortgagee may have incurred. Redemption is an equitable remedy in England, so a person redeeming may be put on terms to do something he is not legally obliged to do. For example, he will be obliged to pay statute-barred arrears of interest as well as those recoverable at law.[17]

In England and Wales and Northern Ireland, if redemption does not occur on the date specified in the mortgage contract, the person redeeming must usually give six months' notice of his intention to redeem unless the agreement provides for a different period or the mortgagee agrees to accept shorter notice. The notice is to allow the mortgagee time to find an alternative investment for his money. The rule of six months' notice does not apply to short term mortgages, such as the usual mortgage by deposit of title deeds, where reasonable notice is all that is required; nor to redemption when the mortgagee has demanded payment or has entered into possession, in which cases there can be redemption without notice.

In Scotland, with regard to the standard security, section 18 of the Conveyancing and Feudal Reform (Scotland) Act 1970 provides as follows:

(1)[18] Subject to the provisions of subsection (1A) of this section, the debtor in a standard security or, where the debtor is not the proprietor, the proprietor of the security subjects shall be entitled to redeem the security on giving two months' notice of his intention to do so, and in conformity with the terms of standard condition 11 and the appropriate Forms of Schedule 5 to this Act.

(1A)[19] The provisions of the foregoing subsection shall be subject

15. *Gordon Grant & Co. Ltd.* v. *Boos* [1926] A.C. 781. See further, Keeton and Sheridan, *Equity*, p. 190.
16. As to the right of a cautioner who pays to a transfer of securities, see pp. 296-7 *post*.
17. *Holmes* v. *Cowcher* [1970] 1 W.L.R. 834.
18. As amended by the Redemption of Standard Securities (Scotland) Act 1971, s. 1(b).
19. Added by s. 1(c) of the Act of 1971.

to any agreement to the contrary, but any right to redeem the security shall be exercisable in conformity with the terms and Forms referred to in that subsection.

(2)[20] Where owing to the death or absence of the creditor, or to any other cause, the debtor in a standard security or, as the case may be, the proprietor of the security subjects (being in either case a person entitled to redeem the security) is unable to obtain a discharge under the foregoing provisions of this section, he may:

(a) where the security was granted in respect of any obligation to repay or pay money, consign in any bank in Scotland, incorporated by or under Act of Parliament or by Royal Charter, the whole amount due to the creditor on redemption, other than any unascertained expenses of the creditor, for the person appearing to have the best rights thereto, and

(b) in any other case, apply to the court for declarator that the whole obligations under the contract to which the security relates have been performed.[21]

(3) On consignation, or on the court granting declarator as aforesaid, a certificate to that effect may be expede by a solicitor in the appropriate form prescribed by Form D of Schedule 5 to this Act, which on being duly recorded shall disburden the interest in land, to which the standard security relates, of that security.

(4) For the purposes of this section, 'whole amount due' means the debt to which the security relates, so far as outstanding, and any other sums due thereunder by way of interest or otherwise.

The first two clauses[22] of standard condition 11 run:

(1) The debtor shall be entitled to exercise his right (if any) to redeem the security on giving notice of his intention to do so, being a notice in writing (hereinafter referred to as a 'notice of redemption').

(2) Nothing in the provisions of this Act shall preclude a creditor from waiving the necessity for a notice of redemption, or from agreeing to a period of notice of less than that to which he is entitled.

That condition cannot be varied by the parties.[23]

20. As amended by s. 1(d) of the Act of 1971.
21. For provision for discharge of a bond and disposition or assignation in security (including a bond of cash credit) where a discharge is not obtainable from the creditor, see the Conveyancing (Scotland) Act 1874, s. 49.
22. Conveyancing and Feudal Reform (Scotland) Act 1970, sch. 3, as amended by the Redemption of Standard Securities (Scotland) Act 1971, s. 1(g).
23. 1970 Act, s. 11(3), as amended by s. 1(a) of the Act of 1971.

## The Duty of the Mortgagee on Redemption

**England and Wales** By the Law of Property Act 1925, section 115, a mortgage of unregistered land may be discharged or transferred by an appropriately worded receipt endorsed on, written at the foot of, or annexed to, the mortgage instrument. Such a receipt operates as a discharge if payment was by the mortgagor or someone on his behalf, but as a transfer of the mortgage if payment was by anyone else, such as a subsequent mortgagee. The duty of the mortgagee to execute a reassignment, surrender, release, or transfer, in lieu of a receipt, is preserved by subsection (4), in the event of his being required to do so. In the case of registered land, a registered charge is discharged by cancellation of the entry on the register.[24]

In general,[25] a person paying off a mortgage may require the mortgagee to transfer the mortgage to someone else. For example, a mortgagor who borrows from A to pay off B may require B to transfer his mortgage security to A. If the mortgagor has obtained better terms from A than he had from B he is able to protect A in that way by clothing him with B's priority over subsequent incumbrancers.[26]

If the mortgagee will not discharge the mortgage when payment is made or offered, the mortgagor or other payer may bring a redemption action. In such an action, either party[27] may be granted an order for sale as an alternative to redemption (if the mortgagor wins) or foreclosure (if the mortgagee wins). If the mortgagee has initiated proceedings, e.g., for foreclosure, the mortgagor may claim redemption in that action without bringing separate proceedings of his own.

An equitable mortgage by deposit of title deeds or of the land certificate is normally discharged by executing a receipt and returning the documents deposited.

**Northern Ireland** The law is the same in general,[28] the main exception being that there is no statutory provision for discharge by

24. Land Registration Act 1925, s. 35.     25. Law of Property Act 1925, s. 95.
26. See further, Keeton and Sheridan, *Equity*, pp. 190–3, and, as to merger on redemption, pp. 193–6.
27. Law of Property Act, 1925, s. 91.
28. The statutory provisions are as follows. Discharge of registered charges: Land Registration Act (Northern Ireland) 1970, s. 49. Right of payer to require transfer instead of reconveyance: Conveyancing Acts 1881, s. 15, and 1882, s. 12. There is no statutory provision for a mortgagor or mortgagee to have an order for sale in a redemption action. There being no foreclosure in Northern Ireland, an unsuccessful redemption action would normally result in an order for sale, or a judgment that no right of redemption existed in the plaintiff.

receipt. Hence, a mortgagee must always reconvey or transfer his security interest in the land by a formal document.

**Scotland** A standard security duly recorded may be discharged or it may be transferred. There are separate forms for the two transactions. Assignation is governed by section 14 of the Conveyancing and Feudal Reform (Scotland) Act 1970, and discharge by section 17. The creditor must transfer or discharge as required by the payer.

The older forms of heritable security required transfers or discharges according to their form.[29] At common law, the creditor secured by an ex facie absolute disposition would have had to reconvey the feudal ownership to the debtor on redemption by him. A simpler procedure was introduced by section 40 of the Conveyancing and Feudal Reform (Scotland) Act 1970, which allows such a security to be discharged, and the land to be vested in the person entitled to it as effectively as if there had been a full conveyance, by a simple attested deed (endorsed on the conveyance to the creditor or separate from it) acknowledging that the disposition was by way of security and that the debt secured by it has been paid off.

**Loss of the Right to Redeem** In all parts of the United Kingdom, a security ceases to be redeemable when one of the following events occurs:

1. The debtor's interest in the property is destroyed by foreclosure, a procedure by which the creditor ceases to hold the property as security and becomes its beneficial owner.
2. The creditor exercises an express, implied or statutory power to sell the property free from the debtor's interest, thus making the purchaser the beneficial owner.
3. The debtor's rights are barred by adverse possession (England and Wales and Northern Ireland) or prescription (Scotland) (in the case of an ex facie absolute disposition).

Foreclosure and sale figure later in this chapter.

In England and Wales[30] and Northern Ireland,[31] when a mortgagee has been in possession of any of the mortgaged land for twelve years, neither the mortgagor nor any person claiming through him can any longer bring an action to redeem the land of which the mortgagee has been in possession for that period; and the mort-

29. As to discharge of a bond and disposition (or assignation) in security, see the Conveyancing (Scotland) Act 1924, s. 29.
30. Limitation Act 1939, s. 12.
31. Statute of Limitations (Northern Ireland) 1958, s. 36.

gagor's title to the land is extinguished.[32] So far as Scotland is concerned, there is no such concept as adverse possession, but a limited similarity is provided by positive prescription. Essentially, this type of prescription operates to buttress a title and not to confer a new one. Possession, by someone who holds under a title expressed to be by way of security, cannot convert the security into ownership. But possession by someone who holds a title ex facie absolute can render the title absolute (positive prescription) and nullify the contractual right to redeem (negative prescription). Difficulty is caused by the period of positive prescription being ten years and that of negative prescription, twenty. It seems to follow that, if there is a security constituted by ex facie absolute disposition, duly recorded in the Register of Sasines, twenty years possession of the disponed land by the creditor, peaceably and without interruption, will put an end to the contractual right to redeem: that, on expiry of ten years' possession by the creditor, he could give an unchallengeable title to a third-party purchaser; but that, if the debtor offered to redeem, after such a purchaser had bought, but before the twenty-year period had expired, the creditor would be liable in damages to the debtor for breach of the latter's contractual right to redeem.[33]

## Remedies of the Creditor to Enforce his Security

The creditor may adopt one (or sometimes more than one at a time) of the following methods of enforcing his security:

1. Appoint a receiver (England and Wales and Northern Ireland) (see next page).
2. Poind the ground (in Scotland, in the case of a security over a feudal title, not made by ex facie absolute disposition).[34]
3. Enter into possession of the land.[35]
4. Sell the land.[36]
5. Foreclose.[37]

Instead of enforcing his security, or, if necessary, in addition to doing so, the creditor may sue the debtor on the contract to pay.

---

32. 1939 Act, s. 16 (England and Wales); 1958 Act, s. 37 (Northern Ireland).
33. Prescription Act 1617; Conveyancing (Scotland) Act 1924, s. 16, as amended by the Conveyancing and Feudal Reform (Scotland) Act 1970, s. 8. It seems that the position will be the same after 24th July 1976, by virtue of the Prescription and Limitation (Scotland) Act 1973, ss. 1 and 8. S. 16 of the 1924 Act will be repealed by the 1973 Act, s. 16(2), (3), and sch. 5, pt. I.
34. See p. 69, *post.*    35. See pp. 54-9, *ante.*
36. See pp. 69-80, *post.*    37. See pp. 80-1, *post.*

He may sue for the whole amount, not enforcing the security except as to what he does not recover, or realise his security and, if not paid in full that way, sue for the balance. But a creditor who has parted with his interest in the land otherwise than by realising his security by sale (i.e., a mortgagee who has assigned his mortgage) cannot sue on the contractual obligation. That is because he cannot perform his own obligations: if the mortgagee exacts payment from the mortgagor, the latter is entitled to the return of the mortgaged property on redemption.

**Example** Agatha mortgages a farm to Benjamin. Later, Agatha sells the farm to Clara, subject to Agatha's debt and Benjamin's security. Then Clara sells the farm to Douglas, again subject to Agatha's debt and Benjamin's security. Douglas grants a second mortgage of the farm to Elizabeth. Subsequently, Benjamin releases, in Douglas's favour, some of the fields of the farm from their burden as security for Agatha's debt. Elizabeth then pays Benjamin off and takes over the mortgage of the unreleased part of the farm. Elizabeth sues Agatha for the amount of the debt. The court will give judgment for Agatha because Elizabeth cannot restore to her on redemption the land released by Benjamin to Douglas.[38]

## Appointment of a Receiver in England and Wales and Northern Ireland

A mortgagee may not wish to be repaid in full, but to enforce his security in respect of arrears of interest or of instalments of capital. In that event, if the mortgaged property is producing income, e.g., it is a large house, the mortgagor living in part of it and having let other floors off as separate flats, the appointment of a receiver is a convenient means for the mortgagee to exact the money he wants and is entitled to. The mortgagee, by appointing a receiver, does not go into possession and incurs no liabilities, for the receiver is normally in law the agent of the mortgagor; but the receiver collects the income and pays the mortgagee what is due to him.

Where the mortgage is by deed the mortgagee has a statutory power,[39] which may be varied, extended[40] or excluded[41] by the

---

38. See *North Albion Property Investment Co. Ltd.* v. *MacBean's Curator Bonis* (1893) 21 R. 90. See also *Mackirdy* v. *Webster's Trustees* (1895) 22 R. 340. The law of England and Wales and Northern Ireland is the same: *Palmer* v. *Hendrie* (1859) 27 Beav. 349. See also Keeton and Sheridan, *Equity*, pp. 238-9.
39. England and Wales: Law of Property Act 1925, s. 101(1) (iii); Northern Ireland: Conveyancing Act 1881, s. 19(1) (iii).
40. 1925 Act, s. 101(3); 1881 Act, s. 19(2).
41. 1925 Act, s. 101(4); 1881 Act, s. 19(3).

deed, to appoint a receiver. As between the parties to the mortgage, the power to appoint a receiver, which must be done in writing,[42] becomes exercisable only if the mortgagee's statutory power of sale has become exercisable,[43] but a person paying money to a receiver gets a valid discharge, without investigating the validity of the appointment, if the receiver was appointed by a mortgagee whose security was constituted by deed.[44] If the mortgagee has no statutory power to appoint a receiver (e.g., because the mortgage was not made by deed), and no express power conferred by the mortgage contract, he may apply to the court to make such an appointment.[45] If a mortgagee, without a statutory or express power to do so, appoints a receiver, such a receiver is the agent of the mortgagee and, if the receiver acts, the mortgagee becomes a mortgagee in possession.[46] In the case of a receiver appointed under the statutory power, he 'shall be deemed to be the agent of the mortgagor; and the mortgagor shall be solely responsible for the receiver's acts or defaults unless the mortgage deed otherwise provides.'[47]

Such a receiver has all the powers of the mortgagor, plus any further powers delegated to him by the mortgagee, to gather in the income he has been appointed to receive.[48] The receiver is remunerated and reimbursed expenses by a commission on what he collects;[49] he must also pay the cost of insurance directed by the mortgagee.[50] His duty[51] is to apply the money he collects in the following order:

    (i)   in discharge of all rents, taxes, rates, and outgoings whatever affecting the mortgaged property;

    (ii)  in keeping down all annual sums or other payments, and the interest on all principal sums, having priority to the mortgage in right whereof he is receiver;

    (iii) in payment of his commission, and of the premiums on fire, life, or other insurances, if any, properly payable under the

---

42. 1925 Act, s. 109(5); 1881 Act, s. 24(5).
43. 1925 Act, s. 109(1); 1881 Act, s. 24(1). As to when the power of sale becomes exercisable, see pp. 70–1, *post*.
44. 1925 Act, s. 109(4); 1881 Act, s. 24(4).
45. The court's inherent jurisdiction to appoint a receiver on the application of an equitable mortgagee has been extended to legal mortagees by statute: see the Judicature (Consolidation) Act 1925, s. 45(1), (2), as to England and Wales, and the Judicature Act (Ireland) 1877, s. 28(8). A mortgagee with power to appoint a receiver out of court will have to pay the costs if he applies to the court unnecessarily, but he may be justified in going to court (e.g., because his power is disputed).
46. See *Lever Finance Ltd.* v. *Needleman's Trustee* [1956] Ch. 375.
47. 1925 Act, s. 109(2); 1881 Act, s. 24(2).
48. 1925 Act, s. 109(3); 1881 Act, s. 24(3).
49. 1925 Act, s. 109(6); 1881 Act, s. 24(6).
50. 1925 Act, s. 109(7); 1881 Act, s. 24(7).
51. 1925 Act, s. 109(8); 1881 Act, s. 24(8).

mortgage deed or under the Act, and the cost of executing necessary or proper repairs directed in writing by the mortgagee;

(iv) in payment of the interest accruing due in respect of any principal money due under the mortgage;

(v) in England and Wales, but not in Northern Ireland, in or towards discharge of the principal money, if so directed by the mortgagee;

(vi) as to the residue, if any, to the mortgagor or other person who, but for the appointment of the receiver, would have been entitled to the income.

The powers of leasing the mortgaged property,[52] and of accepting surrenders of leases,[53] are exercisable by the mortgagee, as if he were in possession, during the period when a receiver is acting; and the mortgagee may delegate these powers to the receiver.[54]

**Poinding the Ground in Scotland**  There is no receivership without possession in Scotland. The creditor under any form of security, if he wishes to intercept the income or to let the land, must go into possession and take over management of the property from the debtor. Alternatively, provided he is not the feudal owner under an ex facie absolute disposition (who obviously cannot poind his own ground), or secured on a lease, a creditor may poind the ground in respect of the heritable subjects of the security, thus attaching or acquiring a preference over the debtor's or his tenants' moveables on the ground in respect of arrears of interest. (As to moveables of any defender, the Law Reform (Diligence) (Scotland) Act 1973 places restrictions on poinding certain household effects. At common law, in the case of tenants' moveables, they can only be attached to the extent of any rent due.)

**Sale by the Mortgagee or at his Instance : England and Wales and Northern Ireland**  Unless varied or extended[55] or excluded[56] by the deed, a mortgage by deed confers on the mortgagee[57] a 'power, when the mortgage money has become due,[58] to sell, or to

52. 1925 Act, s. 99(19); Northern Ireland: Conveyancing Act 1911, s. 3(11).
53. 1925 Act, s. 100(13); 1911 Act, s. 3(11).
54. See further, Keeton and Sheridan, *Equity*, pp. 239–42, 509–17.
55. England and Wales: Law of Property Act 1925, s. 101(3); Northern Ireland: Conveyancing Act 1881, s. 19(2).
56. 1925 Act, s. 101(4); 1881 Act, s. 19(3).
57. See also s. 106 of the 1925 Act; s. 21 of the 1881 Act.
58. I.e., as soon as the legal date for redemption has passed without repayment.

concur with any other person in selling, the mortgaged property, or any part thereof, either subject to prior charges or not, and either together or in lots, by public auction or by private contract, subject to such conditions respecting title, or evidence of title, or other matter as the mortgagee thinks fit, with power to vary any contract for sale, and to buy in at an auction, or to rescind any contract for sale, and to re-sell, without being answerable for any loss occasioned thereby . . .'[59]

The fact that the mortgagee has a statutory power of sale does not mean that he can exercise it. The power does not become exercisable until:[60]

(i) notice requiring payment of the mortgage money has been served on the mortgagor or one of two or more mortgagors, and default has been made in payment of the mortgage money, or of part thereof, for three months after such service; or

(ii) some interest under the mortgage is in arrear and unpaid for two months after becoming due; or

(iii) there has been a breach of some provision contained in the mortgage deed, or in the Act, to be observed or performed by the mortgagor or by some person concurring in making the mortgage, other than a covenant for payment of the mortgage money or interest thereon.

As between the mortgagor and the mortgagee, a sale is wrongful if the power of sale has not become exercisable, but that does not affect the validity of the sale as against a purchaser if the power of sale has arisen. A purchaser, by looking at the mortgage deed and a calendar, can tell whether the legal date for redemption has passed, but he cannot be expected to investigate the state of payments, notices or breaches of covenant between debtor and creditor.

**Example 1** Algernon, the fee simple owner, mortgages Blackacre to Clarence by way of legal mortgage to secure a loan of £5,000, repayable six months after the loan. Twelve months later, Algernon has not repaid the £5,000 and is six months in arrears with payment of interest. Clarence sells Blackacre to Dorothea for £6,500, its full market value. The sale is fully valid, Dorothea acquires a beneficial fee simple in Blackacre,[61] and

59. 1925 Act, s. 101(1) (i); 1881 Act, s. 19(1) (i).
60. 1925 Act, s. 103; 1881 Act, s. 20.
61. England and Wales: see the Law of Property Act 1925, ss. 88, 89 and 101(6).

Algernon is entitled to the surplus of the sale price over his debt to Clarence.

**Example 2** Algernon, the fee simple owner of Blackacre, grants a legal mortgage of it to Clarence to secure a loan of £5,000, repayable six months after the loan. Twelve months later, Algernon has not repaid the £5,000 but Clarence has not asked for it, and Algernon is up to date with payments of interest and is in breach of no obligation under the mortgage or any statute (except that he has not repaid the loan). Clarence sells Blackacre to Dorothea for £6,500, its full market value. The sale is valid as between Algernon and Clarence, on the one hand, and Dorothea, on the other hand, so Dorothea acquires a beneficial fee simple in Blackacre. But as between Algernon, on the one hand and Clarence, on the other hand, the sale is wrongful and Algernon may sue Clarence for any damages he may have suffered.[62]

**Example 3** Algernon, the owner in fee simple, grants Clarence a legal mortgage of Blackacre to secure a loan of £5,000, repayable six months after the loan. Three months later, Clarence sells Blackacre to Dorothea for £6,500, its full market value. The sale is not under the statutory power, as that power has not yet arisen. So the fee simple stays with Algernon and all Dorothea gets is a transfer of Clarence's security for £5,000.

In the case of a sale by a legal mortgagee, the purchaser gets the mortgagor's estate in England and Wales because statute says so; and in Northern Ireland the mortgagee has the legal estate anyway: that passes to the purchaser free from the equity of redemption. The case of a sale under the statutory power where the deed creates an equitable mortgage is not so clear. In *Re White Rose Cottage*[63] Lord Denning M. R. said, obiter, that he saw no reason why an equitable mortgagee in England and Wales, exercising his statutory power of sale, should not be able to convey the legal estate. He did not regard *Re Hodson and Howes' Contract*[64] as authority under the Act of 1925. The other two judges of the Court of Appeal expressed no opinion on that point. In *Re Hodson and Howes' Contract* the Court of Appeal held that the Conveyancing Act 1881, which is still in force in Northern Ireland, conferred no power on the mortgagee to pass the mortgagor's legal estate. Such a mortgagee could therefore convey to the purchaser only his equitable interest, but free from the

---

62. England and Wales: Law of Property Act 1925, s. 104; Northern Ireland: Conveyancing Acts 1881, s. 21 (1), (2) and 1911, s. 5 (1).
63. [1965] Ch. 940.    64. (1887) 35 Ch.D. 668. See below.

mortgagor's right to redeem. Accordingly, in view of the authority on the 1881 Act and the uncertainty on the 1925 Act, an equitable mortgagee whose mortgage is by deed, as well as one whose mortgage is not made by deed, should seek to be given an express power of selling the mortgagor's estate in the land. If there is no statutory or express power of sale, the mortgagee may apply to the court for an order for sale.

When the sale has been completed, the proceeds must be used in the following order:[65]

    (i) to pay off any prior incumbrancers to whose rights the sale was not made subject, or to pay into court a sufficient sum to pay them off;[66]

    (ii) to reimburse the mortgagee who has sold for any expenses he has properly incurred;

    (iii) to pay the mortgagee who has sold all money due in respect of his mortgage.

If the amount is not enough to pay the mortgage debt, the mortgagee who has sold now becomes an unsecured creditor as to the balance of what is due to him. He may sue the mortgagor in contract for the balance or, if the mortgagor is bankrupt, prove in his bankruptcy for the amount. If the selling mortgagee has a balance in his hands after paying himself everything to which he is entitled he must pay it 'to the person entitled to the mortgaged property, or authorised to give receipts for the proceeds of the sale thereof.' If there is a subsequent mortgage, the balance must be paid to the second mortgagee,[67] who must then comply with the statutory order of applying it. If there is no subsequent mortgage, the balance must be paid to the mortgagor or his assignee. If the mortgagee who has sold has been in possession so as to bar the rights of the mortgagor and all subsequent mortgagees under the legislation governing limitation of actions, he can keep the balance because he is the only person entitled to the mortgaged property within the meaning of the Act.[68]

In exercising the power of sale, the mortgagee owes some duty of care to the mortgagor. In the case of sale by a building society, tatute[69] imposes various duties on the vendor, including a duty to

---

65. England and Wales: Law of Property Act 1925, s. 105; Northern Ireland: Conveyancing Act 1881, s. 21(3).

66. See *Samuel Keller (Holdings) Ltd.* v. *Martins Bank Ltd.* [1971] 1 W.L.R. 43 (C.A.).

67. See *West London Commercial Bank* v. *Reliance Permanent Building Soc.* (1885) 29 Ch.D. 954; *Re Thomson's Mortgage Trusts* [1920] 1 Ch. 508.

68. *Young* v. *Clarey* [1948] Ch. 191. See, further, Keeton and Sheridan, *Equity*, pp. 256-7.

69. Great Britain: Building Societies Act 1962, s. 36; Building Societies Act (Northern Ireland) 1967, s. 36.

take reasonable care to ensure that the price at which the estate is sold is the best price which can reasonably be obtained. There is no such statutory duty on other mortgagees, but there is relevant legislation.

The section[70] setting out the statutory power of sales confers it on the mortgagee 'without being answerable for any loss occasioned thereby . . .' Another section[71] states:

> The mortgagee shall not be answerable for any involuntary loss happening on or about the exercise or execution of the power of sale . . . , or of any trust connected therewith, or . . . of any power or provision contained in the mortgage deed.

These enactments clearly preclude liability on the part of the mortgagee for: (*a*) loss occasioned simply because the mortgagee exercises his power of sale or because he does so when he does; and (*b*) accidental loss, i.e., loss not occasioned by the mortgagee's negligence or wilful default. As to the latter, the matter is governed by case law.[72]

The mortgagee is not liable to the mortgagor or subsequent mortgagees on account of his motives or choice of time for realising his security. He may be liable and, if the purchaser is aware of the circumstances, the sale may be set aside, if the mortgagor has tendered what is due in an attempt to redeem before the sale,[73] or in certain cases where the price obtained by the sale is too low. For example, where an auctioneer selling for first mortgagees got too low a price because he misdescribed the property, the first mortgagees were held liable to the second mortgagees for the loss.[74] The principles were reviewed in three leading cases, two English and one Irish: *Kennedy* v. *De Trafford*,[75] *Holohan* v. *Friends Provident and Century Life Office*[76] and *Cuckmere Brick Co. Ltd.* v. *Mutual Finance Ltd.*[77]

In *Kennedy* v. *De Trafford*,[75] two tenants in common mortgaged land for £60,000. After the power of sale became exercisable, the mortgagees, who wished to reduce the amount of their investment, wrote to both tenants in common[78] to the effect that they proposed

70. England and Wales: Law of Property Act 1925, s. 101(1) (i); Northern Ireland: Conveyancing Act 1881, s. 19(1) (i).
71. England and Wales: s. 106(3) of the 1925 Act; Northern Ireland: s. 21(6) of the 1881 Act, as amended by the Conveyancing Act 1911, s. 5(2).
72. See Keeton and Sheridan, *Equity*, pp. 253–6.
73. *Jenkins* v. *Jones* (1860) 2 Giff. 99. Cf. *Duke* v. *Robson* [1973] 1 W.L.R. 267.
74. *Tomlin* v. *Luce* (1889) 43 Ch.D. 191. Cf. *Cuckmere Brick Co. Ltd.* v. *Mutual Finance Ltd.* [1971] Ch. 949.
75. [1897] A.C. 180.      76. [1966] I.R. 1.
77. [1971] Ch. 949.
78. Actually, one of the tenants in common was bankrupt by this time, and the plaintiff was his trustee in bankruptcy.

to sell the land if they could obtain enough for it to cover their principal, interest and costs. Eventually, one of the tenants in common bought the land at such a price, the mortgagees leaving £54,000 of the purchase price on mortgage after the sale was completed. The other tenant in common,[79] who had not raised any objection between getting his letter from the mortgagees and their sale, now sued both the vendors and the purchasers. He failed, because he could not establish either a breach of duty by the mortgagees or a fiduciary duty on the party of the purchaser. Lord Herschell (with whom Lords Macnaghten, Morris and Shand agreed) said:[80]

> ... if a mortgagee in exercising his power of sale exercises it in good faith, without any intention of dealing unfairly by his mortgagor, it would be very difficult indeed, if not impossible, to establish that he had been guilty of any breach of duty towards the mortgagor ... It is very difficult to define exhaustively all that would be included in the words 'good faith,' but I think it would be unreasonable to require the mortgagee to do more than exercise his power of sale in that fashion. Of course, if he wilfully and recklessly deals with the property in such a manner that the interests of the mortgagor are sacrificed, I should say that he had not been exercising his power of sale in good faith.

In *Holohan* v. *Friends Provident and Century Life Office*,[81] the mortgagees, whose power of sale was exercisable, proposed to sell mortgaged premises of which part had been let. They entered into a contract to sell the premises as an investment, i.e., subject to existing tenancies. They had no right to get the tenants out, but the mortgagor suggested trying to buy them out with a view to selling with vacant possession. The mortgagees refused to consider that suggestion, although sale with vacant possession would have produced a much higher price than the sum total of the price subject to tenancies and reasonable compensation to the tenants for quitting. The mortgagor was granted an injunction to restrain the sale, Ó'Dálaigh C. J. (with whom Lavery and Walsh JJ. agreed) saying[82] that the test of propriety of the sale was what a reasonable man would do in the mortgagee's position; that good faith was not enough, there being no reason to doubt the good faith of a reasonable man; and that the reasonable man would bear in mind the interests of the mortgagor and of subsequent incumbrancers and would try to get

79. See footnote 78, p 73, *ante*.    80. [1897] A.C. 185.
81. [1966] I.R. 1.    82 [1966] I.R. 21.

the best price obtainable. While the learned Chief Justice seems to have thought that he was requiring a higher standard than good faith, the conduct of the dependants might well have come within Lord Herschell's description of wilfully and recklessly dealing with the property in such a manner that the interests of the mortgagor are sacrificed.

In *Cuckmere Brick Co. Ltd.* v. *Mutual Finance Ltd.*,[83] land worth much more was sold by a mortgagee's auctioneers for £44,000, there having been inadequate publicity for the fact that there was planning permission for a hundred flats to be built on the land. The plaintiff mortgagors recovered damages from the mortgagees. All three judges of the Court of Appeal examined the authorities fully. Salmon L.J. said:[84]

It is well settled that a mortgagee is not a trustee of the power of sale for the mortgagor. Once the power has accrued, the mortgagee is entitled to exercise it for his own purposes whenever he chooses to do so. It matters not that the moment may be unpropitious and that by waiting a higher price could be obtained. He has the right to realise his security by turning it into money when he likes. Nor, in my view, is there anything to prevent a mortgagee from accepting the best bid he can get at an auction, even though the auction is badly attended and the bidding exceptionally low. Providing none of those adverse factors is due to any fault of the mortgagee, he can do as he likes. If the mortgagee's interests, as he sees them, conflict with those of the mortgagor, the mortgagee can give preference to his own interests, which of course he could not do were he a trustee of the power of sale for the mortgagor . . .

It is impossible to pretend that the state of the authorities on this branch of the law is entirely satisfactory. There are some dicta which suggest that unless a mortgagee acts in bad faith he is safe. His only obligation to the mortgagor is not to cheat him. There are other dicta which suggest that in addition to the duty of acting in good faith, the mortgagee is under a duty to take reasonable care to obtain whatever is the true market value of the mortgaged property at the moment he chooses to sell it . . .

The proposition that the mortgagee owes both duties, in my judgment, represents the true view of the law. Approaching the matter first of all on principle, it is to be observed that if the sale

83. [1971] Ch. 949. Cf. *Palmer* v. *Barclays Bank Ltd.* (1971) 23 P. & C.R. 30.
84. [1971] Ch. 965–6.

yields a surplus over the amount owed under the mortgage, the mortgagee holds this surplus in trust for the mortgagor. If the sale shows a deficiency, the mortgagor has to make it good out of his own pocket. The mortgagor is vitally affected by the result of the sale but its preparation and conduct is left entirely in the hands of the mortgagee. The proximity between them could scarcely be closer. Surely they are 'neighbours.'

A mortgagee exercising his power of sale may not use the transaction to make himself the owner of the property, but only to pay himself what he is owed. Hence, he may not sell to himself, to a nominee for himself[85] or to a servant[86] or agent[87] acting for him in the matter of the sale. But he can sell to persons with whom he has some connection unrelated to the sale, such as a company in which he owns shares,[88] a solicitor employed by him in other business or a subsequent mortgagee.[89]

**Scotland** A creditor intending to realise his security must first serve a notice on the debtor calling it up. If the debt is not paid on the date specified in the notice, the creditor may proceed, among other ways, by selling the land.

In the case of a standard security, in these circumstances, the creditor must proceed under section 19 of the Conveyancing and Feudal Reform (Scotland) Act 1970 to serve a calling-up notice, demanding payment within two months,[90] on the mortgagor or his successor in title.[91] The creditor must also serve a copy of the notice on anyone else against whom he wishes to preserve any right of recourse in respect of the debt. The period of notice may be dispensed with or shortened by the person on whom the notice is served, with the consent of any creditors holding securities ranking equally with or subsequent to that of the creditor serving it. If the debtor does not comply with the notice, the creditor may sell the land.[92] By section 25 of the Act of 1970,[93] the sale may be either by private bargain or by exposure to sale by public roup, 'and in either event it shall be the duty of the creditor to advertise the sale and to

85. *Robertson* v. *Norris* (1858) 4 Jur. N.S. 443.
86. *Martinson* v. *Clowes* (1885) 52 L.T. 706; *Hodson* v. *Deans* [1903] 2 Ch. 647.
87. See *Matthison* v. *Clarke* (1854) 3 Drew. 3.
88. *Farrar* v. *Farrars Ltd.* (1888) 40 Ch.D. 395.
89. *Shaw* v. *Bunny* (1865) 2 De G. J. & S. 468; *Kirkwood* v. *Thompson* (1865) 2 De G. J. & S. 613. See further, Keeton and Sheridan, *Equity*, pp. 254–6.
90. See Form A in sch. 6 to the Act of 1970.
91. In the case of a remediable default [by the debtor, the creditor may seek remedy by notice of default under ss. 21–4 of the Act of 1970.
92. 1970 Act, s. 20(1), (2), and standard condition 10(2), sch. 3.
93. See also s. 30.

take all reasonable steps to ensure that the price at which all or any of the subjects are sold is the best that can be reasonably obtained.' A proper sale duly recorded in the Register of Sasines passes title to the purchaser free from the standard security of the creditor-vendor and free from any equally ranked or subsequent securities.[94] The sale does not affect prior securities, which the selling creditor retains a right to redeem. The order of purposes for which the vendor must apply the proceeds of sale is:[95]

(i) payment of all expenses properly incurred by him in connection with the sale, or any attempted sale;

(ii) payment of the whole amount due under any prior security to which the sale is not made subject;

(iii) payment of the whole amount due under the vendor's security, and payment, in due proportion, of the whole amount due under a security (if any), ranking pari passu with his own security, which has been recorded in the Register of Sasines;

(iv) payment of any amounts due under any securities with a ranking postponed to that of his own security, according to their ranking;

(v) to the person entitled to the security subjects at the time of the sale, or to any person authorised to give receipts for the proceeds of sale thereof.

If unable to make any of these payments, the creditor may consign the amount due in the sheriff court for the person appearing to have the best right to it.

In the case of an ex facie absolute disposition, which is in fact made by way of security, the creditor, as owner of the land, can sell. No express or statutory authorisation is needed by him. He can certainly sell by public roup, can probably sell by private bargain, and can certainly sell without giving the debtor notice of his intention to do so.[96] The proceeds of sale have to be dealt with in the same manner as those received on realisation of a standard security.

In the case of a bond and disposition (or assignation) in security, the statutory form confers upon the creditor an express power of sale on default by the debtor.[97] Unless expressly authorised to sell

94. 1970 Act, ss. 26 and 30.
95. 1970 Act, s. 27.
96. *Aberdeen Trades Council* v. *Ship Constructors' and Shipwrights' Assoc.* 1949 S.C. (H.L.) 45.
97. Titles to Land Consolidation (Scotland) Act 1868, s. 118 (as substituted by the Titles to Land Consolidation (Scotland) Act Amendment Act 1869, s. 6) and s. 119 (as substituted by s. 7 of the Act of 1869 and amended by the Conveyancing (Scotland) Act 1924, s. 25.) See also s. 121 of the Act of 1868 and s. 36 of the Act of 1924. As to calling-

by private bargain, the creditor had to sell by public roup until the enactment of section 35(1) of the Conveyancing and Feudal Reform (Scotland) Act 1970 which provides:

> The creditor in a bond and disposition[98] in security may exercise his power to sell the land disponed in security by way of sale by private bargain for the best price that can be reasonably obtained.

A purchaser from the creditor gets a good title, free from any rights of the debtor,[99] and whether or not there is a surplus after the vendor has paid himself off.[100] A subsequent secured creditor is overreached, though he is, of course, entitled to be paid off out of any surplus.[101]

The purchaser from a creditor secured by one of the old types of express security is not concerned with any irregularity in the conduct of the sale, and gets a good title even if the sale is irregular, but the creditor may be liable in damages to the debtor or to a subsequent incumbrancer in respect of the irregularity.[102] With regard to dispositions registered after the Act came into force, the Conveyancing and Feudal Reform (Scotland) Act 1970, section 38, provides:[103]

> Where a disposition of land is duly recorded in the appropriate Register of Sasines and that disposition bears to be granted in the exercise of a power of sale contained in a deed granting a bond and disposition in security, and the exercise of that power was *ex facie* regular, the title of a *bona fide* purchaser of the land for value shall not be challengeable on the ground that the debt had ceased to exist, unless that fact appeared in the said Register, or was known to the purchaser prior to the payment of the price, or on the ground of any irregularity relating to the sale or in any preliminary procedure thereto; but nothing in the provisions of this subsection shall affect the competency of any claim for

---

up notices, see the 1924 Act, ss. 33–5, and the Conveyancing and Feudal Reform (Scotland) Act 1970, ss. 33 and 34.

98. This includes an assignation: ss. 30(2) and 43(2).

99. Heritable Securities (Scotland) Act 1894, s. 9. The debtor remains liable for any deficiency if the proceeds do not pay off the whole debt.

100. Titles to Land Consolidation (Scotland) Act 1868, s. 123; Conveyancing (Scotland) Acts 1874, s. 48, and 1924, s. 42.

101. Titles to Land Consolidation (Scotland) Act 1868, s. 122, enacting the law as previously laid down in *Wilson* v. *Stirling* (1843) 8 D. 1261.

102. Conveyancing (Scotland) Act 1924, s. 41.

103. By substituting new s. 41(2) in the Conveyancing (Scotland) Act 1924.

damages in respect of the sale of the land against the person exercising the said power.

The selling creditor must account for any surplus to the debtor and other interested parties[104] or consign the surplus.[105]

So far as the vendor's duty, to the debtor and to others interested in the security subjects, is concerned: first, the Building Societies Act 1962 applies to Scotland, so that such a society has a duty under section 36 to take reasonable care to obtain the best price that can reasonably be obtained.[106] Other secured creditors are in much the same position. In relation to a security by ex facie absolute disposition, Lord Thomson said in *Rimmer* v. *Thomas Usher & Son Ltd.*:[107]

> It is not disputed that conventional agreement apart, an *ex facie* absolute disponee in realising by sale the security subjects acts in a dual capacity. He is entitled to sell and in recovering the amount due to him he acts *in rem suam*, but he is also a *quasi* trustee for his debtor to whom he is bound to account for the difference between the price obtained and the amount of the loan and interest due to him. He must not in exercising his power of sale 'do so unfairly and without due regard to the interests of his debtor . . .'

In this case, a term of the minute of agreement allowed the creditors to sell 'on such terms and conditions as they may think proper.' They sold a hotel worth £12,000 for £8,000 and a condition in restraint of trade in their favour. They were held liable to the debtors for the missing £4,000 (presumably the value to the vendors of the restraint of trade). Lord Thomson said:[108]

> In my opinion, the defenders here were under an overriding obligation to the pursuers to exercise their power of sale *bona fide* and with regard to the interests of the pursuers and take such reasonable steps as they considered necessary to obtain a full and fair market price for the subjects.

The position is similar in the case of an express security.[109] On the other hand, there will be no damages for irregularities in the conduct of a sale if the full market price is obtained despite them.[110]

In addition to damages after sale, there may, in an appropriate case, be an interdict to prevent an improper exercise of the power.

104. Titles to Land Consolidation (Scotland) Act 1868, s. 122. See *Adair's Trustee* v. *Rankin* (1895) 22 R. 975.
105. S. 122 of the Act of 1868. See also s. 123.
106. See p. 72, footnote 69, *ante*.
107. 1967 S.L.T. 7. See also *Shrubb* v. *Clark* (1897) 5 S.L.T. 125.
108. 1967 S.L.T. 9.
109. See *Davidson* v. *Scott* 1915 S.C. 924 (bond and disposition in security).
110. *Park* v. *Alliance Heritable Security Co. (Ltd.)* (1880) 7 R. 546.

In *Kerr* v. *M'Arthur's Trustees*,[111] Lord Mackenzie held that a subsequent secured creditor could prevent, by interdict, a prior creditor from selling recklessly, 'at such a season of the year as that purchasers could not be procured, or at such an upset price as to leave little hope to postponed creditors of getting payment . . .'

A creditor cannot sell to himself. In cases where the security was a bond and disposition in security, it has been held that he can neither do that nor sell to a nominee for himself;[112] and that he also cannot appoint someone else to conduct the sale, with a view to buying the property himself.[113] But if the land is being auctioned in lieu of foreclosure under statutory provisions, the creditor may bid.[114]

**Foreclosure** This is a judicial proceeding which ends in an order making the creditor the owner of the property free from any rights of the debtor. It is rarely used in England and Wales or Scotland because of the greater convenience of exercising a statutory or express power of sale. In Northern Ireland, it has fallen into total disuse.

**England and Wales.**[115] Any mortgagee[116] may bring foreclosure proceedings when the mortgagor is in default, or claim foreclosure in proceedings brought by someone else for redemption. The mortgagee seeking foreclosure must bring his action against everyone he wishes to foreclose (which can include the mortgagor and any subsequent mortgagee) or redeem (any prior mortgagee). If foreclosure is granted, the proceedings are adjourned for six months to give the persons the mortgagee seeks to foreclose a chance to redeem. If redemption does not occur during that time, a foreclosure order absolute is made. Even after that, a mortgagor is allowed to bring a redemption action if he starts it within what the court regards as a reasonable time having regard to the circumstances. Furthermore, if the property is less valuable than the debt, and the mortgagee sues the mortgagor for the balance after the foreclosure, the mortgagor has a renewed right to redeem.

The court may order a sale instead of foreclosure at the instance

111. (1848) 11 D. 301.   112. *Taylor* v. *Watson* (1846) 8 D. 400.
113. *Stirling's Trustees* (1865) 3 M. 851.
114. Heritable Securities (Scotland) Act 1894, ss. 8 (as amended by the Conveyancing and Feudal Reform (Scotland) Act 1970, s. 39(1)) and 14.
115. See Keeton and Sheridan, *Equity*, p. 242–9.
116. Except where the mortgage is by way of trust for sale: *Scweitzer* v. *Mayhew* (1862) 31 Beav. 37. The remedy of the mortgagee is then to enforce the trust by obtaining an order for sale. That form of mortgage is obsolete.

of any party.[117] The most likely party to ask for a sale is a defendant subsequent mortgagee.[118]

**Scotland** The owner of a standard security may foreclose.[119] The right to apply to the court for a foreclosure order arises two months after an unsuccessful attempt to sell the land for not more than the debt (plus, if appropriate, sums due on any prior security or security ranking pari passu with that of the applicant).[120] The application must be served on the debtor, the proprietor of the security subjects (if he is not the debtor) and other creditors secured on the same land whose securities were registered in the Register of Sasines during the preceding twenty years.[121] The court may allow the debtor (or proprietor) a period, not exceeding three months, to redeem the security and, subject to that, may order either foreclosure or a renewed attempt to sell the land.[122] If they order a sale, the creditor may buy.[122] The effect of a foreclosure order is that the creditor becomes the purchaser, free from the right to redeem of the creditor, the proprietor or any subsequent secured creditor, at the price at which the land foreclosed was last exposed to sale.[123] The creditor who has foreclosed, if the price he has paid himself is not enough to discharge his debt, can sue the debtor for the balance.[124] He also has a right to redeem prior and equal securities.[125]

Similar rights of foreclosure are given to holders of securities created by bond and disposition (or assignation) in security.[126] A creditor secured by ex facie absolute disposition may contract in the qualifying agreement for power to foreclose, but usually he seeks a declarator of the court, which is not an action of foreclosure, that the debtor by reason of breach of the contract has forfeited his right of redemption under the agreement. That procedure is unusual – normally the creditor merely wishes to sell.

---

117. Law of Property Act 1925, s. 91(2), (4)–(6).
118. For an example of such a request by the successors in title of the mortgagor, see *Silsby* v. *Holliman* [1955] Ch. 552.
119. Standard condition 10(7) which, by virtue of the Conveyancing and Feudal Reform (Scotland) Act 1970, s. 11(3), as amended by the Redemption of Standard Securities (Scotland) Act 1971, s. 1(a), may not be varied by the agreement of the parties.
120. Conveyancing and Feudal Reform (Scotland) Act 1970, s. 28(1).
121. S. 28(3).        122. S. 28(4).
123. S. 28(5), (6).        124. S. 28(7).
125. S. 28(6) (c).
126. Heritable Securities (Scotland) Act 1894, s. 8, as amended by the Conveyancing and Feudal Reform (Scotland) Act 1970, s. 39.

# 7 land: priority of successive mortgages

**England and Wales** In relation to unregistered land, many mortgages can be registered in the register of land charges established in 1925 and maintained under the Land Charges Act 1972. Those which can be registered are:

- (i) a legal mortgage where the mortgagee does not get the title deeds (normally because it is not a first mortgage): such a security is called a 'puisne mortgage';[1]
- (ii) an equitable mortgage by charge on a legal estate, where the mortgagee does not get the title deeds: such a security is called a 'general equitable charge';[2] and
- (iii) a contract to create a legal mortgage, operating as an equitable mortgage: such a security is called an 'estate contract.'[3]

If there are two or more registered mortgages, they rank in order of registration, irrespective of their legal or equitable nature, according to the Law of Property Act 1925, section 97. Unfortunately, that does not seem to be the result according to section 4 of the Land Charges Act 1972 if only puisne mortgages and general equitable charges are involved. That section provides:

(4) A land charge of . . . Class C . . . (other than an estate contract) . . . shall be void as against a purchaser[4] of the land charged with it, or of any interest in such land, unless the land

1. Land Charges Act 1972, s. 2(4)–Class C (i) land charge.
2. Class C (iii) land charge.     3. Class C (iv) land charge.
4. 'Purchaser' includes a mortgagee or chargee: Land Charges Act 1972, s. 17(1).

charge is registered in the appropriate register before the completion of the purchase.

(5) An estate contract . . . shall be void as against a purchaser for money or money's worth of a legal estate in the land charged with it, unless the land charge is registered in the appropriate register before the completion of the purchase.

Some examples will illustrate the operation of the provisions and the difficulties involved.

**Example 1** Blackacre is mortgaged by second mortgage by demise on 1st January 1973 to Aaron. A third mortgage by equitable charge on Blackacre is granted on 1st February 1973 to Beelzebub. Aaron registers his mortgage on 1st March 1973, and Beelzebub registers his on 1st April 1973. According to the Law of Property Act 1925, section 97, Aaron comes before Beelzebub because Aaron registered first. According to the Land Charges Act 1972, section 4(4), Beelzebub comes before Aaron because Aaron's mortgage was unregistered when the mortgage to Beelzebub was granted.

**Example 2** Whiteacre is mortgaged by second mortgage by contract to grant a legal mortgage to Cyril on 1st January 1973. A third mortgage of Whiteacre by equitable charge is granted to Dorothy on 1st February 1973. Neither mortgage is ever registered. There is no relevant statutory provision,[5] so equitable principles prevail, which means that Cyril comes before Dorothy, because the dates of granting of the mortgages govern their priority, unless Cyril has behaved inequitably so as to have enabled Dorothy to be misled into thinking she was getting a second mortgage. (Had Cyril or Dorothy, or both, subsequently registered, priority would have been governed by order of registration.)[6]

Mortgages of land which cannot be registered under the Land Charges Act 1972 are:

(i) Legal and equitable mortgages of a legal estate where the mortgagee gets the title deeds. (Questions of priority involving such mortgages are determined by principles of equity.[7])

(ii) Equitable assignments of legal mortgages. (Again, equitable principles apply to priorities.)

5. The Land Charges Act 1972, s. 4(5), does not protect Dorothy because she does not purchase a legal estate in the land.
6. See further, Keeton and Sheridan, *Equity*, pp. 209–12.
7. See pp. 84–6, *post.*

    (iii)  Mortgages of equitable interests in land. (Priority is in the order in which the mortgagees give notice in writing to the trustees of the settlement, a trust corporation nominated for the purpose,[8] or the estate owner, as appropriate.[9])

    (iv)  Registered charges over registered land. (These rank in order of entry on the register of charges.[10])

    (v)  Other legal mortgages of registered land. (These rank in order of their protection by caution.[11])

    (vi)  Equitable mortgages or submortgages of registered land by deposit of the land or charge certificate. (Questions of priority involving such mortgages are determined by principles of equity.[12])

Mortgages by limited companies are also governed by the Companies Act 1948, sections 95–106. Charges by such companies, in order to be valid, must be registered in the register of company charges. Under the Land Charges Act 1925, section 10(5), such registration had the same effect as registration under the Land Charges Act, but that does not apply to charges (other than floating charges) created after the Law of Property Act 1969 came into force. The effect of section 26 of the 1969 Act, replaced by the Land Charges Act 1972, section 3(7), is that mortgages of land by companies must now be registered under the Land Charges Act as well in order to protect their priority.

The principles of equity[13] may be summarised as follows, so far as they govern the priority of successive mortgages of land.

    (1)  Mortgages rank in the order of their creation.

    (2)  Mortgages of equitable interests in land are an exception in England and Wales after 1925 because the Law of Property Act, section 137 substitutes the order of giving written notice to the trustees of the settlement or other appropriate person.[14]

    (3)  Another exception is that if two equitable mortgages of a legal estate are in competition, the earlier is postponed to the later if the later mortgagee has the better equity. This will occur if the earlier mortgagee has, by his conduct (e.g., giving a receipt before he has been paid) contributed to ignorance on

8. Law of Property Act 1925, s. 138.
9. Law of Property Act 1925, s. 137; *Dearle* v. *Hall* (1823) 3 Russ. 1. See also Keeton and Sheridan, *Equity*, pp. 300–6.
10. Land Registration Act 1925, s. 29.
11. Land Registration Act 1925, s. 106.
12. See 84–6, *post*. See also *Barclays Bank Ltd.* v. *Taylor* [1973] 2 W.L.R. 293.
13. For a full exposition, see Keeton and Sheridan, *Equity*, pp. 213–17.
14. See footnotes 8 and 9 above.

the part of the later mortgagee of the existence or continued existence of the earlier mortgage.[15]

(4) By way of further exception, a bona fide legal mortgagee for value takes free from a prior equitable mortgage of which, at the time of taking his legal mortgage, he had no notice.[16]

(5) The final exception is that an equitable mortgagee takes priority over an earlier legal mortgage if: (a) the legal mortgagee is party to a fraudulent misrepresentation that his mortgage does not exist, or (b) the legal mortgagee leaves the title deeds with, or gives the title deeds to, the mortgagor in order to enable the latter to borrow again, and the mortgagor, when borrowing again, fraudulently suppresses the existence of the legal mortgage.[17]

The case of *McCarthy & Stone Ltd.* v. *Julian S. Hodge and Co. Ltd.*[18] illustrates the application of these principles. Cityfield, the fee simple owners, contracted on 17th February 1964 to sell land to McCarthy and Stone, builders. McCarthy and Stone were, under this agreement, entitled to a conveyance on giving a fortnight's notice on or after 18th March 1964, and Cityfield had rights to compel McCarthy and Stone to complete. On 14th March 1964, Cityfield deposited the title deeds to the land with Hodge, a bank, by way of equitable mortgage; and at the same time Cityfield gave Hodge a power of attorney to execute in their (Hodge's) favour a legal mortgage over the land; and by the same deed, by way of further security, Cityfield declared themselves trustees of the land for Hodge. At that date, Hodge had constructive notice of the contract between Cityfield and McCarthy and Stone. On 13th April 1964, Hodge registered their equitable mortgage under the Companies Act 1948, section 95. On 27th September 1965, McCarthy and Stone registered their agreement as an estate contract under the Land Charges Act 1925, section 10(1) (i.e., as a Class C(iv) land charge). On 21st June 1967, Hodge exercised the power of attorney and gave themselves a legal mortgage. On 3rd October 1967, Cityfield were ordered to be wound up. The fee simple was still vested in Cityfield. McCarthy and Stone claimed to be entitled to the land free from any rights claimed by Hodge. It was held that McCarthy and Stone had

15. See *Rice* v. *Rice* (1854) 2 Drew. 73.
16. As to the nature of notice, see the Law of Property Act 1925, ss. 198 and 199; *Caunce* v. *Caunce* [1969] 1 W.L.R. 286.
17. See *Northern Counties of England Fire Insurance Co.* v. *Whipp* (1884) 26 Ch.D. 482; Law of Property Act 1925, s. 13.
18. [1971] 1 W.L.R. 1547.

priority over Hodge. First, as the contract between Cityfield and McCarthy and Stone was susceptible to an order of specific performance, McCarthy and Stone had an equitable interest which was created before Hodge's equitable mortgage. Secondly, the fact that McCarthy and Stone's rights were not registered as an estate contract, when Cityfield granted the equitable mortgage to Hodge, did not assist Hodge because Hodge were not purchasers of a legal estate.[19] Thirdly, Hodge were not helped by their legal mortgage because: (i) it was not executed until 21st June 1967, and so was subject to McCarthy and Stone's estate contract registered on 27th September 1965 unless it could be related back to some earlier date; (ii) Hodge could not gain priority for their equitable mortgage of 14th March 1964 by adding the legal estate they acquired on 21st June 1967 because, on 14th March 1964, they had constructive notice of the earlier agreement between Cityfield and McCarthy and Stone. Finally, Cityfield's declaration of 14th March 1964 that they held the land on trust for Hodge was inoperative, because, by virtue of the agreement of 17th February 1964, Cityfield already held the land on trust for McCarthy and Stone.

**Northern Ireland**   Since 1707, there has been a register of deeds, now governed by the Registration of Deeds Act (Northern Ireland) 1970. A memorial of any written disposition (including a legal or equitable mortgage) of a legal estate in unregistered land may be registered in the register of deeds (whether the writing is under seal or not). Registered mortgages rank for priority in order of registration. As between two written mortgages, if one is registered and the other not, the registered mortgage takes priority over the unregistered one, unless the unregistered mortgage was made first and the later mortgagee who did register had actual notice of the existence of the unregistered mortgage at the time of taking his later security.

The following priorities are not governed by the Registration of Deeds Act, but by the principles of equity:[20]

  (i)  between two unregistered mortgages;
  (ii) between an unregistrable mortgage (i.e., one by deposit of title deeds without writing) and any other mortgage, whether registered or not;[21]

---

19. See the Land Charges Act 1925, s. 13(2), proviso (Land Charges Act 1972, s. 4(5)), p. 83, *ante*.
20. See pp. 84–6, *ante*.
21. *Re Burke's Estate* (1881) 9 L.R.Ir. 24.

(iii) between two mortgages of an equitable interest under a trust of land.

Registered charges over registered land take effect, under the Land Registration Act (Northern Ireland) 1970, in order of registration in the register of charges. There are also provisions in the Companies Act (Northern Ireland) 1960 for the validity of charges created by companies to depend on registration with the Registrar of Companies.

When applying the equitable principles to priorities of successive mortgages in Northern Ireland, the principle of tacking by getting in the legal estate may come into play. The possibility of tacking is confined to cases not governed by the provisions for registration of deeds, and so rarely arises. This type of tacking (known as the *tabula in naufragio*, in contradistinction to the tacking of further advances), in outline, works in this way: there are two equitable mortgages of the same land; the later equitable mortgagee then acquires the legal estate in the land: the result is that he has acquired priority over the earlier equitable mortagee if, but only if, when he acquired his equitable mortgage, he was without notice of the existence of the earlier equitable mortgage.

**Example**  Belinda, the fee simple owner, mortgages Whiteacre, to secure a loan of £5,000 from Charles, by conveying the fee simple to Charles. Charles registers his mortgage at the registry of deeds. Later, Belinda borrows £1,000 from Dorothy, secured by an equitable charge in Dorothy's favour over Whiteacre. Shortly afterwards, Belinda gives Edward an equitable charge over Whiteacre to secure another loan of £1,000, Edward (being unaware of Dorothy's charge) believing that he is the second mortgagee. Before either Dorothy or Edward registers, Edward learns of Dorothy's charge. Edward redeems Charles's mortgage by paying Charles £5,000. Edward now has the legal fee simple in Whiteacre, and is entitled to a security for £6,000 (what he is due on the legal mortgage he acquired from Charles plus what he is due on his equitable mortgage) in priority to the payment of anything to Dorothy.

Prior to its abolition in England and Wales by the Law of Property Act 1925, section 94, English case law brought this kind of tacking to a high pitch of complication.[22] These cases will be followed in applications of the doctrine of tacking in Northern Ireland. One of the principles is that tacking is not permitted when the

22. See Keeton and Sheridan, *Equity*, pp. 218–20.

equitable mortgagee seeking to tack acquires the legal estate from a bare trustee.

**Example**   Francis, the fee simple owner, agrees to grant a lease of Greenacre to Greta. Greta mortgages her equitable interest, created by the contract, to Harold, and agrees to give Harold a legal mortgage when she is granted the lease. Harold registers the equitable mortgage. Francis then performs his contract with Greta by granting her the lease. Later, Harold writes asking Francis for the lease, but gets no reply. After that, Greta deposits the lease with Ian (who is unaware of the mortgage to Harold) by way of equitable mortgage. Harold then discovers that the lease has been deposited with Ian as security and informs Ian of his (Harold's) mortgage. Ian then gets Greta to grant him a legal mortgage of Greenacre by assigning to him the legal title to the lease. Harold will have priority over Ian because Ian, when he got the legal estate, knew that Greta was trustee of the lease for Harold.[23]

**Scotland**   The preference in ranking of all types of heritable security depends, first, on the agreement, if any, made between the creditors and the debtor and, subject to that, on the dates of registration of the dispositions or assignations or standard securities in the Register of Sasines. (The right to insert conventional ranking clauses when creating standard securities is recognised by the Conveyancing and Feudal Reform (Scotland) Act 1970, section 13(3)(b), and schedule 2, note 5.) In the absence of agreement or registration, ranking is prima facie in order of the creation of the securities, though that order will be varied, if necessary, so as to nullify the advantages of fraud.

The Companies Act 1948, which requires registration of a charge created by a company in the register of company charges, applies in Scotland.

## Marshalling of Securities in England and Wales and Northern Ireland

Marshalling is an equitable process which, coupled with the principle of subrogation, is designed to regulate the situation where one creditor is secured on two properties of the debtor, while a subsequent creditor is secured on only one of those properties. The

23. See *Workingman's Benefit Building Soc.* v. *Dixon* [1908] 1 I.R. 582.

idea is to protect the second creditor from being prejudiced by the whims of the first.

**Example** Robert is the fee simple owner of Blackacre and Yellowacre. He mortgages them both to Susan to secure a loan of £9,000. Later, Robert borrows £3,000 from Thomas and gives him a second mortgage of Blackacre. Robert then becomes insolvent. Blackacre is worth £9,000 and Yellowacre £4,500. If there were no doctrine of marshalling, Susan could realise her security by sale in one of two ways. (1) She could sell Blackacre for £9,000, pay herself off, and release Yellowacre from her security. That would destroy Thomas's security and reduce him to the status of an unsecured creditor. (2) She could sell Blackacre and Yellowacre for £13,500, pay herself off and hand £4,500 to Thomas (entitled to the surplus as second mortgagee of Blackacre), who, in turn, would pay himself off and hand the residue of £1,500 to Robert or his trustee in bankruptcy.

Marshalling prevents Thomas being at Susan's mercy.

It works in this way. If the matter comes before the court before the first mortgagee sells, he will be directed to satisfy himself entirely, or as far as possible, out of the property on which the second mortgagee is not secured, so as to leave the other property, or as much of it as possible, for the second mortgagee. If the matter does not come before the court at that early stage, and the first mortgagee begins by selling the property on which the second mortgagee is secured, and that sale leaves no surplus after the first mortgagee's debt has been paid off, the second mortgage is transferred to the other property.[24]

**Example** In the last example, marshalling makes an adjustment if Susan follows course number (1). Having sold Blackacre and paid herself off, she cannot release Yellowacre to Robert completely. Yellowacre is no longer security for Susan because Robert no longer owes her anything; but Thomas, who has lost his security in Blackacre, now becomes mortgagee of Yellowacre instead. Thomas is said to be subrogated to Susan's rights over Yellowacre to the extent (£3,000) to which Susan has destroyed Thomas's rights over Blackacre.

If there are three mortgagees, there may have to be a different adjustment. If the first mortgagee is secured on both Blackacre and Yellowacre, the second on Blackacre alone and the third on Yellowacre alone, to be fair to the second and third creditors, the first

24. See Keeton and Sheridan, *Equity*, pp. 432–7.

mortgagee must pay himself rateably out of the two properties (i.e., if Blackacre is worth twice as much as Yellowacre, he must cast two-thirds of the burden of his debt on Blackacre and one-third on Yellowacre).[25]

## Catholic and Secondary Securities in Scotland

A catholic security is a prior security over two funds and a secondary security is a subsequent security over one (or, occasionally, both) of these funds. The common-law rule is that the holder of the catholic security must act, in realising his security, so far as possible, so as to preserve the secondary security.

> **Example** Donald is a first mortgagee of Mary's heritage and moveables. James has a second mortgage of Mary's heritage only. Donald must either: (i) satisfy himself out of Mary's moveables as far as possible before touching the heritage; or (ii) satisfy himself out of the heritage and, if necessary, moveables, and, if some moveables are left over, assign his security over the moveables to James.[26]

*Nicol's Trustee* v. *Hill*[27] is an example of the application of this principle to a secondary security over both funds. A granted a heritable security to B, and then gave a second security over the same land to C. B poinded the ground, thereby obtaining a preference over A's moveables for £122 16s 1d. A then went bankrupt. Afterwards, C poinded the ground and so obtained a preference over A's moveables for £24 5s 5d. Finally, B sold the heritage, paying himself in full and handing the balance of the proceeds of sale to C. It was held that C could be preferred over A's ordinary creditors in right of B's £122 16s 1d secured on A's moveables, although both B and C had rights over both funds.

A creditor with two securities may, before the bankruptcy of his debtor, release one security, thus limiting his security to the other property, even if the property over which he retains his rights in security is also subject to a secondary security. In *Morton* (*Liddell's Curator*),[28] A mortgaged property to B, who later assigned his security to C. Subsequently, C obtained from D additional security for the debt owed to him by A. Later on, C became satisfied with

---

25. *Barnes* v. *Racster* (1842) 1 Y. & C.C. 401; *Flint* v. *Howard* [1893] 2 Ch. 54. Ireland: cf. *Re Archer's Estate* [1914] 1 I.R. 285; *Smyth* v. *Toms* [1918] 1 I.R. 338.
26. See *Littlejohn* v. *Black* (1855) 18 D. 207.
27. (1889) 16 R. 416.
28. (1871) 10 M. 292.

his original security, and released D from his security. Four years later, on A's insolvency, E, who was a second mortgagee of the property over which C had retained security, came forward and objected to C's release of D's security. The objection was repelled.

# 8 land: special arrangements

## Mortgages of Settled Land and of Land Held on Trust

**Settled Land in England and Wales**   The tenant for life[1] of settled land, within the meaning of the Settled Land Act 1925, has power to grant a legal mortgage of the fee simple or term of years he holds as tenant for life, but only so as to raise capital money for limited purposes. The purposes consist mainly of buying out incumbrances on the land,[2] paying compensation or costs under statutory provisions[3] and improving the settled land.[4]

The tenant for life may exercise his power of mortgaging so as to make the mortgage money repayable by instalments under the Agricultural Credits Acts,[5] even though the mortgage will therefore be irredeemable until the last instalment is paid.[6]

**Settled Land in Northern Ireland**   The tenant for life of settled land may grant a legal or equitable mortgage of the settled estate in order to raise money for enfranchisement, for equality of exchange or partition or for the discharge of incumbrances.[7]

1. See the Settled Land Act 1925, ss. 19–29, 117(1) (xxvi), (xxviii).
2. Settled Land Act 1925, s. 71.
3. Settled Land Act 1925, s. 71; Coast Protection Act 1949, s. 11(2) (*a*) (coast protection charges and expenses incurred in carrying out a works scheme); Landlord and Tenant Act 1954, s. 8(5) and sch. 2, para. 6, as amended by the Rent Act 1957, s. 21(2) (cost of carrying out initial repairs in accordance with an agreement or determination under the Act, or expenses thereunder); Coal Mining (Subsidence) Act 1957, s. 11(7) (sums payable by a licensee to the National Coal Board to compensate the Board for expenditure on repairing damage caused by subsidence); Leasehold Reform Act 1967, s. 6(5) and sch. 2, para. 9(1) (expenses of proceedings and compensation).
4. Settled Land Act 1925, ss. 71 and 83 and sch. 3.      5. See p. 96, *post.*
6. Agricultural Credits Act 1932, s. 3.
7. Settled Land Acts 1882, s. 18, and 1890, s. 11. See also the *Survey of the Land Law of Northern Ireland* (1971), p. 45, para. 122, and p. 47, para. 127.

**Settled Land in Scotland**   Since the enactment of the Entail (Scotland) Act 1914, section 2, it has not been permissible to execute entails of land in Scotland. Securities over pre-1914 entailed estates are seldom encountered. What follows is a very brief summary of the main statutory provisions relating to them.

The heir of entail, if of full age and in possession of the settled land, may charge the estate with debts or incumbrances.[8] He requires the authority of the Court of Session[9] and also, in general, the consents of his apparent successors in title.[10] These consents are not required where the heir of entail, with the authority of the Court of Session, grants a bond and disposition in security or (now) a standard security[11] to secure the payment of debts which he could lawfully charge on the fee;[12] and there are also provisions[13] for the Court of Session to dispense with consents in difficult cases.

The heir of entail may also grant a bond and disposition in security or (now) a standard security[11] to secure the cost of improvements.[14] He needs the authority of either the Court of Session[15] or the sheriff.[16]

Finally, the heir of entail who is liable to pay charges to the younger child of a previous heir may charge the land by bond and disposition in security[17] or (now) standard security.[18] He may charge the land either in favour of the child or in favour of someone advancing the money to the child.[19]

A security granted by an heir of entail may contain a power of sale in the ordinary form.[20] A creditor's express power of sale is, however, limited in its exercise to selling a portion of the estate sufficient to pay the debt.[21] If the sale produces a surplus after payment of the debt, it is to be invested in land to be entailed, unless the surplus is less than £200, in which case it is payable to the heir of entail beneficially.

8. Law of Entail (Scotland) Act 1848, ss. 4, 6; Entail (Scotland) Act 1882, s. 4.
9. Law of Entail (Scotland) Act 1848, s. 4.
10. Law of Entail (Scotland) Act 1848, s. 4.
11. Conveyancing and Feudal Reform (Scotland) Act 1970, s. 9(5).
12. Entail Amendment (Scotland) Act 1868, s. 11.
13. Entail Amendment (Scotland) Act 1875, ss. 5, 6; Entail (Scotland) Act 1882, ss. 13-15.
14. Law of Entail (Scotland) Act 1848, ss. 18, 19; Entail Amendment (Scotland) Act 1875, ss. 7-9; Entail Amendment (Scotland) Act 1878, ss. 3-4; Entail (Scotland) Act 1882, ss. 4, 6(4).
15. Law of Entail (Scotland) Act 1848, s. 18; Entail (Scotland) Act 1882, s. 6(1).
16. Entail (Scotland) Act 1882, ss. 5, 6(1).
17. Law of Entail (Scotland) Act 1848, ss. 21-3; Entail (Scotland) Act 1882, s. 4.
18. Conveyancing and Feudal Reform (Scotland) Act 1970, s. 9(5).
19. Entails (Scotland) Act 1853, s. 7.
20. Entails (Scotland) Act 1853, s. 23.     21. Law of Entail (Scotland) Act 1848, s. 30.

The Entail (Scotland) Act 1882, section 18, governs securities in favour of the creditors of an heir who could disentail.

**Land Held on Trust in England and Wales and Northern Ireland**   In the case of land held on trust for sale,[22] the trustees have all the mortgaging powers of a tenant for life of settled land.[23] Where land is held on trust, and the trust is neither for sale nor by way of settling the land, the trustees may mortgage it to raise capital money for any purpose for which the trustees are authorised by the trust instrument or by law[24] to apply capital money.[25] This power applies to trusts of all other kinds of property as well as to trusts of land. A personal representative may also grant a mortgage of land.[26]

**Land Held on Trust in Scotland**   There is no difference between a trust for sale and any other trust, with regard to rights in security, nor is there any difference between trusts of land and trusts of moveables. All trustees have power, 'where such acts are not at variance with the terms or purposes of the trust,' to 'borrow money on the security of the trust estate or any part thereof, heritable as well as moveable.'[27] To borrow lawfully in a way which is at variance with the trust, the trustees must have the authority of the court.[28] If trustees grant a security, which is at variance with the terms of purposes of the trust, but without a grant of power by the court, the security is valid but the trustees are liable to the beneficiaries for breach of trust.[29] An executor dative has all the same powers of granting security as a trustee has.[30]

**Mortgages by Co-owners (Including Husband and Wife)**
**England and Wales**   Where there are co-owners of land, whether husband and wife or not, there is a trust for sale[31] or a strict settlement,[32] so the powers of mortgaging which the co-owners have is that of trustees[33] or of a tenant for life.[34]

---

22. England and Wales: Law of Property Act 1925, s. 28; Northern Ireland: Settled Land Acts 1882, s. 63, and 1884, s. 7 (the court may by order confer the powers on the tenant for life under the trust for sale).
23. See p. 92, *ante*.     24. E.g., the power of advancement.
25. England and Wales: Trustee Act 1925, s. 16; Trustee Act (Northern Ireland) 1958, s. 16.
26. See the Administration of Estates Act 1925, s. 39(1) (i) (England and Wales); Administration of Estates Act (Northern Ireland) 1955, s. 40(4).
27. Trusts (Scotland) Act 1921, s. 4(1) (*d*).     28. S. 5 of the Act of 1921.
29. Trusts (Scotland) Act 1961, s. 2.     30. Succession (Scotland) Act 1964, s. 20.
31. Law of Property Act 1925, ss. 34–7.     32. Settled Land Act 1925, s. 19(2).
33. See above.     34. See p. 92, *ante*.

Difficulties arise when one spouse (usually the husband, so that is the terminology used here, but it works the other way round when the wife owns the title) owns the legal title to the matrimonial home and the wife appears to have no proprietary rights in it, so that there is no co-ownership and no trust for sale, but either: (i) the husband who holds the legal title has been helped by contributions from the wife in acquiring it; or (ii) the husband deserts the wife, leaving her in occupation of the house. In the case of the husband's mortgagee who wishes to sell or take possession of the land, there may be a contest of priorities.

With regard to case (i), it would appear that, unless she has protected herself under the Matrimonial Homes Act 1967,[35] the wife cannot resist eviction by the mortgagee but can claim an appropriate share of any proceeds of sale.[36] The wife's equity amounts to a right to share when the house is disposed of. By the Matrimonial Proceedings and Property Act 1970, section 37, a wife gets a beneficial interest in a matrimonial home owned by a husband if she contributes to improving it.

Independently of statute, a deserted wife has a right to reside in the matrimonial home, but that right prevails only against her husband (and his agents) and will not protect her against her husband's mortgagee.[37] By the Matrimonial Homes Act 1967, section 1, where the husband owns the title to the dwelling, the wife has a right not to be evicted or, if she is not in occupation, she has a right to enter with leave of the court. By section 2, the wife's right is a charge on the husband's title. In the case of unregistered land, that charge is registrable as a Class F land charge under the Land Charges Act 1972, section 2(1), (7);[38] in the case of registered land, the charge may be protected by caution. The effect of registration of a land charge is to give actual notice to persons dealing with the land.[39] Accordingly, a mortgagee who takes a legal mortgage from the husband after registration of the wife's charge will take subject to it unless the wife joins in the mortgage. Similarly, registration of the wife's charge makes her right in the matrimonial home equivalent to a second mortgage with regard to a prior mortgagee who is seeking to take further advances (section 2(8) of the Act of 1967).

---

35. See below.
36. See *Caunce* v. *Caunce* [1969] 1 W.L.R. 286; Hayton, 'Overriding Rights of Occupiers of Matrimonial Homes' (1969) 33 *Conveyancer* 254.
37. *National Provincial Bank Ltd.* v. *Ainsworth* [1965] A.C. 1165.
38. See also s. 4(8).
39. Law of Property Act 1925, s. 198.

By virtue of section 1(5) of the Act of 1967, the wife can redeem the mortgage, but that does not require the mortgagee to join her as a defendant in proceedings for possession.[40]

**Northern Ireland**　　There are no special rules for mortgages by co-owners; nor does co-ownership of land which is not settled land cause a trust for sale to come into existence.[41] There is no legislation governing the rights of spouses in a matrimonial home so the position is as it was in England and Wales before 1967.[42]

**Scotland**　　There are no special rules for security given by co-owners or of premises which constitute a matrimonial home.

## Mortgages of Agricultural Land

**England and Wales**　　The Agricultural Holdings Act 1948 gives a tenant of agricultural land certain rights to compensation from his landlord on the termination of the tenant's occupancy. By section 66 of that Act, if the tenant holds under a lease made by a mortgagor in possession, the lease not being one binding on the mortgagee, and the mortgagee goes into possession, the tenant's right to compensation from the mortgagor takes priority over the right of the mortgagee to pay himself. That section also provides that if such a tenancy is from year to year or for a period not exceeding twenty-one years, a mortgagee seeking possession of the land must give the tenant six months notice; and if the tenant is ejected when the notice expires, he gets compensation. The Act[43] also makes it impossible for a mortgage of agricultural land to exclude the powers given by the Law of Property Act 1925, section 99, to a mortgagor in possession to grant leases.

The Agricultural Credits Act 1928, section 1, provided for the establishment of a company – the Agricultural Mortgage Corporation – to make loans on agricultural land on terms most favourable to the borrowers; and for the government to make loans to the company. By section 2(3) (c), a mortgage granted to the company may express the loan to be repayable by equal yearly or half-yearly instalments of capital and interest spread over a period not exceeding sixty years. Section 2 of the Agricultural Credits Act 1932 says

40. *Hastings and Thanet Building Soc.* v. *Goddard* [1970] 1 W.L.R. 1544.
41. But see the proposals for statutory trusts in the *Survey of the Land Law of Northern Ireland* (1971), pp. 51–5, paras. 140–57.
42. See p. 95, *ante.*　　43. S. 95 and sch. 7, para. 2: see p. 39, footnote 35, *ante.*

that such a provision is not rendered invalid by virtue of the mortgagor being unable to redeem his land during the period of repayment, notwithstanding any rule of equity to the contrary.[44]

**Northern Ireland** There are virtually no special rules relating to mortgages of agricultural land. The only relevant legislation is the Development Loans (Agriculture and Fisheries) Act (Northern Ireland) 1968. By section 1, there is set up the Agricultural Loans Fund, from which the Ministry may make loans upon security for certain purposes of agriculture, forestry and rural industry listed in the first schedule.[45] A mortgage to secure such a loan may contain a provision making it irredeemable except upon specified terms and conditions.[46]

**Scotland** The Agricultural Credits (Scotland) Act 1929, sections 1 and 2, corresponds to sections 1 and 2 of the Act of 1928 in force in England and Wales.[47]

## Sub-Mortgages

Throughout the United Kingdom, a secured creditor may raise money on the strength of his security. If a mortgagee has a temporary need for a loan of less than he has lent to the mortgagor, he may not wish to realise or transfer his security. In that event, the mortgagee may mortgage his mortgage, and that is a sub-mortgage. For example, in England and Wales, a legal mortgagee by demise may grant a legal sub-mortgage by sub-demise or charge or an equitable sub-mortgage by deposit of title deeds or charge. In Scotland, there is no specific provision for a sub-security to be created out of a standard security (though there is no difficulty with the older forms of heritable security). Section 14 of the Conveyancing and Feudal Reform (Scotland) Act 1970 provides for the transfer, in whole or in part, of a standard security duly recorded, and there seems to be no reason in principle why the transferor should not reserve a power of redemption in any such assignation.

---

44. By s. 3 of the Act of 1932, such provisions for repayment and postponement or redemption may be included in mortgages granted by tenants for life of settled land, trustees and personal representatives: see pp. 92, 94, *ante*.
45. As to loans for fishery development, see s. 5.
46. S. 2(2) (*c*).    47. See p. 96, *ante*.

## Enforcement of Judgments

In England and Wales,[48] it is provided by the Administration of Justice Act 1956, section 35, that the High Court and county courts may, for the purpose of enforcing a judgment awarding a sum of money, make an order charging that sum upon land belonging to the judgment debtor. In general, such a charge has the same effect as an equitable charge created by the debtor in writing.[49] This does not mean that, if the debtor is a company, the charging order has to be registered in the register of company charges.[50]

The only property against which a charging order can be made under the Act of 1956 is land. Accordingly, no order can be made against the beneficial interest of a co-owner because co-owners hold their land on trust for sale, their beneficial interests being in proceeds of sale, not in land.[51] On the other hand, if there are two co-owners who hold on trust (for sale for themselves), and the judgment is against both of them, a charging order can be made because the two co-owners, as trustees, have power to charge the legal estate, which is land.[52]

## Mortgages to Moneylenders

There are no special rules relating to mortgages as such, when the mortgagee is a moneylender, but there are two special rules which apply to loans, including loans secured by mortgage or otherwise, made by moneylenders. These rules apply throughout the United Kingdom.

The first rule is that there is statutory provision,[53] replacing an earlier equitable jurisdiction, for the court to grant relief against harsh and unconscionable terms, including terms providing for excessive interest. An obligation to pay interest at a rate of more than 48% per annum is presumed to be harsh and unconscionable until the contrary is proved.[54] That means that the burden of justifying

48. See also the Judgments (Enforcement) Act (Northern Ireland) 1969, ss. 46–50. There is no similar mechanism in Scotland.
49. S. 35 makes a charging order registrable as a writ or order affecting land, not as a land charge. See the Land Charges Act 1972, s. 6; Land Registration Act 1925, ss. 54–6.
50. *Re Overseas Aviation Engineering (G.B.) Ltd.* [1963] Ch. 24.
51. *Irani Finance Ltd.* v. *Singh* [1971] Ch. 59.
52. *National Westminster Bank Ltd.* v. *Allen* [1971] 2 Q.B. 718.
53. Money-lenders Act 1900, s. 1.
54. Great Britain: Moneylenders Act 1927, s. 10; Money-lenders Act (Northern Ireland) 1933, s. 10.

a rate of over 48% is on the moneylender, while the burden of showing a rate of 48% or less to be harsh and unconscionable is on the borrower. What is a justifiable rate of interest will depend on, among other things, whether the loan is secured and, if so, the adequacy of the security.

The second rule is that a moneylender is not allowed to charge compound interest (though he may have interest on arrears of interest).[55]

If discretionary relief is granted to a borrower, he will be excused from performing the harsh and unconscionable terms of the contract of loan, but he will have to repay the amount he has borrowed, together with reasonable interest.[56] Sometimes, however, a money-lending transaction is void, e.g., because there is no note or memorandum of the terms as required by statute. In such a case, the lender cannot usually recover even the amount he has lent. An interesting exception is provided by subrogation, as in *Congresbury Motors Ltd.* v. *Anglo-Belge Finance Co. Ltd.*[57] In that case, the defendant moneylenders lent £46,000 to the borrower by paying most of it direct to the vendors from whom the borrowers were buying land. The land was conveyed to the borrowers, who gave the defendants a legal mortgage by charge to secure the £46,000. The loan and the mortgage were both void because there was no memorandum satisfying the Moneylenders Act 1927, section 6 (there was a memorandum, but it was defective as it omitted the date of the loan). Had the vendors conveyed the land and not been paid, they would have had a lien over the land for the price. The Court of Appeal held that, having paid the vendors, the moneylenders were subrogated to the unpaid vendor's lien (for £45,086 18s 5d). A considerably extended application of this doctrine occurred in *Coptic Ltd.* v. *Bailey*.[58] The defendant bought land, borrowing part of the purchase price and giving the lender a legal mortgage. Later, the defendant borrowed more from the plaintiff, a moneylender, purported to give him a legal mortgage, and paid off the first lender. The loan by the moneylender and the second legal mortgage to him were void. Nevertheless, it was held that the plaintiff could recover the amount of his loan from the defendant on one of two grounds. First, the lender was subrogated to the vendor's lien for unpaid purchase money and that lien by subrogation was not lost

---

55. 1927 Act, s. 7 (Great Britain); 1933 Act, s. 7 (Northern Ireland).
56. See *B. S. Lyle Ltd.* v. *Pearson* [1941] 2 K.B. 391.
57. [1971] Ch. 81. Cf. *Capital Finance Co. Ltd.* v. *Stokes* [1969] 1 Ch. 261.
58. [1972] Ch. 446. Cf. *Capital Finance Co. Ltd.* v. *Stokes* [1969] 1 Ch. 261.

by taking a valid legal mortgage; when the moneylender lent money to pay off the first lender, he became subrogated in his turn to the unpaid vendor's lien. Or, secondly, when the plaintiff lent money to pay off the first mortgage he became entitled to have the first (valid) legal mortgage kept alive for assignment to him. This decision goes rather far in keeping alive an unpaid vendor's lien where the vendor has been paid and the lender has got what he bargained for, namely a valid legal mortgage. It may be doubted whether it will be followed.

## Mortgages to Co-Lenders (Including Trustees)

**Loans by Several Lenders in Their Own Right**  In England and Wales and Northern Ireland, if two or more persons together lend money on mortgage, taking the security as joint tenants, they hold the mortgage on trust for themselves as tenants in common in equity in proportion to the amounts they contributed to the loan.[59] This is to avoid the rule that on the death of a joint tenant the property accrues to the survivor or survivors, a rule which is inappropriate to a commercial transaction such as a mortgage, and which does not apply to tenancies in common. But as against the mortgagor, the mortgage remains a joint mortgage, and he can obtain a valid discharge from the survivor or survivors or the personal representative of the last survivor (subject to the terms of the mortgage).[60] There are no such rules in Scotland.

**Loans by Trustees**  The powers of investment of trustees depend in the first instance on the terms of the trust instrument. If not extended or curtailed by that instrument, the power to lend money on mortgage is set out, for all parts of the United Kingdom, by the Trustee Investments Act 1961, section 1(1) and schedule 1, part II, paragraph 13.[61] They are empowered to invest in mortgages of freehold property in England and Wales or Northern Ireland and of leasehold property in those countries of which the unexpired term at the time of investment is not less than sixty years, and in

59. See *Morley* v. *Bird* (1798) 3 Ves. 628; *Re Jackson* (1887) 34 Ch.D. 732.
60. England and Wales: Law of Property Act 1925, s. 111; Northern Ireland: Conveyancing Act 1881, s. 61.
61. These provisions govern the position in Northern Ireland by virtue of the Trustee Act (Northern Ireland) 1958, s. 1, and the Trustee (Amendment) Act (Northern Ireland) 1962.

loans on heritable security in Scotland. Before making such an investment, trustees are bound to obtain and consider proper advice on the question whether the investment is satisfactory having regard to two factors the trustees are bound to take into account.[62] These are: (a) the need for diversification of investments of the trust, in so far as is appropriate to the circumstances of the trust; and (b) the suitability to the trust of investments of the description of the investment proposed and of the investment proposed as an investment of that description.[63] Co-trustees lending money hold the security as joint tenants, the right of survivorship being convenient.

If the security proves inadequate, trustees are not liable for breach of trust if they have complied with the Trustee Investments Act 1961 and if they were acting upon a report as to the value of the property made by a person whom they reasonably believed to be an able practical surveyor or valuer instructed and employed independently of the owner of the property, and they did not lend more than two-thirds of the value of the property as expressed in the report, and the loan was made under the advice of the surveyor or valuer expressed in the report.[64] If the trustees lend too much, but the security would have been a valid investment for a smaller amount, they are liable only for loss in respect of the excess over what they could properly have lent.[65]

## Life Insurance, Taxation and Subsidies

From the point of view of repayment and redemption, mortgages fall into three main categories:

(1) those where the loan is made for a specified period, no repayment of capital being obligatory on the mortgagor until the end of the period so long as interest is punctually paid in the meantime (though the mortgagor may have the right to redeem earlier on giving due notice);

(2) those where the loan is repayable by instalments, each instalment representing partly a repayment of capital and partly interest on the outstanding balance, the instalments

62. Trustee Investments Act 1961, s. 6(2).   63. Trustee Investments Act 1961, s. 6(1).
64. England and Wales: Trustee Act 1925, s. 8(1); Trustee Act (Northern Ireland) 1958, s. 8(1); Trusts (Scotland) Act 1921, s. 30. As to England and Wales and Northern Ireland, see further, Keeton, *The Law of Trusts*, 9th ed., pp. 253-5, 433-4, and Irish Supplement (Sheridan), pp. 35-7; Keeton, *Modern Developments in the Law of Trusts*, pp. 62-5.
65. Trustee Act 1925, s. 9 (England and Wales); Trustee Act (Northern Ireland) 1958, s. 9; Trusts (Scotland) Act 1921, s. 29.

being equal in amount so that the period of the mortgage may vary with variations in interest rates, the mortgagor only being liable to repay the capital sum as a whole if called upon by the mortgagee after the mortgagor has committed some breach of contract such as a failure to pay instalments (the mortgagor, however, having the right to redeem by giving due notice);

(3) a variant of (2) in one of the following ways: (*a*) that the interest is fixed, so that the period of repayment is fixed; (*b*) that if interest rates vary, the amounts of instalments vary, so that the period of repayment is fixed; (*c*) that the mortgagor may not redeem until the last instalment is due.

The second of these varieties is the commonest type of building society mortgage, and either (2) or one of the variants listed under (3) is usual with mortgages to friendly societies, industrial and provident societies, employers and many other lenders. Type 3(*c*) is rarely met outside agricultural mortgages. Type (1) is usual for short-term mortgages (especially to banks), commercial loans (e.g., by a parent company to a subsidiary company for the purpose of financing a capital development) and building society mortgages linked with life endowment insurance.

**Income Tax**  So long as a loan (whether secured or not) is for the purpose of buying or improving land, it qualifies for relief from income tax. That is to say, the interest paid in a year is deducted from the borrower's income for that year when computing his taxable income.[66] If the loan is secured, it makes no difference to the tax position what type of security it is, though in the case of an instalment mortgage the calculation of the amount of each instalment attributable to interest may involve quite difficult arithmetic. It follows that the higher the income of the borrower the less will be his net outlay, and a person whose income is too low to be taxable derives no advantage at all from tax relief. Money borrowed for a purpose outside the statutory list will not qualify for tax relief on the first £35 interest unless it is a borrowing of working capital for a business, trade or profession. If a wealthy landowner, for example, borrows money by mortgaging his land, so that he can invest the

66. Income and Corporation Taxes Act 1970, s. 57, replaced by the Finance Act 1972, s. 75 and sch. 9. That section provides that interest on loans for other purposes also qualifies for income tax relief: (*a*) if, and to the extent that, the interest exceeds £35 a year; and (*b*) provided the rate of interest is a reasonable commercial rate. See also s. 76 of the Act of 1972.

borrowed amount in shares, he cannot deduct the first £35 of annual mortgage interest from the dividends on the shares when computing his taxable income.

**Life Insurance**   Life insurance policies can be linked with loans in all sorts of ways, both for the better protection of the lender and for the greater tax advantage of the borrower. Any lender may insure his debtor's life so as to protect himself against the debt becoming bad due to the borrower's premature death; the insurance would be for the amount of the debt. A debtor may take out an insurance policy on his own life and mortgage it to secure the debt.

A life insurance policy may provide for payment of a sum only on death; or it may provide in addition for a lump sum or an annuity to be paid on survival to a specified age. It may provide for a fixed sum or for a minimum sum plus a share in the profits of the insurance company to be added periodically (e.g., each year), the latter being called a policy 'with profits.' The premium may be a single one paid when taking out the policy or, more usually, premiums may be payable throughout the period from the inception of the policy until its maturity. Such periodical premiums are usually payable monthly or annually.

All kinds of lump sum life insurance have their function in relation to security over land. From the point of view of the mortgagee of a dwelling-house, for example, where the mortgagor is a husband with children, insurance of his life by the mortgagor and assignment of the insurance policy to the mortgagee by way of security will save the mortgagee the trouble of realising his security if the mortgagor dies and the widow cannot afford to redeem, and ensures that the widow and children will not be put out of their home. In the case of a borrower who has a sum of money but uncertain prospects of a stable or increasing income, a single-premium policy will minimise the risk of default.

In general, life insurance qualifies for relief from income tax. In respect of a policy on the life of the taxpayer or on the life of his wife, two-fifths of the amount of premiums paid in a year are deducted from the taxpayer's income when computing his taxable income.[67]

Because of the benefits to the mortgagor and his family and the benefits to the mortgagee, borrowers in the relatively high income group who buy houses through a building society loan quite often

67. Income and Corporation Taxes Act 1970, s. 19.

do so by a fixed-term loan coupled with a life insurance endowment policy. For example, the husband is buying a house for £12,000. He borrows £8,000 from a building society, repayable twenty years later. In the meantime, he pays interest, on which he gets tax relief. He also takes out an insurance policy for £8,000 with profits, the sum assured to be paid on his death or survival for twenty years. In the meantime, he pays monthly premiums, on which he gets tax relief. If he has chosen his insurance company wisely, and he survives the twenty years, the amount paid to him by the insurance company (including accumulated profits) should then be enough to pay off the £8,000 to the building society and reimburse him for a good deal of the interest and premiums. In other words, the difference between (a) the sum of the amount of the loan to be repaid, the interest and the premiums; and (b) the sum of the policy moneys and the tax relief; should be less than £8,000. If he dies before the twenty years are up, the bargain may be even better, in financial terms, from the point of view of the mortgagor's family, because less has been paid in premiums and interest. (A contract of insurance is a contract uberrimae fidei, i.e., the proposer must declare all material facts; and in cases of life insurance, the insurance company usually require a medical examination.)

**Option Mortgages** In Great Britain, but not in Northern Ireland, there was introduced in 1967 a subsidy option for house purchasers whose income situation is such that they derive little or no benefit from the tax relief on interest. In certain cases, the borrower is allowed to opt for a subsidised rate of interest, but then he can claim no tax relief at all. For the person paying no income tax, the subsidy is obviously a beneficial option (if, indeed, his financial standing is sufficiently good for him to get a loan at all). For the person paying a low rate of income tax, it may be a matter of fine judgment whether he is better off with a subsidy or with tax relief.

The right to opt applies, under the Housing Subsidies Act 1967, section 24,[68] to a loan, repayable by instalments, made by a qualifying lender,[69] on the security of a legal estate, for the purpose of acquiring a dwelling, acquiring a site for one, constructing one, converting a building to a dwelling or improving a dwelling.

---

68. See also s. 25, s. 26 (as amended by the Income and Corporation Taxes Act 1970, s. 537(2) and sch. 15, para. 11, pt. II) and s. 26A (added by the Housing Act 1969, s. 79(2)).
69. See p. 105, post.

If he opts for the subsidy, the borrower's interest is reduced either: (*a*) *to* 4% per annum; or (*b*) *by* 2% per annum;[70] whichever reduction is less.[71] (In respect of any instalment representing interest only, the figures are: (*a*) $4\frac{1}{4}$%; and (*b*) $1\frac{3}{4}$%.) The difference between the rate of interest due under the contract and the lower rate of interest the mortgagor has opted to pay is given as a subsidy by the Minister[72] to the lender.[73]

Qualifying lenders[74] are local authorities, certain building societies,[75] such other building societies, insurance companies and friendly societies as the Minister[72] may prescribe, development corporations and the Commission for the New Towns.

## Loans by Local Authorities

By section 1 of the Small Dwellings Acquisition Act 1899, which applies throughout the United Kingdom,[76] a local authority may lend money, repayable by instalments over a period not exceeding thirty years,[77] to a resident in a house in their area, for the purpose of enabling him to acquire the ownership of that house, the value of the house being £5,000 or less.[78] The local authority must be satisfied as to the borrower's residence or intention to reside in the house, and that he does not already own one, and as to the value, title and state of the house; and they must take a mortgage.[79]

When the borrower has acquired the title to the house, until he has repaid the loan, he is subject to the following obligations: (*a*) to pay his instalments punctually; (*b*) to live in the house;[80] (*c*) to

70. The 2% may be raised by the Ministers acting jointly, with Treasury approval: Housing Act 1969, s. 78. (As to who the Ministers are, see footnote 73, below.)
71. Housing Subsidies Act 1967, s. 28.
72. The Minister of Housing and Local Government, the Secretary of State for Scotland or the Secretary of State for Wales: s. 32(2) of the Act of 1967.
73. Ss. 24 and 33 of the Act of 1967.     74. S. 27 of the Act of 1967.
75. See the House Purchase and Housing Act 1959, s. 1.
76. See also the Housing, Town Planning, etc., Act 1919, s. 49(*b*) (England and Wales); Housing, Town Planning, etc. (Scotland) Act 1919, s. 39; Housing, etc. Act 1923, s. 24 and sch. 3 (Great Britain); Housing (Miscellaneous Provisions) and Rent Restriction Law (Amendment) Act (Northern Ireland) 1956, s. 25(1), (2).
77. Fifty years in Northern Ireland: Housing (Ireland) Act 1919, s. 34.
78. Housing Act 1949, s. 44(1) (England and Wales); Housing (Scotland) Act 1949, s. 39; Small Dwellings Acquisition Act (Northern Ireland) 1947, s. 1(2); Small Dwellings Acquisition (Market Value) Order (Northern Ireland) 1954: S.R. & O. (N.I.) 1954 No. 145.
79. 1899 Act, s. 2; Law of Property (Amendment) Act 1924, s. 9 and sch. 9 (England and Wales); Conveyancing and Feudal Reform (Scotland) Act 1970, s. 9(7).
80. See also s. 7 of the Act 1899 (Great Britain); Housing Act (Northern Ireland) 1923, s. 5(*c*).

insure against fire; (*d*) to keep the house in good repair; (*e*) not to sell intoxicating liquors in it or to commit a nuisance to adjacent houses; and (*f*) to allow entry at reasonable times to a person authorised by the mortgagee to check that the obligations are being carried out (1899 Act, section 3(1)). The borrower may transfer his interest in the house, with the permission of the mortgagee[81] (which permission must not be unreasonably withheld), and the transferee will take subject to the same obligations (1899 Act, section 3(2)). If the condition as to residence is broken, the mortgagee may take possession of the house; and if any of the other conditions is broken, the mortgagee may either take possession or order sale of the house without taking possession (1899 Act, section 3(3)).[82] If the breach does not consist of default in payment of an instalment, before realising the security the mortgagee must serve on the mortgagor a notice calling on him to comply with the condition; then, if the mortgagor undertakes in writing within fourteen days to do so, and does so within two months, the mortgagee must not take possession or order a sale (1899 Act, section 3(4)). If the breach is non-payment of an instalment, no notice need be given; but if the mortgagee sues for possession, the mortgagor cannot be put out if he brings himself up to date with payments by the time of the court hearing.[83]

When a mortgagee does take possession, the mortgagor's title to the house vests in the mortgagee, who may keep it or sell it (1899 Act, section 5(1)). The mortgagee must then pay the mortgagor either a sum agreed between them or the value of the interest the mortgagee acquires in the house less what is owing by the mortgagor on the mortgage (1899 Act, section 5(2)). That means that the local authority mortgagee, by taking possession, is in effect foreclosing the mortgage summarily: a quite different effect from the taking of possession by any other kind of mortgagee. That was one of the factors in the decision in *Alnwick R.D.C.* v. *Taylor*.[84] The analogy with foreclosure was also significant in *Mexborough U.D.C.* v. *Harrison*.[85] There, the mortgagor abandoned the house, and the local authority took possession and let it to a tenant. The local authority then sued the mortgagor to recover the principal sum and

---

81. Permission is not required for the creation of a subsequent mortgage: s. 4(2) of the 1899 Act.
82. As to the bankruptcy of the mortgagor or his death insolvent, see s. 3(5) of the 1899 Act.
83. *Alnwick R.D.C.* v. *Taylor* [1966] Ch. 355.
84. [1966] Ch. 355.    85. [1964] 1 W.L.R. 733.

other money due to them under the mortgage. It was held that, by analogy to foreclosure of ordinary mortgages, the mortgagor, having been sued on the contractual obligation to pay, had a renewed right to redeem. If he did not redeem, the local authority could recover what was due under the mortgage (including the costs of the action), less the value of the house.

When a mortgagee orders the sale of a house without taking possession, the house must be put up for sale by auction; the local authority is paid off out of the proceeds and any balance must be handed over to the mortgagor (1899 Act, section 6(1)). But if the local authority cannot sell the house at an auction for enough to pay themselves in full, they may take possession of the house and are then not liable to pay anything to the mortgagor (1899 Act, section 6(2)). In *Re Brown's Mortgage*,[86] the mortgagor died and his widow, who was his administratrix, asked the local authority to foreclose, as she did not want to have any further responsibilities with regard to the property, and handed over the keys of the house to the town clerk. The local authority put the house up for sale by auction, but it was not sold, so they took possession. Later the value of the property rose, and the local authority now proposed to sell the house for more than the debt and pay the balance to the mortgagor's widow. It was held that the local authority could not do that: if they sold the house, they must keep the whole of the proceeds of the sale. Section 6(2) states: '. . . they shall not be liable to pay any sum to the proprietor.' Because a local authority are trustees for the ratepayers, they cannot make any payment they are not liable to make (unless authorised by statute). In *Re Caunter's Charge*,[87] on the other hand, section 6(2) fell to be considered in relation to a second mortgagee. The mortgagor bought his house for £2,250 by borrowing £1,800 from the local authority on a first mortgage, and by borrowing the balance of £450 from the vendor on a second mortgage. Eventually, the mortgagor defaulted in payments to the local authority and disappeared. The local authority put the house up for sale by auction, but the reserve price was not reached, so they took possession. Later, they sold the house for more than was due under their first mortgage, and claimed to keep all the proceeds, paying nothing to the second mortgagee. Danckwerts J. did not approve of Cohen J.'s decision in *Re Brown's Mortgage*, but was able to distinguish it. The second mortgagee was not the proprietor; the Act (section 4(2)) specifically referred to second

86. [1945] Ch. 166.    87. [1960] Ch. 491.

mortgages; and there was nothing in the Act which required the second mortgagee to be deprived of his right to repayment by reason of the default of the mortgagor. Consequently, the second mortgagee's right remained unless disposed of by due process of law, as, for instance, by full foreclosure proceedings. So the second mortgagee was entitled to payment by the local authority out of their proceeds of sale.

In Northern Ireland, there are two extensions of this scheme. Local authorities may advance loans on mortgage not only for the purchase but also for the construction of small dwellings.[88] They may make the loan by instalments during the building operations, advancing up to 80% of the value of the work done at the time of the advance.[89] Secondly, local authorities are no longer the sole source of public finance for housing purposes. By the Housing Executive Act (Northern Ireland) 1971, section 14:

The [Housing] Executive may, subject to such conditions as the Ministry may specify, advance money by way of mortgage to any person for the purposes of—

    (a) acquiring or constructing a house;

    (b) converting a building into a house or acquiring buildings for that purpose;

    (c) altering, enlarging, repairing or improving a house.

## The Rent Acts

**Great Britain** Restriction of amounts of rent for dwelling-houses which are let, and restraint of the landlord's powers to evict tenants of dwellings subject to rent restriction, are governed by two schemes under the Rent Act 1968 (as to England and Wales) and the Rent (Scotland) Act 1971. One scheme, which relates to what are called 'regulated tenancies,' was introduced in 1965, and provides for the fixing of fair rents. The other scheme, which relates to what are called 'controlled tenancies,' was originally a measure of the first world war and was put substantially on its present footing in 1920. Controlled tenancies are tenancies of houses which were restricted before 1965 and which have not been changed over to the system of regulated tenancies. Control consists of pegging the rent payable at

88. Housing Act (Northern Ireland) 1923, s. 5(a), which makes a consequential amendment in the residence requirement.
89. Housing Act (Northern Ireland) 1923, s. 5(e); Housing (Miscellaneous Provisions) and Rent Restriction Law (Amendment) Act (Northern Ireland) 1956, s. 25(3), (4).

the date on which the house became subject to control, or at which the house was first let thereafter if it was not let on that date, subject to certain permitted increases specified in the legislation. All remaining controlled tenancies will have been converted to regulated tenancies by the middle of 1975.[90]

If a dwelling subject to rent *control* is mortgaged by the landlord, the security is also *controlled* (by virtue of the Rent Act 1968, section 93, and the Rent (Scotland) Act 1971, section 110). These are securities which, before 1968 (England and Wales) or 1971 (Scotland) were governed by the Act of 1920.[91] The control consists of restrictions on raising the rate of interest payable to the creditor and on the creditor enforcing his security.[92]

In respect of *regulated* tenancies, if the landlord has mortgaged the dwelling, the security is usually also *regulated* if it was granted before 8th December 1965[93] or, in the case of a long tenancy in England and Wales becoming regulated by the Leasehold Reform Act 1967, section 39, 28th November 1967.[94] By section 94(1) of the Rent Act 1968,[95] a mortgage which is not controlled is regulated if it is a legal mortgage of, or including, a dwelling let on or subject to a regulated tenancy, in such circumstances that the regulated tenancy is binding on the mortgagee, unless:

(a) the rateable value of the mortgaged dwelling or dwellings is less than one-tenth of that of all the land comprised in the mortgage; or

(b) the mortgagor is in breach of any covenant except one for repayment of the principal money otherwise than by instalments.

These provisions are applied to Scotland, under the appropriate amendment of the terms used, by section 111 of the Rent (Scotland) Act 1971.

The court is empowered[96] to vary the terms of a regulated mortgage in cases of severe financial hardship to the mortgagor.

90. Housing Finance Act 1972, Part IV, especially s. 35, and s. 89; Housing (Financial Provisions) (Scotland) Act 1972, Part V, especially ss. 34–6.
91. The repealed Acts which formerly governed controlled mortgages are: the Increase of Rent and Mortgage Interest (Restrictions) Act 1920, ss. 4, 7, 12(1) (b), (4)–(6), 14 and 18; Rent and Mortgage Interest Restrictions Act 1923, s. 14; Rent and Mortgage Interest Restrictions (Amendment) Act 1933, s. 9; and the Rent and Mortgage Interest Restrictions Act 1939.
92. Rent Act 1968, ss. 96–9 and sch. 12; Rent (Scotland) Act 1971, ss. 113–16 and sch. 16.
93. Rent Act 1968, s. 93(1); Rent (Scotland) Act 1971, s. 110(1).
94. Rent Act 1968, s. 93(4).
95. And s. 111 of the Rent (Scotland) Act 1971.
96. Rent Act 1968, s. 95; Rent (Scotland) Act 1971, s. 112.

**Northern Ireland**  There are only controlled mortgages,[97] there being no regulated tenancies and no recent legislation similar to that in Great Britain.

---

97. These are governed by the Increase of Rent and Mortgage Interest (Restrictions) Act 1920, the Rent and Mortgage Interest (Restrictions) Act (Northern Ireland) 1940, ss. 1–5 and 10, and the Housing (Miscellaneous Provisions) and Rent Restriction Law (Amendment) Act (Northern Ireland) 1956, s. 57.

# securities over personal chattels (corporeal moveables)

Goods and chattels about the house – personal effects such as clothes and furniture – are not usually given as security for a loan: often they are not valuable enough, or not easily saleable. If items of household equipment are acquired on credit, that is usually arranged by hire-purchase, which is not a type of security – the customer does not acquire a proprietary right until the last instalment is paid – or by some similar arrangement such as a credit sale or a conditional sale. If money is borrowed to buy a car or household goods, it is usually borrowed from a bank by way of unsecured overdraft on a current account (or by what are commonly called nowadays 'personal loans'). Personal belongings of a small but valuable nature, such as watches and jewellery, may be pawned[1] to raise money, and valuable contents of a house may (except in Scotland) be mortgaged along with the house itself. However, much the most frequent employment of chattels personal (to use the technical term of England and Wales and Northern Ireland), or corporeal moveables (the technical term of Scotland), as security is in commerce, to raise money for business purposes.

There is virtually no limit to the variety of circumstances in which borrowing may be necessary in trade, or to the varieties of property that may be used as security. A middle-man dealing in goods may use the goods as security to borrow in order to pay for them, with a view to repaying the loan when the goods have been re-sold. A manufacturer may raise working capital on the security of his plant.

1. See pp. 144–74, *post*.

A hotelier may finance his operations by borrowing on the security of the furnishings of the hotel. A farmer may stock his farm by using money lent to him on the security of livestock and farming implements. A firm running a fleet of lorries or aeroplanes[2] may buy the vehicles by borrowing on the security of them. A company running any kind of trading business may finance itself by raising loans on the security of its stock-in-trade, or even on the security of its whole undertaking (premises, plant, stock, goodwill, book debts and so forth). These are examples, not intended to be exhaustive, and many other examples will present themselves in the course of this chapter.

Leaving aside, for the moment, security given by private individuals over personal possessions, e.g., by pawning them, and referring particularly to commercial use of goods and other moveable property as security: there are two features of this type of property as security which differentiate it from land and which pose problems of law different from those associated with mortgages of real property and heritable securities.

First, in respect of most property other than land there are no title deeds or registers of titles or conveyances. A landowner who has secured a loan on his property, and continues to live on it with all the appearance of being the absolute owner, cannot readily swindle a purchaser into buying the land in ignorance of the lender's rights over the security because the lender will generally be protected in one of the following ways:

(i) by being registered as a chargee or by holding the land certificate as a depositee, if the land is registered land in England and Wales or Northern Ireland (or by having a caution entered in respect of an unregistered mortgage over registered land in England and Wales);

(ii) by holding the title deeds to the mortgagor's unregistered estate or registering a land charge over it in England and Wales;

(iii) by holding the title deeds to the mortgagor's unregistered estate or registering in the registry of deeds in Northern Ireland;

(iv) by registration in the Register of Sasines, or entering into possession of the land where the security is a short lease, in Scotland.

In the absence of title deeds, the only safety for the creditor

2. As to security over aircraft, see p. 118, *post*, and as to security over ships and their freight and cargo, see pp. 175–203, *post*.

secured on property is for him to take possession of the property, or to provide him with a register of securities which a purchaser from the borrower ignores at his peril. The very mobility of goods, coupled with the easy assumption that the person with control of them is the owner, makes it hazardous to take security of this kind without getting possession of the goods, some similar control over them, or a registrable security. To all intents and purposes, the law in all parts of the United Kingdom nowadays recognises only two types of security over moveable property: that which is registered and that which gives the lender physical control.

Secondly, in commerce, it is necessary to deal with many of the types of property over which security is given. When a factory owner gives security over his machinery, that machinery will be left in position (though it may have to be replaced at long intervals). But when a wholesaler gives security over his stock-in-trade, the continuance of the business (and hence the well-being of the creditor as well as that of the debtor) requires that the wholesaler should be able to sell the goods to a retailer, free from the creditor's security, so as to make profits and pay his debts. Similarly, the owner of vehicles used for carriage of goods or passengers must be free to move them around in the course of business. The latter situation requires that the vehicles remain in the possession of the borrower, and argues for security by registered transaction. The former situation requires not merely that the lender should not get possession of the goods but even that they be disposable by the borrower free from rights of security. For this purpose the floating charge[3] was devised.

In this chapter, the following types of security over personal chattels (corporeal moveables) are dealt with:

  (i)   mortgages of chattels in England and Wales and Northern Ireland;
 (ii)   rights in security over corporeal moveables in Scotland by ex facie absolute assignation or assignation in security;
(iii)   floating charges throughout the United Kingdom;
 (iv)   agricultural charges in Great Britain;
  (v)   pledge or pawn throughout the United Kingdom.[4]

---

3. See pp. 126–43, *post.*
4. Security on the transfer of documents of title to goods: pp. 151–5, *post*; security over and in connection with ships: pp. 175–203, *post*; liens and rights of retention: pp. 204–38, *post.*

## Mortgages of Chattels in England and Wales and Northern Ireland

At common law, no formalities were required for the creation of a mortgage over a chattel.[5] The arrangement could be written or oral, the mortgagee taking possession or leaving it with the mortgagor. From the point of view of the mortgagee such a security (whether oral or in writing) was hazardous if the mortgagor remained in possession. The mortgagor might dispose of the chattel unlawfully without much hindrance; and if the mortgagor went bankrupt, the unsecured creditors might well displace the mortgagee by calling upon the doctrine of reputed ownership. In order to allow a more serviceable security over chattels left in the debtor's possession, legislation provided for registration. Security over chattels can still be given validly without writing or registration if possession is passed to the lender, i.e., it is a pledge[6] or unregistrable mortgage.

**Bills of Sale**   The basic statute now in force in England and Wales, replacing earlier legislation, is the Bills of Sale Act 1878.[7] A bill of sale is not necessarily a document creating a security. The expression includes, among other things, assignments, transfers, declarations of trust without transfer, inventories of goods with receipt attached, or receipts for purchase-money of goods and other assurances of personal chattels[8] (not including ships, bills of lading, transfers in the ordinary course of business and various other types of transaction).[9] All the transactions listed may be by way of out-and-out disposition or by way of security (i.e., subject to redemption). Personal chattels in this context include fixtures and growing crops, when separately assigned or mortgaged,[10] and trade machinery.[11] A document giving a right of distress by way of security is a bill of sale unless it is a mining lease, a lease by a mortgagee in possession to the mortgagor at a fair and reasonable rent[12] or a document giving a power of distress by way of indemnity against a rent or any

5. A mortgage of a moveable windmill, in writing but not under seal, the mortgagor retaining possession, was upheld in *Flory* v. *Denny* (1852) 7 Ex. 581.
6. See pp. 144–74, *post*.
7. Northern Ireland: Bills of Sale (Ireland) Act 1879.
8. England and Wales: Bills of Sale Act 1878, s. 4; Bankruptcy Act 1914, s. 3; Northern Ireland: Bills of Sale (Ireland) Act 1879, s. 4.
9. England and Wales: Bills of Sale Acts 1878, s. 4, and 1891, s. 1; Northern Ireland: Bills of Sale (Ireland) Act 1879, s. 4.
10. 1878 Act, s. 4; 1879 Act, s. 4.     11. 1878 Act, s. 5; 1879 Act, s. 5.
12. 1878 Act, s. 6; 1879 Act, s. 6.

part thereof payable in respect of any land or against the breach of any covenant or condition in relation to land.[13]

A bill of sale given by way of security must be attested by one witness not a party to it[14] and registered[15] within seven days of its execution (or, in the case of a bill made outside the country, within seven days of the date when it should have arrived in the country in the ordinary course of post if posted immediately after its execution), and must set forth the consideration for which it was given; otherwise it will be void.[16] A bill by way of security is void, too, if given in consideration of an advance of less than £30.[17] It is also void – (a) except in the case of a bill giving security over growing crops or replacement fixtures:[18] (i) unless it has a schedule or inventory of chattels comprised in it;[19] (ii) as to any chattels not listed in the schedule or inventory;[19] (iii) as to any chattels which are listed but of which the grantor was not the true owner at the time of the execution of the bill;[20] (b) if it is not in the form given in the schedule to the Act.[21]

The general position of the parties is similar (so far as differences in the types of property permit) to that of parties to a legal mortgage of an estate in land. The mortgagor has both a legal and an equitable right to redeem. The mortgagee may bring foreclosure proceedings to put an end to the right of redemption. The mortgagee will not usually have a statutory power of sale, because the mortgage will not usually be by deed, but a power of sale may be given expressly in the bill of sale. If there is no express or statutory power of sale, there may be power implied by law: there are some dicta[22] that such a power exists, but there appears to be no direct authority. There are statutory restrictions[23] on the mortgagee's power to seize a mortgaged chattel, and the court is empowered to grant relief.

Bills of sale requiring registration under the Bills of Sale Acts do not include: (a) a charge registrable under the Companies Acts;[24]

13. England and Wales: Law of Property Act 1925, s. 189(1).
14. England and Wales: Bills of Sale Act (1878) Amendment Act 1882, ss. 3, 10; Northern Ireland: Bills of Sale (Ireland) Act (1879) Amendment Act 1883, ss. 3, 10.
15. As to registration in England and Wales, see the 1878 Act, ss. 10–17; 1882 Act, s. 11; Administration of Justice Act 1925, s. 23(2); Northern Ireland: 1879 Act, ss. 10–17, 1883 Act, s. 11.
16. 1882 Act, s. 8; 1883 Act, s. 8.     17. 1882 Act, s. 12; 1883 Act, s. 12.
18. 1882 Act, s. 6; 1883 Act, s. 6.
19. 1882 Act, s. 4; 1883 Act, s. 4.
20. 1882 Act, s. 5; 1883 Act, s. 5.
21. 1882 Act, s. 9; 1883 Act, s. 9.
22. See, e.g., dicta of Stirling and Cozens-Hardy L. JJ. in *Deverges* v. *Sandeman, Clark & Co.* [1902] 1 Ch. 579.     23. 1882 Act, s. 7; 1883 Act, s. 7.
24. *Read* v. *Joannon* (1890) 25 Q.B.D. 300; *Re Standard Manufacturing Co.* [1891] 1 Ch. 627; *Re Royal Marine Hotel Co. (Kingstown) Ltd.* [1895] 1 I.R. 368. As to registration of company charges, see pp. 119–20, *post.*

(b) an instrument creating or evidencing a fixed or floating charge on the assets of a registered society if application for the recording of the charge is made to the friendly societies central office;[25] (c) in England and Wales, an agricultural charge;[26] (d) a pledge[27] or oral mortgage;[28] or (e) a common law lien.[29] In *Morris* v. *Delobbel-Flipo*[29] a contract between a principal and his agent employed to sell the principal's goods gave the agent a right to retain goods in his possession as security for his expenses. It was held that the agent had no right in equity or charge by way of security over the goods within the legislation on bills of sale, so the contract did not require registration. The agent had no right to get any goods, but only to retain those which were in his possession.

Apart from those exceptions, any documentary transaction of loan on security of chattels (other than ships and aircraft in the United Kingdom nationality register) is a bill of sale, void for non-registration, however it may be dressed up to appear. If, for example, the owner of goods sells them to someone and agrees to take them back on hire-purchase, and the real object of the transaction is to provide an advance on security, no title to the goods passes to the 'purchaser,' though the advance is recoverable from the 'vendor' in a quasi-contractual action.[30] On the other hand, a genuine sale by the owner of chattels followed by a hiring or hire-purchase back to the vendor, not intended as a transaction of loan on security, is not a bill of sale and does not require registration in order to be valid.[31]

If the borrower on security of a bill of sale goes bankrupt without having defaulted in payments due to the lender, the doctrine of reputed ownership applies to goods subject to the bill.[32]

25. England and Wales: Industrial and Provident Societies Act 1967, s. 1; Industrial and Provident Societies Act (Northern Ireland) 1969, s. 29.
26. Agricultural Credits Act 1928, ss. 8(1), 14; Agricultural Marketing Act 1958, s. 15(5). As to agricultural charges, see pp. 143–4, *post.*
27. *Ex parte Hubbard* (1886) 17 Q.B.D. 690; *Hilton* v. *Tucker* (1888) 39 Ch.D. 669; *Waight* v. *Waight* [1952] P. 282.
28. An oral agreement to grant a bill of sale is not itself registrable as a bill of sale: *Ex parte Hauxwell* (1883) 23 Ch.D. 626.
29. *Morris* v. *Delobbel-Flipo* [1892] 2 Ch. 352.
30. *Cochrane* v. *Matthews* (1878) 10 Ch.D. 80n.; *Ex parte Odell* (1878) 10 Ch.D. 76; *Manchester, Sheffield and Lincolnshire Railway Co.* v. *North Central Wagon Co.* (1888) 13 App. Cas. 554; *Re Watson* (1890) 25 Q.B.D. 27; *Beckett* v. *Tower Assets Co.* [1891] 1 Q.B. 638; *Madell* v. *Thomas & Co.* [1891] 2 Q.B. 230; *Maas* v. *Pepper* [1905] A.C. 102; *Polsky* v. *S. and A. Services* [1951] 1 All E.R. 185 and 1062; *North Central Wagon Finance Co. Ltd.* v. *Brailsford* [1962] 1 W.L.R. 1288.
31. *Redhead* v. *Westwood* (1888) 59 L.T. 293; *Re Yarrow* (1889) 59 L.J.Q.B. 18; *Victoria Dairy Co. (of Worthing)* v. *West* (1895) 11 T.L.R. 233 (not a security despite an express right of redemption); *Staffs Motor Guarantee Ltd.* v. *British Wagon Co. Ltd.* [1934] 2 K.B. 305; *Snook* v. *London and West Riding Investments Ltd.* [1967] 2 Q.B. 786.
32. *Re Ginger* [1897] 2 Q.B. 461; *Hollinshead* v. *P. and H. Egan Ltd.* [1913] A.C. 564.

**Methods of Mortgaging Chattels Personal**  To create a legal mortgage of a chattel it is necessary to vest the legal title in the mortgagee. Title to chattels (other than ships) can be passed by: (*a*) delivery; (*b*) sale; or (*c*) deed. If the title is passed as security, with a contractual right to redeem, the transaction is a legal mortgage. First, it would be possible to mortgage a chattel by delivery coupled with an oral contract. That would be unusual, for the mortgagor normally wishes to retain possession: if he does not, he will usually give security by delivering possession as a pledge, which is simpler than delivering ownership as a mortgage. Secondly, it is manifestly not possible to mortgage by sale. But it is the bill of sale which corresponds: a written agreement to pass the title as security, duly registered. Finally, a deed, though seldom employed for mortgaging a chattel, can be so used. It, too, would require registration as a bill of sale. It would have the advantage, from the mortgagee's point of view, of importing the statutory powers of mortgagees (e.g., to appoint a receiver of the income of the mortgaged property, or to sell it). One would be most likely to find a deed used if the chattel to be mortgaged is income-producing and of high value, such as an aeroplane.

The legal owner of chattels may also grant an equitable mortgage. That, if done in writing (whether or not under seal), will be a bill of sale requiring registration. It may occur in one of two ways: (*a*) the owner, by contract, charges his chattel in equity with repayment of a loan; or (*b*) a borrower, to whom a loan is made now, contracts for a legal mortgage over a chattel, as security for that loan, but, though the contract is susceptible to a decree of specific performance in principle, the legal mortgage does not yet take effect. In *Holroyd* v. *Marshall*[33] the owner of a mill got a loan and gave a mortgage of machinery and, in that mortgage, agreed that machinery to be installed thereafter would be security for that loan. Later, he did instal machinery. It was held that the new machinery became security in equity when acquired. The contract could be specifically enforced, so the machinery was held on trust for the equitable mortgagee. There is no equitable mortgage if the contract is merely to grant a bill of sale in the future, or if it is not one of which specific performance can be ordered. Whether a mortgage of a chattel is legal or equitable does not make any practical difference to the rights of the parties.

33. (1862) 10 H.L.C. 191.

**Mortgages of Aircraft**   The Civil Aviation Act 1968, section 16, gave power to legislate by Order in Council on this subject. That power was exercised by the Mortgaging of Aircraft Order 1972 (S.I. 1972 No. 1268), which applies throughout the United Kingdom. By article 4 of the Order, a mortgage of an aircraft may be registered in a register kept by the Civil Aviation Authority. The Order allows for such registration of a mortgage which includes a store of spare parts for the aircraft, but not any other floating charge (articles 2(2), 3). The system applies only to aircraft registered in the United Kingdom nationality register (article 3), but removal of an aircraft from that register does not affect any mortgage, or registration of any mortgage, made when the aircraft was so registered (article 12). So far as England and Wales and Northern Ireland are concerned, the Bills of Sale Acts no longer apply to aircraft in the United Kingdom nationality register (article 16 (1)).

Registration of aircraft mortgages affects their place in the system of priorities but not any other aspect of them. Article 13 makes registration 'express notice,' but also states that registration is not evidence of validity. A registered mortgage is not affected by the aircraft owner's bankruptcy, even if the aircraft is in the mortgagor's possession or reputed ownership; and the mortgagee prevails over unsecured creditors (article 15). A registered mortgage has priority over an unregistered mortgage (article 14(1)); and two or more registered mortgages rank in the order of their registration (article 14(2)); but these provisions do not give a registered mortgage priority over a possessory lien for the price of work done on the aircraft (article 14(5)).

## Mortgages by Persons other than the Legal Owner

There are three classes of case when a person without title, without the authority of the owner, wrongfully as against the owner, can mortgage a chattel so as to pass a good security to the creditor: (*a*) where a mercantile agent, in possession of the goods with the owner's consent, exceeds his authority;[34] (*b*) where the vendor of goods, after selling them, is in possession and deals with them, as if he were the owner, in favour of a third party acting in good faith and without notice of the previous sale;[35] (*c*) where, for any other reason (such

34. Factors Act 1889: see pp. 168–72, *post*.
35. Sale of Goods Act 1893, s. 25(1): see p. 166, footnote 265, *post*.

as handing over documents relating to the goods) the owner has so enabled someone else (a cheat) to pose as owner, and so deal with innocent third parties, that the true owner is estopped, as against the third party, from denying that the cheat is owner of the goods.

In the case of a person who has an equitable interest in a chattel: (a) if he is a beneficiary under a trust of the chattel, it being income-producing or held under a trust for sale or with a power of sale, he may mortgage his chose in action;[36] (b) if he is entitled in equity in some other way, e.g., as an equitable mortgagee, he may charge his interest or assign it by bill of sale.

## Company Charges

Throughout the United Kingdom provision exists for the registration of mortgages and other charges created by limited liability companies over their assets. This legislation applies whether the charge is over a specified asset or is a floating charge;[37] whether the property involved is land (heritage),[38] chattels (corporeal moveables) or incorporeal personalty (incorporeal moveables);[39] and whether the charge is legal or equitable.

If a company creates any kind of charge over all or any of its property of a kind covered by the legislation,[40] that charge must be registered, within 21 days of its creation, with the registrar of companies; otherwise the charge will be void as against the liquidator and creditors. The following charges require registration:

    (i)   a charge securing any issue of debentures (not in Scotland);

    (ii)  a charge on uncalled share capital;

    (iii) a charge evidenced by a document, which if made by an individual, would require registration as a bill of sale (not in Scotland);

    (iv) a charge on land;

36. Choses in action as security: see pp. 277–83, post.
37. Floating charges: see pp. 126–43, post.
38. Land as security: see pp. 16–110, ante.
39. Incorporeal property as security: see pp. 244–83, post.
40. Companies Act 1948, s. 95 (England and Wales); Companies Act 1948, s. 106A (Scotland), added by the Companies (Floating Charges) (Scotland) Act 1961, s. 6 and sch. 2, replaced by the Companies (Floating Charges and Receivers) (Scotland) Act 1972, s. 6 and sch.; Companies Act (Northern Ireland) 1960, s. 93. See also *Ladenburg & Co.* v. *Goodwin, Ferreira & Co. Ltd.* [1912] 3 K.B. 275.

    (v)   a charge on book debts;[41]

   (vi)  a floating charge;

  (vii)  a charge on calls made but not paid;

 (viii)  a charge on a ship or aircraft[42] or a share in a ship;

   (ix)  a charge on goodwill, a patent, a licence under a patent, a trademark, a copyright or a licence under a copyright.

A company is also required to keep a register of the charges it creates,[43] but the validity of a charge does not depend on the company carrying out that obligation. A charge not registered with the registrar of companies is valid between the company and the chargee: it is for the liquidator, not the company, to challenge it.[44]

What is in substance a charge, within the statutory list, requires registration, even if an attempt is made to disguise the transaction in some form other than that of a charge.[45] But in a genuine assignment, e.g., of hire-purchase contracts to a finance company, there is no reason to import a right of redemption, and hence there is no need to register the assignment as a charge.[46] The same applies to a company genuinely selling a chattel and taking it back on hire-purchase.[47]

A vendor's lien is not registrable under section 95 of the Companies Act 1948,[48] but if an unpaid vendor gives up his lien over the land and takes a mortgage in its place, such a mortgage is void if unregistered.[49]

---

41. Book debts are such debts as are commonly entered in books (whether actually entered or not, and whether due or payable at some future date): *Independent Automatic Sales Ltd.* v. *Knowles & Foster* [1962] 1 W.L.R. 974; *Paul & Frank Ltd.* v. *Discount Bank (Overseas) Ltd.* [1967] Ch. 348. As to mortgages of debts, see pp. 270–83, *post.*

42. The references to aircraft in ss. 95(2) (*h*) and 106A(2) (*d*) of the 1948 Act and s. 93(2) (*h*) of the 1960 Act were added by the Mortgaging of Aircraft Order 1972 (S.I. 1972 No. 1268), art. 16(2).

43. Companies Act 1948, s. 104 (England and Wales); Companies Act 1948, s. 106I (Scotland), added by the Companies (Floating Charges) (Scotland) Act 1961, s. 6 and sch. 2, replaced by the Companies (Floating Charges and Receivers) (Scotland) Act 1972, s. 6 and sch.; Companies Act (Northern Ireland) 1960, s. 102.

44. *Independent Automatic Sales Ltd.* v. *Knowles & Foster* [1962] 1 W.L.R. 974. As to irregularities in the process of registering, see *Re C. L. Nye Ltd.* [1971] Ch. 442.

45. See, e.g., *Re Old Bushmills Distillery Co. Ltd.* [1896] 1 I.R. 301.

46. *Re George Inglefield Ltd.* [1933] Ch. 1. See also *Coveney* v. *H. S. Persse Ltd.* [1901] 1 I.R. 194.

47. *Stoneleigh Finance Ltd.* v. *Phillips* [1965] 2 Q.B. 537. See also *Yorkshire Railway Wagon Co.* v. *Maclure* (1882) 21 Ch.D. 309, where the issue was one of ultra vires.

48. *London and Cheshire Insurance Co. Ltd.* v. *Laplagrene Property Co. Ltd.* [1971] Ch. 499.

49. *Capital Finance Co. Ltd.* v. *Stokes* [1969] 1 Ch. 261.

## Rights in Security over Corporeal Moveables in Scotland

With the sole exception of securities over ships or connected with shipping, the common law of Scotland recognises no security over corporeal moveables unless possession of the article is transferred to or already with the creditor. Exceptions have been created by statute, viz., agricultural charges,[50] floating charges[50] and mortgages of aircraft,[50] but there is no provision for registration of bills of sale. In *Stiven* v. *Scott*[51] the borrower purported to give the lenders security over some parcels of flax. The borrower marked the parcels which were to be security for the lenders, but they remained in his possession. It was held in the Court of Session that the lenders had no security. Lord President Inglis, with whom the other members of the court agreed, said (p. 930):

> Now, it is needless for me to say that as a matter of law that made no security at all. If it was intended to be a contract of pledge we all know that that real contract cannot be completed or made available without actual delivery of the subject pledged by the pledger to the pledgee; and if it was anything else than a pledge I am really quite at a loss to know what it is, for I know of no other way in which a security can be made over goods or moveables except by real contract or pledge.[52]

The commonest type of security given over corporeal moveables is the pledge.[53] The other possibilities (apart from ships and statutory inventions) are:

(i) assignation in security with delivery of possession[54] (which will be security for advances made on or before the occasion of granting it);

(ii) ex facie absolute assignation with delivery of possession[55] and with an agreement for redemption on repayment (which will be security for all sums due to the creditor[56]).

---

50. As to ships, see pp. 175–203, *post*; agricultural charges, pp. 143–4, *post*; floating charges, pp. 126–43, *post*; aircraft, p. 118, *post*.
51. (1871) 9 M. 923.
52. See also *Anderson* v. *M'Call* (1866) 4 M. 765; *Mackinnon* v. *Max Nanson and Co.* (1868) 6 M. 974; *Jones & Co's Trustee* v. *Allan* (1901) 4 F. 374.
53. See pp. 144–74, *post*.
54. See *Clark* v. *Liquidators of the West Calder Oil Co.* (1882) 9 R. 1017.
55. See *Heritable Securities Investment Assoc. (Ltd.)* v. *Wingate & Co.'s Trustee* (1880) 7 R. 1094.
56. *Hamilton* v. *Western Bank of Scotland* (1856) 19 D. 152.

In each case, the rights and remedies of the parties are the same (so far as differences between heritage and moveables will permit) as those of parties to the corresponding types of heritable security.

Physical possession may be given to the lender or to someone on his behalf. In *Union Bank of Scotland* v. *Mackenzie*[57] the bank was secured on a mill, but not on the moveable machinery in the mill. After the occupier of the mill was sequestrated, his trustee and the bank agreed that the bank would advance the value of the machinery and would have security over it. The mill and the machinery were then offered together for leasing. A purchaser of the machinery went into possession of the mill, but no formal lease was granted to him. It was held that the purchaser took possession as the bank's tenant, and that that completed the bank's security over the moveables. In *Moore* v. *Gledden*[58] there was a pledge by a contractor of his plant to the owner of the land on which the work was to be done. It was held that, although the contractor used the plant, possession passed to the pledgee because that was the contract and the plant was on his land. In *Stiven* v. *Cowan*,[59] on the other hand, also involving a mill owner who purported to give security to his creditor over the mill and the moveables in it, the lender took possession of the mill and its contents on a Saturday and, on the Sunday, purported to lease the whole lot back to the debtor, who thereupon went back into possession. It was held that the lender had no security over the moveables. Possession had not really passed to him. The former owner (who was known as the owner) had in effect been left in possession.

If moveables are not in the custody of the lender or borrower but are being held by a third party to the borrower's order, the borrower is in possession. This possession may be transferred by making the custodier hold to the lender's order. If goods are in a warehouse or store, the possession of the goods may be given to the creditor, so as to complete his security, by informing the warehouse-keeper or store-keeper that he is to hold the goods on behalf of the creditor.

Just as possession may be taken by a tenant on behalf of his landlord, so may possession be taken by an agent on behalf of his principal. But it is only in exceptional cases that a borrower remaining in possession can be the agent of the creditor so that the bor-

---

57. (1865) 3 M. 765.
58. (1869) 7 M. 1016. See also *Orr's Trustee* v. *Tullis* (1870) 8 M. 936.
59. (1878) 15 S.L.R. 422. See also *Rennet* v. *Mathieson* (1903) 5 F. 591.

rower's possession becomes that of the creditor. *Moore* v. *Gledden*[60] and *Orr's Trustee* v. *Tullis*[61] show that it is possible. Those cases, when contrasted with *Stiven* v. *Cowan*,[62] demonstrate that, for the protection of unsecured creditors, the real question is whether the debtor is in possession in circumstances in which he is likely to be believed to be the owner. If the owner of a house is left in possession of his furniture, people will assume he still owns the furniture even if he has tried to assign them in security. On the other hand, if the lessee of a hotel assigns his furniture in security and hires it back to use in the hotel, his possession may be held to be that of the creditor because he could well have been the lessee, not the owner, of the furniture all the time. Similarly, while an independent store-keeper may be authorised to hold for a new possessor, a borrower does not give a lender possession of goods by ordering his own (i.e., the borrower's) store-keeper to hold goods for the lender.[63]

In *Rhind's Trustee* v. *Robertson & Baxter*[64] the owner of wines and spirits had them in a warehouse to which there were two keys – one held by the owner and one by the excise officer. The owner borrowed money and gave the lender delivery orders in respect of the liquor, these orders being addressed to the excise officer, who entered the transfer in his books. It was held that that did not constitute delivery of the goods to the lender, who therefore had no security. One can deliver goods by handing over keys. If there had been only one key to the warehouse in *Rhind's Trustee* v. *Robertson & Baxter*, and if it had been handed over to the lender of the money in order to give him security over the goods in the warehouse, possession of the wines and spirits would have passed to the lender. But not every delivery of keys to premises is delivery of possession of the contents of those premises. For example, delivery of the keys of a house to someone as house agent to show prospective buyers around will not pass possession of the moveables in the house to the agent (even if the owner of the house has purported to assign those moveables to the house agent as security for a loan).[65]

The delivery order in *Rhind's Trustee* v. *Robertson & Baxter*[66] was ineffectual to perfect the lender's security, as delivery did not take place; and a delivery order is not a document of title. Nevertheless

60. (1869) 7 M. 1016. See p. 122, *ante*.   61. (1870) 9 M. 936.
62. (1878) 15 S.L.R. 422. See p. 122, *ante*.
63. *Anderson* v. *M'Call* (1866) 4 M. 765. See also *Dobell, Beckett & Co.* v. *Neilson* (1904) 7 F. 281.
64. (1891) 18 R. 623.
65. See *Pattison's Trustee* v. *Liston* (1893) 20 R. 806.
66. (1891) 18 R. 623. See above.

a delivery order may be useful as it enables the holder to obtain delivery (sometimes even if he is not entitled to delivery and has obtained the delivery order improperly). In *H. D. Pochin & Co.* v. *Robinows & Marjoribanks*,[67] P & Co. agreed to buy iron from A. Then P & Co. employed B as a broker to find a purchaser for the iron. B falsely told P & Co. that he had found a purchaser whereupon P & Co. gave B a delivery order for A to deliver the iron to B. B endorsed the delivery order to R & M as security for a loan. R & M used the delivery order to obtain delivery of the iron from A. It was held that P & Co. could not recover the iron from R & M without repaying the loan they had made to B. P & Co. had put B in a position to commit the fraud of dealing with the goods as owner.

Because it is frequently desirable, in the eyes of borrowers and lenders alike, that the borrower should remain in possession of corporeal moveables over which he has tried to give the lender security, so that the borrower may use them to earn money to pay off his debts, the parties to a loan sometimes try to dress up security as some other transaction. Knowing, or sometimes not knowing, that the lender gets no security without possession, the parties sometimes pretend that there has been an outright sale to the lender and that the borrower is left in possession in some other character than as owner. These attempts always fail. If the substance of the transaction is that the moveables are being used as security for a loan, then, because the creditor does not take possession, he gets no security. In *Rennet* v. *Mathieson*[68] the deal was expressed to be a sale of his plant by a tenant to his landlord followed by the landlord hiring out the plant to his tenant. It was held that this was intended to be by way of security given by the tenant, so there was no sale passing the property in the plant to the landlord, and, as there was no actual transfer of possession to the landlord, there was no security. In *Scottish Transit Trust Ltd.* v. *Scottish Land Cultivators Ltd.*[69] the defenders, owners of some lorries, needed both ready cash and the use of the lorries. They entered into an agreement which was in the form of a sale of the lorries to the pursuers and an agreement to buy the lorries back from the pursuers by hire-purchase. The defenders were in possession of the lorries throughout. They fell into arrears with payments under the agreement, whereupon the pursuers

---

67. (1869) 7 M. 622.   68. (1903) 5 F. 591.
69. 1955 S.C. 254. See also *Pattison's Trustee* v. *Liston* (1893) 20 R. 806; *Robertson* v. *Hall's Trustee* (1896) 24 R. 120; *Jones & Co.'s Trustee* v. *Allan* (1901) 4 F. 374; *Hepburn* v. *Law* 1914 S.C. 918; *Newbigging* v. *Ritchie's Trustee* 1930 S.C. 273; *G. and C. Finance Corp. Ltd.* v. *Brown* 1961 S.L.T. 408.

claimed both the lorries and the unpaid instalments. It was held that there had been no sale[70] because the arrangement was intended to operate by way of security. So the pursuers could not recover the lorries. But they could recover the unpaid money: they had made a valid unsecured loan.

On the other hand, there may be a genuine sale. An owner of moveables may raise money by selling them. If such a transaction is not intended as a mere security, title will pass to the purchaser even though the vendor remains in possession. There may be difficult questions of fact, if the person in possession of the goods goes bankrupt, whether he is an owner who has given an abortive security or a former owner who has sold. In *Robertson* v. *M'Intyre*[71] G was tenant of a factory and machinery, the owners being his sisters. G owned the power looms in the factory. Being pressed for money, he sold the looms to his sisters and continued to be their tenant (now tenant of the looms as well) at the same rent. His sisters granted G a new lease, covering the looms as well, but again at the same rent, five months after the sale. Six months after the grant of the new lease, G went bankrupt. It was held that the looms had been genuinely sold to the sisters, so G's trustee in his sequestration had no claim to them. Lord Justice-Clerk Moncrieff said[72] that the doctrine of reputed ownership was no longer of much importance. A change in the possession of the moveables was not necessary 'so long as the transaction is an honest one.'

The provisions of the Mortgaging of Aircraft Order 1972 (S.I. 1972 No. 1268, p. 118, *ante*) apply to Scotland with suitable modification of its terms as they apply in the rest of the United Kingdom. Schedule 2 to the Order contains the adaptation provisions for Scotland. In particular, paragraph 3 of part 1 of that schedule lays down that a mortgage is valid without delivery of the aircraft, while paragraph 8 deals with the powers of the creditor if the debtor defaults.

---

70. A sale of goods passes property to the purchaser without delivery unless the transaction is intended to operate by way of security: Sale of Goods Act 1893, s. 61 (4).
71. (1882) 9 R. 772. See also *Darling* v. *Wilson's Trustee* (1887) 15 R. 180; *Scott* v. *Scott's Trustee* (1889) 16 R. 504; *Liquidator of West Lothian Oil Co. Ltd.* v. *Mair* (1892) 20 R. 64; *Gavin's Trustee* v. *Fraser* 1920 S.C. 674.
72. 9 R. 778, the other judges concurring.

## Floating Charges

Floating charges are a creature of equity in England and Wales and Northern Ireland; in Scotland they were introduced by statute in 1961. The typical floating charge is one which is created by a limited company over all its assets (but such a charge can be created by chargors other than companies and need not extend to all the chargor's assets). The charge floats in the sense that the assets of the company can be dealt with in the ordinary course of business notwithstanding the creation of the charge. The assets can be disposed of. Acquisition of new assets subjects them to the charge. So long as the charge floats, the chargee has no right to be secured over any specific asset belonging to the chargor. If, however, the chargee becomes entitled to enforce his security, the charge ceases to float: it is said to crystallise. It then becomes a fixed charge on the assets the chargor has at that moment. As evidence of his floating charge, the chargee is given a document called a debenture (though debentures are not confined to floating charges).

In *Re Panama, New Zealand and Australian Royal Mail Co.*[73] the steamship company issued debentures expressed to 'charge the said undertaking, and all sums of money arising therefrom . . .' When the company was being wound up, the effect of this charge was disputed, and Giffard L.J. said:[74]

> . . . the word 'undertaking' had reference to all the property of the company, not only which existed at the date of the debenture, but which afterwards might become the property of the company. And I take the object and meaning of the debenture to be this, that the word 'undertaking' necessarily infers that the company will go on, and that the debenture holder could not interfere until either the interest which was due was unpaid, or until the period had arrived for payment of his principal, and that principal was unpaid . . . But the moment the company comes to be wound up, and the property has to be realised, that moment the rights of these parties, beyond all question, attach.

In *Governments Stock and Other Securities Investment Co. Ltd.* v. *Manila Railway Co. Ltd.*[75] Lord Macnaghten said:

---

73. (1870) L.R. 5 Ch. App. 318. See also *Gardner* v. *London Chatham and Dover Railway Co. (No. 1)* (1867) L.R. 2 Ch. App. 201.
74. L.R. 5 Ch. App. 322–3. See also *Re Florence Land and Public Works Co.* (1878) 10 Ch.D. 530.    75. [1897] A.C. 81, 86.

A floating security is an equitable charge on the assets for the time being of a going concern. It attaches to the subject charged in the varying condition in which it happens to be from time to time. It is of the essence of such a charge that it remains dormant until the undertaking charged ceases to be a going concern, or until the person in whose favour the charge is created intervenes. His right to intervene may of course be suspended by agreement. But if there is no agreement for suspension, he may exercise his right whenever he pleases after default.

The same learned judge, in *Illingworth* v. *Houldsworth*,[76] said:

A specific charge, I think, is one that without more fastens on ascertained and definite property or property capable of being ascertained and defined; a floating charge, on the other hand, is ambulatory and shifting in its nature, hovering over and so to speak floating with the property which it is intended to affect until some event occurs or some act is done which causes it to settle and fasten on the subject of the charge within its reach and grasp.

## Who Can Create a Floating Charge

Throughout the United Kingdom, a floating charge may be created by a company registered under the Companies Acts or by a registered friendly society. The essential protection, for anyone dealing with a company, from the possibility that its apparent prosperity may be a sham is provided by legislation invalidating company charges which are not registered.[77] Similar provisions exist for registration of charges created by registered friendly societies.[77] In England and Wales, a farmer may create an agricultural charge in the nature of a floating charge,[77] and provisions exist for registering agricultural charges. But in Northern Ireland there is no legislation for agricultural charges, while in Scotland the Acts introducing floating charges[77] provide only for their creation by companies and by registered friendly societies.

In principle, in England and Wales and Northern Ireland, there seems to be no reason why a floating charge should not be created by partners or an individual running a business. The difficulty is one of machinery: registers of bills of sale, land and other property

76. [1904] A.C. 355, 358.
77. As to registration of company charges, see pp. 119–20 *ante*; registration of charges by friendly societies, p. 116, footnote 25, *ante*; agricultural charges, pp. 143–4, *post*; legislation on floating charges in Scotland, p. 130, *post*; mortgages of aircraft including a store of spare parts, p. 118, *ante*.

must record the precise property charged: there is no suitable register for floating charges. In point of fact, no cases are to be found in the reports of attempts by partnerships or one-man businesses to create floating charges.

For simplicity of exposition, floating charges will from now on be assumed to be created by limited companies.

**Property Which Can be Subject to a Floating Charge**  Generally a company creating a floating charge comprises its whole undertaking in the charge. Such a charge will float over the land, plant, stock, debts owed to the company, uncalled share capital, goodwill and other incorporeal property such as patents, or such of these as the company may own.

Alternatively, a company may include in a floating charge only some of its property, e.g., a floating charge by a retail company over its stock but not over its premises or goodwill.

Since a floating charge may comprise land and incorporeal property as well as chattels (corporeal moveables), such a charge involves considerations wider than the title of this chapter. Since, however, it is stock which provides the prime example of assets which are acquired and disposed of in the ordinary course of business, it is in relation to dealing with goods that a floating charge has its greatest practical value.

**The Nature of Debentures**  A debenture is a document issued by a company evidencing its indebtedness. It is not specifically related to security. A debenture may be evidence of an unsecured loan, a loan secured by fixed charge or a loan secured by floating charge.

If a company borrows from one lender, such as a bank, it may issue a single debenture. When a company seeks to raise a large loan by public subscription, it may create a series of debentures, say 10,000 debentures of £100 each, all ranking equally, to raise £1,000,000. If the loan is secured by floating charge, all the lenders rank as equal co-chargees although they obviously do not lend their money and acquire their debentures simultaneously. It is more usual in such cases to issue debenture stock, which has the same legal effect but is usually transferable in any amounts.

With large numbers of debenture holders all secured by one floating charge, there can be difficulties in securing action. Meetings are necessary. To avoid these complications and possibly dangerous loss of time, it is usual for the company to charge its property only in favour of trustees who will hold the title to the charge, the individual creditors being their beneficiaries.

A floating charge on all a company's property, if the company owns any land, is an interest in land, in which case a contract to assign a debenture must be evidenced in writing.[78]

**Registration**   Company charges in general require registration,[79] and this requirement extends to floating charges. A floating charge which is not registered within twenty-one days of its creation is void as against the liquidator and creditors of the company.[80]

**Creation Shortly Before Winding Up**   A floating charge is also void if created within twelve months of the winding up of the company, except as to cash paid by the chargee to the company at the time of the creation of the charge or subsequently and in consideration of the charge, and except as to interest at 5% per annum or such other rate as may be prescribed by the Treasury (Great Britain) or the Secretary of State for Northern Ireland; unless it is proved that the company was solvent immediately after the creation of the charge.[81]

If a floating charge is void for having been made too soon before winding up, that does not mean that the debenture itself is void: only that the debt is unsecured. So if the company repaid the loan before the commencement of winding up, the liquidator cannot recover the money from the creditor unless there has been a fraudulent preference.[82]

For money to be paid at the creation of the charge, there is no strict requirement of simultaneity. Money paid by the chargee to the company before the charge is imposed will be regarded as having been paid at the time of the creation of the charge if paid in reliance

78. *Driver* v. *Broad* [1893] 1 Q.B. 744.
79. See pp. 119–20, *ante*.
80. England and Wales: Companies Act 1948, s. 95. Scotland: Companies Act 1948, s. 106A; *Archibald Campbell, Hope & King Ltd.* 1967 S.C. 21; *Scottish and Newcastle Breweries Ltd.* v. *Liquidator of Rathburne Hotel Co. Ltd.* 1970 S.C. 215. Northern Ireland: Companies Act (Northern Ireland) 1960, s. 93; *Revere Trust Ltd.* v. *Wellington Handkerchief Works Ltd.* [1931] N.I. 55; *Re White & Shannon Ltd.* [1965] N.I. 15.
81. Great Britain: Companies Act 1948, s. 322 (amended as to Scotland by the Companies (Floating Charges and Receivers) (Scotland) Act 1972, s. 8); Companies Act (Northern Ireland) 1960, s. 290. See also *Revere Trust Ltd.* v. *Wellington Handkerchief Works Ltd.* [1931] N.I.55.
82. *Re Parkes Garage (Swadlincote) Ltd.* [1929] 1 Ch. 139.

on the impending creation of the charge and if the charge is created within a reasonable time of the receipt of the cash, the payment and the charge being bona fide parts of a single transaction.[83]

In *Re Yeovil Glove Co. Ltd.*[84] a question arose as to whether money had been paid to the company subsequently to the creation of the charge. A debenture creating a floating charge was given to a bank to secure the company's overdraft, and winding up of the company commenced within a year. Had nothing else happened, the floating charge would have been void. In fact, between the charge and the winding up, the amount of the overdraft remained about the same, but much more than that amount had been paid in and drawn out by the company. It was held[85] that the sums paid in by the company had paid off the overdraft that existed when the floating charge was given, and that the overdraft (i.e., all the indebtedness to the bank) at the time of the winding up was in respect of money paid to the company after the creation of the charge.

**The Introduction of Floating Charges to Scotland** The common law of Scotland did not countenance floating charges because of the general rule that there could be no rights in security over corporeal moveables unless possession was transferred to the creditor.[86] By the Companies (Floating Charges) (Scotland) Act 1961, section 1(1), later replaced by the Companies (Floating Charges and Receivers) (Scotland) Act 1972, section 1, an incorporated company or registered friendly society[87] can create floating charges over heritable and moveable property.[88] The appropriate form was originally provided by section 2 of the 1961 Act and the first schedule, but section 2 of the 1972 Act allows more flexibility. If heritage is affected, there is no need to record the charge in the Register of Sasines.[89]

In general, the legislation is taken to have introduced the floating charge as known in England and Wales, with all its features consistent with the legislation, even though they may not fit neatly into

83. *Re Columbian Fireproofing Co. Ltd.* [1910] 2 Ch. 120; *Re Olderfleet Shipbuilding and Engineering Co. Ltd.* [1922] 1 I.R. 26; *Re F. and E. Stanton Ltd.* [1929] 1 Ch. 180.
84. [1965] Ch. 148.
85. Applying the rule in *Clayton's Case* (1816) 1 Mer. 572.
86. See pp. 121–5, *ante*.
87. Industrial and Provident Societies Act 1967, s. 3 and sch., as amended by the Companies (Floating Charges and Receivers) (Scotland) Act 1972, s. 10.
88. See also Wilson, 'Floating Charges' (1962) *Scots Law Times* 53; note, 'Registration and Ranking of Floating and other Charges' (1962) *S.L.T.* 73; *Amalgamated Securities Ltd.* 1967 S.C. 56.
89. 1961 Act, s. 3; 1972 Act, s. 3.

the concepts of the general law of Scotland. In two respects, the 1961 Act made floating charges in Scotland different from those known in the rest of the United Kingdom, namely, with regard to when they crystallise[90] and with regard to priority of ranking.[90]

**The Right to Redeem and Clogs on that Right**  Whether the company has a right to redeem a floating charge and, if so, when, depends on the terms of the debenture. Legislation, which applies to fixed charges as well as to floating charges, makes inapplicable to debentures the equitable rule[90] that there must be a substantial right to redeem within a reasonable time. By the Companies Act 1948, section 89, which applies throughout Great Britain:[91]

A condition contained in any debentures or in any deed for securing any debentures . . . shall not be invalid by reason only that the debentures are thereby made irredeemable or redeemable only on the happening of a contingency, however remote, or on the expiration of a period, however long, any rule of equity to the contrary notwithstanding.

The question whether a collateral advantage accorded to the chargee over and above his right to be repaid, is void if it infringes the equitable principles governing collateral advantages in mortgage deeds,[92] appears to be settled in the affirmative by *Kreglinger* v. *New Patagonia Meat and Cold Storage Co. Ltd.*[93] However, in that case the collateral advantage was upheld as not infringing the rules of equity, and that has been true of other collateral advantages given with floating charges.[94]

As chargees, lenders secured by a floating charge have the same right to redeem a prior mortgage as a subsequent mortgagee has.[95] In *Wallace* v. *Evershed*[96] a company mortgaged its freehold estate in land. Later, the company created a floating charge over all its property. The legal mortgagee brought a foreclosure action, in which he joined the debenture holders as parties. It was held that the debenture holders were properly made defendants and that they had a right to redeem the legal mortgage.

---

90. As to crystallisation, see pp. 132, *post*; priority, pp. 142–3, *post*; equitable right to redeem, pp. 16–17, 45–7, *ante*.
91. Northern Ireland: Companies Act (Northern Ireland) 1960, s. 88.
92. See pp. 47–50, *ante*    93. [1914] A.C. 25.
94. See *De Beers Consolidated Mines Ltd.* v. *British South Africa Co.* [1912] A.C. 52; *Re Cuban Land and Development Co. (1911) Ltd.* [1921] 2 Ch. 147.
95. See pp. 60–1, *ante*.    96. [1899] 1 Ch. 891.

**Carrying on Business While the Charge is Floating** The intention behind the creation of a floating charge is that the company shall be free to carry on its business unimpeded by the charge until the charge crystallises, i.e., until the debenture holders become entitled to realise their security. Sometimes the debentures expressly say that; but it is nevertheless the case if the debentures are silent on the matter. On the other hand, the debentures may impose a restriction on the company's activities. A restriction met with some frequency is a term in a debenture creating a floating charge to the effect that the company will not create any fixed charges, over property comprised in the floating charge, so as to give the fixed charge priority over or equal ranking with the floating charge.[97]

In the absence of restrictions contained in the instrument creating a floating charge, the company is free to carry on business in the ordinary way, dealing with property subject to the charge and acquiring property which will become subject to the charge. A company which has given a floating charge over its entire undertaking can sell property in the ordinary course of business.[98] The purchaser takes the property free from the charge; the money he pays the company becomes subject to the charge; if the company spend the money on a new typewriter, that machine will become subject to the charge and the vendor of it will take the money from the company free from the charge. The company could quite well have used the money, instead of buying a typewriter with it, to pay off unsecured debts.[99] In fact, they probably raised the money on the floating charge for the purposes of the ordinary course of their business, capital and current. If the debentures do not prohibit it (and sometimes, unlawfully but effectively, even if they do prohibit it[100]), the company can go to the length of granting a fixed charge, in the ordinary course of business, over property comprised in the floating charge. The result of that is, if the company is later wound up, that the fixed charge will have priority, as to the asset on which it is fixed, over the floating charge.

> **Example** A company owning and operating a factory create a floating charge expressed to be a first charge on all the company's property. Later, the company, in the ordinary course of business give someone else an equitable mortgage, by deposit of

97. As to the effect of such restrictions, see the section on priorities, pp. 139–41, *post*.
98. See *Hamer* v. *London City and Midland Bank Ltd.* (1918) 87 L.J. K.B. 973.
99. *Willmott* v. *London Celluloid Co.* (1886) 36 Ch.D. 147.
100. See pp. 139–41, *post*.

title deeds, of the factory premises. The court will hold that the equitable mortgagee has priority over the debenture holders because the equitable mortgage was made before the floating charge crystallised and at that time the company could deal with their property in the ordinary course of business.[101]

Similar principles apply to the acquisition of property after a floating charge has been created. There is nothing to stop a company buying an equity of redemption, i.e., buying a property with a mortgage already on it so that the newly acquired property becomes subject to the floating charge only as a second charge. In *Re Connolly Bros. Ltd.* (*No. 2*)[102] a company, having given a floating charge, bought land and arranged to pay for it by borrowing money on the security of a charge on the land. (The debenture had a term that the company were not to make any subsequent charge with priority over the floating charge.) The loan was made to the company, who paid out of it the balance of the purchase price to the vendor of the land, and the title deeds were taken by the solicitor (who was acting for all the parties) to hold for the lender. It was held that she (the lender on the fixed charge) had priority over the debenture holder, despite the terms of the debenture as to priority, because all that the company acquired, and hence all that become subject to the floating charge, was the equity of redemption in the land.

In *Re Roundwood Colliery Co.*[103] it was held that the company's landlord could distrain for rent on chattels covered by a floating charge which had not yet crystallised.

## When A Floating Charge Crystallises

In Scotland, under the 1961 Act, a floating charge always crystallised when the winding up of the company commenced and in no other circumstances.[104] Under the Companies (Floating Charges and Receivers) (Scotland) Act 1972, Part II, it also attaches to specific property on the appointment of a receiver.

In England and Wales and Northern Ireland there are other events which can make a floating charge crystallise. Apart from

---

101. See *Re Hamilton's Windsor Ironworks* (1879) 12 Ch.D. 707; *Wheatley* v. *Silkstone and Haigh Moor Coal Co.* (1885) 29 Ch.D. 715; *Ward* v. *Royal Exchange Shipping Co. Ltd.* (1887) 58 L.T. 174; *Cox Moore* v. *Peruvian Corp. Ltd.* [1908] 1 Ch. 604.
102. [1912] 2 Ch. 25. See also *Rother Iron Works Ltd.* v. *Canterbury Precision Engineers Ltd.* [1973] 2 W.L.R. 281.
103. [1897] 1 Ch. 373.
104. Companies (Floating Charges) (Scotland) Act 1961, s. 1(2). See also *National Commercial Bank of Scotland Ltd.* v. *Liquidators of Telford Grier Mackay & Co. Ltd.* 1969 S.C. 181.

winding up and the appointment of a receiver, that happens if the company stops business for any reason.

**Winding up**  A floating charge crystallises on winding up of the company, whether the charge is redeemable or not. If debentures creating a floating charge specify a date for repayment, the charge crystallises on the winding up of the company, even if that is before the specified date. The sum owed thereupon becomes immediately repayable, and so the security is realisable, although there could be no suit for the debt.[105] This is so even if the debenture states that the floating charge will crystallise on winding up in some circumstances and the company is actually wound up in other circumstances.[106]

**Stopping business without being wound up**  A sale of the whole of its undertaking by a company is not a transaction in the ordinary course of business. Such a sale causes a floating charge to crystallise because the company is no longer a going concern. The debenture holders can secure the appointment of a receiver and an injunction against the purchaser of the undertaking to restrain him from dealing with the assets except in the ordinary course of business.[107] No such proceedings are available to the debenture holders if the company, acting within its powers, has sold a large part, but not the whole, of its undertaking, continuing as a going concern. That was decided in *Re Borax Co.*,[108] where Lord Alverstone C.J. said (pp. 337–8):

> ... in order to enable the debenture holder to insist on payment of his debentures in such a case as this [a floating charge] he must shew, either that the act complained of is ultra vires, or that, to use the language of Lord Macnaghten, 'the undertaking has ceased to be a going concern,' or that the terms of the debenture which he holds give him the express right to veto or negative the operations which the company are proposing to carry out within their powers.

**Appointment of a receiver**  When the court, in a debenture holders' action, appoints a receiver, in respect of a floating charge on which there has been default by the company, the charge crystallises.[109] Mere default by the company in a payment secured

105. *Hodson* v. *Tea Co.* (1880) 14 Ch. D. 859; *Wallace* v. *Universal Automatic Machines Co.* [1894] 2 Ch. 547.
106. *Re Crompton & Co. Ltd.* [1914] 1 Ch. 954.
107. *Hubbuck* v. *Helms* (1887) 56 L.J. Ch. 536.       108. [1901] 1 Ch. 326.
109. *Re Griffin Hotel Co. Ltd.* [1941] Ch. 129. Scotland: Companies (Floating Charges and Receivers) (Scotland) Act 1972, ss. 11(2), 12(2), 14.

by the charge does not make it crystallise, nor does a demand by the debenture holder for payment. Default by the company entitles the chargee to a receiver; until he secures the appointment, the charge does not crystallise,[110] nor can the debenture holder give notice to seize any particular asset of the company. In *Edward Nelson & Co. Ltd.* v. *Faber & Co.*[111] Joyce J. said:

> ... a debenture such as this does not cease to be a floating security, or, to use another expression, does not become an active security, until the company has been wound up, or stops business, or a receiver has been appointed at the instance of the debenture-holders, and it follows that, even after the interest payable on such debentures has been in arrear for the time specified, the company can deal with the property in the ordinary course of business until the company has been wound up, or stops business, or a receiver has been appointed.

There are circumstances in which a receiver can be appointed without making the charges become fixed. If there has been no default by the company to the debenture holders, but the company is insolvent, the court will appoint a receiver on the application of the debenture holders.[112] This is to protect their security (as will be done for mortgagees) and does not make the floating charge crystallise: that must wait for default, winding up or otherwise ceasing to be a going concern.

In Scotland, but not elsewhere in the United Kingdom unless expressly authorised in the debenture, the chargee under a floating charge can appoint a receiver without going to court: Companies (Floating Charges and Receivers) (Scotland) Act 1972, section 11(1). This he may do, in writing with a copy to the registrar of companies (section 13(1)), either in accordance with the document creating the charge or, if that document is silent on the matter: if (*a*) twenty-one days pass without repayment after he demands the whole or part of the principal sum secured; or (*b*) interest is at least two months in arrear; or (*c*) a winding-up order or resolution is made or passed; or (*d*) a receiver has been appointed by virtue of any other floating charge (section 12(1)).

---

110. *Robson* v. *Smith* [1895] 2 Ch. 118; *Evans* v. *Rival Granite Quarries Ltd.* [1910] 2 K.B. 979. As to what amounts to the appointment of a receiver, see *Windsor Refrigerator Co. Ltd.* v. *Branch Nominees Ltd.* [1961] Ch. 375; *R. A. Cripps & Son Ltd.* v. *Wickenden* [1973] 1 W.L.R. 944. See also *Griffiths* v. *Secretary of State for Social Services* [1973] 3 W.L.R. 831.
111. [1903] 2 K.B. 367, 376-7.
112. *Makins* v. *Percy Ibotson & Sons* [1891] 1 Ch. 133; *McMahon* v. *North Kent Ironworks Co.* [1891] 2 Ch. 148; *Edwards* v. *Standard Rolling Stock Syndicate* [1893] 1 Ch. 574; Companies (Floating Charges and Receivers) (Scotland) Act 1972, s. 12 (2).

The powers of a receiver in Scotland as to getting in and realising the property subject to the charge are set out in section 15 of the Act of 1972. A person transacting with the receiver is not concerned to inquire whether any event has happened authorising the receiver to act (section 15(3)). The receiver is deemed to be the agent of the company as to property attached by the floating charge by virtue of which he is appointed (section 17(1)). Section 16 governs the priorities between two or more receivers appointed under different floating charges. The order in which the receiver must apply assets is set out in section 20 as follows: (1) prior secured creditors; (2) the costs of the receivership; (3) preferential creditors under section 19; (4) the chargee who appointed him; (5) in the case of a balance: (a) another receiver; (b) a subsequent secured creditor, secured by fixed charge on property comprised in the floating charge; (c) the company or its liquidator.

**The Effect of a Floating Charge Crystallising**   When a floating charge crystallises it becomes a fixed charge on all the assets of the company, or, in the case of a charge which is not imposed on the whole undertaking, a fixed charge on all the assets of a class comprised in the charge, owned by the company at the moment of crystallisation.

In the case of goods, the charge applies to goods which have been taken in execution but not yet sold.[113] In *Davey & Co.* v. *Williamson & Sons Ltd.*[114] it was held that the chargee had priority over the execution creditor in respect of such goods even though the charge had not crystallised. In fact, the company had ceased to be a going concern; moreover, the debenture specified the levying of execution as an event upon which the charge could be made to crystallise. A contrast is provided in the case of money paid to a sheriff to get goods back. If goods belonging to the company are taken in execution by the sheriff, and then the company pay the debt to the sheriff and get the goods back, and finally the floating charge crystallises, the execution creditor is entitled to the money paid to the sheriff for him. The debenture holders cannot get the money back because it represents payment of a debt in the ordinary course of business.[115]

The rights of the secured creditor are to the property in the form in which it came into the hands of the company, subject to equities.

113. *Re Opera Ltd.* [1891] 3 Ch. 260; *Taunton* v. *Sheriff of Warwickshire* [1895] 2 Ch. 319. 114. [1898] 2 Q.B. 194.
115. *Robinson* v. *Burnell's Vienna Bakery Co. Ltd.* [1904] 2 K.B. 624; *Heaton and Dugard Ltd.* v. *Cutting Bros. Ltd.* [1925] 1 K.B. 655.

For example, an unsecured creditor may have a right of set-off relating to a book debt which becomes subject to the floating charge.

**Example**  Vending Co. Ltd. give Banking Co. Ltd. a floating charge over their entire undertaking. Later, in the ordinary course of business, Vending Co. Ltd. come to owe Buying Co. Ltd. £200 under a contract. Buying Co. Ltd. are unsecured creditors. Later still, Buying Co. Ltd. order goods priced at £300 from Vending Co. Ltd. Then Vending Co. Ltd. default on their obligations under the debenture and Banking Co. Ltd. appoint a receiver under an express power to do so given to them by the debenture. After that, Vending Co. Ltd. deliver the goods to Buying Co. Ltd., who pay the receiver £100. The receiver sues Buying Co. Ltd. for £200 (the balance of the price). The court will hold the defendants not liable because they had a right to set off the debt owed to them by Vending Co. Ltd. against the price of the goods, and the chargee could have no greater right than the chargor.[116]

Apart from any express terms of the instrument creating the charge, and apart from securing the appointment by the court of a receiver, the main remedy of the chargee is foreclosure. He can foreclose on all property comprised in the charge, including un-called capital, notwithstanding the difficulty that only the company itself can call up that capital.[117] But if there are several debenture holders secured by the same charge, there can be no foreclosure order unless all the chargees are parties to the action. If one is not, the court will order a sale in a foreclosure action by the others, as it is undesirable to vest the ownership of property in an absent person who may not want it.[118]

In the terms used in England and Wales and Northern Ireland, a floating charge is not a mortgage for the purposes of mortgagees' statutory powers. It has been held[119] that, even if made by deed (and a debenture usually is under seal) a floating charge does not give the debenture holder a mortgagee's statutory power of sale. The argument seems to apply with equal force to a mortgagee's other statutory powers. Hence, any powers exercisable otherwise than through an application to the court must be expressly created by the instrument of charge.

---

116. See *Rother Iron Works Ltd.* v. *Canterbury Precision Engineers Ltd.* [1973] 2 W.L.R. 281. See also *Re Connolly Bros. Ltd.* (*No. 2*) [1912] 2 Ch. 25, p. 133, *ante.* Cf *George Barker (Transport) Ltd.* v. *Eynon* [1973] 1 W.L.R. 1461.
117. *Sadler* v. *Worley* [1894] 2 Ch. 170.      118. *Re Continental Oxygen Co.* [1897] 1 Ch. 511.
119. *Blaker* v. *Herts and Essex Waterworks Co.* (1889) 41 Ch. D. 399.

**Priorities in Relation to Floating Charges: England and Wales and Northern Ireland** In general, two or more floating charges rank in order of the dates of their creation (while two or more debentures secured by the same charge rank equally, even if issued on different dates). In *Re Benjamin Cope & Sons Ltd.*[120] the company issued a first series of debentures secured by a floating charge, and later issued a second series of debentures secured by a second floating charge. The second series of debentures was expressed to rank pari passu with the first series, but it was held that the first series had priority over the second. On the other hand, in *Re Automatic Bottle Makers Ltd.*[121] the debenture trust deed, secured by floating charge, reserved the right to the company to charge some of their assets (comprised in the floating charge) so as to give priority over the floating charge. The company subsequently charged those assets by a second floating charged expressed to have priority over the first. The court, though approving *Re Benjamin Cope & Sons Ltd.*, held that the second charge did indeed have priority over the first.

Sometimes there is a conflict between a floating charge and a prior equity. In general, equities rank in order of their creation, so the owner of the prior equity will prevail. This was held to be the case in *Re Morrison, Jones & Taylor Ltd.*[122] where the prior equity was that of a vendor to the company on hire-purchase of a fixture to remove it because of failure to complete payments. The position of the holder of a floating charge, in this respect, is similar to that of a mortgagee of land to which the fixture has become attached. In *Re Samuel Allen & Sons Ltd.*[123] the owner of premises (a company) took machinery on hire purchase and fixed it to the land. Subsequently, the company gave an equitable mortgage of the premises, by deposit of title deeds, to a bank who had no notice of the hire-purchase agreement. The machinery was included in the bank's mortgage because it had become part of the land by annexation. It was held that the owner (the vendor) had a right to remove it for non-payment which prevailed over the bank's later equity. By and large, this principle applies only so long as the mortgagor is in possession of the premises (as a company which has given a floating charge will normally be in possession of any premises comprised in the charge). If the mortgagee goes into possession, he determines the licence of the owner of the fixture to come on the land and

120. [1914] 1 Ch. 800.    121. [1926] Ch. 412.
122. [1914] 1 Ch. 50.    123. [1907] 1 Ch. 575.

repossess the thing for non-payment of hire-purchase instalments, notwithstanding that by the contract the vendor is to remain the owner until the full price has been paid, that it is still a chattel as between vendor and hire-purchaser and that it was wrongful of the mortgagor to make it land as between him and the mortgagee.[124] Even if the mortgagor is still in possession, the mortgagee has been held entitled, as against the owner-vendor, to fixed machinery being bought on hire-purchase by the mortgagor where the mortgagor had covenanted, in the mortgage, not to remove any fixtures included in the security without the written consent of the mortgagee.[125]

The commonest priority problems arise between the holder of a floating charge which has crystallised and a subsequent mortgagee (or other incumbrancer) secured by a fixed charge on one of the assets comprised in the floating charge. The problems arise out of a term, quite usual in debentures, excluding the power of the company to grant a charge to rank in priority to, or equally with, the floating charge. No problem will usually arise if the subsequent mortgagee realises his security before the floating charge crystallises, because the asset will then have disappeared in the ordinary course of business before the debenture holders' security fastens upon it. But if the floating charge crystallises and the debenture holders are then in competition with a fixed security over one of their assets, there can be a problem. If the company have purported to give the later mortgagee priority over the floating charge, or equal ranking with it, in breach of a term in the debenture, that may give the debenture holders a cause of action against the company (not of much value because, by hypothesis, the company is not going to be able to pay its unsecured creditors in full, otherwise the secured creditors would not be fighting over the assets), but it does not follow from that that the debenture holders necessarily have priority over the subsequent mortgagee. The position depends essentially on notice.

If the later taker of a fixed charge takes it with notice of the term in the debentures as to priority, the debenture holders come first. In *Re Robert Stephenson & Co. Ltd.*[126] there was a floating charge excluding the company's power to charge its property so as to give the later chargee priority to or equality with the floating charge. The

---

124. *Hobson* v. *Gorringe* [1897] 1 Ch. 182; *Reynolds* v. *Ashby & Son* [1904] A.C. 466.
125. *Ellis* v. *Glover & Hobson Ltd.* [1908] 1 K.B. 388.
126. [1913] 2 Ch. 201.

company later acquired freehold lands and gave a specific mortgage of them, expressed to be subject to the floating charge. When the floating charge crystallised, it was held that the debenture holders had priority over the mortgagee. In *Cox* v. *Dublin City Distillery Co.*[127] the company gave a floating charge over their whole undertaking, the debentures stipulating that no later charges were to be given priority over them. After that, the company pledged whisky to a bank to secure advances. The bank were held to have notice of the terms of the debentures, because they were themselves registered holders of some of those debentures, and therefore it was held that the floating charge had priority over the pledge.

A floating charge is an equitable security and it is therefore displaced in favour of a subsequent legal mortgage of one of the assets without notice of the term as to priorities. Even a later equitable mortgage without notice will normally have priority over the debenture holders, because documents of title will have been left with the company (in the case of land or other property to which there are title deeds), and the indicia of ownership of other property (possession, in the case of goods) will have been left with the company, so that the ordinary course of business can be carried on. It is notice of the terms of the debentures, not of their existence, which is operative in this context. In *English and Scottish Mercantile Investment Co. Ltd.* v. *Brunton*[128] there was a mortgage of moneys due on an insurance policy comprised in an earlier floating charge. The mortgagee's solicitor knew there were debentures but did not know of the term in them against the company giving priority to later mortgages. In fact, he was told by the managing director of the company that there was nothing in the debentures to affect his client's security. So it was held that the solicitor (and therefore his client) did not get constructive notice of the terms about priority and that the mortgage ranked before the floating charge. Notice of a debenture is merely notice that the company owes money. A debenture may or may not create a charge; if it does, it may or may not contain a term about the priority of subsequent charges.

In *Re Castell & Brown Ltd.*[129] the debentures creating a floating

127. [1906] 1 I.R. 446. See also *Re Old Bushmills Distillery Co. Ltd.* [1896] 1 I.R. 301, a similar case except that the whisky was mortgaged, not pledged.
128. [1892] 2 Q.B. 700. See also *Re Standard Rotary Machine Co. Ltd.* (1906) 95 L.T. 829, a similar case except that the mortgage was of shares in another company.
129. [1898] 1 Ch. 315. See also *Coveney* v. *H. S. Persse Ltd.* [1910] 1 I.R. 194, a similar case except that the mortgagee without notice was secured on whisky.

charge prohibited the company from making a later mortgage to have priority over the debentures. Subsequently the company deposited title deeds to land included in the charge with a bank by way of equitable mortgage. The bank had no notice of the debentures – it was held that they had no duty to inquire – and, although their mortgage was only equitable, they were held to have priority over the debenture holders because the title deeds had been left with the company, thus enabling them to pose as owners of unincumbered land. Another case to the like effect is *Re Valletort Sanitary Steam Laundry Co. Ltd.*[130] It was there held that the mortgagee bank did not acquire notice of the contents of the debentures merely because some debentures had been deposited with them as security by a customer. Another point arose in that case. After they took their mortgage, the bank were issued with a debenture (a new issue, not one of the first series) which referred to the earlier debentures. That was held not to give the bank notice of the terms of the earlier debentures; consequently, the bank were able to claim priority over the first debentures even for further advances on security of their mortgage made after they got their debenture.

A later equity also prevails over the floating charge if it is not created by the company. The common term in the debenture precludes the company from giving someone else priority. In *Brunton* v. *Electrical Engineering Corp.*[131] title deeds to land comprised in a floating charge were in the possession of the company's solicitor, who claimed a lien over them for unpaid costs. It was held that he had priority over the debenture holders because his lien arose by operation of law and was not a charge created by the company.

The Companies Act 1948, section 319,[132] lists the preferential payments to be made on the winding up of a company in priority to all other debts. By section 94[133] the same payments are to be made in priority to payments to the debenture holders if, the company not being wound up, the debenture holders, being secured by a floating charge: (i) appoint a receiver under an express or statutory power; or (ii) procure the appointment of a receiver by the court; or (iii) take possession, or have possession taken on their

---

1 30. [1903] 2 Ch. 654.    131. [1892] 1 Ch. 434.
132. Applicable throughout Great Britain. Equivalent legislation: Companies Act (Northern Ireland) 1960, s. 287.
133. Applicable throughout Great Britain. See also the Companies (Floating Charges and Receivers) (Scotland) Act 1972, s. 19. Equivalent legislation: Companies Act (Northern Ireland) 1960, s. 92. See also *Inland Revenue Commissioners* v. *Goldblatt* [1972] Ch. 498.

behalf, of any property comprised in or subject to the charge. Failure to make the preferential payments gives rise to an action in tort, even if no other debts are paid.[134]

**Ranking of Floating Charges in Scotland**    Apart from sections 94 and 319 of the Companies Act 1948,[135] this matter is governed primarily by the Companies (Floating Charges and Receivers) (Scotland) Act 1972, sections 1 and 5, replacing similar but not identical provisions in the Act of 1961. When a floating charge crystallises, it does so subject to the rights of: (*a*) a person who has effectually executed diligence on any property comprised in the charge; (*b*) a holder of a fixed security, on such property, having priority over the floating charge; and (*c*) a holder of a floating charge, on such property, having priority over the other floating charge.

Subject to the express terms of the floating charge, a fixed security has priority over a floating charge if: (i) the fixed security arises by operation of law (e.g., a lien); or (ii) the fixed security was made before the commencement of the Act. If the fixed security is made by agreement, and after the Act came into force, it still has priority over the floating charge unless: (i) the floating charge was registered[136] before the fixed security was constituted as a real right; and (ii) the instrument creating the floating charge prohibited the company from creating a fixed security with priority over the floating charge or so as to rank equally with it. Two or more floating charges rank in the order of their registration unless the instruments creating them say they are to rank equally. They also rank equally if the registrar receives them both for registration by the same post.

If a registered friendly society has created both a floating charge and an agricultural charge,[137] and some or all of its assets are subject to both charges, the two charges rank in the order of their registration, as if they were both floating charges, and as if the agricultural charge had been registered under the 1961 Act at the time

---

134. *Woods* v. *Winksill* [1913] 2 Ch. 303; *Re Glyncorrwg Colliery Co. Ltd.* [1926] Ch. 951; *Westminster Corp.* v. *Haste* [1950] Ch. 442; *Inland Revenue Commissioners* v. *Goldblatt* [1972] Ch. 498.

135. See pp. 141–2, *ante.*

136. With the Assistant Registrar of Friendly Societies for Scotland, in the case of a floating charge created by a registered society: Industrial and Provident Societies Act 1967, s. 3(2) and sch.

137. As to agricultural charges, see pp. 143–4, *post.*

when it was registered under the Agricultural Credits (Scotland) Act 1929. That is the effect of the Industrial and Provident Societies Act 1967, section 3.

## Agricultural Charges

An entirely new type of security, available only to farmers (England and Wales) and to agricultural societies[138] (Scotland), was introduced in Great Britain in the late 1920s. There is no equivalent in Northern Ireland. A farmer, for this purpose, is a person (other than a corporation) who, as tenant or owner of an agricultural holding, cultivates the holding for profit. This type of activity comprises horticulture and the use of land for any purpose of husbandry inclusive of the keeping or breeding of livestock, poultry or bees, and the growth of fruit, vegetables and the like.

A farmer[139] may, by instrument in writing, create in favour of a bank approved by the minister what is called an agricultural charge.[140] That is a charge on all or any of the farming stock[141] and other agricultural assets[142] as security for loans. In England and Wales an agricultural charge may be either a fixed charge or a floating charge, or it may be both together, but in Scotland it may only be a fixed charge. A fixed charge over or including livestock may include progeny born after the date of the charge and, in the case of plant, may include new plant substituted for the plant specified in the charge. The debt secured may be either a specified amount or a fluctuating sum advanced on current account, with or without limit. In the case of a fluctuating amount, the charge is not redeemed merely by the account ceasing to be in debit, so a subsequent overdraft will still be secured.

A fixed charge gives the chargee bank the right to take possession of the property charged, on default in the farmer's obligations, and to sell it, if not redeemed within five days of seizure (or a shorter period, if so specified in the charge), paying any surplus proceeds of sale, after satisfying the debt, to the farmer.[143] If the farmer sells any property comprised in the charge, he must account to the bank

138. See the Agricultural Credits (Scotland) Act 1929, s. 9(1).
139. In Scotland, an agricultural society.
140. Agricultural Credits Act 1928, s. 5; Agricultural Credits (Scotland) Act 1929, s. 5.
141. Crops or other agricultural or horticultural produce, growing or severed, natural or processed; livestock; seeds and manures; vehicles, machinery and other plant; fixtures.
142. A tenant's right to compensation for improvements, damage by game, disturbance or otherwise, and any other tenant right.
143. 1928 Act, s. 6; 1929 Act, s. 6.

for the proceeds, but the purchaser is not concerned to see that that is done, even if he knows of the existence of the charge.

In England and Wales, a floating charge given by a farmer has a similar effect to that of a floating charge created by a company.[144] The charge becomes fixed on the happening of one of the following events: (*a*) the farmer's bankruptcy; (*b*) the farmer's death; (*c*) dissolution of the partnership if the charge is given by partners; (*d*) the bank giving notice in writing in accordance with a term of the contract of charge.[145] The position of the farmer, if he sells property subject to the charge, is that he must account to the bank for the proceeds unless he spends them on property which becomes subject to the charge.

Agricultural charges are void as against third parties unless registered,[146] and two or more charges rank for priority in order of registration.[147] In England and Wales, if a farmer has given a floating charge he cannot give a fixed charge or bill of sale over any property included in the floating charge.[148] An agricultural charge is not itself a bill of sale.[149]

In England and Wales, a tenant of an agricultural holding cannot be restrained by his contract of tenancy from creating an agricultural charge.[150]

By virtue of section 14 of the Agricultural Credits Act 1928, a registered agricultural society in England and Wales, if it gives a bank a floating charge on farming stock, may register it as if it were an agricultural charge, and also register it with the friendly societies central office. If that is done, the charge is not a bill of sale requiring registration as such. The Agricultural Marketing Act 1958, section 15(5), allows an agricultural marketing board to give a bank a floating charge to be treated in the same manner as an agricultural charge. In Scotland, too, an agricultural marketing board may give a charge to be treated as an agricultural charge.[151]

## Pledge or Pawn

**Nature of the Transaction** 'Pledge' and 'pawn' are two words with the same meaning: a security based on possession. It may be more usual to refer to pawning when the lender is a pawnbroker, and to pledging when he is not, but the law has no such technical

144. See pp. 126–43, *ante.*    145. 1928 Act, s. 7.
146. 1928 Act, s. 9; 1929 Act, s. 8.    147. 1928 Act, s. 8(2); 1929 Act, s. 7.
148. 1928 Act, s. 8(3).    149. 1928 Act, s. 8(1).
150. 1928 Act, s. 13.    151. Agricultural Marketing Act 1958, s. 15(6).

distinction in its nomenclature. Sometimes the act of pledging is referred to (more frequently in Scotland than in other parts of the United Kingdom) as 'impignoration,' from the term of Roman law, *pignus*, which is closely related to the English common law pledge and even more closely related to that of Scottish common law.

The distinction between a mortgage of a chattel (corporeal moveable) and a pledge is that the security of a mortgagee is the ownership of the thing, while the security of a pledgee is its possession.[152] A mortgagee may take possession of the thing mortgaged, to enforce or protect his security, but he does so by virtue of having the title; a pledgee is given possession as his security, the pledgor retaining the title. The nature of the transaction of pledge is similar throughout the United Kingdom, though there are minor differences between the law of Scotland, on the one hand, and the law of England and Wales and Northern Ireland, on the other hand, particularly with regard to the pledgee's power of sale to enforce his security.[153]

Only chattels (corporeal moveables) may be pledged. Any type of such property may be pledged. The commonest pledges are of goods, but documents such as share certificates are sometimes pledged.[154] Land and incorporeal property cannot be pledged. In the case of land in England and Wales and Northern Ireland, deposit of the title deeds to land to secure a loan operates as an equitable mortgage: it operates as a pledge of the documents themselves as well, but that is of little or no practical significance.[155] There seems to be no limit to the use of moveables as pledges. One pledgor was so eccentric as to use for his security half a £50 bank note.[156]

A pledge does not require registration as a bill of sale[157] (or as a company charge[158]). The legislation on bills of sale[159] is not concerned with a distinction between mortgages and pledges as such, but with a distinction between securities with possession and those without. The policy of the legislation is to preclude a borrower from giving a misleading impression of affluence, by requiring public registration of other persons' interests in things of which the borrower is in possession. If possession is given to the lender, there is no

---

152. See *Ryall* v. *Rolle* (1749) 1 Atk. 165.
153. See pp. 158–9, *post*. (A comprehensive book, though an out-of-date one, on all kinds of security in Scotland is Gloag and Irvine, *Law of Rights in Security* (1897).)
154. This chapter is concerned only with chattels (corporeal moveables). A pledge of share certificates gives some rights over the shares themselves. See pp. 249–52, *post*.
155. See p. 27, *ante*.     156. *Taylor* v. *Chester* (1869) L.R. 4 Q.B. 309.
157. See pp. 114–16, *ante*.     158. See pp. 119–20, *ante*.
159. Not applicable in Scotland.

need for registration. In *Ex parte Hubbard*[160] there was a pledge of two tricycles, which were delivered to the pledgee. The parties made a document regulating their rights. That document was held not to be a bill of sale, as it did not give the pledgee a right to possession of the tricycles (he already had possession). Consequently, it was not void for departing from the statutory form required for bills of sale. In fact, it is not possible to give written permission to take possession of goods as security for a debt because such a document is within the definition of a bill of sale, a bill of sale is void if not in the statutory form, and that kind of document cannot be put into that form.[161] There are only two choices for the person seeking security over goods: to get actual possession of the goods[162] or to get on the appropriate register.

There is one classification of pledges which is of legal importance: into those governed by the legislation on pawnbrokers, and those (whether given to pawnbrokers or not) which are outside the statutes.

**Legislation on Pawnbrokers**  In Great Britain, pawnbrokers are governed primarily by the Pawnbrokers Acts 1872 and 1960. Corresponding legislation, differing in some particulars, is contained in the Pawnbrokers Act (Northern Ireland) 1954. These Acts provide for the registration and licensing of pawnbrokers, and create many criminal offences. They are dealt with in this book only to the extent to which they govern the rights of the parties to a transaction. Pawns which do not come within the Acts are governed by principles of the common law and equity, and these principles apply also to pawns regulated by the Acts in so far as they relate to matters not covered by the Acts and in so far as they are consistent with the legislation.

The Acts apply:

    (*a*) in Great Britain, to all loans of less than £5 made by a pawnbroker, and, in the absence of a special contract,[163] to all loans made by a pawnbroker of between £5 and £50;[164]

    (*b*) in Northern Ireland, to all loans not exceeding £50 made by a pawnbroker.[165]

Pawnbrokers are required to keep and use certain documents. In

---

160. (1886) 17 Q.B.D. 690.    161. *Ex parte Parsons* (1886) 16 Q.B.D. 532.
162. As to the various kinds of possession and the modes of obtaining it, see pp. 147–55, *post*.
163. Pawnbrokers Acts 1872, s. 24, and 1960, s. 1.
164. Pawnbrokers Acts 1872, s. 10, and 1960, s. 1.
165. Pawnbrokers Act (Northern Ireland) 1954, s. 2.

particular, they must keep a pledge book and a sale book recording sales of pledges for loans of above 50p.[166] A pawnbroker must not take a pledge without giving a pawn ticket.[167] In *Fergusson* v. *Norman*,[168] where a pawnbroker did not comply with the provisions of the Act then in force as to recording and bookkeeping, it was held that the pawn was void and that the pawnor's trustees in bankruptcy could recover the goods. The Acts also specify the profits and charges a pawnbroker is permitted to make.[169] He must not take a pawn from someone apparently under fourteen years old (Great Britain)[170] or sixteen years old (Northern Ireland),[171] whether the young person is trying to pawn his own property or is acting as agent for someone else.

**The Requirement of Possession by the Pledgee**  There is no valid pledge unless the pledgee has possession of the article, though his taking possession may be contemporaneous with the incurring of the debt or before or after it.[172] If the article is in the possession of someone other than the owner, e.g., for safe custody, a pledge comes into existence if the person in possession later makes the owner a loan and it is agreed that the article is to be held as security for it. If there is a debt, and an article is later pledged as security for it, the pledge takes effect when possession is transferred. If a loan is made and it is then agreed that something will be pledged as security, the pledge is effectual from the time (whether then or later) when the pledgee gets possession.

The most obvious way of giving possession is for the debtor to hand over the article to the creditor.[173] But that is not always possible or expedient, and possession is not the same as custody. Something in the custody of a servant or agent may be in the possession of the master or principal. It is even possible for the pledgor to be the pledgee's servant or agent for this purpose, though that situation is obviously pregnant with the risk of fraud. In the

---

166. Great Britain: 1872 Act, s. 12 and sch. 3, and 1960 Act, s. 6 and sch.; Northern Ireland: 1954 Act, s. 10 and sch. 1 and 2.
167. Great Britain: 1872 Act, s. 14; Northern Ireland: 1954 Act, s. 12.
168. (1838) 5 Bing. N.C. 76.
169. Great Britain: 1872 Act, s. 15 and sch. 4, and 1960 Act, ss. 4 and 7 and sch.; Northern Ireland: 1954 Act, s. 15 and sch. 3.
170. England and Wales: Children and Young Persons Act 1933, s. 8. See also the Metropolitan Police Act 1839, s. 50. Scotland: Children and Young Persons (Scotland) Act 1937, s. 19.
171. Pawnbrokers Act (Northern Ireland) 1954, s. 25(a).
172. See *Hilton* v. *Tucker* (1888) 39 Ch. D. 669.
173. See *Ex parte Hodgkin* (1875) L.R. 20 Eq. 746.

case of very bulky goods, it may not be expedient to move them, and possession may be given to the pledgee by giving him the keys of the place where they are stored. Possession consists substantially of having either the custody and control of the goods or, if someone else (such as a warehouse-keeper) has the custody, having the control in the sense of a right to take delivery or to specify how the custodian must deal with the goods. Where goods are in transit, they may be pledged by notifying the carrier to deliver them to the order of the pledgee or by delivery of the bill of lading.

**Goods in the custody of the pledgor or on his premises**    In *Hilton* v. *Tucker*[174] the owner of some pictures borrowed on the security of them. He rented a room in the museum of the Archaeological Society and put the pictures there. The key to the room normally stayed with the hall porter. The borrower told the lender that the key was entirely at his disposal and that the pictures were to be regarded as in his possession. The borrower, however, could get the key and enter the room, which he did to keep the room in order and dust the pictures. It was held that the lender had possession of the pictures and therefore that they had been validly pledged. It may be doubted, however, whether that decision is right: it is difficult to see why the pictures were in the possession of the lender rather than in that of the borrower when both parties had equal access to the key and the borrower was the tenant of the room. It is also difficult to reconcile the decision with the later one of the House of Lords, on appeal from Ireland, in *Dublin City Distillery (Great Brunswick Street, Dublin) Ltd.* v. *Doherty*.[175] The distillery company borrowed money from Doherty and purported to give him security over whisky which was in the company's warehouse. As is usual in such cases, access to the warehouse was available only to the company and the excise officer acting together, the door having two locks. When the loan was made, the company entered Doherty's name against the whisky intended as security, in their stock book. They also gave him an invoice and a document stating that the whisky (of which the document gave particulars) was deliverable to Doherty or his assigns. The excise officer was not told of the transaction. As it was not registered in the register of company charges, the security was valid only if it was a pledge. This it was held not to be on the ground that possession had not been delivered to the lender. (Incidentally, the company had, with Doherty's permission, sold some of the whisky alleged to have been pledged to him, and

174. (1888) 39 Ch. D. 669.    175. [1914] A.C. 823.

substituted other whisky against his name in the stock book, so that the transaction looked rather like an unregistered floating charge. But the determining factor was that the people who could actually get at the whisky were still the company in concert with the excise officer.) If, on the other hand, only the creditor has the key and hence access and control, there will be a valid pledge even if the premises belong to the debtor. In *Wrightson* v. *McArthur and Hutchisons (1919) Ltd.*[176] the company wished to give some of their stock, £5,000 worth of buttons and thread, as security. They put it into two rooms in their premises, locked the rooms, gave the keys to the creditor and also gave him a letter of authority to remove the goods as desired. The company subsequently went into liquidation, whereupon the liquidator contended that the security was void for lack of registration. It was held to be a valid pledge: possession had passed to the creditor by a combination of the delivery of the keys and the grant of a licence to come on the land to reach the doors and remove the goods.

If the goods are simply left with the borrower, there ought to be no pledge. *Martin* v. *Reid*,[177] in so far as it indicates the contrary, is probably no longer of authority. That was a case of a pledge of a house, a van, a cart and two sets of harness. The cart and one set of harness were left with the pledgor because the pledgee had nowhere to put them, but the pledgee was given the right to take them when he wanted. It was held that possession had passed to the creditor, so that there was a valid pledge. However, since the leaving of the cart and the harness with the debtor was exactly within the mischief of the legislation on bills of sale, the decision ought to have gone the other way.

After goods have been placed in the possession of the pledgee, the pledge ought to be lost if they are handed back to the pledgor. Yet a different result was achieved in *Reeves* v. *Capper*.[178] The captain of a ship pledged his chronometer, which was then in the hands of the makers, to the owners of his ship as security for a loan of £50. Then the captain got the chronometer and handed it to the shipowners' clerk, who gave it back to the captain to take on his voyage. After the voyage had been completed, the captain took his chronometer back to the makers and asked them to hold it for a creditor of the captain's (i.e., a creditor other than the shipowners) as security, which induced that creditor to refrain from pressing for payment. It

176. [1921] 2 K.B. 807.   177. (1862) 11 C.B.N.S. 730.
178. (1838) 5 Bing. N.C. 136.

was apparently held that there had been a mortgage of the chronometer, not a pledge, to the shipowners, who had priority over the second security because they did not lose their security by giving the use of the chronometer to the captain for his voyage. It also appears to have been held that, if the shipowners' security was a pledge, they did not part with possession but only gave a licence to use the chronometer. In the words of Tindal C.J.,[179] '. . . the possession of Captain Wilson was still the possession of Messrs. Capper.' It is submitted that this is a word-game which does not reflect commercial realities. What is required of this branch of the law is that it should facilitate the raising of loans on security while protecting persons from dealing with the debtor on the footing that he is the absolute owner of the property on which the creditor claims security. If the property is to be in the hands of the debtor, the security should be invalid unless registered as a bill of sale. However, *Reeves* v. *Capper* has been cited frequently without disapproval and with only one or two isolated expressions of judicial doubt. What can be said in its favour is that a person dealing with a sea-captain over a chronometer might well consider that he could be the owner, or he could be a hirer, or he could be using a chronometer belonging to the owners of the ship, and the creditor ought to make inquiries before accepting such such an article as security.

**Goods in a third party's warehouse**  In the absence of any special transaction, these goods are in the possession of the owner because he is entitled to instruct the warehouseman how to deal with them (subject, of course, to paying the charges for warehousing). The owner can pledge them and deliver possession to the pledgee by instructing the warehouse-keeper to hold the goods to the order of the pledgee instead of to the order of the owner. In *Grigg* v. *National Guardian Assurance Co.*[180] there was held to be a valid pledge where the owner of goods in a warehouse borrowed money and gave the warehouseman a document requesting him to deliver to the lenders or their order 'all property warehoused with you in my name on payment of your charges.'

**Goods in transit**  Bills of lading are in a special position.[181] If goods are in transit, but are not the subject of a bill of lading, the position of the carrier is similar to that of a warehouse-keeper. In *Re Hall*[182] the consignee of leather sent by train gave the invoice and

---

179. 5 Bing. N.C. 141.
180. [1891] 3 Ch. 206. See also *Young* v. *Lambert* (1870) L.R. 3 P.C. 142.
181. See pp. 152–5, *post*.    182. (1884) 14 Q.B.D. 386.

a delivery order, addressed to the railway company, to a bank to secure an advance. The bank informed the railway company. When the leather arrived, the railway company sent the bank an advice note stating that they held the goods to the order of the bank. At that time, the bank made an advance to the consignee. It was held that the parties had made a valid pledge of the leather, not a bill of sale requiring registration.

**Documents giving a right to possession by way of security**
If documentary right to possession is given by way of security, that will be void if it is not registered as a bill of sale or if it is not in the statutory form laid down for bills of sale. In *Charlesworth* v. *Mills*[183] goods were in the hands of a sheriff's officer. The owner got a loan and sought to pledge the goods. A written agreement was made between the owner, the sheriff and the lender, under which the sheriff agreed to hold the goods for the lender. It was held that there had been a pledge and that possession had passed and that, since the agreement was not the title to the goods, that document was not a bill of sale. (This paragraph does not apply to Scotland.)

**Documents of title to goods**    There are only two types of document of title to goods: bills of sale[184] (in England and Wales and Northern Ireland) and bills of lading[185] (throughout the United Kingdom). A document of title is a document which, if handed over, endorsed, with the intention of assigning the goods to which it relates, passes the property in the goods to the assignee without physical delivery of the goods, regardless of whose custody the goods are in and whether or not the custodian is informed of the change of ownership. If handed over by way of pledge, delivery of the documents of title operates to pledge the goods to which they relate and to pass possession of the goods to the pledgee. Many other documents are made in relation to goods, such as carriers' receipts, dispatch notes, invoices, arrival advices, warehouse receipts and bankers' receipts for safe custody. None of these is a document of title. To pledge the goods to which they refer it is necessary either to execute a bill of sale and register it or to secure that the custodian will hold the goods to the pledgee's order. Accordingly, if a pledge without a bill of sale is desired, and the goods are in the custody of a third party, if no question of action by a mercantile agent[186] is involved, either there must be a pledge of a bill of lading or the custodian must be instructed to hold for the pledgee as possessor.

183. [1892] A.C. 231.    184. See pp. 114–16, *ante*.
185. See pp. 152–5, *post*.    186. See pp. 168–72, *post*.

The case of *Official Assignee of Madras* v. *Mercantile Bank of India Ltd.*[187] is often cited in English cases, as English law is discussed by the Privy Council. But the actual decision turned on the law of Madras. In that case it was held that a pledge of documents of title to ground nuts amounted to a pledge of the goods (which is English law), but it was also held that the document in question in that case, a railway receipt which was pledged by the consignee, was a document of title (which is not English law). The Privy Council held, further, that when the pledgee bank handed over the receipt to the consignee, so that he could effect delivery of the goods into the possession of the pledgee, the latter had parted with custody, not possession, so that the pledge was not lost (in English law that depends on the circumstances). Here, the railway company refused to deliver the goods to the consignee when he presented the receipt because he did not pay the freight. Their lordships thought that even if the receipt was not a document of title, but only a token of authority to receive possession, its transfer as security for a loan created an equitable charge over the goods, at least between the parties, so as to bind the consignee's trustee in bankruptcy.

**Bills of Lading**   A bill of lading is a document relating to goods sent by ship. It is a receipt for the goods given by the captain of the ship to the consignor, with an undertaking to deliver the goods to the consignee on payment of the freight. The consignee may be named in the bill of lading, and he is commonly an importing purchaser. The name of the consignee may be left to be endorsed on the bill by the consignor, or the latter may be named as consignee, leaving him free to endorse the bill later to the person who is actually to receive delivery. The bill of lading will be sent to the consignee, who can use it as a document of title. When the goods are unloaded from the ship, the consignee or his endorsee may take possession, or the goods may be discharged into a quayside wharf to await delivery on payment of warehouse charges (and, of course, freight). While the goods are at sea or in a warehouse at the port of arrival, the consignee will frequently need a bridging loan to pay the purchase price of the goods, the freight on them and other charges, in advance of receiving the proceeds he expects from resales. For that money he may well go to a bank and borrow on security of handing over the endorsed bill of lading. Bills of lading can be used for that purpose until delivery of the goods is taken from the ship or warehouse. Endorsement of a

187. [1935] A.C. 53.

bill of lading intended to pass the title to the goods to the endorsee will operate to pass that title, while endorsement (whether to a named person or in blank) and delivery by way of pledge operates to pledge the goods themselves and to pass their possession to the pledgee.[188] The pledgee is then entitled to take delivery, or to give someone else authority to take delivery, and can bring an action for conversion against the carrier or warehouseman if he wrongfully delivers the goods to the original consignee without a delivery order from the pledgee.[189]

In Scotland, where there is no legislation on bills of sale and where there are no securities over corporeal moveables (apart from registered floating charges, mortgages of aircraft and agricultural charges) without transfer of possession to the creditor, endorsement and delivery of a bill of lading may be used by way of security either to pledge the goods or in support of an assignation in security, since the holder of the bill of lading has possession of the goods. In *Thomas Hayman & Son* v. *M'Lintock*[190] flour pledged by pledge of the bill of lading was, after being landed, mixed in a warehouse with other flour belonging to the pledgee, so as to be indistinguishable. It was held that the pledgee had a claim to the number of bags specified in the bill of lading. In *Price & Pierce Ltd.* v. *Bank of Scotland*[191] there was an assignation in security by the purchaser of timber which was being stored by a third party. The purchaser handed the lender the endorsed bill of lading and a delivery order, and the lender notified the storekeeper. It was held that the lender had a title to the timber which prevailed, on the bankruptcy of the purchaser, over the vendor's right to rescind the sale for misrepresentation.

The bank or other lender having his pledge, a difficulty arises: the loan will not be repaid unless the goods are sold; the borrower, not the lender, is the professional dealer in the goods, likely to get the best price; the borrower needs to get the goods in order to sell them; to get the goods, the borrower needs to have the bill of lading or a delivery order; but to protect his security, the lender needs to hang on to possession of the goods. Since commerce could not be carried on under any system of law without a certain amount of trust in the good faith of the parties, some degree of control over the goods has to be conceded to the borrower. One of two things will commonly happen. First, if the borrower needs to have the goods himself in

188. *Sewell* v. *Burdick* (1884) 10 App. Cas. 74; *The Odessa* [1916] 1 A.C. 145. See also *Harris* v. *Birch* (1842) 9 M. & W. 591.
189. *Bristol and West of England Bank* v. *Midland Railway Co.* [1891] 2 Q.B. 653.
190. 1907 S.C. 936.      191. 1910 S.C. 1095, affirmed 1912 S.C. (H.L.) 19.

order to sell them, the lender will give him a delivery order, on production of which he can obtain the goods from the carrier or warehouse-keeper. Secondly, if the borrower does not need the goods, but needs authority to deliver them to a purchaser, the lender may hand the bill of lading back to the borrower to sell the goods and authorise delivery of them as the lender's agent. In either case, the borrower will probably be required to give the lender a trust receipt, i.e., a document undertaking to hold the proceeds of sale on trust for the lender until the debt secured by the pledge has been paid off. In such a case, the borrower is considered to be in possession of the goods as agent for the lender; as the possession is still the lender's, his pledge remains, at least as against the borrower, the borrower's ordinary creditors and his trustee in bankruptcy or (in the case of a company) liquidator.

In Scotland, where a pledgee has no power of sale of the goods pledged unless such a power is expressly granted to him by the agreement,[192] this situation went to the House of Lords in *North-Western Bank Ltd.* v. *Poynter, Son, & Macdonalds*.[193] Goods were pledged by delivery to the bank of the bill of lading, together with a grant of a power of sale. Later, the bank asked the pledger, as the bank's agent, to sell the goods. It was held that, by parting with the bill of lading to the pledger, the bank had not lost their pledge because, first, the pledger was the pledgee's agent in the sale and, secondly, this was not a mere pledge but a pledge coupled with a power of sale.

In England and Wales and Northern Ireland, a pledgee always has a power of sale.[194] In *Re David Allester Ltd.*[195] a bank were given a pledge of seed by delivery of the bill of lading. Later, so that the seed could be sold, they gave the bill back to the owner company and obtained from them a trust receipt. The company went into liquidation. It was held that the bank had retained their pledge, and that the security was not void for non-registration because the pledge was not changed into a bill of sale type of transaction by the giving of the trust receipt.

However, the trust receipt is not a matter of public knowledge, even if one is given. The fact that the owner of the goods is in possession of them as the pledgee's agent can easily be concealed. Having put the borrower in control of the goods, the lender will

192. See p. 159, *post.*
193. [1895] A.C. 56, extensively discussed by Rodger, 'Pledge of Bills of Lading' (1971) *Juridical Review* 193.
194. See pp. 158–9, *post.*     195. [1922] 2 Ch. 211.

have to cede priority to any bona fide purchaser for value of the goods who believes that the owner can give an unincumbered title. So, if the borrower has the bill of lading in order to sell the goods as the lender's agent, but instead he pledges them by endorsing and delivering the bill to another lender who is unaware of the first pledge, the second pledgee will prevail over the first. The only way a pledgee can protect himself completely is to cling to the bill of lading, authorise the borrower to sell, and give delivery orders himself (not allow the borrower to do so) only in favour of purchasers who pay or undertake to pay the purchase price direct to the pledgee.

An unsatisfactory Scottish authority which goes to show the dangers is *Tod & Son* v. *Merchant Banking Co. of London (Ltd.)*[196]. A purchaser of esparto grass from abroad was given a blank bill of lading. He endorsed and delivered it to his bankers as security for a loan of the purchase-money. The bankers were thus held to have a legal title to the goods, but whether they were regarded as having a possessory title as pledgees or as having ownership by way of assignation in security is not clear. The bankers allowed the borrower to sell *as owners* and they (the bankers) gave delivery orders when required. It was held that the bankers had lost their security over the parts of the cargo so sold.

**Redemption of Pledges**   The rights of the parties vary according to whether the transaction is governed by the Pawnbrokers Acts or not.

**Under the Pawnbrokers Acts**   In Great Britain, a pledge may be redeemed within six months of being made, plus a further period of grace of seven days.[197] In Northern Ireland, that is also the position with regard to pledges for loans of less than £3, but the period for loans of £3–£5 is nine months, and that for loans of over £5 a year, plus the seven days of grace in each case.[198] In Great Britain, but not in Northern Ireland, if the pledge is not redeemed by the end of the days of grace, the article becomes the absolute property of the pawnbroker if the loan was of £2 or less.[199] If the loan was more than that (or, in Northern Ireland, was of any amount[200]), and the pledge is not redeemed when the period of grace runs out, it remains redeemable until the pawnbroker exercises his power of

---

196. (1883) 10 R. 1009.    197. Pawnbrokers Acts 1872, s. 16 and 1960, s. 2.
198. Pawnbrokers Act (Northern Ireland) 1954, s. 16.
199. 1872 Act, s. 17; 1960 Act, ss. 2 and 3.    200. 1954 Act, s. 17.

sale.[201] A person producing the pawn ticket is presumed to be entitled to redeem and, if he turns out to be a thief or cheat, the pawnbroker is not liable for having delivered the article to him.[202] Furthermore, the pawnbroker is not liable to deliver the article to someone claiming to redeem unless he produces the pawn ticket,[203] but the Acts do lay down a procedure for the benefit of people who lose the tickets.

**Pledges outside the Pawnbrokers Acts**   If the agreement of pledge specifies a date for redemption, the pledgor can redeem on that date or thereafter until the pledgee enforces his security by sale.[204] In *Franklin* v. *Neate*[205] the pledge was of a chronometer, with power to the pledgee to sell if it was not redeemed within a year. After the year had passed and the chronometer had not been redeemed, the pledgor sold it to the plaintiff, who tried to redeem. The pawnbroker having refused to part with it, it was held that the plaintiff could sue him for conversion. The pledgor had the legal title, subject to the pawnbroker's rights, and, as the pawnbroker had not exercised his power of sale, could pass the legal right to redeem to the plaintiff. As the right to redeem was legal, not equitable, the action was at common law for conversion.

If there is a pledge with no date specified for redemption, the position is not entirely clear. In a commercial transaction, it is unlikely that so obvious a term would be omitted from the contract. If it were, presumably there would be an implied term that if redemption did not occur within a reasonable time, the pledgee could sell, though it might be prudent for him to seek a court order for sale. If a small article is pawned, it seems that, in the absence of a specified date for payment of the debt, the pawnor has his lifetime to redeem. In *Ratcliff* v. *Davis*[206] a hatband set with diamonds was pawned for £25, no date being set for redemption. The pawnee's wife, acting as her husband's agent, delivered the hatband to the defendant (quite why, it is not clear). The pawnee died, after which the plaintiff, as owner, tried to redeem the article from the pawnee's widow, his executrix. She refused, and, when the plaintiff demanded

---

201. 1872 Act, s. 18; 1960 Act, ss. 2 and 3. As to the pawnbroker's power of sale, see p.158, *post*.
202. Great Britain: 1872 Act, s. 25; Northern Ireland: 1954 Act, s. 19.
203. Great Britain: 1872 Act, s. 26; see also the 1872 Act, s. 29 and the 1960 Act, s. 5. Northern Ireland: 1954 Act, s. 19.
204. As to the pledgee's power of sale, see pp. 158-9, *post*.
205. (1844) 13 M. & W. 481.
206. (1611) Yelv. 178. See also *Kemp* v. *Westbrook* (1749) 1 Ves. Sen. 278; *Martin* v. *Reid* (1862) 11 C.B.N.S. 730, 736-7, *per* Willes J., obiter.

the hatband from the defendant, he too refused to give it up. It was held that the defendant was liable for conversion, but that the widow could recover £25 from the plaintiff. The plaintiff had his lifetime to redeem; if he had died, the pawn would have been irredeemable (i.e., the executrix could have sold the hatband).

Clearly, on redeeming, the pledgor must pay the pledgee all the money secured by the pledge. On principle, in order to redeem, the pledgor ought not to have to pay the pledgee any debts not secured by the pledge he seeks to redeem. *Demainbray* v. *Metcalfe*[207] contains a suggestion that the pledgor must pay his unsecured debts to the pledgee too, before he can redeem, on the principle that he who seeks equity must do equity. The reports of this case contain different versions of the facts, so that it is a confused and therefore not very persuasive authority, but the equitable principle does seem to be only a secondary ground for the decision. The primary ground was that all the debts were in fact intended by the parties to be secured by the pledge. The secondary ground seems wrong for two reasons: (i) the equitable principle does not require the payment of unsecured debts on redemption, unless they were intended to be secured (e.g., because they were originally secured but have become statute-barred); (ii) the right to redeem a pawn is legal, not equitable (unlike the usual position with respect to a mortgage in England and Wales and Northern Ireland), so equitable principles were inapplicable.

In the case of a joint pledge, all the pledgors must join in redeeming. In *Harper* v. *Godsell*[208] there was a pledge of wine by four partners as co-owners. The assignee of three of them was held unable to redeem or recover the wine without joining the fourth.

**The Rights of the Pledgee**  First of all, the pledgee has possession of the thing pledged, and the right to retain possession until the debt is paid. If necessary, he can sue a third party, to recover possession of the article pledged, without joining the pledgor as a party.[209] Secondly, the pledgee may have a right of sale if the debt is not paid.[210] Finally, if he is not paid in due time, the pledgee can sue on the contract to pay. For example, if a pawnbroker, exercising his power of sale properly, sells an unredeemed pledge for less than the

207. (1715) 2 Vern. 691 and 698. See p. 162, *post.*  208. (1870) L.R. 5 Q.B. 422.
209. *Saville* v. *Tankred* (1748) 1 Ves. Sen. 101.
210. As to the power of sale, see pp. 158-9, *post.*

sum secured by it, he can recover the balance of the debt from the borrower unless that right is excluded by the contract.[211]

**The Pledgee's Power of Sale**    At common law, the pledgee has a power of sale in England and Wales and Northern Ireland, but not in Scotland. Throughout the United Kingdom there is a power of sale of pledges governed by the Pawnbrokers Acts.

**Pawnbrokers Acts**    In Great Britain, once a pawn for more than £2 has become irredeemable, the pawnbroker may sell it by public auction, at which he may bid and buy.[212] He does not need a power of sale of pawns for £2 or less, as he becomes the owner when the pawn becomes irredeemable.[213] In Northern Ireland, where there is no special rule for pawns for small debts, the power of sale extends to all pawns for which the date of redemption has passed.[214] In Great Britain, if the pawn is sold for more than the amount of the debt, the pawnbroker must pay the surplus to the holder of the pawn ticket if that person demands the surplus within three years of the sale – but he may set the surplus off against losses on sales of pledges made by the same person if the losses are made within a year before or after the sale producing the surplus.[215]

**Other pledges in England and Wales and Northern Ireland**
Once the period of redeemability has expired, there is a power of sale.[216] As soon as the pledgee enters into a valid contract of sale, the pledgor in default loses his right to redeem.[217] If the pledgee sells before the end of the contractual period for redemption, he is guilty of conversion. In *Johnson* v. *Stear*[218] 243 cases of brandy were pledged by depositing the relevant dock warrant with the lender. The day before the date for redemption, the pledgee sold the brandy; he handed the dock warrant to the purchaser on the following day (redemption day); and the purchaser took possession of the brandy the day after. It was held that the pledgee was liable for conversion of the brandy (by handing over the dock warrant too soon), but only nominal damages were awarded because the borrower had had no intention of redeeming. In *Pigot* v. *Cubley*[219] a pledge of two

---

211. *Jones* v. *Marshall* (1889) 24 Q.B.D. 269.
212. Pawnbrokers Acts 1872, s. 19 and sch. 5., and 1960, s. 3.
213. See p. 155, *ante*.        214. Pawnbrokers Act (Northern Ireland) 1954, s. 18.
215. Pawnbrokers Acts 1872, s. 22, and 1960, s. 3. There are no corresponding statutory provisions in Northern Ireland.
216. *Lockwood* v. *Ewer* (1742) 9 Mod. 275; *Pothonier* v. *Dawson* (1816) Holt N.P. 383.
217. *The Ningchow* [1916] P. 221.        218. (1863) 15 C.B.N.S. 330.
219. (1864) 15 C.B.N.S. 701.

pictures was at first redeemable on a specified date, but the parties agreed later on an indefinite extension of the time for repayment. Later still, the lender demanded repayment of more than was due. The sum asked not being paid, he sold the pictures. The borrower tried to redeem and, having failed, recovered damages for conversion. The arrangement for an extension of time for repayment could have been terminated by proper notice. On the other hand, a sale by a pledgee on the bankruptcy of the pledgor, without demand or notice, even if wrongful, gives no right of action for damages to the bankrupt's trustee in bankruptcy because no damage has been suffered.[220]

It seems that the pawnbroker has no right of set-off at common law. If he sells some pledges for more than the amount advanced on them and other pledges by the same pledgor for less, the common law requires the pawnbroker to account for the surpluses without deduction for the deficits.[221] However, the pledgee could sue for the balance due in the cases of deficit, and there may be an equitable right of set-off since the Judicature Acts.

**Pledges in Scotland not governed by the Pawnbrokers Acts** There is no common law power of sale. Accordingly, the pledgee can sell only if there is an express power granted by the contract of pledge or if he obtains a court order for sale. Alternatively, he may arrange for the pledger to sell the article to a purchaser who will pay off the loan out of the price.

**Foreclosure** Except in cases where the pawnbroker becomes the owner of small unredeemed pledges under the Pawnbrokers Acts in Great Britain, there is no right of a pledgee to become the owner of pledged goods on default by the borrower. A pledge is not a mortgage, the pledgee has only a possessory title, and there can be no proceedings for foreclosure. In *Fraser* v. *Byas*[222] the pledge was of a picture of the Madonna and Child attributed to Dürer. On non-payment of the debt, it was held that the pledgee could not foreclose: there must be either redemption or sale, the pledgor and the pledgee each being given liberty to bid at any sale.

## Loss, Damage, Depreciation and Use of Goods While Pledged

**Loss or damage by fire** In cases governed by the Pawnbrokers Acts, if a pledge is destroyed or damaged by fire during the period

220. *Halliday* v. *Holgate* (1868) L.R. 3 Ex. 299.
221. *Dobree* v. *Norcliffe* (1870) 23 L.T. 552.
222. (1895) 11 T.L.R. 481. See also *Carter* v. *Wake* (1877) 4 Ch. D. 605, p. 250, *post*.

for redemption, the pawnbroker is liable to pay the pledgor the value of the thing pledged less the amount of the loan and the pawnbroker's permissible profit.[223] The value is calculated as the amount of the loan plus the amount of the profit plus 25% of the amount of the loan, and for the amount of the value so calculated the pawnbroker is authorised to insure the pledge.

It seems that, in cases outside the Pawnbrokers Acts, a pledgee is not liable for damage to the goods caused by 'an accidental fire without his default, neglect or wilful misbehaviour.'[224] In the Irish case of *Foley* v. *O'Hara*,[225] where goods deposited with a pawnbroker (outside the Acts) were destroyed by fire, it was held, first, that a pawnbroker's duty is to use ordinary diligence in the care of the thing pledged; secondly, that res ipsa loquitur: the fire was itself prima facie evidence of negligence; and finally, that the presumption had not been displaced by the evidence, so that the pawnbroker was liable for the difference between the value of the goods and the amount lent on them.

**Other depreciation**   Under the Pawnbrokers Acts,[226] the pawnbroker is liable for depreciation due to his default, neglect or wilful misbehaviour. In cases outside the Acts, the position is the same as that of liability for fire.

**Use**   It appears that a pledgee may make proper use of the goods (e.g., milk cows), but not misuse them, i.e., wear them out (e.g., wear clothes).[227] A pledgee may apparently wear things that do not deteriorate with use, e.g., jewellery. If she keeps them laid up in proper custody, she is not answerable for loss if she takes reasonable care, and if she is not answerable, she can still enforce payment of the debt if the pledge is stolen. But if she wears jewels, the pledgee takes the full risk of loss and is liable even if she is robbed.[228] A pledgee certainly must not consume a pledge, however tempting. In *Cooke* v. *Haddon*,[229] when the pledgor sought to redeem four cases of champagne he discovered that some of the wine had been drunk. It was held that the pledgor could recover the value of the pledged

223. Great Britain: Pawnbrokers Act 1872, s. 27; Pawnbrokers Act (Northern Ireland) 1954, s. 20.
224. *Per* Lord Campbell C. J., the other judges concurring, *Syred* v. *Carruthers* (1858) E.B. & E. 469, 473. The pawnbroker was held not liable, partly on the basis of the common law and partly on that of an Act then in force respecting pawnbrokers.
225. (1920) 54 I.L.T.R. 167.
226. Great Britain: Pawnbrokers Act 1872, s. 28; Pawnbrokers Act (Northern Ireland) 1954, s. 21.
227. *Mores* v. *Conham* (1610) Owen 123.
228. See the judgment of Holt C. J. in *Coggs* v. *Bernard* (1703) 2 Ld. Raym. 909.
229. (1862) 3 F. & F. 229.

goods without deducting the debt due to the pledgee: by using the goods up, the pledgee had forfeited his security. But a mere assertion by the pledgee that he had bought the goods and is the owner, not a pledgee, does not entitle the pledgor to recover the goods without tendering repayment.[230]

**Seizure**  If a pawnbroker's landlord distrains for rent on goods pledged, that is wrongful, and the pawnbroker can recover the full value of the goods.[231] That is because distress would lead to sale of the goods, which would only be in order if they had become irredeemable. But the pawnee has an assignable interest, subject to the rights of the pawnor. Consequently, a pawnbroker's interest in redeemable pledges may be taken in execution for a judgment creditor of the pawnbroker (who will then get the pawnee's rights, not interfering with those of the pawnor).[232]

## Assignment and Sub-Pledge

**Assignment and Sub-Pledge**  Like a mortgagee, a pledgee has an assignable interest in the property on which his debt is secured. He may, for example, assign the pledge to someone (other than the pledgor) who pays off the debt.[223] The assignee will get exactly the rights of the assignor, namely, possession subject to redemption and the power to enforce his security by the appropriate means if the debtor defaults.

A pledgee can validly sub-pledge the goods, though if he borrows more than he has lent he cannot increase the burden of the head pledgor.

**Example**  Alfred borrows £30 from Boris on security of a pledge of a camera worth £75, the loan being for a year. Six months later, Boris borrows £45 from Cyril on security of a pledge of the camera, that loan also being for a year. Six months after that, Alfred seeks to get his camera back from Cyril. The court will hold that Alfred can redeem by paying off his £30 debt to Boris.[234]

In *Donald* v. *Suckling*[235] Mellor J. said:

> . . . although [the pledgee] cannot confer on any third person a better title or a greater interest than he possesses, yet, if nevertheless he does pledge the goods to a third person for a greater

230. *Yungmann* v. *Briesemann* (1892) 67 L.T. 642.
231. *Swire* v. *Leach* (1865) 18 C.B.N.S. 479.      232. *Re Rollason* (1887) 34 Ch. D. 495.
233. *Mores* v. *Conham* (1610) Owen 123.
234. See *Donald* v. *Suckling* (1866) L.R. 1 Q.B. 585 (pledge of debentures); *Blundell-Leigh* v. *Attenborough* [1921] 3 K.B. 235 (jewellery).
235. (1866) L.R. 1 Q.B. 585, 610.

interest than he possesses, such an act does not *annihilate the contract of pledge* between himself and the pawnor; but that the transaction is simply inoperative as against the original pawnor, *who upon tender of the sum secured immediately becomes entitled to the possession of the goods* . . .

And Blackburn J. said:[236]

. . . the subpledging of the goods, held in security for money, before the money is due, is not in general so inconsistent with the contract as to amount to a renunciation of that contract.

The case of *Demainbray* v. *Metcalfe*,[237] in so far as it is irreconcilable with *Donald* v. *Suckling*, is probably of no authority. As reported by Vernon, there was a pawn of jewellery, followed by a sub-pawn by the pawnee to secure a larger sum, followed by the bankruptcy of the head pawnee upon which it was held that, in order to redeem, the head pawnor must pay all sums due from the head pawnee to the sub-pawnee. Some other reporters give the same version, but elsewhere[238] there is no mention of a sub-pawn and the only question reported was whether the pawnor had to pay the pawnee, as a condition of redemption, sums lent to the pawnor, after the pawn was made, the further advances being made without the parties referring to the question whether the new loans were unsecured or by way of additional burden on the jewellery.[239]

A lienee cannot give a sub-security by way of pledge. In *M'Combie* v. *Davies*[240] an agent having a lien over tobacco belonging to his principal for money owed[241] was held unable to give a valid pledge of the tobacco for a loan to himself (the agent). The principal could recover the tobacco from the third party without paying what was due to the agent on the lien because such a lien is personal.

**Pledges by Persons Not Owners of the Goods** Chattels (corporeal moveables) being mobile, and being frequently found in the possession or custody of someone other than the owner, a person lending on security of a pledge, at least where the pledgor does not produce documents of title, runs the risk that the pledgor is in no position to pass a possessory security. He may, for example, be a thief, a hirer, a tenant for life under a trust or an agent.

If a pledgee takes possession of goods from someone who has no right to give it, e.g., if stolen goods are pawned, the owner may

236. L.R. 1 Q.B. 615.   237. (1715) 2 Vern. 691 and 698.
238. E.g., Prec. Ch. 419.   239. See p. 157, *ante*.
240. (1805) 7 East 5.   241. As to such liens themselves, see pp. 204–28, *post*.

recover them from the pledgee without paying back what the pledgee has advanced.[242] That is so even if the transaction is one within the Pawnbrokers Acts. In *Singer Manufacturing Co.* v. *Clark*[243] the hirer of a sewing machine pawned it for less than £2. The plaintiffs, the owners, discovered the whereabouts of the sewing machine and asked the pawnbroker to give it back to them. He declined to part with it then, but later he allowed the machine to be redeemed by the producer of the pawn ticket. The plaintiffs recovered damages from the pawnbroker for conversion. It was held that the owners had a common law title which was not removed by the Pawnbrokers Act 1872, sections 25–6, which presume the holder of the pawn ticket to be entitled to redeem and protect the pawnbroker if he allows the ticket-holder to redeem and someone else later turns out to be entitled to do so. They do not protect the pawnbroker against an owner who has not authorised the pledge, for the owner is not seeking to redeem but to recover his property without paying the debt. A person who is entitled to redeem, but cannot produce the pawn ticket, is protected by section 29. The owner can use that procedure in these circumstances if he wishes, but he can, if he prefers, assert his paramount title.[244] In *Burrows* v. *Barnes*[245] A hired out a bicycle to B. B pawned it to C and did not redeem by the due date. C put the bicycle up for sale and, at the auction, bought it himself. Later, C sold it to D. D took the bicycle to A for repair. A recognised it and refused to give it back to D. It was held that A could keep the bicycle: D had no title as against him. Sections 16–19 of the Pawnbrokers Act 1872[246] regulate only the relations between B and C.

If goods are pledged by a thief, and the owner cannot get them back, perhaps because the pawnbroker has sold them to someone who cannot be traced, the owner can recover damages from the pawnbroker for conversion.[247] If the pawnbroker has sold the goods and the purchaser is made to give them back to the owner, the purchaser has no cause of action against the pawnbroker in the absence of an express warranty of title. In *Morley* v. *Attenborough*[248] a harp was pawned and not redeemed, so it was sold by auction at the instance of the pawnbroker. It then transpired that the pawnor had

242. *Packer* v. *Gillies* (1806) 2 Camp. 336 n.    243. (1879) 5 Ex. D. 37.
244. See also *Leicester & Co.* v. *Cherryman* [1907] 2 K.B. 101.
245. (1900) 82 L.T. 721.    246. See p. 155, *ante*.
247. *Williams* v. *Barton* (1825) 3 Bing. 139; *Kingsford* v. *Merry* (1856) 1 H. & N. 503.
See also *Higgons* v. *Burton* (1857) 26 L.J. Ex. 342.
248. (1849) 3 Ex. 500.

hired the harp, and the owner recovered it from the purchaser. It was held that the purchaser had no action for breach of contract against the pawnbroker. There was no implied warranty of title: the vendor had only sold what he had, i.e., rights under an irredeemable pledge, because it had been made clear at the auction that the goods for sale were irredeemable pledges. It was thought that the purchaser might recover the purchase price from the pawnbroker as on a consideration that had totally failed in an appropriate case, but that had not been argued in this one.

If the pledgee comes to know that the pledge was wrongful, he is entitled to refuse redemption by the pawnor and return the article to the owner. In *Cheesman* v. *Exall*[249] the plaintiff, owner of plate, assigned it for value by bill of sale, but remained in possession of it.[250] Four years later, a judgment against the plaintiff for debt was being executed, at which time the plaintiff pledged the plate to the defendant. When the plaintiff tendered repayment to the defendant, the latter refused to part with the plate except to the purchaser under the bill of sale. It was held that the defendant was not liable to the plaintiff for conversion. Pollock C.B., the other barons agreeing, said[251] that, in the absence of any special contract:

> ... the person who pledges impliedly undertakes that the property pledged is his own; and if it turns out not to be so, the pledgee may restore it to the lawful owner.

**Property pledged by someone who has acquired it by fraud** A person who steals property gets no title. One who acquires it by false pretences gets a title voidable by the victim of the fraud. If that title is passed on, before being rescinded, to a bona fide purchaser for value without notice of the defect in the title, the purchaser takes free from the right to avoid the title. A pledgee is a purchaser for value for this purpose. In *Whitehorn Bros.* v. *Davison*[252] the plaintiffs sold a pearl necklace on credit to a pearl dealer who had fraudulently misrepresented to them that he had a customer to buy it and that that customer normally got six months credit. The dealer pledged the necklace with the defendant as security for a loan then made and for money already owing. The dealer having absconded, the plaintiffs sued the defendant for return of the neck-

---

249. (1851) 6 Ex. 341.
250. As to a pledge by a vendor in possession nowadays, see pp. 166–7, *post.*
251. 6 Ex. 343.
252. [1911] 1 K.B. 463. See also *Attenborough* v. *London and St. Katharine's Dock Co.* (1878) 3 C.P.D. 450; *Phillips* v. *Brooks Ltd.* [1919] 2 K.B. 243; *London Jewellers Ltd.* v. *Attenborough* [1934] 2 K.B. 206.

lace or its value. The defendant succeeded because he took from a pledgor with a voidable title, without notice of the defect. The burden of proving notice or bad faith on the part of the pledgee was held to rest on the plaintiff.

**Property pledged by a hirer**   Pledge by a hirer of goods is the same as pledge by a thief.[253] Where the hirer is in possession under a hire-purchase agreement, as opposed to a mere agreement for hire, he can pass some rights but cannot give a pledgee a title of full effect against the owner. In *Helby* v. *Matthews*,[254] where a piano was pledged by such a hirer, the owners obtained judgment against the pledgee for return of it. The position, however, is not always as straightforward as that. In *Belsize Motor Supply Co.* v. *Cox*[255] the hirer of a taxicab on hire-purchase pledged it to the defendant, who believed the pledgor to be the owner. It was held to be a pledge of the pledgor's rights (even though the assignment was a breach of the hire-purchase agreement). The result was that when the owners sued the defendant for return of the cab or its value, he could either return the cab or, if he kept it, pay the sum unpaid under the hire-purchase agreement (not the full value of the cab).

**Pledge by a tenant for life**   In *Hoare* v. *Parker*[256] plate was pawned by the tenant for life of it. The pawnee had no notice of the settlement. It was held that, on the death of the pawnor, the remainderman could get the plate back from the pawnee without paying the debt.

**Pledge by executors or trustees**   One of several executors has full authority to deal with the estate, so can create a valid pledge. One of several trustees cannot act without the others. When administration of an estate is completed, the executors become trustees of any undistributed assets.[257] In *Attenborough & Son* v. *Solomon*[258] the residuary account of the executors had been passed in 1879. In 1892, one of the executors still had in his possession some silver plate, part of the residuary estate. He pawned it in that year, to raise money for his personal purposes, without the knowledge of his co-executor, the pawnbrokers having no reason to believe that the pawnor was not the absolute owner. In 1907, the pawnor died, and a new trustee of the residuary estate was appointed in his place. In 1908, the fact of the pawning was discovered by the trustees,

253. See *Morley* v. *Attenborough* (1849) 3 Ex. 500 (p. 163, *ante*); *Singer Manufacturing Co.* v. *Clark* (1879) 5 Ex. D. 37 (p. 163, *ante*); *Burrows* v. *Barnes* (1900) 82 L.T. 721.
254. [1895] A.C. 471.
255. [1914] 1 K.B. 244.
256. (1788) 2 T.R. 376.
257. See, further, Keeton and Sheridan, *Equity*, pp. 285–6.    258. [1913] A.C. 76.

who successfully sued the pawnbrokers for the return of the plate. The executors had been functus officio in 1879, so they had become trustees long before the pawning in 1892. Only the trustees acting together could part with any title, so the pawnbrokers got nothing.

**Pledge by a purchaser in possession** If someone has bought goods, but has not paid for them, for has not finished paying for them, the vendor has certain rights.[259] These are best protected by retaining possession. If the purchaser is allowed possession of the goods, or of documents of title to them, he can give a valid pledge of the goods, overriding any interest of the vendor, to a pledgee in good faith not having notice of any lien or other right of the original seller in respect of the goods.[260] The effect of the pledge is the same as if it had been made by a mercantile agent in possession of the goods or of documents of title relating to them.[261]

A person who has taken goods on sale or return is a purchaser in possession if there is no stipulation to the contrary.[262] In *Percy Edwards (Ltd.)* v. *Vaughan*[263] a necklace was delivered on sale or return, and pledged by the deliveree. It was held that the pledge was not valid because, by the agreement, property was to pass to the pledgor only if he paid cash by a specified date.

**Pledge by a vendor in possession** If a vendor has sold goods but has possession of those goods or of documents of title relating to them, delivery or transfer of those goods or documents of title[264] by the vendor or his mercantile agent[261] under a sale, pledge or other disposition, or agreement for a sale, pledge or other disposition, to a person receiving them in good faith and without notice of the prior sale, is as effective as if the vendor had been expressly authorised by the owner to make the disposition.[265] If the vendor has sold the goods to someone who lets them back to the vendor on hire-purchase, the vendor can make a good pledge. If the vendor remains in possession, it does not matter, for this purpose, in what

259. As to an unpaid vendor's rights, see pp. 225–8, *post*.
260. Factors Act 1889, s. 9; Sale of Goods Act 1893, s. 25(2). The sections apply to a sale, pledge or other disposition by the purchaser. They do not apply to a buyer under a conditional sale agreement: Hire Purchase Act 1965, s. 54 (England and Wales); Hire-Purchase (Scotland) Act 1965, s. 50; Hire Purchase Act (Northern Ireland) 1966, s. 54. A conditional sale is one of payment by instalments, the property to remain in the buyer until such conditions as to payment of instalments or otherwise as may be specified in the agreement are fulfilled (s. 1(1)).
261. As to pledges by mercantile agents, see pp. 168–72, *post*.
262. As to valid pledges in such cases, see pp. 167–8, *post*.
263. (1910) 26 T.L.R. 545.
264. As to documents of title in other cases, see pp. 152–5, *ante*.
265. Factors Act 1889, s. 8; Sale of Goods Act 1893, s. 25(1).

capacity he so remains. He may be a bailee from the purchaser, but he is still a vendor in possession.[266] In *City Fur Manufacturing Co. Ltd. v. Fureenbond (Brokers) London Ltd.*[267] it was held that the vendor was in possession of goods, for the purpose of making a valid pledge of them, if someone else (not the purchaser or the pledgee) was holding them to his order. Here, the goods were furs in a warehouse belonging to the person who had sold them to the vendor.

**Pledge of goods taken on approval or on sale or return**

Where there is a contract for the sale of specific or ascertained goods, the property in them is transferred to the buyer at such time as the parties to the contract intend it to be transferred.[268] If the purchaser takes goods on approval, what is generally meant is that they are delivered to the purchaser on the understanding that he will have a reasonable time to try them out and that, at the end of that time, he will either return them or keep and pay for them. If a purchaser (commonly a retail trader) takes goods on sale or return, what is generally meant is that the goods are delivered to the purchaser on the understanding that he will either sell and pay for them or return them to the vendor. In either case, if the purchaser pledges the goods before paying for them, the question whether the pledge is binding on the vendor (so that he is an unsecured creditor of the purchaser for the price) or not (so that he can recover the goods from the pledgee without redeeming the pledge) depends on whether the property in the goods has (i) passed to the purchaser before or at the moment when he makes the pledge, or (ii) remained in the vendor. That, in turn, depends on the intention of the parties to the sale.[268] If they have not made their intention clear, help is to be derived from the Sale of Goods Act 1893, section 18, which provides:

> Unless a contrary intention appears, the following are rules for ascertaining the intention of the parties as to the time at which the property in the goods is to pass to the buyer . . .

> Rule 4. When goods are delivered to the buyer on approval or 'on sale or return' or other similar terms the property therein passes to the buyer:

> (*a*) When he signifies his approval or acceptance to the seller or does any act adopting the transaction:

> (*b*) If he does not signify his approval or acceptance to the seller but retains the goods without giving notice of rejection,

---

266. *Worcester Works Finance Ltd.* v. *Cooden Engineering Co. Ltd.* [1972] 1 Q.B. 210.
267. [1937] 1 All E.R. 799.     268. Sale of Goods Act 1893, s. 17(1).

then, if a time has been fixed for the return of the goods, on the expiration of that time, and, if no time has been fixed, on the expiration of a reasonable time. What is a reasonable time is a question of fact.

In Scotland, in *Brown* v. *Marr*,[269] a jeweller obtained watches and jewellery on sale or return and promptly pawned them. It was held that the pawnbrokers got valid pledges, binding on the pledger's vendor, because the jeweller had become the owner of the goods: he adopted the sale and gave up his right to return the goods when he dealt with them by pawning them. Later cases in England and Wales came to the same conclusion.[270]

In *Weiner* v. *Smith*[271] the contract of sale on sale or return, once again of jewellery, provided that the property in the goods was not to pass to the purchaser until he paid cash or the vendor agreed to give him credit. Without paying cash or obtaining credit, the purchaser parted with the jewels. He handed them for sale to someone else, who represented that he had a customer for them; but this person had no customer and did not sell the jewellery, but pledged it. It was held that the pledge was invalid as against the original vendor, who could therefore recover the goods from the pledgee. Rule 4 in section 18 of the Sale of Goods Act 1893 had been excluded by a contrary intention.

**Pledge of goods by an agent employed to sell or buy them**
If the owner of goods employs an agent to sell them, and the agent pledges them instead, for a personal loan, the question whether the pledge is binding on the principal (so as to leave him only with redress against his agent) or not (so that he can recover the goods from the pledgee without redeeming the pledge) depends on whether the agent is a mercantile agent acting in the ordinary course of business.

Mercantile agents are governed by the Factors Act 1889, applicable throughout the United Kingdom, having been extended to Scotland by the Factors (Scotland) Act 1890, section 1. The expression 'mercantile agent' is defined in section 1(1) of the Act of 1889 as meaning:

> . . . a mercantile agent having in the customary course of his business as such agent authority either to sell goods, or to consign

269. (1880) 7 R. 427. See also *Bryce* v. *Ehrmann* (1904) 7 F. 5.
270. *Kirkham* v. *Attenborough* [1897] 1 Q.B. 201; *London Jewellers Ltd.* v. *Attenborough* [1934] 2 K.B. 206.
271. [1906] 2 K.B. 574. See also *Percy Edwards (Ltd.)* v. *Vaughan* (1910) 26 T.L.R. 545 (p. 166, *ante*).

goods for the purpose of sale, or to buy goods, or to raise money on the security of goods . . .

By section 2(1):

> Where a mercantile agent is, with the consent of the owner,[272] in possession[273] of goods or of the documents of title[274] to goods, any sale, pledge, or other disposition of goods, made by him when acting in the ordinary course of business of a mercantile agent, shall . . . be as valid as if he were expressly authorised by the owner of the goods to make the same; provided that the person taking under the disposition acts in good faith, and has not at the time of the disposition notice that the person making the disposition has not authority to make the same.

It follows from this section that, if the elements set out in it are present, a pledge of his principal's property by an agent, to secure a personal loan to the agent, is binding on the principal, even though not authorised,[275] even if expressly prohibited by the principal, whether or not the pledgee knows he is dealing with an agent.[276] But nothing in the Factors Act makes the transaction rightful as between principal and agent.[277] The two problems which most frequently arise are: (*a*) When is an agent a mercantile agent? (*b*) What is the ordinary course of business?

One example of a mercantile agent is a commercial traveller. In *Weiner* v. *Harris*[278] a manufacturing jeweller gave goods to a commercial traveller 'on sale or return,' the traveller to be remunerated by getting half the profits on sales. The traveller pledged goods with a moneylender, and that pledge was held binding on the manufacturer. The words 'on sale or return' did not reflect the true position of a commercial traveller, employed as an agent only for sale of the goods, therefore he was a commercial agent. It was never envisaged (as the provision for remuneration helped to show) that the agent could become the purchaser, and you cannot change the nature of a transaction by what you call it. Consequently, the

272. If a mercantile agent is in possession of goods, the consent of the owner is presumed until the contrary is proved: s. 2(4). If there was consent at first, but it has come to an end, the sale, pledge or other disposition is as valid as if the consent had continued, if the pledgee (etc.) took without notice that the consent had ended: s. 2(2).
273. A person is deemed to be in possession of goods or documents of title if they are in his custody or held by any person subject to his control or for him or on his behalf: s. 1(2)
274. These include a bill of lading, dock warrant, warehouse-keeper's certificate, warrant or order for delivery of goods and any other document used in the ordinary course of business as proof of possession or control of goods or authorising the possessor of the document to transfer or receive goods: s. 1(4). See also s. 2(3).
275. See *Midwood* v. *Kelly* (1902) 36 I.L.T.R. 58.
276. *Oppenheimer* v. *Attenborough & Son* [1908] 1 K.B. 221, p. 171, *post*.
277. Factors Act 1889, s. 12.     278. [1910] 1 K.B. 285.

manufacturer, as owner, could redeem. Had the traveller been a buyer on sale or return, the pledge would have been invalid, and the manufacturer would have been able to recover the goods without redeeming, because the agreement made it clear that no property in the goods was to pass until they were paid for.[279] The crucial factor is that the person in possession of the goods should have power, as agent for the owner, to sell them. In *Mehta* v. *Sutton*[280] a pledge of pearls was held invalid, because the agent who made it had no authority to sell the pearls, but only to introduce prospective purchasers to his principal. Hence, he was not a mercantile agent within the Factors Act.

*Lloyds Bank Ltd.* v. *Bank of America National Trust and Savings Assoc.*[281] concerned goods pledged to a bank by a company by transfer of the bills of lading coupled with an express power to the bank to deal with the goods as if they were the absolute owners. The bank gave the company the bills of lading back, against a trust receipt,[282] so that the company could sell the goods and pay the bank off out of the proceeds. The company did not sell the goods, but fraudulently pledged them to a second bank. It was held that the second bank got a good title as against the first bank under the Factors Act. If the company and the first bank were co-owners of the goods, there was nothing in the Act to stop one co-owner being the mercantile agent of both of them. Alternatively, the bank were the owners and the company were their mercantile agents.

A warehouseman is not a mercantile agent. In *Cole* v. *North Western Bank*[283] Edwin Slee had two businesses: warehouseman and woolbroker. Wool was deposited in his warehouse by the plaintiff to await the latter's instructions as to its disposal. Slee purported to pledge or mortgage the wool to the bank for £7,000 and absconded It was held that the pledge or mortgage was invalid because Slee was not an agent in possession of goods for the purposes of the Factors Act 1842, section 1, and the same reasoning would lead to the conclusion that he would not be a mercantile agent under the Act of 1889. Similarly, a hirer of a lorry is not in possession of it as the mercantile agent of the owner, even if the hirer is a dealer in second-hand lorries.[284] In the case of a servant who has the goods of his employer, he would not usually be a mercantile agent.[285] If

279. As to pledges of goods held on sale or return, see pp. 167–8, *ante*.
280. (1913) 109 L.T. 529.     281. [1938] 2 K.B. 147.
282. As to this type of transaction, see pp. 154–5, *ante*.     283. (1875) L.R. 10 C.P. 354.
284. *Staffs Motor Guarantee Ltd.* v. *British Wagon Co. Ltd.* [1934] 2 K.B. 305.
285. See *Lamb* v. *Attenborough* (1862) 1 B. & S. 831.

the servant were employed as a salesman, he might be a mercantile agent, but a question would then arise as to whether the employer or the servant was in possession of the goods, which is a question of fact.

What is the ordinary course of business of a mercantile agent was considered in *Oppenheimer* v. *Attenborough & Son*.[286] There, a diamond merchant entrusted diamonds to a diamond broker to sell them to a named merchant. The broker pledged them to the defendants, who did not know that the pledgor was not the owner, and the pledge was held valid. A custom in the trade that agents employed to sell diamonds had no authority to pledge them did not affect the operation of the Factors Act (any more than the principal's express prohibition of pledging would affect it). Buckley L.J. said[287] that the phrase 'when acting in the ordinary course of business of a mercantile agent':

> means, 'acting in such a way as a mercantile agent acting in the ordinary course of business of a mercantile agent would act'; that is to say, within business hours, at a proper place of business, and in other respects in the ordinary way in which a mercantile agent would act, so that there is nothing to lead the pledgee to suppose that anything wrong is being done, or to give him notice that the disposition is one which the mercantile agent had no authority to make.

In *De Gorter* v. *George Attenborough and Son*[288] a diamond broker employed to sell diamonds got a friend to pawn them with the defendant pawnbrokers. This pawn was held invalid, and the owners recovered the diamonds from the defendants, because it is not in the ordinary course of business to send a friend. The ordinary course is for the mercantile agent to go himself or to send his clerk. In *Waddington and Sons* v. *Neale and Sons*[289] a mercantile agent was employed to sell pianos for cash or on hire purchase. He actually sent a piano to some auctioneers, and got an advance from them against the proceeds of sale. That arrangement was held not to be a pledge of the piano anyway, but it was also held that, in sending the piano for sale by auction, the agent had not been acting in the ordinary course of business of a mercantile agent.

Section 2(1) of the Factors Act 1889 relates to a mercantile agent in possession of documents of title as well as to an agent in possession

---

286. [1908] 1 K.B. 221. See also *Janesich* v. *George Attenborough and Son* (1910) 102 L.T. 605.
287. [1908] 1 K.B. 230-1.   288. (1904) 21 T.L.R. 19.
289. (1907) 96 L.T. 786.

of goods. By section 3, a pledge of the documents of title is deemed to be a pledge of the goods themselves. That last proposition applies as a general proposition of the law of the United Kingdom, but outside the Factors Act only a bill of lading is a document of title to goods. Section 1(4) of the Act contains a much wider definition of documents of title,[290] so as to include, for example a warehouse-keeper's certificate. It follows that goods can be pledged by a mercantile agent by pledging documents of a kind whose pledge by the owner would not operate to pledge the goods. In *Inglis* v. *Robertson & Baxter*[291] the owner, to secure a loan, deposited with the lender warrants from a warehouse-keeper bearing that whisky in the warehouse was held to the order of the owner. The lender did not intimate the facts to the warehouse-keeper, so it was held that the lender did not prevail, as to the whisky, over the owner's other unsecured creditors. Section 3 of the Factors Act does not apply to an owner. Had the warrants been deposited with the lender by a mercantile agent, the lender would have had a pledge of the whisky under the Act; had the warehouse-keeper been instructed to hold the whisky to the order of the lender, the latter would have had a pledge at common law.[292]

**Pledges and Priorities**   Normally no problems of ranking will arise as between a pledgee of goods and another creditor secured on the same goods because of the possession in the pledgee and the notoriety gained by registration in respect of other securities in goods. Occasionally, however, problems arise, usually out of either: (*a*) fraud on the part of the pledgor; or (*b*) the fact that the creditor claiming adversely to the pledgee has a security which, arising by operation of law and not by contract, is not of a registrable variety.

In *Meyerstein* v. *Barber*[293] there were two pledges of the same cotton, which was made possible by the existence (as is usual) of three copies of the bill of lading. Two copies were handed to the first pledgee and the third copy was used for the second pledge, made to a lender without notice of the first pledge. When the second pledgee heard of the existence of the earlier pledge, he sold the cotton. It was held that the first pledgee could recover the proceeds of sale as money received to his use or damages for conversion. As he had already parted with possession of the goods, the pledgor could not pass it to the second pledgee. After the first pledge,

290. See n. p. 169, footnote 274, *ante*.      291. [1898] A.C. 616.
292. See p. 150, *ante*.      293. (1866) L.R. 3 C.P. 38 and 661.

the pledgor could only deal with what he had, viz. a right to redeem the cotton, which would have required a bill of sale.

A first pledgee will only be postponed to a second when the first has contributed, intentionally or carelessly, to the pledgor's capacity to mislead the second pledgee into thinking there is no prior incumbrance on the goods. In *Babcock* v. *Lawson*[294] there was a pledge of flour in a warehouse. The pledgors made a second pledge by concealing the first. They pretended to the first pledgees that the second ones had bought the flour and, undertaking to pay the first pledgees the proceeds of sale, they thus obtained a delivery order from the first pledgees. Armed with the delivery order, the second pledgees obtained possession of the flour and, not having been repaid by the pledgors, sold it. It was held that the second pledgees could keep the proceeds of sale. The first pledgees lost their pledge when they revested the whole property in the pledgors for sale. The first pledgees could, as against the pledgor, have revoked the delivery order on the ground of fraud, but they could not do that as against the second pledgees because the latter were bona fide purchasers for value without notice of the fraud.[295]

Sometimes there is a contest between a pledgee and a vendor claiming a right of stopping goods in transit. The unpaid vendor who has consigned goods by a carrier to a purchaser has a right, if the buyer becomes insolvent, to retake the goods, at any time before they are delivered to the consignee, or to notify the carrier to return them to him or to hold them to his order.[296] It may be that goods have been shipped, that they have been pledged by pledge of the bill of lading, and that the vendor then tries to exercise his right of stoppage in transitu. In such a case, the pledgee takes priority over the vendor.[297] But the vendor's right of stoppage in transitu is not destroyed by the pledge of the bill of lading. It take effect in equity so as to entitle the vendor to any balance of the proceeds of sale there may be, if the pledgee sells the goods, after the amount secured by the pledge has been paid off. The pledgee is not allowed to use that surplus to pay himself unsecured debts due from the consignee of the goods.[298]

294. (1879) 4 Q.B.D. 394; (1880) 5 Q.B.D. 284.
295. As to the second pledgee gaining priority because the first pledgee constitutes the pledgor his mercantile agent, see pp. 154–5, 168–72, *ante*. As to a pledgee losing his pledge, as against the pledgor's unsecured creditors, by parting with the goods or the bill of lading, see pp. 154–5, *ante*.
296. As to the details of the right of stoppage in transitu, see pp. 226–7, *post*.
297. *Re Westzinthus* (1833) 5 B. & Ad. 817; Sale of Goods Act 1893, s. 47.
298. *Spalding* v. *Ruding* (1846) 15 L.J. Ch. 374; *Kemp* v. *Falk* (1882) 7 App. Cas. 573.

By the Factors Act 1889, section 10, where a document of title[299] is transferred to a person as buyer or owner of the goods, and he transfers it to a person who takes it in good faith and for valuable consideration, the last transfer has the same effect for defeating a vendor's lien[300] or right of stoppage in transitu as a transfer of a bill of lading has for defeating a right of stoppage in transitu. By the Factors (Scotland) Act 1890, section 1, lien means and includes a right of retention, and vendor's lien means and includes any right of retention, competent to the original owner or vendor.

---

299. As to the meaning of this expression in the Act, see p. 169, footnote 274, *ante*.
300. As to a vendor's lien, see pp. 225–6, *post*.

# securities over and connected with ships

Ships differ from most other chattels (corporeal moveable property) in a number of ways which, being significant commercially, have given rise to special rules of law. On the whole, they are bigger, more valuable and more mobile than most other chattels. They are frequently employed away from their home country, and their employment is often hazardous in terms of both the perils of the sea and the commercial outcome of the venture in which they are engaged. They have been in use for longer than any other kind of vehicle now employed for the carriage of goods or passengers, and the law relating to ships is of ancient origins, tending to vary only in points of detail from one country to another. Trains, lorries, buses and aircraft have not been assimilated legally to ships, though some of the legal issues to which their use gives rise are similar to those involving ships. For example, the bill of lading as a document which can be used to pass the title to goods which have been shipped, or to pledge them,[1] has no counterpart in documents relating to goods which have been sent by air, rail or road: these latter documents evidence merely possession or a right to take delivery; they become an instrument of passing property, e.g., to a pledgee, only in the hands of a mercantile agent.[2]

Unlike other chattels, ships cannot be transferred by delivery. Also unlike other chattels, title to ships is registered. Ships are also divisible, so far as title is concerned, into shares. There are sixty-four shares in a ship, and a person can be registered as owner of

1. See pp. 152–5, *ante*.    2. See pp. 168–72, *ante*.

any number of sixty-fourths from one to the whole ship. Transfer of a ship or a share in it is by bill of sale perfected by altering the register.

The normal method of raising money to pay for a ship, or to raise working capital to use the ship, is to mortgage the ship or the shares in it owned by the mortgagor.[3] In addition, the following kinds of security may be created by agreement of the parties to a shipping transaction:

(a) mortgage of the freight;[4]

(b) mortgage of the cargo;[5]

(c) hypothecation of the ship and freight (bottomry) and cargo (respondentia) to raise money to meet emergencies in the course of a voyage.

Apart from the agreement of the parties, security over a ship or its associated assets may come into existence in the form of either: (i) a possessory lien;[6] or (ii) a maritime lien.[7]

## Mortgages of Ships

Ships and shares in ships may be the subject of a legal mortgage (anywhere in the United Kingdom) or of an equitable mortgage (in England and Wales and Northern Ireland). Other chattels can, in general, only be mortgaged by bill of sale registered under the Bills of Sale Acts[8] (in England, Wales and Northern Ireland) or by assignation in security or ex facie absolute assignation, with delivery of possession (in Scotland).[9] The Bills of Sale Acts expressly do not apply to ships or vessels. This has led to one interesting lacuna. The idea of excluding mortgages of ships and vessels from the necessity of registration under the Bills of Sale Acts was that such mortgages (unless equitable) were registrable in the register of ships. But not all vessels are registered. In *Gapp* v. *Bond*[10] there was a mortgage of a dumb barge propelled by oars, used for carrying goods on the River Thames. It was held that the barge was a vessel, so that by virtue of section 4 of the Bills of Sale Act 1878 the mortgage was not registrable as a bill of sale, although the barge was not a registered vessel so that the mortgage could not be registered anywhere.

Ships in course of construction, not yet registered, are presumably

3. See below.    4. See pp. 187–8, *post*.
5. See p. 187, *post*.    6. See pp. 198–9, *post*.
7. See pp. 194–8, *post*.
8. See pp. 114–16, *ante*. As to mortgages of aircraft, see p. 118, *ante*.
9. See pp. 121–5, *ante*.    10. (1887) 19 Q.B.D. 200.

treated like other chattels. In *Ex parte Hodgkin*[11] a shipbuilder with an unfinished ship lodged the builder's certificate with a bank as security for a loan. That was held to be a valid equitable mortgage of the nascent ship. The bank had taken possession of it, so the transaction might properly have been regarded as one of pledge. There seems no reason in law why one should not pledge a finished and registered ship, but the owner is unlikely to try that as it would preclude him from using the vessel to earn the money to pay off the loan. But ships are to be found as other types of security than mortgages or securities peculiar to ships. A shipping company which gives a floating charge over its whole undertaking will have subjected its ships to the charge.

**Form of Legal Mortgage**  The Merchant Shipping Act 1894 applies throughout the United Kingdom. By section 31(1), a ship or a share in a ship may be mortgaged[12] and, on production of the instrument of mortgage, the registrar of the ship's port of registration must record the mortgage in the register book. Subsection (2) requires the registrar to record successive mortgages in the order in which the instruments are produced to him for that purpose. When a mortgage is paid off, it is discharged by cancellation of the entry in the register.[13]

Section 34 provides that the mortgagee is not to be treated as the owner of the ship or share except so far as is necessary for the purpose of making the property effective security.[14]

**Equitable Mortgages in England and Wales and Northern Ireland**  The general principles of equity apply to ships in much the same way as they apply to land. Hence, any transaction intended to make the ship stand as security by way of mortgage, but not constituted by registered legal mortgage, will take effect as an equitable mortgage.[15] However, legislation has diminished the efficacy of equitable mortgages of ships, as against third parties, when compared with the efficacy of equitable mortgages of land. According to the principles of equity,[16] a person taking a legal mort-

---

11. (1875) L.R. 20 Eq. 746.    12. The form is form B in sch. 1.
13. Section 32. See also *Bell* v. *Blyth* (1868) L.R. 4 Ch. App. 136; *The Rose* (1873) L.R. 4 A. & E. 6.
14. As to the rights, remedies and liabilities of the mortgagee, see pp. 180–4, *post.*
15. Cf. *Jackson* v. *Vernon* (1789) 1 H. Bl. 114; *Gardner* v. *Cazenove* (1856) 1 H. & N. 423; *Ward* v. *Beck* (1863) 13 C.B.N.S. 668.
16. See pp. 84–6, *ante.*

gage will take it subject to any prior equitable interest of which he has notice at the time of the grant of the legal mortgage. In relation to mortgages of land, to the extent to which reliance on notice has been replaced by reliance on registration, equitable mortgages have become registrable. The opposite has happened with regard to ships. Equitable mortgages cannot be registered; and a registered owner or mortgagee takes free from equitable interests even if he has notice of them.

That effect is achieved by the Merchant Shipping Act 1894, sections 56 and 57, which provide:

56. No notice of any trust, express, implied, or constructive, shall be entered in the register book or be receivable by the registrar, and, subject to any rights and powers appearing by the register book to be vested in any other person, the registered owner of a ship or of a share therein shall have power absolutely to dispose in any manner in this Act provided of the ship or share, and to give effectual receipts for any money paid or advanced by way of consideration.

57. The expression 'beneficial interest' where used in this part of this Act, includes interests arising under contract and other equitable interests; and the intention of this Act is, that without prejudice to the provisions of this Act for preventing notice of trusts from being entered in the register book or received by the registrar, and without prejudice to the powers of disposition and of giving receipts conferred by this Act on registered owners and mortgagees, and without prejudice to the provisions of this Act relating to the exclusion of unqualified persons from the ownership of British ships, interests arising under contracts or other equitable interests may be enforced by or against owners and mortgagees of ships in respect of their interest therein in the same manner as in respect of any other personal property.

The upshot of that legislation is that an equitable mortgage of a ship or share, made by the registered owner, constitutes no security for the lender as against anyone to whom the registered owner, earlier or later, grants a legal, registered mortgage, or against anyone who later becomes the registered owner. For that reason it was held in *Black* v. *Williams*,[17] decided on earlier similar legislation, that a registered mortgagee prevailed over a prior floating charge even though he had notice of it. Similarly, a legal mortgagee, who grants an equitable sub-mortgage, gives the sub-mortgagee no protection

17. [1895] 1 Ch. 408.

against anyone who becomes registered as a transferee of the mortgage, or of the ship if the mortgagee exercises his power of sale.

On the other hand, the equitable mortgage is enforceable against the mortgagor, which will include his trustee in bankruptcy, so that the equitable mortgagee is by no means reduced to the status of an unsecured creditor. Moreover, the equitable mortgage will usually be efficacious as against any third party whose interest is also equitable. Finally, if the equitable mortgagee gets wind that the mortgagor is selling to someone whose ownership will be registered, though the purchaser will take free from the equitable interest, the equitable mortgagee will be able to claim the proceeds of sale to the extent of what is due to him on his mortgage.

What is a mortgage and what is a transfer depends on the intention of the parties and not on the form of the transaction. Applying that principle, an apparent co-owner has been held to be a mortgagee.[18]

In the remainder of this section on mortgages of ships, the mortgage will be assumed to be a registered mortgage (except for express references to equitable mortgages in relation to priorities[19]).

**Property Comprised in a Mortgage**    If a ship is mortgaged, there may be a question, should the security come to be enforced, as to the rights of the mortgagee over fittings, such as machinery or furniture, or over other things on the ship, such as moveable equipment or stores.

The first resort for resolving such a question is to the terms of the mortgage instrument, which may contain express provision. In *The Humourous*[20] the mortgage was of a fishing vessel 'and her appurtenances.' That was held to pass nets on board at the time when the mortgagee took possession, in so far as they were nets appropriated to that ship at the time of the mortgage or replacements for nets so appropriated, but not to pass any other nets that happened to be on board.

Secondly, without express provision, a mortgage of a ship will pass all property necessary for the operation of the vessel. In *Coltman* v. *Chamberlain*[21] the mortgage was also of a fishing vessel, but it made no reference to appurtenances. That mortgage was held to give the mortgagee rights, when he took possession, over all articles necessary to navigation or to fishing which were on board at the time of the

18. *The Innisfallen* (1866) L.R. 1 A. & E. 72.
19. As to priorities, see pp. 184–7, *post*.
20. [1933] P. 109.    21. (1890) 25 Q.B.D. 328.

mortgage or were brought on later in substitution for articles there at the date of the mortgage.

The security of the mortgagee will also include the right to enforce payment by claiming income earned by the ship.[22]

**Rights of Possession and Management**   It is unusual for any mortgagee to take possession of the mortgaged property unless he needs to enforce his security. However, he usually has a right to take possession if he wishes. In the case of a ship, the mortgagee has no general right to possession.[23] He can take it only if: (*a*) the mortgagor has defaulted in payments or in some other respect under the mortgage; or (*b*) if the mortgagor is so managing the ship as to build up liabilities on her.[24] The rights of a mortgagee of a majority of the shares in a ship are the same as those of a mortgagee of the whole ship,[25] but a mortgagee of half the shares or less cannot take possession of her.

The general right to manage the ship and to receive the income of her, and the general liability for outgoings on her, is vested in the mortgagor if he is in possession or in the mortgagee if the latter should be in possession.[26]

**Mortgagee not in possession**   If the mortgagor is in possession, he has the general right of management. He can use the vessel himself or enter into charterparties[27] in respect of her.

The mortgagee cannot object to a charterparty, and oust the charterer by taking possession of the ship, so long as the mortgagor's management of her is not prejudicial to the mortgagee's security.[28] In *The Fanchon*[29] it was held that a charterparty granted by a mortgagor in possession did not impair the mortgagee's security merely because it would result in the ship going out of the jurisdiction, thus putting complications in the way of enforcing the security. But in the Scottish case of *Laming & Co.* v. *Seater*[30] a mortgagee was held to be entitled (by interdict if necessary) to prevent a charterer

22. As to when the mortgagee can make such a claim, see pp. 181–2, *post.*
23. See the Merchant Shipping Act 1894, s. 34, p. 177, *ante.*
24. *The Manor* [1907] P. 339.    25. *Japp* v. *Campbell* (1887) 57 L.J.Q.B. 79.
26. *Keith* v. *Burrows* (1877) 2 App. Cas. 636.
27. A charterparty is a written contract by which the owner of a ship undertakes carriage of goods in her, or hires out the whole ship for a voyage or for a period to a merchant who will carry his own goods in her or engage in contracts for the carriage of goods or passengers for that voyage or period.
28. *Collins* v. *Lamport* (1864) 4 De G.J. & S. 500; *The Maxima* (1878) 39 L.T. 112; *Cory, Bros. & Co.* v. *Stewart* (1886) 2 T.L.R. 508; *The Blanche* (1887) 58 L.T. 592.
29. (1880) 5 P.D. 173.    30. (1889) 16 R. 828.

taking the ship to sea uninsured, the obligation to insure her being on the owner. Similarly, the mortgagee made a successful objection to charterparties in *Law Guarantee and Trust Soc.* v. *Russian Bank for Foreign Trade.*[31] They were for the carriage of coals from Barry to Vladivostock during the war between Russia and Japan. The mortgagee was successful despite the fact that the ships in question had already reached Asian ports at the time of the action (there had been concealment by fraud in getting the vessels away).

A mortgagee has a right to freight.[32] Generally, if the mortgagor is in possession and has made a charterparty the mortgagee does not become entitled to the freight unless he takes possession of the ship.[33] But it seems that, if the mortgagor defaults, the mortgagee, without taking possession, can intercept the freight by directing the charterer to pay it direct to him.[34] On the other hand, the mortgagee cannot recover from the mortgagor freight he has allowed the mortgagor to receive.[34] A mortgagee's right to freight takes preference over a prior assignment of the freight by the owner, if the mortgagee took his mortgage without notice of the assignment.[34]

A mortgagee does not incur liabilities on the ship when he is not in possession. He is not, for example, liable to pay for goods, such as equipment for the vessel, supplied on credit to a mortgagor in possession,[35] or for necessaries supplied, unless the master ordered them as the mortgagee's agent,[36] or for repairs.[37] On the other hand, the mortgagor may so manage the ship as to create liens or bottomry bonds which will have priority as incumbrances over the mortgage.[38]

**Mortgagee in possession** When a mortgagee enters into possession of a ship, he becomes entitled to receive freight in the course of being earned.[39] His entitlement extends also to freight already earned but which does not become payable by the charterer or the consignee of goods until after the taking of possession.[40] The

31. [1905] 1 K.B. 815.
32. Freight is payment due to the owner of a ship under a charterparty for carrying goods or as hire for the whole ship.
33. As to freight earned before he takes possession, see below.
34. See *Wilson* v. *Wilson* (1872) L.R. 14 Eq. 32.
35. *Baker* v. *Buckle* (1822) 7 Moo. C.P. 349.
36. *Twentyman* v. *Hart* (1816) 1 Stark. 366.
37. *Jackson* v. *Vernon* (1789) 1 H. Bl. 114; *Briggs* v. *Wilkinson* (1827) 7 B. & C. 30; *The Harriet* (1868) 18 L.T. 804. Ireland: *Harries* v. *Handy* (1851) 3 Ir. Jur. 290. Scotland: *Tyne Dock Engineering Co. Ltd.* v. *Royal Bank of Scotland Ltd.* 1974 S.L.T. 57.
38. As to priorities between mortgagees and lienees, see pp. 185-6, *post*; as to bottomry bonds, see pp. 186-7, *post*.
39. See *Kerswill* v. *Bishop* (1832) 2 C. & J. 529; *Keith* v. *Burrows* (1877) 2 App. Cas. 636; *The Fairport* (1884) 10 P.D. 13.
40. *Rusden* v. *Pope* (1868) L.R. 3 Ex. 269; *Shillito* v. *Biggart* [1903] 1 K.B. 683.

mortgagee may then claim the full amount of freight from charterers without allowing them to deduct anything for advances they had made to the mortgagor in possession for ship's disbursements.[41] The mortgagee's right to receive freight earned but due later prevails over the title of an express assignee of the freight where the mortgagor in possession made the assignment after the mortgage but before the mortgagee took possession.[42] It also prevails over the ship's husband's[43] claim on freight for disbursements.[44] The ship's husband's lien is possessory, i.e., a right to retain freight he has received, not a right to claim freight.

Charterparties made by a mortgagor in possession, in so far as they are binding on the mortgagee when made, remain binding on him after he goes into possession.[45] The question whether he would be bound by a charterparty, whether prejudicial to his security or not, if it was entered into by the owner before creating the mortgage and the mortgagee had notice of it when taking the mortgage, has never been authoritatively answered.[46]

The position of a mortgagee in possession in relation to liability for the outgoings of the ship is similar to that of an owner in possession. That is to say, he is liable for what is done as agent of himself. In the Scottish case of *Havilland, Routh & Co.* v. *Thomson*[47] it was held that a mortgagee in possession was liable in respect of advances and disbursements made on account of the ship in a foreign port, even if the mortgagee's attorney, having received the advances, did not in fact apply them for the service of the ship. On the other hand, the mortgagee is not liable to pay for necessaries supplied to the ship on credit if the master did not order them as his agent.[48]

A mortgagee in possession of a ship, like a mortgagee in possession of land,[49] is bound to account to the mortgagor for his use of her. In *Marriott* v. *Anchor Reversionary Co.*[50] mortgagees who employed the ship in a hazardous and speculative manner, so as to depreciate her value, ending up by selling her for a small sum, were held liable

41. *Tanner* v. *Phillips* (1872) 42 L.J. Ch. 125.
42. *Brown* v. *Tanner* (1868) L.R. 3 Ch. App. 597. Ireland: *Dobbyn* v. *Comerford* (1860) 10 Ir. Ch. Rep. 327.
43. A ship's husband is a general agent of the owners as to the employment of the vessel, and to see that she is well repaired, equipped, stocked and manned.
44. *Beynon & Co.* v. *Godden & Son* (1878) 3 Ex. D. 263.
45. *The Heather Bell* [1901] P. 272.
46. A purchaser with notice of a charterparty is not bound by it: *Port Line Ltd.* v. *Ben Line Steamers Ltd.* [1958] 2 Q.B. 146.
47. (1864) 3 M. 313. See also *The Ripon City* [1898] P. 78.
48. *The Troubadour* (1866) L.R. 1 A. & E. 302; *The Two Ellens* (1871) L.R. 3 A. & E. 345.
49. See pp. 58–9, *ante.*      50. (1861) 3 De G. F. & J. 177.

to account to the mortgagor for the value of the ship and fittings as they had been at the time the mortgagees took possession.

**Redemption** To redeem, as with a mortgage of any other property, the mortgagor of a ship must pay principal, interest and costs due to the mortgagee. If the mortgagor redeems when the mortgagee has started to sell the ship, he must pay the mortgagee his costs so far incurred in the sale.[51]

There seems little doubt that the equitable rule against clogs on the equity of redemption[52] applies to mortgages of ships, but in those cases[53] in which it has been considered there has been held to be no clog.

**Remedies of the Mortgagee** Apart from taking possession of the ship,[54] the main power of the mortgagee to realise his security is to sell her. While foreclosure may be technically possible, attempts to foreclose do not occur in practice. If he wishes to receive freight without taking possession, the mortgagee may notify persons from whom freight is to become due[55] or appoint or procure appointment by the court of a receiver.[56]

**Sale** By the Merchant Shipping Act 1894, section 35,[57] a first or only registered mortgagee has power to sell the mortgaged ship or share. A second or subsequent mortgagee also has that power, but must not sell without either the concurrence of all prior mortgagees or an order of the court.

If the mortgagor tenders the amount due and tries to redeem, but the mortgagee nevertheless sells the ship, the mortgagee is liable in damages to the mortgagor, the amount of the damages being the difference between the value of the ship at the time of the sale and the amount of the mortgage debt.[58] In *Fletcher and Campbell* v. *City Marine Finance Ltd.*[59] that rule was applied where the person seeking to pay off the mortgage debt was not the mortgagor, but the beneficial owner of a yacht, for whom the mortgagor held her on trust.

It would seem that in a mortgagee's sale the purchaser will take the ship free from any charterparty, or other agreement as to the

---

51. *Wilkes* v. *Saunion* (1877) 7 Ch. D. 188.
52. See pp. 45–7, *ante*.
53. *The Benwell Tower* (1895) 72 L.T. 664; *Reeve* v. *Lisle* [1902] A.C. 461.
54. See pp. 180–3, *ante*.    55. See p. 181, *ante*.
56. *Burn* v. *Herlofson* (1887) 56 L.T. 722.
57. See also *Clydesdale Bank Ltd.* v. *Walker & Bain* 1926 S.C. 72.
58. *M'Larty* v. *Middleton* (1861) 4 L.T. 852.    59. [1968] 2 Lloyd's Rep. 520.

use of the ship, made by the mortgagor when in possession, whether he has notice of it or not. Otherwise, the mortgagee's power of sale would be restricted;[60] moreover, a purchaser from the mortgagor would not be bound.[61]

If there is any surplus after the mortgagee selling has paid himself off out of the proceeds of sale, he must account for it to the subsequent mortgagee,[62] if any, or to the mortgagor or his successor in title. In paying himself off, the mortgagee is entitled to the costs of his sale, but not to charge for his own trouble or time in the matter.[63]

Equitable principles apply to sales of mortgaged ships as they apply to sales of mortgaged land.[64] Moreover, if the mortgage of the ship is by deed, the statutory powers of the mortgagee set out in the Law of Property Act 1925 will be available in England and Wales.

**Priorities: Registered mortgages**  Two or more registered mortgages of the same ship or share rank for priority in the order in which they were registered, without regard to any question of notice (Merchant Shipping Act 1894, section 33).

**Foreign mortgages**  Equitable principles have been applied in the nineteenth century, though nowadays, with rapid international communications, there seems no reason to excuse failure to inspect a foreign register. In *Hooper* v. *Gumm*[65] the dispute involved an American ship, mortgaged in the United States. The mortgagees allowed the owners to take her to England for sale without disclosing the existence of the mortgage. It was held that, as the mortgagees had suppressed their mortgage, the purchaser (being without notice) took free from it.

**Further advances**  The question of when a prior mortgagee is allowed to tack fresh loans to his security, so as to make them repayable in priority to a subsequent mortgage made before the further advances, is governed by the same principles and authorities as those applicable to mortgages of land.[66]

**Registered and equitable mortgages**  There are no equitable mortgages in Scotland, though there could be a contest between the mortgagee of a ship and the holder of a debenture

60. *The Celtic King* [1894] P. 175.
61. *Port Line Ltd.* v. *Ben Line Steamers Ltd.* [1958] 2 Q.B. 146.
62. *Tanner* v. *Heard* (1857) 23 Beav. 555; *Banner* v. *Berridge* (1881) 18 Ch. D. 254.
63. *The Benwell Tower* (1895) 72 L.T. 664.
64. See pp. 73–6, *ante*.
65. (1867) L.R. 2 Ch. App. 282. See also *Mocatta* v. *Murgatroyd* (1717) 1 P. Wms. 393.
66. See pp. 32–6, *ante*; *The Benwell Tower* (1895) 72 L.T. 664.

secured by floating charge in any part of the United Kingdom.[67] In England and Wales and Northern Ireland, the relations between an equitable mortgagee and a registered mortgagee of a ship or share are concluded by sections 56 and 57 of the Merchant Shipping Act 1894.[68] The registered mortgagee will have priority over the equitable mortgagee, irrespective of notice.

Similarly, a purchaser from a registered owner takes free from an equitable mortgage, even if he has notice of it. Hence, it was held in *Barclay & Co. Ltd.* v. *Poole*,[69] the registered owner of shares in a ship could sell them and contract for the purchasers to apply the money without regard to an unregistered mortgage. The feature of that case is that the purchase-money was not to be paid to the selling mortgagor. If any of it is payable to him, the unregistered mortgagee is entitled to intercept it.

Paradoxically, the tabula in naufragio was invented for land. Aptly, it was applied as an equitable principle to ships. In *Liverpool Marine Credit Co.* v. *Wilson*[70] there was a first mortgage of a ship; followed by a second (equitable) mortgage of the freight; followed by a further (equitable) charge of the ship and freight to the first mortgagee. The first mortgagee went into possession of the ship, thus becoming entitled at law to the freight.[71] It was held that, if he had no notice of the second mortgage when he took the third mortgage, the first mortgagee was entitled to be paid everything due on his first and third securities before anything was paid to the intervening incumbrancer. This kind of tacking has been virtually abolished in England and Wales,[72] but in the more hazardous waters of Northern Ireland it remains possible.[73]

**Two or more equitable mortgages**  The priorities inter se of two or more equitable mortgages in England and Wales and Northern Ireland are governed by the general principles of equity.[74] The same applies to the relations between an equitable mortgagee and the owner of any other equitable interest. For example, in *Burgis* v. *Constantine*[75] there was an equitable mortgage of a ship, the owner-mortgagor being a trustee under a resulting trust. It was held that the beneficiaries under the trust had priority over the mortgagee because the equities were equal, so the first in time prevailed.

---

67. See pp. 138–42, *ante*.     68. See p. 178, *ante*.
69. [1907] 2 Ch. 284.
70. (1872) L.R. 7 Ch. App. 507. See pp. 87–8, *ante*.
71. See pp. 181–2, *ante*.     72. See p. 87, *ante*.
73. See pp. 87–8, *ante*.     74. See pp. 84–6, *ante*.
75. [1908] 2 K.B. 484.

**Registered mortgages and rights of retention**  The holder of a possessory lien over a ship[76] for work done for a mortgagor in possession ranks in priority to a mortgagee (whenever the mortgage was made). In *The Sherbro*[77] the mortgagee brought an action for sale of the ship. Material men[78] had a possessory lien over her (i.e., a right to retain possession of the ship until their bill was paid). The sale of the vessel only produced enough money to pay the material men. Consequently, the mortgagee was left with no contribution towards his debt. But it was held that he was entitled to be paid the costs of the proceedings for sale before any money went to the material men.

On the other hand, a mortgagee ranks before a creditor employed by the mortgagor in possession, such as a repairer,[79] supplier of necessaries,[80] or ship's husband,[81] who would have a right of retention if he were in possession of the ship or freight, but who has no possessory lien because he is not. In relation to freight, the mortgagee similarly ranks before stevedores' claim to wages.[82]

**Registered mortgages and maritime liens**  The holder of a maritime lien over a ship[83] ranks in priority to a mortgagee (whenever the mortgage was made). In *The Feronia*[84] it was held that the master's lien for disbursements[85] had priority over the mortgage notwithstanding that the master was part owner of the ship.

The position of repairers and suppliers of materials is anomalous. If not in possession claiming a possessory lien, they have no maritime lien by virtue of having done the repairs, but they acquire a lien if they sue the ship.[86] Consequently, repairers employed by the mortgagor will rank before or after the mortgagee according as they commence their action in rem before or after the making of the mortgage.[87]

**Registered mortgages and bottomry bonds**  A bottomry bond[88] has priority to a registered mortgage made before the grant-

---

76. Possessory liens: see pp. 198–9, *post*.
77. (1883) 52 L.J.P. 28. See also *Williams* v. *Allsup* (1861) 10 C.B.N.S. 417.
78. Repairers and maintainers of ships and their equipment and suppliers of equipment.
79. *The Scio* (1867) L.R. 1 A. & E. 353; *The Zigurds* [1932] P. 113.
80. *The Zigurds* [1932] P. 113.      81. *Beynon & Co.* v. *Godden & Son* (1878) 3 Ex. D. 263.
82. *The Zigurds* [1932] P. 113.      83. Maritime liens: see pp. 195–8, *post*.
84. (1868) L.R. 2 A. & E. 65. See also *The Aline* (1839) 1 W. Rob. 111; *The Daring* (1868) L.R. 2 A. & E. 260; *The Hope* (1873) 28 L.T. 287; *The Leoborg* (1963) 107 S.J. 1004.
85. Master's lien for disbursements: see p. 196, *post*.
86. As to the nature of maritime liens and actions in rem against ships, see pp. 195–6, *post*.
87. See *The Neptune* (1835) 3 Knapp 94; *The Pacific* (1864) Br. & L. 243; *The Scio* (1867) L.R. 1 A. & E. 353; *The Harriet* (1868) 18 L.T. 804.
88. Bottomry bonds and respondentia: see pp. 188–94, *post*.

ing of the bond. If not enforced within a reasonable time after the end of the voyage, the bond will lose its priority, at least if the mortgagee is prejudiced by the laches.[89]

A lien not arising from agreement has priority over securities created by contract. If, for example, there is a registered mortgage (the mortgagor remaining in possession), followed by a bottomry bond given by the master, followed by a collision causing damage to another ship, the order of entitlement to payment is: (1) the holder of the maritime lien for damage; (2) the bondholder; (3) the mortgagee.[90]

## Mortgages of Cargo

In the strict sense of mortgage, the transfer by the owner of title subject to redemption, there is no fundamental difference between cargo which has been shipped and any other goods.[91] Security over cargo on board ship may be given by the master by bond of respondentia,[92] but that is not a mortgage. It is unusual to mortgage goods because it is more convenient to pledge them.[93] The only special feature of a ship's cargo is that the master issues a bill of lading,[94] which can be used to pledge the goods without giving notice to the physical custodian.

## Mortgages of Freight

The right to be paid freight is one example of a chose in action (in Scotland, incorporeal moveable property). Freight may be mortgaged separately from the ship, or the right to it may go with a mortgage of the ship.[95] If mortgaged, the mortgage must be by the person entitled to receive it, i.e., the owner of the ship or someone to whom he has assigned the freight. The master of a vessel may grant security over the freight by a bottomry bond,[96] but that is not a mortgage. The master, unless he is authorised to do so by the owner of the freight, cannot grant an ordinary mortgage of it.[97] Freight may become subject to liens,[98] but those are not mortgages either.

89. See *The Royal Arch* (1857) Swab. 269; *The Helgoland* (1859) Swab. 491.
90. *The Aline* (1839) 1 W. Rob. 111.
91. Mortgages of goods: see pp. 114–20, *ante*.       92. See pp. 188–94, *ante*.
93. See pp. 144–73, *ante*.       94. See pp. 152–5, *ante*.
95. As to the right to freight of a mortgagee of a ship, see pp. 181–2, *ante*.
96. See pp. 188–93, *post*.       97. *Reynolds* v. *Jex* (1865) 7 B. & S. 86.
98. See pp. 196–8, 227–8, *post*.

A mortgage of freight alone is made like other mortgages of rights to receive sums of money,[99] by written assignment with a proviso for redemption, notice in writing of the assignment normally being given to the person who will have to make payment. In *Gardner* v. *Lachlan*[100] it was held that the mortgage was valid where notice was given to the mortgagor's agent who was going to receive the freight from the charterer, although no notice was given to the charterer himself. If there are successive mortgages of the same freight, these rank for priority in the order in which notice of them is given to the person who will pay the freight.[101] The mortgagee is entitled to be paid the freight in full, the charterer or consignee (or whoever is liable to pay) having no right to set off a debt due to him from the mortgagor.[102]

## Bottomry Bonds and Bonds of Respondentia

A bottomry bond is a document issued, usually by the master of a vessel, hypothecating her as security for an advance made to enable a voyage then in progress to be completed. It may extend to charging the freight as well, and usually does. When the cargo is charged, the transaction is known as *respondentia*. There are no significant differences in the law governing bottomry from that governing respondentia, and it is quite usual to use the expression *bottomry bond* to cover both types of hypothecation. A single bottomry bond may secure the loan on ship, freight and cargo.

Such a bond is expressed to make the money repayable after, and contingently upon, the completion of the voyage. The other main respects in which that type of security differs from a mortgage are: (*a*) the master has only implied authority, from his position and the circumstances, to hypothecate the ship, freight and cargo, whereas a mortgage, if not made by the owner, would have to be made by his agent expressly authorised; (*b*) there must be a necessity to raise the money in that way in order to complete the voyage; and (*c*) the remedy of an unpaid bondholder is not sale, but an action in rem against the ship or its cargo or both.

An action in rem against a ship is one which commences with the arrest of the ship. If the action succeeds, and the debt is not paid

---

99. See pp. 270–83, *post.*     100. (1838) 4 My. & Cr. 129.
101. *Smith* v. *Owners of S.S. Zigurds* [1934] A.C. 209.
102. *Weguelin* v. *Cellier* (1873) L.R. 6 H.L. 286.

by the owner, the ship will be sold under order of the court. The proceeds are then used to pay off creditors secured on the ship in the order of their ranking, any balance belonging to the owner.

Normally, a bottomry bond is given by the master when he is in a foreign port, having had to incur some expense such as repairs, necessary for the continuation of the voyage, and having no other means of raising the funds required. There have been exceptional cases where a bottomry bond has been upheld when granted by the owner, without the master joining in, when the owner happened to be on board;[103] or by a consul when there was no master. In *The Cynthia*[104] there had been a mutiny, resulting in the murder of the master and all the British crew except two seamen. Four Mexicans remained on board and brought her to Campeachy. The British consul there executed a bottomry bond to raise the money to enable the ship to continue her voyage with a new crew. That bond was upheld. The more usual course would have been for the consul to begin by appointing a new master. At the other extreme, bonds have been upheld when granted by the master over an English ship in a port in Great Britain.[105] The development of both modern systems of communications and modern systems of finance have made bottomry bonds less common than they used to be, but they are by no means extinct.

**The Necessity to Raise the Money** A bottomry bond is void if it was not necessary to raise the money,[106] and also if the lender did not make reasonable inquiries whether there was any necessity or not.[107] It cannot be used to raise money for supplies which do not come within the category of necessaries;[108] and if the money is partly for necessaries and partly for other expenditure the bond will be partly valid and partly void.[109] In *The Serafina*[110] it was held that a bottomry bond could not be used to raise the money to pay the premium to insure the ship, because insurance, though prudent, was not necessary, so that it was not within the implied authority of the master.

The necessity must relate to the voyage on which the vessel is

103. *The Duke of Bedford* (1829) 2 Hagg. 294.
104. (1852) 3 L.T. 682; 6 L.T. 165; 20 L.T.O.S. 54.
105. *The Providence* (1783) Burr. 330; *The Trident* (1839) 1 W. Rob. 29. See also *La Ysabel* (1812) 1 Dods. 273 (hypothecation of a Spanish ship in a Spanish port).
106. *The Reliance* (1833) 3 Hagg. 66; *The Pontida* (1884) 9 P.D. 177.
107. *The Orelia* (1833) 3 Hagg. 75; *Soares v. Rahn* (1838) 3 Moo. P.C. 1.
108. *Gore v. Gardiner* (1840) 3 Moo. P.C. 79.
109. *Smith v. Gould* (1842) 4 Moo. P.C. 21.    110. (1864) Br. & L. 277.

engaged when the bottomry bond is granted.[111] In The Edmond[112] it was held that the master could not raise money on bottomry on the homeward voyage in order to pay charges relating to the outward cargo.

**The Necessity to Raise the Money by Bottomry** A bottomry bond will be held invalid if there were other resources available to the master to pay for what he needed to complete the voyage. In The Faithful[113] it was held invalid on the ground that the ship had, in the port in question, an agent who could have accommodated the master; and that the lender either knew that or ought to have known. In Heathorn v. Darling[114] the bottomry bond was held invalid because the lender did not use reasonable diligence to find out whether the master could acquire supplies on the personal credit of the owner.

When someone is approached to lend money on bottomry, he should therefore try to ascertain both (i) whether the expenditure proposed by the master is necessary for the continuation of the voyage; and (ii) whether the master so lacks funds and credit that he needs to resort to a bottomry bond. Having satisfied himself as to both these, the lender may safely advance the money on a bottomry bond (safely, that is, so far as the validity of the bond is concerned); or advance the money on the understanding that a bottomry bond will be executed before the ship sails; and he need not supervise the spending of the money to ensure that it goes on necessaries. But a lender who lends on personal credit without an agreement for a bottomry bond, and who afterwards gets cold feet about the quality of the personal credit of the master or owner, cannot turn round and ask for security by way of a bottomry bond. Such a bond is void to the extent to which it is given to secure the repayment of money already advanced on personal credit, or to secure payment for goods or services supplied or undertaken on personal credit.[115] On the other hand, a bottomry bond may validly be given to raise money to pay for repairs which have already been executed.[116]

111. The Lochiel (1843) 2 W. Rob. 34; The Osmanli (1849) 3 W. Rob. 198.
112. (1860) Lush. 57.
113. (1862) 31 L.J.P.M. & A. 81. See also The Sydney Cove (1815) 2 Dods. 1; Dobson v. Lyall (1837) 6 L.J. Ch. 115; Lyall v. Hicks (1859) 27 Beav. 616; The Karnak (1868) L.R. 2 A. & E. 289.
114. (1836) 1 Moo. P.C. 5. See also Soares v. Rahn (1838) 3 Moo. P.C. 1.
115. The Augusta (1813) 1 Dods. 283; The Hersey (1837) 3 Hagg. 404; Gore v. Gardiner (1840) 3 Moo. P.C. 79; The Wave (1851) 17 L.T.O.S. 285. See also The North Star (1860) Lush. 45; The Ida (1872) L.R. 3 A. & E. 542.
116. Droege & Co. v. Suart (1869) L.R. 2 P.C. 505.

**A Bottomry Bond Must Be Contingent on the Voyage** The idea of a bottomry bond is that the lender takes the risk of the voyage. The bond specifies the voyage and the date of payment after the arrival of the ship at the port of destination, and the terms are that the lender is to be paid neither his loan nor his bottomry premium (interest) if the ship is lost before completing the voyage specified.[117] In *Anderston Foundry Co.* v. *Law*[118] it was left open whether a bond could validly be given for payment in a port before the end of the voyage. There, for repairs done in Rio de Janeiro to a ship bound from Glasgow to Bombay via Melbourne, a bond of respondentia for payment in Melbourne was given over cargo consigned to Bombay.

If the voyage is not completed but the ship is not lost, the money due on the bond becomes payable when the voyage is abandoned. In *The Elephanta*[119] a bottomry bond was given, and later the ship was damaged. She was not repaired, but was sold, and so never completed the voyage. Some cargo was thrown overboard; some was sold; the rest was delivered by another ship. It was held that the bond was enforceable against the proceeds of sale of the ship and cargo and against the cargo which was delivered.

If the lender does not take the risk of the voyage, the security is, if anything, a mortgage and not a bottomry bond.[120] But if a document is intended to be a bottomry bond, and is so in substance, it will be so construed even if it contains some phrases more apt to be found in some other type of security.[121]

**Communication with the Owner** Before hypothecating the ship by bottomry bond, the master must communicate with the owner, or attempt to do so, unless circumstances such as the need for great speed render that impracticable.[122] The purpose is to enable the owner to give alternative instructions. The master may hypothecate cargo to pay for repairs to the ship,[123] but if he grants a bond of respondentia for any valid purpose, he has the same duty of

---

117. *The James W. Elwell* [1921] P. 351. See also *Simonds* v. *Hodgson* (1832) 3 B. & Ad. 50. Scotland: *Alexander and George Miller & Co.* v. *Potter, Wilson & Co.* (1875) 3 R. 105.
118. (1869) 7 M. 836.     119. (1852) 18 L.T.O.S. 249.
120. *Stainbank* v. *Fenning* (1852) 11 C.B. 51; *Stainbank* v. *Shepard* (1853) 13 C.B. 418; *The Indomitable* (1859) Swab. 446.
121. *The Haabet* [1899] P. 295.
122. *Glascott* v. *Lang* (1847) 2 Ph. 310; *The Wave* (1851) 17 L.T.O.S. 285; *Wallace* v. *Fielden* (1851) 7 Moo. P.C. 398; *The Nuova Loanese* (1852) 3 L.T. 154; *Barron* v. *Stewart* (1870) L.R. 3 P.C. 199. Cf. *Smith* v. *Bank of New South Wales* (1872) L.R. 4 P.C. 194 (Ireland).
123. *The Gratitudine* (1801) 3 C. Rob. 240.

communicating with the owner of the cargo as he has to communicate with the shipowner when hypothecating the vessel.[124] In
*Dymond* v. *Scott*[125] the master of a vessel in Leith, carrying cargo
belonging to owners in Newcastle, purported to grant repairers of
the ship a bottomry bond over her, her freight and her cargo for
£500. The bond was held to be ineffective in respect of the cargo
because: (*a*) it was unfair in that the master had neither funds nor
credit for repayment; and (*b*) the owners of the cargo did not
consent – they either refused or were not asked, as they should have
been because Newcastle is accessible from Leith. Bonds of respondentia have been held valid without any communication with the
owner of the cargo when speed was necessary to salve the cargo[126]
and when, for some other reason, it would have taken too long to get
an answer.[127]

In communication with the cargo owner, it is enough to send
details of the damage to the vessel.[128] In *The Onward*,[129] on the other
hand, a bottomry bond was held invalid as to the cargo because the
communication by the lenders (the ship's agents) in Mauritius
omitted the information which would have indicated that bottomry
might be necessary. A similar case is the decision of the Privy
Council on appeal from Ceylon in *Kleinwort, Cohen & Co.* v. *Cassa
Marittima of Genoa*,[130] where the master, who did communicate with
the owners of the cargo, failed to state the details of the need for the
expenditure and of the need for hypothecation, despite the owners'
repeated requests.

**Reimbursement of Cargo Owner by Shipowner**    If the master
borrows on bottomry of ship, freight and cargo for the repair of the
ship, and the bond is enforced against the cargo because the debt
is more than the value of the ship and the freight, the master has
acted as agent of the owner of the ship and it follows that the shipowner must indemnify the cargo owner unless there is some provision
to the contrary in the bill of lading.[131]

---

124. *The Bonaparte* (1853) 8 Moo. P.C. 459; *Duranty* v. *Judah Hart & Co.* (1864) 2 Moo.
P.C.N.S. 289; *Droege & Co.* v. *Suart* (1869) L.R. 2 P.C. 505; *The Onward* (1873) L.R.
4 A. & E. 38. See also *Kleinwort, Cohen & Co.* v. *Cassa Marittima of Genoa* (1877) 2 App. Cas.
156.
125. (1877) 5 R. 196.        126. *Cargo ex Sultan* (1859) Swab. 504.
127. *The Olivier* (1862) Lush. 484; *The Lizzie* (1868) L.R. 2 A. & E. 254.
128. *The Bonaparte* (1853) 8 Moo. P.C. 459.
129. (1873) L.R. 4 A. & E. 38.        130. (1877) 2 App. Cas. 156.
131. *Benson* v. *Duncan* (1849) 3 Ex. 644; *Anderston Foundry Co.* v. *Law* (1869) 7 M. 836.

**Bottomry Bonds Hypothecating Mortgaged Ships** The holder of a bottomry bond granted while the mortgagor is in possession of the vessel is under no duty to inform the mortgagee of the existence of the bond.[132] Nor is a bottomry bond invalidated because the voyage was engaged in by the mortgagor contrary to the terms of the mortgage: the lender on the bond is not concerned with such considerations.[133] On the other hand, it was held in *The St George*[134] that it was desirable for notice to be given to the mortgagee, if practicable, when making a hypothecation by bottomry. It was also decided in that case that section 34[135] of the Merchant Shipping Act 1894 presented no obstacle to bottomry by a mortgagor in possession. In fact the bond, which was upheld, was taken by a lender who was registered as managing owner of the ship and who was also a director of the company, the mortgagors, who actually owned her.[136]

**Scrutiny of the Terms of Bottomry Bonds** Apart from the possibility that a bond may be struck down as being unfair,[137] the court may hold a bond valid but adjust its terms. As the lender takes the risk of the voyage, he is entitled to a maritime premium which, to be commensurate with the risk, is allowed to be high in comparison with rates of interest normally considered appropriate with safer securities such as mortgages of land. But if the amount payable to the lender is extortionate, it can be reduced to a reasonable level.[138] The jurisdiction is not confined to the premium. In *The Glenmanna*[139] there was a bond of respondentia to secure payment of charges for unloading, storing and trans-shipping the cargo; the charges were high, and the court reduced the amount payable to the amount of reasonable charges.

**Priorities** After some uncertainty in the earlier cases, it has been settled[140] that where there are two or more bottomry bonds they rank in the opposite order to that of their creation, i.e., a later bond has priority over an earlier one.

132. *The Helgoland* (1859) Swab. 491.    133. *The Mary Ann* (1865) L.R. 1 A. & E. 13.
134. [1926] P. 217.    135. See p. 177, *ante.*
136. As to ranking of bonds and mortgages, see pp. 186–7, *ante.*
137. See, e.g., *Dymond* v. *Scott* (1877) 5 R. 196, p. 192, *ante.*
138. *The Roderick Dhu* (1856) Swab. 177; *The Huntley* (1860) Lush. 24; *The Pontida* (1884) 9 P.D. 177.
139. (1860) Lush. 115. See also *The Fortuna* (1861) 4 L.T. 840 (Ireland).
140. *The Rhadamanthe* (1813) 1 Dods. 201; *The Betsey* (1813) 1 Dods. 289; *The Sydney Cove* (1815) 2 Dods. 1; *The Priscilla* (1859) Lush. 1.

If one bond covers ship, freight and cargo, the lender must resort to the ship and freight before proceeding against the cargo.[141] If there is a bottomry bond over ship and freight only, followed by a second bond over ship, freight and cargo, the holder of the second bond must exhaust the ship and freight before touching the cargo: there will be no marshalling in favour of the first bondholder.[141]

In *The Daring*[142] it was held that the owners of part of the cargo covered by a bond could not oppose the payment of wages to the master in priority to the holders of the bottomry bond. A bottomry bond ranks after a master's lien for wages on a later voyage, but before his lien for wages earned prior to the execution of the bond.[143] In *The Cornelia Henrietta*[144] the holder of a bond was held not to be entitled to pay the wages of the crew, and add the amount to his security, without the prior approval of the court. Finally, in *The St Lawrence*[145] a person who, at the request of the master, paid dock dues at the port of discharge, was held entitled to be paid in priority to the holder of a bottomry bond.

## Liens

Liens over or in connection with ships fall into various classes. First, there is the maritime lien. That is a security over the ship and freight for payments due under a contract, for the cost of salvage or for damage caused by a ship. The rights of a lienee are similar to those of the holder of a bottomry bond. Indeed, the only difference is that a bottomry bond expressly hypothecates a ship, while a maritime lien arises by operation of law. The lienee may bring an action in rem against the ship or its freight or both, which means that in the last resort he will be paid out of the proceeds if the ship is sold either in his action or otherwise. Such a lien arises as soon as the payment is due. Secondly, there are liens which do not arise until the creditor has established in court his claim in rem. Because it does not attach without an action, it is not a maritime lien, but it resembles such a lien in that the right of the creditor is to sue the ship in rem. Finally, there are possessory, or common-law, liens over ships. That is, there is no right of action in rem, but merely a right

---

141. *The Priscilla* (1859) Lush. 1.
142. (1868) L.R. 2 A. & E. 260. See also *The Edward Oliver* (1867) L.R. 1 A. & E. 379; *The Eugènie* (1873) L.R. 4 A. & E. 123.
143. *The Hope* (1873) 28 L.T. 287.     144. (1866) L.R. 1 A. & E. 51.
145. (1880) 5 P.D. 250.

not to hand over possession of the vessel until payment. No special rules apply merely because the chattel concerned is a ship.[146]

**Maritime Liens**   In *The Ripon City*[147] Gorell Barnes J. said:

The law now recognises maritime liens in certain classes of claims, the principal being bottomry, salvage, wages, master's wages disbursements and liabilities and damage . . . such a lien is a privileged claim upon a vessel in respect of service done to it, or injury caused by it, to be carried into effect by legal process. It is a right acquired by one over a thing belonging to another – a jus in re alienâ. It is, so to speak, a subtraction from the absolute property of the owner in the thing. This right must, therefore, in some way have been derived from the owner. The person who has acquired the right cannot be deprived of it by alienation of the thing by the owner. It does not follow that a right to a personal claim against the owner of the res always coexists with a right against the res. The right against the res may be conferred on such terms or in such circumstances that a person acquiring that right obtains the security of the res alone, and no rights against the owner thereof personally. A simple illustration of this is the case of bottomry.

A maritime lien is security for the amount due plus the cost of enforcing the lien.[148] Being enforced by action in rem, the lien binds the ship despite changes of ownership.[149] It is only lost on a change of owners of the vessel if that occurs on sale in an action in rem.[150] A maritime lien is also lost by laches, i.e., undue delay in enforcing it.[151] That was accepted in *The Kong Magnus*,[152] where laches was regarded as being such delay is to cause the relevant evidence to be lost. It is a question of fact in each case whether the merits can still be gone into after the delay. In *The Kong Magnus* the lien was for damage caused by a collision, and an action to enforce it was allowed after eleven years.

One does not acquire a lien merely by supplying a ship. In *El Argentino*[153] it was held that the unpaid vendor of coal had no lien over the freight earned by using that coal because he had no proprietary interest in the coal.

146. As to common-law liens generally, see pp. 204–28, *post*.
147. [1897] P. 226, 242–3.
148. *Re Rio Grande Do Sul Steamship Co.* (1877) 5 Ch. D. 282.
149. *The Margaret* (1835) 3 Hagg. 238; *The Goulandris* [1927] P. 182.
150. *The Goulandris* [1927] P. 182.
151. *The Europa* (1863) 2 Moo. P.C.N.S. 1.
152. [1891] P. 223. See also *The Charles Amelia* (1868) L.R. 2 A. & E. 330.
153. [1909] P. 236.

**Seaman's lien for wages**  A seaman has a maritime lien for his wages over the ship[154] and her freight,[155] though not over the cargo she carries.[156] That lien cannot be forfeited by agreement.[157]

Wages are payment for a seaman's normal work on the ship during a voyage. There is no lien for payments due under a special contract. In *The Riby Grove*[158] it was held that a seaman had no lien for remuneration consisting of a share of the proceeds of a whaling voyage, while in *The British Trade*[159] there was equally held to be no lien for damages for wrongful dismissal where the contract was a special one in that it contained terms other than employment for a voyage and the rate of pay.

A seaman is a member of the crew (not including the master). A ship's husband has no lien for his wages, even if he does some of his work on board: it is not ship's work, so he is not a seaman.[160] In *Inter-Islands Exporters Ltd.* v. *Berna Steamship Co. Ltd.*[161] ships' riggers supplied two of their own men to work on a ship in dock. The men were held not seamen because they were not members of the crew, but servants of the riggers, and hence they had no lien over the vessel for wages.

**Master's lien for wages**  The master of a ship has the same lien for wages as a seaman has.[162] The sum secured has been held[163] to include national insurance contributions paid by the master when the owner of the ship had agreed to pay them. But, as with a seaman, the lien does not cover payments under a special contract.[164] Furthermore, it was decided in *The Bangor Castle*[165] that the master's lien for wages does not prevail against a mortgagee of the ship if the master has guaranteed payment of the mortgage debt.

**Master's lien for disbursements and liabilities**  The master of a ship has the same lien for the recovery of disbursements or liabilities properly made or incurred by him on account of the ship as he has for his wages.[166]

**Undertaker's lien**  Certain types of undertaker providing services for a ship, such as pilotage, have a maritime lien for their

154. Scotland: *The Golden Star* (1682) Mor. 6259; Ireland: *The Costante* (1851) 18 L.T.O.S. 20.
155. Scotland: *Sands* v. *Scott* (1708) Mor. 6261.
156. *The Lady Durham* (1835) 3 Hagg. 196.
157. Merchant Shipping Act 1894, s. 156.
158. (1843) 2 W. Rob. 52.       159. [1924] P. 104.
160. *The Ruby (No. 2)* [1898] P. 59.       161. 1960 S.L.T. 21.
162. Merchant Shipping Act 1894, s. 167(1). See also *The Tagus* [1903] P. 44.
163. *The Gee-Whiz* [1951] 1 All. E.R. 876.
164. *The British Trade* [1924] P. 104, above.
165. (1896) 74 L.T. 768.
166. Merchant Shipping Act 1894, s. 167(2). See also *The Tagus* [1903] P. 44.

unpaid rates. By the Harbours, Docks and Piers Clauses Act 1847, section 44, undertakers of the types indicated in the title to the Act have a possessory lien over a ship for unpaid rates, coupled with a power to sell her. That might be interpreted to create a maritime lien.[167]

**Salvor's lien**  Someone who salves a vessel or her contents after an accident has a maritime lien for the value of the salvage work.[168] There is, however, no lien for a charge for towing a ship, not by way of salvage, but simply for speeding her up in and out of harbour.[169]

**Lien for damage**  There is a maritime lien over a ship and her freight[170] for damage done by her to another ship or to other property, even if the defendant vessel is under the control of charterers, who employ the crew,[171] and even if she is in the control of some other independent contractor, such as agents for the sale of boats.[172] The owner of the damaged vessel or other property damaged may bring an action in rem against the ship responsible for the collision, whosoever possession she comes into.[173] There is no lien over the cargo being carried in the delinquent vessel, even if it belongs to the shipowner.[174]

The Harbours, Docks and Piers Clauses Act 1847, section 74, gives port undertakers a possessory lien for damage done by a ship to their installations. In *The Merle*[175] it was held that that section also gave them a maritime lien.

If a ship has been wrecked and the owners remain in possession of the wreck, but the port authority in whose harbour the wreck lies undertake the duty of protecting other shipping, then, if another vessel collides with her, the owners of the wreck are not liable unless they have been negligent themselves, so there is no maritime lien over her.[176] Furthermore, there is no maritime lien for damage caused by the crew otherwise than through the instrumentality of the ship. In *Currie* v. *M'Knight's Executors*[177] there was held to be no lien for the damage caused to a ship's cables when the crew of

---

167. Cf. *The Merle* (1874) 31 L.T. 447, below.
168. It has been held in Scotland that a salvor may not retain a ship in order to enforce payment if the owner has offered to consign: *Mackenzie* v. *Steam Herring Fleet Ltd.* (1903) 10 S.L.T. 734.
169. *Westrup* v. *Great Yarmouth Steam Carrying Co.* (1889) 43 Ch. D. 241.
170. *The Orpheus* (1871) L.R. 3 A. & E. 308.
171. *The Lemington* (1874) 32 L.T. 69.     172. *The Ruby Queen* (1861) Lush. 266.
173. *The Bold Buccleugh* (1851) 7 Moo. P.C. 267; *The Europa* (1863) 2 Moo. P.C.N.S. 1.
174. *The Victor* (1860) Lush. 72.     175. (1874) 31 L.T. 447.
176. *Owners of the S.S. Utopia* v. *Owners and Master of S.S. Primula* [1893] A.C. 492.
177. [1897] A.C. 97.

another ship cut through them in order to let their vessel get to sea.

**Supplier of necessaries**   A person who supplies necessaries to a vessel in a port in her country of registration has no maritime lien for the price, either at common law or under section 167(2) of the Merchant Shipping Act 1894.[178] In England and Wales it has been held[179] that there is no equitable lien either.

### Lien Attaching on Successful Suit

There appears to be only one variety of such a lien: that of the material men. Suppliers of materials for the ship, such as cables, have no maritime lien over the vessel for the amount of their unpaid bill. They have, however, a right to sue the ship in rem, and they acquire a lien over her if they establish their claim.[180] The time when the lien attaches will be significant if other securities arise or are granted over the vessel in the period between the supply of the material and the successful action in rem for its price.[181]

### The Possessory Lien of Repairers

Shipwrights who repair a vessel have no maritime lien for their charges, nor have they a cause of action in rem against the ship or her freight. In *The Harriet*[182] there was a mortgage of a three-quarters share in the ship. The owner of the other quarter share managed her, and had repairs done. Later, the mortgagee realised his security by selling the ship. It was held that, because the repairers had no maritime lien, the mortgagee was entitled to three-quarters of the proceeds of sale without any deduction towards the cost of the repairs.

People who repair chattels have a possessory lien for the cost of the repairs.[183] That is to say, the repairer is entitled to refuse to return the chattel to the owner after repair until his bill has been paid. In this respect, a ship is the same as any other chattel.[184] It has been held in Scotland[185] that the shipowner is entitled to delivery of the vessel on consignation of what is due to the repairer. The amount

178. England and Wales: *Northcote* v. *Owners of the Heinrich Björn* (1886) 11 App. Cas. 270. Scotland: *Clydesdale Bank Ltd.* v. *Walker & Bain* 1926 S.C. 72. See also *John Wood & Co.* v. *Hamilton* (1789) 3 Pat. App. 148; *Constant* v. *Christensen* 1912 S.C. 1371. For s. 167(2) of the 1894 Act, see p. 196, footnote 166, *ante*.
179. *The Aneroid* (1877) 2 P.D. 189.
180. *The Neptune* (1835) 3 Knapp 94; *The Pacific* (1864) Br. & L. 243.
181. As to priorities in relation to liens, see pp. 199–201, *post*.
182. (1868) 18 L.T. 804.
183. As to repairers' liens, generally, see pp. 221–4, *post*.
184. *Ex parte Bland* (1814) 2 Rose 91; *Franklin* v. *Hosier* (1821) 4 B. & Ald. 341. Two persons may perhaps be in possession simultaneously: see *Earle's Shipbuilding & Engineering Co. Ltd.* v. *Aktieselskabet D/S Geflon* (1922) 10 Lloyd's Rep. 305.
185. *Garscadden* v. *Ardrossan Dry Dock and Shipbuilding Co. Ltd.* 1910 S.C. 178.

due does not include costs incurred by the repairer in enforcing his possessory lien. He cannot add to his bill an amount for the cost of keeping the ship in his dock for that purpose.[186]

To have the lien, the shipwright must have the ship delivered into his possession, and the lien lasts only as long as he retains possession. Who is in possession is a question of fact. It is not necessary that the vessel should come into the repairers' premises. In *The Rellim*[187] it was held that the repairers had a possessory lien by virtue of the owners having brought the ship to a public dock, intending to put the repairers in possession, actually handing the repairers control of her. In *Barr v. Cooper*[188] it was held that repairers who had a ship on their premises did not lose their lien by moving her to a public dock, to complete the repairs there, so long as they did not hand possession back to the owners. But if they part with possession, the repairers lose their lien over the ship.[189] The court has no jurisdiction to allow them to retain their lien on ceasing to be in possession.[190]

**Liens and Subrogation**  If someone other than the shipowner voluntarily pays a lienee what is due to him, the lien is not thereby transferred to the payer, at any rate where the payment is made without the authority of the court.[191] However, there are cases where the court has authorised the holder of a bottomry bond to pay seamen's wages,[192] or dues for pilotage, towage, etc.,[193] and be subrogated to the payee's lien.

**Liens and Priorities**  The priority of ranking where there are two or more liens[194] depends on certain general principles. First, the preserver of the res ranks first. For example, a salvor will rank before the crew. Secondly, persons whose involvement is involuntary will rank before those who have a choice. For example, a lien for damage will rank before seamen who subsequently earn wages.

186. *Somes v. British Empire Shipping Co.* (1860) 8 H.L.C. 338.
187. (1922) 39 T.L.R. 41.
188. (1875) 2 R. (H.L.) 14.
189. *Ex parte Bland* (1814) 2 Rose 91. See also *Olsen & Ugelstad v. G. T. Gray & Co.* (1921) 9 Lloyd's Rep. 565.
190. *The Gaupen* [1925] W.N. 138; *The Ally* [1952] 2 Lloyd's Rep. 427.
191. *The Janet Wilson* (1857) Swab. 261 (master paying seamen's wages); *The Cornelia Henrietta* (1866) L.R. 1 A. & E. 51 (bondholder paying seamen's wages); *The Lyons* (1887) 57 L.T. 818 (payer of seamen's wages); *The Petone* [1917] P. 198 (person paying seamen's wages and reimbursing master for disbursements); *The Leoborg* (*No. 2*) [1964] 1 Lloyd's Rep. 380. See also *Clark v. Bowring and Co.* 1908 S.C. 1168.
192. *The Kammerhevie Rosenkrants* (1822) 1 Hagg. 62.
193. *The Fair Haven* (1866) L.R. 1 A. & E. 67.
194. As to liens in relation to mortgages, see pp. 185-6, *ante*; as to liens in relation to bottomry bonds, see p. 194, *ante*.

Thirdly, the producer of a fund for payment will rank first for payment of his costs of doing so. For example, a lienee who sells the ship will get his costs before the proceeds can go towards payment of a lienee whose lien ranks before that of the lienee who carried out the sale.[195] Finally, liens of the same type and quality rank equally or pari passu.

**Two or more salvors** In *The Veritas*[196] the first salvors brought the vessel into the Mersey. Then the vessel was involved in a collision. The second salvors tried to beach her to prevent her sinking in deep water. In the course of that operation, the vessel damaged a landing stage belonging to the Mersey Docks and Harbour Board. It was held that the order of priority was: (i) the lien, or right of action in rem, of the Board, because their involvement, unlike that of the salvors, was involuntary; (ii) the second salvors, because they were preserving the res for the first salvors; (iii) the first salvors.

**Salvage lien and lien for damage** If a vessel is involved in a collision so as to be liable for damage to the other vessel, sinks and is raised by salvors, the lien of the salvors ranks before the lien for damage because the salvors have produced the res for the damage lien to attach to.[197] In *The Inna*[198] the cargo exploded, sinking the ship and damaging warehouses in Poole harbour. The ship was salved. The salvage lien was held to rank before the lien for damage. The reason the lien for damage came before those of the salvors in *The Veritas*[199] is that the damage in that case was caused during salvage.

**Salvage and crew's wages** A salvage lien has priority over a lien for wages earned before the salvage.[200]

**Damage and wages** In *The Elin*[201] it was held that a lien over a foreign ship for damage caused by her took precedence over the seamen's lien for wages earned since the collision, as it would be unjust to allow the owner to pay out of the ship what he was obliged to pay anyway. In the Irish case of *The Carlota*[202] on the other hand, a lien for wages earned before the collision was held to have priority, after the ship had later been sold, over the lien for damage, in respect of the proceeds of sale.

---

195. *The Immacolata Concezione* (1883) 9 P.D. 37.
196. [1901] P. 304.    197. *The Sea Spray* [1907] P. 133.
198. [1938] P. 148.    199. [1901] P. 304, above.
200. *The Sabina* (1843) 7 Jur. 182.
201. (1883) 8 P.D. 129. See also *The Duna* (1861) 5 L.T. 217 (Ireland).
202. (1849) 4 Ir. Jur. 237.

**Two or more liens for damage** If there are successive collisions, the liens rank pari passu.[203]

**Undertakers and necessaries men** A lien for dock dues ranks equally with one for the supply of necessaries.[204]

**Crew and necessaries men** The seamen's lien for wages ranks before a lien for the supply of necessaries.[205]

**Crew and master** It was held in *The Mons*[206] that (*a*) the crew's lien had priority over the master's; (*b*) the master's lien for wages ranked equally with his lien for disbursements; and (*c*) two masters of the same ship ranked *pari passu.*

**Master as agent and creditor** In *The Heinrich*[207] a solicitor's lien for costs was held to have priority over: (*a*) necessaries supplied later and (*b*) the master's lien for wages, the solicitor having been employed by the master; while in *The Jenny Lind*[208] the master (who was also part owner of the ship) having ordered necessaries, the suppliers were held to have priority over the master's lien for wages.

**Two or more necessaries men** As this lien only arises on establishing a claim in litigation,[209] the prior petens, i.e., the first to establish his claim, would normally come first, but if they both establish their claim together they rank pari passu,[210] as do they if the second commences his action in rem before the first to sue gets a final order.[211]

**Possessory and maritime liens** A possessory lien held by repairers of a ship ranks after maritime liens already attached to the vessel when she comes into the possession of the shipwrights and ranks before maritime liens which attach to her after she comes into their possession. For example, their possessory lien will take effect subject to a lien in favour of the salvors who brought her in for repair[212] and subject to a lien for seamen's wages[213] which were attached to her when the ship entered the shipwrights' yard, but before a lien for seamen's wages earned after the shipwrights took possession of her.[214]

---

203. *The Stream Fisher* [1927] P. 73.    204. *The Charger* [1968] 1 W.L.R. 1707.
205. *The Queen (No. 2)* (1869) 19 L.T. 706.    206. [1932] P. 109.
207. (1872) L.R. 3 A. & E. 505.    208. (1872) L.R. 3 A. & E. 529.
209. See p. 198, *ante.*    210. *The Queen (No. 2)* (1869) 19 L.T. 706.
211. *The Africano* [1894] P. 141.
212. *The Gustaf* (1862) Lush. 506; *The Russland* [1924] P. 55.
213. *The Gustaf* (1862) Lush. 506; *The Immacolata Concezione* (1883) 9 P.D. 37; *The Tergeste* [1903] P. 26.
214. *The Gustaf* (1862) Lush. 506; *The Tergeste* [1903] P. 26.

**Lien Over Cargo For Freight**   A shipowner has a lien over (i.e., a right to retain and sell) cargo in order to recover freight due on it. In *Youle* v. *Cochrane*[215] it was held that the shipowner had that right even if the goods were shipped by a sub-freighter under some arrangement as to payment otherwise than on delivery. There, one-third of the freight was paid by the sub-freighter to the charterer at the time of shipment of the goods, but the consignee paid the whole amount to the master when they arrived. It was held that the consignee could not get back one-third of what he had paid because the master could have refused to deliver without payment in full. In *M'Lean* v. *Fleming*[216] the shipowner's right of retention of cargo for freight included a right to retain it for freight to be paid for empty space on board where a full cargo was not provided; but it was queried whether that right would prevail against a bona fide assignee of the bill of lading without notice that freight was due on more than his cargo. A similar decision was arrived at in *Lamb* v. *Kaselack, Alsen & Co.*[217] In that case, the main cargo was guano, claimed by the consignee. A cargo of plastic clay, which filled the rest of the boat, was not claimed by anyone, and its sale did not realise enough to pay the freight on it. It was held that the balance was secured by a right to retain the guano.

The lien extends to unloaded goods if it is protected in the appropriate way. By the Merchant Shipping Act 1894, section 494, if, when goods are landed from a ship and placed in the custody of a wharfinger or warehouseman, the shipowner gives the custodian notice in writing that the goods are to remain subject to a lien for freight or other charges payable to the shipowner, to an amount mentioned in the notice, the goods continue to be subject to any such lien they were subject to before unloading. The custodian must retain the goods until the lien is discharged or, if he does not, make good to the shipowner any loss thereby occasioned to him. By section 495, such a lien is discharged upon: (i) production to the custodian of a receipt, and delivery to him of a copy, or production of a release of the freight; or (ii) deposit by the owner of the goods with the custodian of the amount of money claimed by the shipowner. In this latter case,[218] the discharge is without prejudice to the shipowner's other remedies for recovery of the freight. By section 497, if the lien is not discharged within ninety days (or, in the case of perishable goods, such shorter period as the custodian thinks fit),

---

215. (1868) 6 M. 427.    216. (1871) L.R. 2 Sc. App. 128.
217. (1882) 9 R. 482.    218. See also s. 496; Arbitration Act 1950, s. 29.

the custodian may – and, if required by the shipowner, must – sell the goods by auction; or sell at least enough of the goods to pay the charges specified in section 498.[219] Before the sale, the custodian must advertise and, if he knows the address, notify the owner of the goods. A bona fide purchaser at such a sale gets a good title even if no notice of the sale is given to the owner. By section 498, the proceeds of sale go to pay: (i) customs and excise duties, if the goods are sold for home use; (ii) the expenses of the sale; (iii) the custodian and the shipowner according to their agreement or, if they have no agreement: (a) the custodian's charges and (b) the freight. If there is any surplus, it goes to the owner of the goods.

Section 499 provides that, if goods are placed in the custody of a wharfinger or warehouseman by a shipowner because the owner does not take delivery, the custodian has a lien on the goods for his rent and expenses.

219. See below.

# 11 liens and rights of retention

## Introduction

No rigid distinction is drawn, in the language of the law, between a lien and a right of retention. In Scotland, it used to be stated that a lien was a right over the property of someone else (for example, the lien of an unpaid solicitor over his client's title deeds), while a right of retention was a power to hold back and keep possession of one's own property in derogation of someone else's right to acquire it.[1] The only example of a right of retention in this restricted sense ceased to exist in Scotland with the enactment of the Sale of Goods Act 1893. At common law, an agreement to sell goods did not pass the property: the title passed to the purchaser only on delivery of the goods. If the vendor was not paid the purchase price, he had a right to retain the goods even though the contractual date for delivery had arrived. By the common law of England and Wales and Ireland, on the other hand, a contract to sell goods passed the title to the buyer. An unpaid vendor who did not deliver would be exercising a lien over the purchaser's goods. The English rule was embodied in the Sale of Goods Act 1893, which applies throughout the United Kingdom. Outside Scotland, while 'lien' is the more usual word, that term and 'right of retention' seem to be used synonymously in relation to chattels or money.

What differentiates a lien or right of retention from all other kinds of security is that it does not arise from the express or implied agreement of the parties, but is held to exist as a matter of law in

1. For a general discussion of terminology in Scotland, see Gloag and Irvine, *Law of Rights in Security*, pp. 329–30.

connection with certain types of commercial relationship. A lienee is a person to whom the owner of the property has not given security but who is to be treated as if he were a secured creditor.

One very significant classification, therefore, of liens is according to the type of security the lien gives.

In Scotland, apart from maritime liens,[2] there are four types of security which arise by operation of law:

(1)    A right to refuse to hand back a debtor's moveable property, of which the creditor is in possession, until the debt is paid (e.g., a solicitor's lien for fees over his client's title deeds);

(2)    a right to refuse to hand back a debtor's moveable property, of which the creditor is in possession, until the debt is paid, and, in the last resort, if the debt is not otherwise satisfied, to sell the article in question, or have it sold, and put the proceeds towards liquidating the debt (e.g., an innkeeper's lien for his charges over his guest's luggage);

(3)    a right to deduct from a debtor's money, of which the creditor is in possession, the amount of the debt (e.g., a solicitor's lien for fees over damages recovered for his client and paid into the solicitor's bank account);

(4)    a right to retake possession of goods on their way from the creditor to the debtor and either retain them until the debt is paid or sell them (an unpaid vendor's right of stoppage in transitu).

In England and Wales and Northern Ireland, liens may be classified as: (1) maritime;[2] (2) common law; (3) equitable. Common law liens are possessory liens of the four types mentioned in the last paragraph as existing (in addition to maritime liens) in Scotland. Equitable liens are not based on a right to retain possession or to retake possession and do not apply to chattels. They are all right to be treated as if one were an equitable mortgagee by charge over a debtor's land or incorporeal property. The example most frequently met in practice is the lien of an unpaid vendor for the price.[3]

Liens may also be classified as special and general. A special lien – the commoner type – is a security for the payment of a particular debt connected with the property over which the lien is being claimed. For instance, a garage proprietor has a lien over a car he has repaired for the charge for the repairs, but he cannot refuse to redeliver the car to the owner merely because the latter owes him some other debt (e.g., for petrol previously supplied on credit). A

2. See pp. 194-8, *ante.*    3. See pp. 226, 228-31, *post*

general lien – quite a rare security – is for a general balance owed to the creditor. A factor employed, for example, to sell goods has a lien on the goods of his principal in his possession not only for commission earned on sale of those goods, but for all sums owed to him arising out of his employment as a factor.

In the remainder of this chapter, liens are classified according to the relationships and occasions which give rise to them.

## Solicitor's Lien

Apart from any express security he may have been given, there are three main ways in which a solicitor may be secured on his client's property in respect of professional charges. First, he has a lien over his client's documents in his possession. Secondly, he has a lien over his client's funds in his control or under the control of the court. Thirdly, for charges incurred in litigation, the court may charge the client's property in his favour.

**Lien Over Documents**  The solicitor has a general lien over client's documents, i.e., a right to refuse to part with them until he is paid.[4] Commonly, these documents are title deeds to land, which have come into the solicitor's possession in the course of a conveyancing transaction, but the lien is not confined to title deeds. Such documents are not marketable by the solicitor, e.g., he has no lien over the land if the documents are title deeds, so that his security consists of a capacity to inconvenience the client, who may not be able to conduct his affairs without getting the documents back. The client is not allowed to circumvent the lien by examining the documents and memorising or copying them.[5]

**What the lien secures**  The solicitor is entitled to retain possession of the documents until he has been paid what the client owes him for professional services.[6] It is a general lien, i.e., it extends to all such debts, not just fees for any transactions to which the documents in question relate,[7] and includes charges arising before

---

4. See, for general statements of the law: *Re Hawkes* [1898] 2 Ch. 1; *Re Rapid Road Transit Co.* [1909] 1 Ch. 96. Scotland: *Liquidation of John Smith & Sons, Rutherglen, Ltd.* (1893) 1 S.L. T. 273. Ireland: *Re Watters* (1881) 7 L.R. Ir. 531. *Re Harvey's Estate* (1886) 17 L.R. Ir. 65; *Re Vahy* (1893) 28 I.L.T.R. 140; *Re Stannard's Estate* [1897] 1 I.R. 415; *Carroll v. Fleming* (1923) 57 I.L. T.R. 75.
5. *Re Biggs and Roche* (1897) 41 S.J. 277.
6. Scotland: *Drummond v. Muirhead & Guthrie Smith* (1900) 2 F. 585. Ireland: see *Porter v. Bennett* (1897) 33 I.L. T.R. 7.
7. *Ex parte Sterling* (1809) 16 Ves. 258; *Colmer v. Ede* (1870) 40 L.J. Ch. 185.

or after the documents in question came into existence[8] or into the possession of the solicitor. The solicitor may exercise his lien only in respect of taxable costs, charges and expenses, and not in respect of other debts owed to him by his client,[9] such as advances made by him to his client[10] or disbursements made as factor for his client,[11] though it has been held[12] by the Court of Session in Scotland that a solicitor has a lien for sums expended the better to secure himself in respect of advances to his client. Scottish Courts have also decided[13] that the right to retain title deeds extends to securing payment of the costs of a successful action brought by the solicitor against the client for fees.

The solicitor is entitled (under the law of England and Wales and Northern Ireland)[14] to a lien to secure statute-barred debts as well as those enforceable by action.

**What documents may be retained.** Title deeds to land are the commonest subjects of a lien simply because they are the documents which most commonly come into the hands of a solicitor. The solicitor can also exert his lien over other documents if they come into his possession (or were created by him), such as business records or other company documents.[15] They must, however, be his client's documents. In *Liquidator of the Garpel Hoematite Co. Ltd.* v. *Andrew*[16] the Court of Session held that a solicitor could not have a right of retention of a company's register of shareholders (because such a register is required by law to be available for public access on the company's premises) or of share transfers (because those were not the property of the client company).

The lien is not restricted to papers which have some intrinsic value to the client. In *Hughes* v. *Hughes*[17] the Court of Appeal held that it could exist over the papers in a divorce case.

On the other hand, it cannot be exerted so as to interfere with

8. *Re Dee Estates Ltd.* [1911] 2 Ch. 85.
9. *Re Galland* (1885) 31 Ch. D. 296.
10. *Re Taylor, Stileman & Underwood* [1891] 1 Ch. 590.
11. Scotland: *Largue* v. *Urquhart* (1883) 10 R. 1229 (payment by solicitor in Banff to solicitor in Edinburgh for conducting litigation in the Court of Session); England and Wales: *Re Walker* (1893) 68 L.T. 517 (no lien for solicitor in his capacity as land agent).
12. *Palmer* v. *Lee* (1880) 7 R. 651.
13. *Gray* v. *Graham* (1855) 2 Macq. 435. Cf. *M'Tavish* v. *Pedie* (1828) 6 S. 593.
14. See *Curwen* v. *Milburn* (1889) 42 Ch. D. 424; *Re Brockman* [1909] 2 Ch. 170.
15. *Re Capital Fire Insurance Assoc.* (1883) 24 Ch. D. 408; *Re Rapid Road Transit Co.* [1909] 1 Ch. 96.
16. (1886) 4 M. 617. England and Wales: *Re Capital Fire Insurance Assoc.* (1883) 24 Ch. D. 408. Ireland: *Gerty* v. *Mann* (1891) 29 L.R. Ir. 7.
17. [1958] P. 224.

litigation.[18] The public interest in justice requires that documents needed in court be produced. The solicitor with a lien over such documents may be ordered to hand them over, which will usually be done only if the debtor client (unless he settles the solicitor's bill) pays the amount claimed into court or provides alternative security or on the terms that the solicitor parting with the documents shall not lose his lien and that the documents will be returned to him when the purpose for which he had to produce them has been achieved.[19]

**Assignment of lien**  In general, debts can be assigned by the creditor. If a solicitor assigns a debt secured by a lien on his client's documents, he can pass the lien to the assignee by handing over possession of the documents.[20]

**Avoidance of lien by provision of alternative security**  If, at the outset, the client gives an express security to his solicitor for his charges, the lien may be precluded from coming into existence. Similarly, if a lien already exists, it may cease on the provision of alternative express security. In the absence of express agreement to that effect, whether the provision of the other security avoids the lien depends on the circumstances. The authorities are not unanimous on the question of what circumstances are relevant. One view is that the lien is avoided if the other security is more advantageous than the lien (unless the lien is expressly reserved); the other, that the lien is avoided only if the other security is inconsistent with it.[21]

In any event, if the client owes several sums to his solicitor, and gives him an express security for a particular debt, the solicitor retains a general lien over the client's papers as to the rest of the money owed.[22]

In Scotland, it has been held[23] that the solicitor cannot be

---

18. *Belaney* v. *Ffrench* (1873) L.R. 8 Ch. App. 918; *Re Boughton* (1883) 23 Ch. D. 169; *Re Capital Fire Insurance Assoc.* (1883) 24 Ch. D. 408; *Re Galland* (1885) 31 Ch. D. 296; *Boden* v. *Hensby* [1892] 1 Ch. 101; *Re Hawkes* [1898] 2 Ch. 1; *Dessau* v. *Peters, Rushton & Co. Ltd.* [1922] 1 Ch. 1. Scotland: see *Callman* v. *Bell* (1793) Mor. 6255.

19. Scotland: see *Skinner* v. *Balfour's Trustee* (1865) 3 M. 867; *W. Adam & Winchester* v. *White's Trustee* (1884) 11 R. 863; *Liquidator of James Donaldson & Co. Ltd.* v. *White & Park* 1908 S.C. 309; *Garden Haig Scott & Wallace* v. *Stevenson's Trustee* 1962 S.C. 51. Ireland: see *Re Wade's Estate* [1900] 1 I.R. 211; *Re Ardtully Copper Mines Ltd.* (1915) 50 I.L.T.R. 95.

20. *Bull* v. *Faulkner* (1848) 2 De G. & Sm. 772.

21. See *Re Taylor, Stileman & Underwood* [1891] 1 Ch. 590; *Bissill* v. *Bradford and District Tramways Co. (Ltd.)* (1893) 9 T.L.R. 337; *Re Douglas Norman & Co.* [1898] 1 Ch. 199; *Re Morris* [1908] 1 K.B. 473. Scotland: in *Palmer* v. *Lee* (1880) 7 R. 651 it was held that the solicitor did not lose his lien by taking a bill of exchange, and giving a receipt for the amount due, if the bill was dishonoured at maturity. Ireland: *Brownlow* v. *Keatinge* (1840) 2 Ir. Eq. Rep. 243.

22. *Re Morris* [1908] 1 K.B. 473.

23. *Ferguson* v. *Grant* (1856) 18 D. 536. Cautionary obligations: see pp. 284–310, *post*.

compelled to give up deeds, over which he claims a lien, in return for the security of caution (at least, if there are no special circumstances). It was pointed out that the right of retention was superior to caution in that its irritant power was a spur to speedy settlement, though inferior in that the deeds could not be sold to provide cash. In the same year, in *Drysdale* v. *Howden*,[24] the Court of Session ordered the solicitor to give his client her deeds, thus defeating his lien, where the solicitor's account was disputed. It was important for the client to get her deeds quickly and she was willing to consign the amount claimed. It was suggested that caution would have been adequate instead of consignation.

It has been held in Ireland, in *Re Aikin's Estate*,[25] that the solicitor does not lose his lien over the papers by suing the client for the amount due.

**Loss of lien by parting with the papers**   The lien depends on possession, so that if the solicitor parts with possession of the papers, except to someone who will hold them on his behalf, he ceases to be secured on them. In *Caldwell* v. *Sumpters*,[26] the Court of Appeal held that a solicitor did not lose his lien over deeds when he sent them to his former client's new solicitor on terms that the latter was to hold them to his (the creditor's) order.

In Scotland, in *Renny* v. *Kemp*,[27] a similar position was taken up. It was there held that a solicitor did not lose his lien by parting with deeds to another solicitor who gave a receipt stating that he had borrowed them. Even if the second solicitor handed the deeds to the client's trustee in his sequestration, the first solicitor would still be regarded as in possession of them. In the Scottish appeal case of *Gray* v. *Graham*,[28] the House of Lords held that a solicitor who had a lien over the deeds relating to three estates, and who released one set of deeds, retained his lien over the other two sets for the whole amount owed.

**Failure of lien by papers not being held on account of debtor**   If the solicitor comes into possession of documents otherwise than in the capacity of solicitor to the debtor, he will get no lien over them. In *National Bank of Scotland Ltd.* v. *Thomas White & Park*,[29] the lien was claimed by a solicitor to a landowner who had

24. (1856) 18 D. 863.     25. [1894] 1 I.R. 225.
26. [1972] Ch. 478.     27. (1841) 3 D. 1134.
28. (1855) 2 Macq. 435.
29. 1909 S.C. 1308. Ireland: see *Smith* v. *Chichester* (1842) 2 Dr. & War. 393; *Blunden* v. *Desart* (1842) 2 Dr. & War. 405, where Sugden L.C. carried out a general survey of this lien; *Molesworth* v. *Robbins* (1845) 2 Jo. & Lat. 358; *Re Stannard's Estate* [1897] 1 I.R. 415; *Belfast Artisans' Mutual Benefit Building Soc.* v. *Parsons* (1906) 40 I.L.T.R. 221; *Rath* v. *M'Mullan* [1916] 1 I.R. 349.

granted another creditor rights in security over the land and who owed the solicitor money as fees. The solicitor came into possession of the title deeds of the land as agent for an assignee of the secured creditor. The Court of Session held that the solicitor could not retain the deeds as against a creditor with a subsequent security over the land (i.e., a species of assignee of the debtor's rights in the land) because he did not get possession of them as agent of the debtor. The same applies if the solicitor comes into possession of the deeds on his own account. In *Garden Haig Scott & Wallace* v. *Stevenson's Trustee*,[30] the Court of Session decided that a solicitor had no lien over deeds which he held as creditor secured on the land to which they related, even if he had them as agent of the debtor (the client who owed him fees) too.

A lien may come to an end upon similar considerations. A solicitor loses his lien over deeds if he comes to hold them on behalf of someone other than the debtor. Many of the reported cases have arisen out of a solicitor acting for more than one party to a transaction.

> **Example** Desdemona owes fees to her solicitor, Ophelia. Ophelia has a lien over the title deeds to Elsinore Castle, land owned by Desdemona. Desdemona mortgages Elsinore Castle to Portia. Ophelia acts for Desdemona and Portia in the mortgage transaction. Ophelia has been in possession of the deeds throughout, but the court will hold that she has lost her lien for Desdemona's debt because she now has the deeds as Portia's agent.[31]

A solicitor may also lose his lien because someone asserts a right to the deeds superior to that of the indebted client.

> **Example** Oliver has a client, Peter, who is the mortgagee of Endacre. Oliver has a lien over the title deeds to Endacre for sums owed by Peter on account of work done by Oliver in connection with transactions relating to Endacre during the currency of the mortgage. Derek redeems Endacre. The court will hold that Oliver has no right to retain the title deeds as against Derek.[32]

The principle seems to be that the solicitor gets a lien only over what the client can bind. The Court of Appeal in Chancery held,

---

30. 1962 S.C. 51. England and Wales: see *Sheffield* v. *Eden* (1878) 10 Ch. D. 291.
31. See *Re Snell* (1877) 6 Ch. D. 105; *Re Mason and Taylor* (1878) 10 Ch. D. 729; *Re Nicholson* (1883) 53 L.J. Ch. 302; *Barratt* v. *Gough-Thomas* [1951] Ch. 242. See also *Ex parte Fuller* (1881) 16 Ch. D. 617; *Meguerditchian* v. *Lightbound* [1917] 2 K.B. 298. Scotland: *Tawse* v. *Rigg* (1904) 6 F. 544; *Liquidator of Lochee Sawmills Co. Ltd.* v. *Stevenson* 1908 S.C. 559.
32. See *Wakefield* v. *Newbon* (1844) 6 Q.B. 276; *Re Llewellin* [1891] 3 Ch. 145.

in *Pelly* v. *Wathen*,[33] that if a solicitor acted for the owner of mortgaged land, the rights of the mortgagee would have priority over any lien the solicitor obtained as against his client. That principle is furthered in Scotland by legislation. The Conveyancing (Scotland) Act 1924, section 27, provides that a law agent or notary public, acting for the proprietor or creditors or others, whose rights in or over land conveyed in security are postponed to those of the creditor in such heritable security, cannot acquire over the writs and evidents as against the secured creditor any right of hypothec, lien or retention after the date of recording the heritable security.

In the Scottish case of *Liquidator of Weir & Wilson Ltd.* v. *Turnbull & Findlay*,[34] where land had been given as security, the title deeds were with the secured creditor's solicitor. The Court of Session held that he had no lien as against the debtor, who needed the deeds in order to sell the land (subject to the rights in security) even though the purchaser was the secured creditor. Lord President Dunedin said (p. 1010):

> I know of no authority, and I see no principle, on which a security holder, having got the titles for the purpose of making good his security, should be allowed to give them to his law-agents for the purpose of raising up a fund of credit with his law-agents for all accounts between him and them *hinc inde*.

This contrasts with the decision in *Paul* v. *Meikle*[35] that the solicitor has a lien against the owner of the land, even if that person is not his client, if the land belonged to his client when the right arose. Despite the contrast, the principle is the same: the client had all the right in the land when the lien came into existence. The purchaser from the client does not suffer any loss: he can get his deeds by paying the debt to the solicitor and can then deduct that amount from the purchase price of the land.

**Lien Over Funds**  In so far as a solicitor has a lien over funds he holds for his client,[36] to secure payment for his professional services, it amounts to a right to deduct his charges from what he must account to his client for. There is no difference between a right to retain money until one is paid and paying oneself.

---

33. (1851) 1 De G.M. & G. 16.    34. 1911 S.C. 1006.
35. (1868) 7 M. 235. See also *Hamilton's Creditors* (1781) Mor. 6253. In *Menzies* v. *Murdoch* (1841) 4 D. 257 it was held that a solicitor got a lien even as against a creditor who could stop the client dealing with the land to which the deeds related (the client being the proprietor of the land).
36. See *Cormack* v. *Beisly* (1858) 3 De G. & J. 157; *Loescher* v. *Dean* [1950] Ch. 491.

In addition to funds he holds, a solicitor has a lien over funds in court to which his client has become entitled in litigation.[37] The client will be entitled, usually, either because he is the successful plaintiff, and the money was paid in by the defendant, or because he paid the money in himself as defendant, and the plaintiff has lost. This is not a general lien: it extends only to securing the payment of the solicitor's costs in the suit that produced or preserved the fund,[38] including statute-barred costs,[39] and embracing the case where the client is an infant.[40] The nature of this lien is a right to be paid out of the fund before any of it is handed over to the client.

The lien is not confined to funds to which the client has become entitled under a judgment. In *Ross* v. *Buxton*[41] Stirling J. reviewed the authorities and held that it attached also to money to be paid out to the plaintiff under a compromise. This has been applied to compromise of an arbitration[42] as well as of a suit.

No lien exists over a fund which is neither in the possession of the solicitor nor in court.[43] Nor does a solicitor ever acquire a lien over property other than a fund of money (such as land or goods) which is recovered or successfully defended in litigation. But the lien does extend to a sum ordered to be paid by one party to another by way of costs,[44] as well as to sums awarded as damages.

**Charge Imposed by the Court** Because there was no common law lien for a solicitor's costs over property recovered or defended in litigation, apart from a fund in the solicitor's possession or in court, statutory protection has been enacted. By the Solicitors Act 1957, section 72,[45] replacing earlier legislation operating in England and Wales, power is conferred upon the court to give a solicitor employed in litigation a charge on property recovered or preserved in the action or proceeding, for the taxed costs of the litigation. If

37. *Re Born* [1900] 2 Ch. 433. Ireland: *Plunkett* v. *Lee* (1903) 37 I.L.T.R. 232; *Re Maloney* [1928] I.R. 155.
38. *Bozon* v. *Bolland* (1839) 4 My. & Cr. 354; *Mackenzie* v. *Mackintosh* (1891) 64 L.T. 706.
39. *Higgins* v. *Scott* (1831) 2 B. & Ad. 413. But the lien itself is lost by laches: Ireland: *Browne* v. *Dempsey* (1903) 37 I.L.T.R. 135.
40. *Re Wright's Trust* [1901] 1 Ch. 317.　　41. (1889) 42 Ch. D. 190.
42. *Re Meter Cabs Ltd.* [1911] 2 Ch. 557.
43. Scotland: see *Stephen* v. *Smith* (1830) 8 S. 847; *Cullen* v. *Smith* (1845) 8 D. 77. Ireland: *Savage* v. *James* (1875) I.R. 9 Eq. 357.
44. *Campbell* v. *Campbell* [1941] 1 All E.R. 274.
45. Northern Ireland: Legal Practitioners (Ireland) Act 1876, s. 3; Scotland: Solicitors (Scotland) Act 1933, s. 43. In England and Wales, under the Arbitration Act 1950, s. 18(5), the High Court may charge property recovered or preserved by arbitration.

the court, in its discretion, does impose the charge, all dealings with the property by the client thereafter are subject to the charge except dealings in favour of a bona fide purchaser for value without notice of the charge.[46] It seems that one solicitor's lien over a fund in court has priority over another solicitor's charging order on it.[47]

## Other Agents' Liens Over Paper

**Banker's Lien**  A bank has a general lien on its customer's securities in the possession of the bank, unless the lien is excluded by the circumstances of the bank's possession. The lien is a right to refuse to give up the securities until any balance due to the bank by the customer is paid. The lien applies to documents of title, such as title deeds and share certificates, and to paper representing a right to money. As Lord President Inglis said in *Robertson's Trustee* v. *Royal Bank of Scotland*,[48] the bank has a right of retention of '. . . all unappropriated negotiable instruments belonging to the customer in the hands of the banker for securing his balance on general account.'[49]

The general lien does not extend to securities deposited for a specific purpose, e.g., for safe custody.[50] Nor has a bank a general lien over documents deposited to secure a specified amount. In *Vanderzee* v. *Willis*[51] the documents were given to the bank to secure a fluctuating overdraft up to £1,000. The customer died owing the Bank £1,541. It was held that his personal representative could redeem the documents on paying the bank £1,000.

Sometimes the cases exhibit confusion between a banker's *lien* and his right of *set-off* (or *compensation*, as it is called in Scotland). A banker's lien is a general possessory lien over paper; a right to keep a sum of money, instead of paying it out to a customer, because the

---

46. Scotland: except dealings in favour of a bona fide purchaser or lender.
47. Ireland: *Hickey* v. *Hickey* (1917) 51 I.L. T.R. 185. Legal aid fund's charge without court order: England and Wales: Legal Aid Act 1974, s. 9(6); *Till* v. *Till* (1974), *The Times* newspaper, 25th January. See also: Legal Aid (Scotland) Act 1967, s. 3(4); Legal Aid and Advice Act (Northern Ireland) 1965, s. 3.
48. (1890) 18 R. 12, 16. See also *Muir* v. *Royal Bank of Scotland* (1893) 20 R. 887.
49. England and Wales: see *Re European Bank* (1872) L.R. 8 Ch. App. 41; *Misa* v. *Currie* (1876) 1 App. Cas. 554. Cf. *National Westminster Bank Ltd.* v. *Halesowen Presswork & Assemblies Ltd.* [1972] A.C. 785, 802, *per* Lord Dilhorne, 810–11 *per* Lord Cross. See also the Bills of Exchange Act 1882, s. 27(3), in force throughout the United Kingdom.
50. *Brandao* v. *Barnett* (1846) 12 Cl. & Fin. 787.
51. (1789) 3 Bro. C.C. 21. See also *Re Bowes* (1886) 33 Ch. D. 586.

customer is indebted to the bank, is a right of set-off or compensation. In any case the money belongs to the bank, and you cannot have a lien over your own property; what the bank has in these cases is a right not to pay a debt but to strike a balance on mutual dealings.[52]

**Stockbroker's Lien** A stockbroker has a general lien over documents in his possession, relating to shares owned by his client, for all amounts due to him in respect of dealings with shares.[53] As with all liens, they give way to contrary agreement, and to circumstances negativing a general lien in the manner the paper comes into the creditor's possession. Moreover, the lien can only be over the client's interest in the shares. In *Peat* v. *Clayton*,[54] where the client first made an equitable assignment of shares and then sent the share certificates to his broker to sell the shares, the equitable assignee was held to have priority over the broker's lien.

**Accountant's Lien** It would seem from *Ex parte Southall*[55] that an accountant has a special lien on his client's books in his possession, i.e., a right to refuse to part with them until he is paid the fee for the work for which he was given those books.

While case-law on this subject is scanty in England and Wales, there are several Scottish cases. There is ample authority for the existence of the lien.[56] There is also no doubt that the lien is not a general one, i.e., it does not extend to fees for previous work on the same books (after which the accountant returned the books to his client).[57] If the client is a company in liquidation, the accountant must give the books up to the liquidator, but he does not lose his lien by doing so if he reserves his lien or acts under an order of the court.[58] The lien is only as between accountant and client: an

---

52. Ireland: see *Re Morris* [1922] I. R. 136. In the following Scottish cases, where the terminology of right of retention was used, the decisions really were that the respective bankers had no right of compensation: *Paul* v. *Royal Bank of Scotland* (1869) 7 M. 361; *Gray's Trustees* v. *Royal Bank of Scotland* (1895) 23 R. 199; *Anderson* v. *North of Scotland Bank Ltd.* (1901) 4 F. 49.

53. *Jones* v. *Peppercorne* (1858) Johns. 430; *Re London and Globe Finance Corp.* [1902] 2 Ch. 416. Scotland: *Glendinning* v. *John D. Hope & Co.* 1911 S.C. (H.L.) 73.

54. [1906] 1 Ch. 659.    55. (1848) 17 L.J. Bcy 21.

56. See *Stewart* v. *Stevenson* (1828) 6 S. 591; *Bruce* v. *Irvine* (1835) 13 S. 437; *Meikle* v. *Smith's Trustee* (1880) 8 R. 69; *Liquidation of John Smith & Sons, Rutherglen, Ltd.* (1893) 1 S.L.T. 273; *Liquidator of the Scottish Workmen's Assurance Co. Ltd.* v. *Waddell* 1910 S.C. 670; *Train & M'Intyre Ltd.* v. *Forbes* 1925 S.L.T. 286.    57. *Morrison* (1901) 9 S.L.T. 34.

58. *Liquidator of the Scottish Workmen's Assurance Co. Ltd.* v. *Waddell* 1910 S.C. 670; *Train & M'Intyre Ltd.* v. *Forbes* 1925 S.L.T. 286.

accountant in employment cannot retain his employer's books – in fact, in the servant's custody, the books are in the employer's possession.[59] In *Gladstone* v. *McCallum*,[60] where a company secretary was held to have no right to detain the company's minute book, Lord McLaren said:

> Retention, as I understand it, is the right of an owner of property to withhold delivery of it under an unexecuted contract of sale or agreement of a similar nature, until the price due to him has been paid, or the counter obligation fulfilled. Lien, again, is the right of a person who is not the owner of property but is in possession of it on a lawful title, and whole right of lien, if it is not a general one – of which class of lien there are not many examples – is a right to retain the property until he has been compensated for something which he has done to it.

### Landowner's Factor's Lien in Scotland

A landowner's factor on his estates has a right to retain the documents relating to those estates until his salary is paid and he is reimbursed for outgoings.[61] The right prevails only against the landowner: the factor cannot refuse to hand documents over to a mortgagee.[62]

When a landowner's factor collects rent, he has a right to retain thereout the amount of advances made by him as factor.[63]

### Other Agents' Liens

**Auctioneer's Lien**   The Court of Appeal held in *Webb* v. *Smith*[64] that an auctioneer had a lien over the proceeds of sale to the extent of his charges in conducting the transaction. As against the highest bidder, the auctioneer has a lien over the goods for the purchase-price. If the purchaser will not take delivery, the auctioneer can sue for the price, even if he has already been paid part of it, enough to cover his commission and charges.[65]

An auctioneer is a factor, so he has a lien over goods sent to him for sale in respect of a general balance arising out of advances he made to his principal against future proceeds of sale.[66] On the other hand, he has no common law right against goods or proceeds

59. *Martin* v. *Boyd* (1882) 19 S.L.R. 447.
60. (1896) 23 R. 783, 785. See also *Barnton Hotel Co. Ltd.* v. *Cook* (1899) 1 F. 1190 (minute book and other papers: no lien against the employing company).
61. *Robertson* v. *Ross* (1887) 15 R. 67.   62. *Macrae* v. *Leith* 1913 S.C. 901.
63. *Stevenson, Lauder & Gilchrist* v. *Dawson* (1896) 23 R. 496.
64. (1885) 30 Ch. D. 192.   65. *Chelmsford Auctions Ltd.* v. *Poole* [1973] Q.B. 542.
66. *Neillay's Trustee* v. *Hutcheson* (1881) 8 R. 489. Factor's Lien: see p. 216, *post*.

of sale in respect of a sum due to him under a contract having nothing to do with auctions,[67] (though in England and Wales and Northern Ireland he may have an equitable set-off).

**Factor's Lien** A factor[68] has a general lien over goods which are in his possession as factor, for any balance owed to him as factor,[69] even if the factor is obliged by his contract with the principal to sell the goods at a stipulated price,[70] and whether the goods are with him for sale or after purchase for his principal.

There is no lien over goods for servants or agents who are not factors. A servant who has custody of his master's goods for the purpose of working on them has no right to detain them in order to provoke payment of disbursements or wages (in such cases the master remains in possession).[71] An agent (who is not a factor) to whom goods are delivered for his principal has no right to hold on to them or stop them in transit merely because he is surety for his principal's obligation to pay the price.[72] A commercial traveller, if he must hand over his gross takings to his employer under a contract of employment, is an unsecured creditor for his commission on his employer's bankruptcy,[73] though in appropriate circumstances a commercial traveller is a factor.[74]

In order for a factor to obtain a lien over goods, the possession of the asset must arise out of his activities as factor. In *Dixon* v. *Stansfeld*[75] the agent was held to have no lien over an insurance policy he had arranged for his principal because, although he had acted as factor for the insured in the past, this time the policy was not one insuring goods he was employed to sell or buy, so he had no general lien for a balance due to him as factor. (He had no special lien on the policy as broker because the insured owed him nothing on that transaction, the premium having been reimbursed.)

No lien arises until the goods come into the possession of the factor.[76] Even if the goods are on the factor's premises, there is no

---

67. *Brown* v. *Smith* (1893) 1 S.L.T. 158.    68. See pp. 168–72, *ante*.
69. *Kruger* v. *Wilcox* (1755) Amb. 252. Scotland: *John McCall and Co.* v. *James Black and Co.* (1824) 2 Sh. App. 188; *Moore's Universal Carving-Machine Co. Ltd.* v. *Austin* (1896) 4 S.L.T. 38. See also *Wilmot* v. *Wilson* (1841) 3 D. 815, where a broker who effected insurance for his principal was held to have a general lien over the policy.
70. *Stevens* v. *Biller* (1883) 25 Ch. D. 31.    71. *Burns* v. *Bruce* (1799) Hume 29.
72. *Louson* v. *Craik* (1842) 4 D. 1452.
73. *Brown and Co's Trustee* v. *Osler's Assignee* (1855) 17 D. 1011.
74. See pp. 169–70, *ante*.
75. (1850) 10 C.B. 398. Scotland: see *John McCall & Co.* v. *James Black & Co.* (1824) 2 Sh. App. 188.
76. *Kinloch* v. *Craig* (1790) 3 T.R. 783.

lien if he is not rightfully in possession of them as against his principal[77] (as, for example, where he steals them from a vendor who was holding them to his principal's order). The lien is lost if the factor parts with possession of the goods.[78]

In *Houghton* v. *Matthews*[79] it was held that a factor had no lien over goods of one principal for sums owed to him by a second principal, or for sums owed by the first principal to the second principal, or for debts arising before his employment as factor.

If the factor has a lien over goods he has bought for his principal, his right is to refuse to deliver them to the principal until he is paid. He has no right, as against his principal, to enforce the lien by sale. Nevertheless, a sale, if in the ordinary course of business, would pass a good title to the purchaser under the Factors Act 1889.[80] If the factor has a lien over goods given to him by his principal for sale, he can, in general, sell them (because that is the purpose of his authority) and reimburse himself out of the proceeds before remitting the balance to his principal.[81] In *Smart* v. *Sandars*[82] it was held that the factor could not enforce his lien by sale if the principal had revoked his authority to sell. In effect, that means that the sale would be wrongful as against the principal, but the buyer would get a good title if the sale came within the Factors Act 1889.[83]

In the Scottish case of *Miller* v. *M'Nair*[84] a factor sold goods and asked the purchaser to pay his principal direct. The purchaser accepted a bill of exchange drawn by the principal for the price. It was held that the factor could not later require the purchaser to pay him (the factor), instead of returning the bill of exchange to the principal after acceptance, because the principal owed the factor money on another transaction. There were alternative grounds for that decision. Either: (i) the agent had no lien because the sum was owed by the principal on a non-factorial debt; or (ii) the acceptance of the bill of exchange was equivalent to paying, so the purchaser no longer owed anything he could be asked to pay.

**Consignee dealing with factor** By the Factors Act 1889, section 7, if the owner of goods has given possession of them to another person for the purpose of consignment or sale, or has

---

77. *Taylor* v. *Robinson* (1818) 8 Taunt. 648.    78. *Kruger* v. *Wilcox* (1755) Amb. 252.
79. (1803) 3 Bos. & P. 485.    80. See pp. 168–72, *ante*.
81. Scotland: *Sibbald* v. *Gibson* (1852) 15 D. 217. In *Gairdner* v. *Alexander Milne and Co.* (1858) 20 D. 565 that principle was applied to a purchase transaction. The principal having gone bankrupt, the factor was allowed to pay himself out of money paid to him under a policy insuring a cargo he had bought and which was lost at sea.
82. (1848) 5 C.B. 895.    83. See p. 169, *ante*.
84. (1852) 14 D. 955.

shipped goods in the name of another person, and the consignee is without notice that the person in possession of the goods does not own them, then the consignee, in respect of advances made to or for the use of the person in possession of the goods, has the same lien[85] on the goods as if the person in possession of them were the owner.

## Innkeeper's Lien

When a traveller stays as a guest at a hotel, the innkeeper has a lien, over the belongings the guest brings with him, for the amount of the bill. This lien is general in the sense that each item of the guest's luggage is security for the whole bill, not just for any costs attributable to storing the particular item;[86] but it is special in the sense that the lien is only for the charge for board and lodging and storage of goods, and does not cover repayment of loans to the guest or of disbursements made for him.[87] The right to retain the belongings exists even when the reason for the guest not paying the bill is that the charges exceeded what had been agreed on.[88] An innkeeper has no lien for the cost of looking after goods for someone who is not a guest.[89] Nor has an innkeeper a lien on the guest himself or the clothes he is wearing, so he cannot lock the guest up or strip him naked.[90]

The goods need not belong to the person who is liable to pay the bill. In *Gordon* v. *Silber*[91] husband and wife stayed together at a hotel on the husband's account. The husband went off without paying and it was held that, although the wife was not the debtor, the innkeeper had a lien over all the luggage of husband and wife, even if some of it belonged to the wife (the innkeeper not having to try to distinguish his from hers). In *Robins & Co.* v. *Gray*[92] the Court of Appeal held that the lien extended to luggage of a commercial traveller which the innkeeper knew to belong to the guest's employer; while in *Snead* v. *Watkins*,[93] where the guest was formerly an attorney's clerk, the innkeeper was held to have a lien over a letter book, belonging to the attorney, that the guest brought with him. The Court of Exchequer Chamber, in *Threfall* v. *Borwick*,[94] held

85. By the Factors (Scotland) Act 1890, s.1, lien means and includes a right of retention.
86. *Mulliner* v. *Florence* (1878) 3 Q.B.D. 484.
87. *Chesham Automobile Supply (Ltd.)* v. *Beresford Hotel (Birchington) (Ltd.)* (1913) 29 T.L.R 584.
88. *M'Kichen* v. *Muir* (1849) Shaw J. 223.   89. *Smith* v. *Dearlove* (1848) 6 C.B. 132.
90. *Sunbolf* v. *Alford* (1838) 3 M. & W. 248.   91. (1890) 25 Q.B.D. 491.
92. [1895] 2 Q.B. 501.   93. (1856) 1 C.B.N.S. 267.
94. (1875) L.R. 10 Q.B. 210.

that an innkeeper had a lien over a piano a guest brought with him, the piano being in fact hired by the guest, though the innkeeper thought he owned it. Whether the innkeeper could have refused to accept the piano into his hotel (which he probably could not if he had room for it) was irrelevant because he did accept it.

In all these cases where the guest brings luggage he does not own with him, the innkeeper's lien prevails against the owner, who can get his property back only by settling the hotel bill. That rule applies even to stolen property the thief brings with him when he arrives at the hotel.[95] On the other hand, no lien attaches to goods which are not brought by the guest, but which are brought him after his arrival, and which the innkeeper knows to be someone else's property. In *Broadwood* v. *Granara*[96] a professional pianist (the aptly named M. Hababier) had already booked in at a hotel when he was lent a piano by the manufacturers. The innkeeper was held, on that principle, to have no lien over the instrument.

Reversing the previous common law rule, it has been laid down by statute[97] that an innkeeper has no lien on any vehicle, or property left in a vehicle, or on any horse or other live animal or its harness or equipment.

If the innkeeper lets the property out of his custody, he loses his lien. Whether he loses it, or prevents it arising, by taking express alternative security for payment of the bill depends on agreement or other circumstances showing an intention to rely on the other security to the exclusion of the lien. In *Angus* v. *McLachlan*[98] the taking by the innkeeper of an equitable mortgage of a share in a ship was held not to destroy his lien because there was nothing in the mortgage or the circumstances of its creation that was inconsistent with the continuance of the lien.

At common law, the lien of the innkeeper was simply a right to retain possession of the goods until they were redeemed by paying the bill. The Innkeepers Act 1878, which applies throughout the United Kingdom, adds a power of sale. It provides that, in addition to his lien, the landlord, proprietor, keeper or manager of a hotel, inn or licensed public house may sell by auction any goods deposited with him, or left in the house he keeps, to satisfy a debt for board or lodging. The goods must have been with him, and the debt unpaid, for at least six weeks. The vendor must advertise the auction at least a month beforehand. If the sale produces more than the amount of

95. *Marsh* v. *Commissioner of Police* [1945] K.B. 43.     96. (1854) 10 Ex. 417.
97. Great Britain: Hotel Proprietors Act 1956, s. 2(2); Hotel Proprietors Act (Northern Ireland) 1958, s. 2(2).
98. (1883) 23 Ch. D. 330.

the debt (after paying the expenses of the sale), the surplus is payable on demand to the person who deposited or left the goods in the vendor's house. This power of sale may only be exercised to secure payment of a debt in respect of which the innkeeper could have retained the property under his lien. In *Chesham Automobile Supply (Ltd.)* v. *Beresford Hotel (Birchington) (Ltd.)*,[99] it was held that an innkeeper did not lose his lien by sending the article away for repair, in preparation for selling it under his statutory power, as he retained charge of it. Furthermore, the period during which the article was off his premises for repair counted towards the six weeks the goods had to be left with him before he could auction them.

## Lien for Storage Charges

A keeper of a warehouse or other depository, such as a railway left luggage office, has a special lien on the goods he stores, which is a right to retain possession of them until the charge for storing them has been paid.[100] There is no right to sell the goods, but it has been held[101] in Scotland that, if the goods would deteriorate by retention (as in the case of maize which would rot), the court may order a sale, shifting the storekeeper's preference to the proceeds.[102]

If the person who brings the goods for storage is not the owner, the lien will prevail against the owner if the depositor was acting with express or implied authority. In *Singer Manufacturing Co.* v. *London and South Western Railway Co.*[103] the hirer of a sewing machine deposited it in the cloakroom at Waterloo Station and did not come back to collect it. The owners were held unable to recover the machine without paying the cloakroom charges. It was reasonable (and not prohibited) for the hirer to take the sewing machine by train and deposit it in a station cloakroom.

In *Dirks* v. *Richards*[104] a demand by the storekeeper for the payment of debts due to him from a third party as well as the storage charges, as a condition of returning the chattel, was held to be a waiver of the lien for storage charges because it amounted to a denial that the owner was the depositor.

---

99. (1913) 29 T.L.R. 584.    100. *Laurie* v. *Denny's Trustee* (1853) 15 D. 404.
101. *Parker* v. *Andrew Brown & Co.* (1878) 5 R. 979.    102. England and Wales: see p. 224, *post*.    103. [1894] 1 Q.B. 833.    104. (1842) Car. & M. 626.

## Lien for Carriage

An unpaid carrier of goods has a lien for his charges.[105] In the absence of special circumstances, this is a special lien, consisting of the right to retain possession of each article until the charge for carrying that article has been paid.[106]

In *Wolf* v. *Summers*[107] it was held that the master of a ship had a lien on the luggage of a passenger to secure payment of his passage money. The parents of this lien are the carrier's lien for charges for goods and the innkeeper's lien for the bill for hospitality.

## Lien for Packing

Packers of goods have a general lien. That is to say, a packer may refuse to return goods to his customer until he is paid what is due to him for packing those goods or other goods of the same customer.[108]

## Lien for Improving Goods

When the owner of goods, or someone else with authority to do so, takes them to someone else to work on them, the person who has done the work has a lien on them for the cost of any improvement. The earlier authorities in England and Wales were reviewed, and in several instances disapproved, by Lord Ellenborough C.J., giving the judgment of the Court of Kings Bench in *Chase* v. *Westmore*.[109] In that case there was a contract for grinding wheat. The miller was held to have a lien over the wheat, when ground, for the price of grinding it, whether the wheat was delivered for grinding all at once or in parcels, if there was one contract for the entire work. The lien would be for the agreed price, if any; if none was agreed, the lien would be for a reasonable price. A contrast is provided by the Court

---

105. As to a shipowner's lien for freight, see pp. 202–3, *ante*.
106. *Skinner* v. *Upshaw* (1701) 2 Ld. Raym.7 52; *George Barker (Transport) Ltd.* v. *Eynon* [1973] 1 W.L.R. 1461. Scotland: *Stevenson* v. *Likly* (1824) 3 S. 204. In *Alexander M. Peebles and Son* v. *Caledonian Railway Co.* (1875) 2 R. 346 the Court of Session held that a carrier had no right of retention under the Railway Clauses Consolidation (Scotland) Act 1845, s. 90 (right to detain and sell carriages and goods to satisfy tolls on them or on others belonging to the same owner), as against an onerous consignee, for a general balance due from the consignor.
107. (1811) 2 Camp. 631.
108. See *Ex parte Deeze* (1748) 1 Atk. 228; *Re Witt* (1876) 2 Ch. D. 489. Scotland: *Leck, Cowan & Co's Trustee* v. *J. M'Murray & Co's Assignee* (1878) 5 R. 770.
109. (1816) 5 M. & S. 180.

of Appeal decision in *Cassils & Co.* v. *Holden Wood Bleaching Co. Ltd.*[110] There, the C. Co., who owned some lumps of calico, sent them to the P. Co. for printing. The P. Co., without authority from the C. Co., sent the calico to the H. Co. for bleaching. It was held that the H. Co. had no lien over the cloth for (i) sums due to them from the P. Co.; (ii) the cost of bleaching, because the C. Co. had contracted with the P. Co. for payment for an entire process – bleaching, dyeing, printing and finishing – and therefore owed no one an identifiable sum for the bleaching stage of that process.

The lien is only over goods the subject of the contract. In Scotland, in *Brown* v. *Sommerville*,[111] it was held that a printer had no right to retain his customer's plates to secure payment of his printing bill. He would have had a right to refuse to deliver the finished printing until paid, but he had not improved the plates. That might have been enough to dispose of *Mitchell* v. *Z. Heys & Sons*,[112] but that case was actually decided on a different ground. M let out copper rollers to J, calico printers, who had no printing works. J sent their own cloth to H, together with M's rollers, to be printed. It was held that H had no lien over the rollers for the cost of printing the calico because, although H thought the rollers belonged to J, they belonged to M and M had not contributed to H's belief.

When the bailee has a lien over goods he has improved, it is a special lien, i.e., it secures only charges for work done on the goods retained and does not extend to debts for other work in the absence of special agreement or trade custom;[113] though it has also been held[114] that the special lien is not waived by making an unfounded claim of a general one.

In *Hatton* v. *Car Maintenance Co. Ltd.*[115] it was held that there could be no lien over a motor car for a charge for maintaining it in its current condition, no improvement being involved. There are quite a few cases on horses dealing with this distinction. In general, there is no lien over them for the cost of their keep, though such a lien may arise by special contract;[116] but there would be a common law lien for charges for veterinary attention, training a racehorse,[117] or

---

110. (1914) 84 L.J.K.B. 834.    111. (1844) 6 D. 1267.    112. (1894) 21 R. 600.
113. *Green* v. *Farmer* (1768) 4 Burr. 2214; *Scarfe* v. *Morgan* (1838) 4 M. & W. 270; *Lilley* v. *Barnsley* (1844) 1 Car. & K. 344. Scotland: *Harper* v. *Faulds* (1791) Mor. 2666; *Smith* v. *Aikman* (1859) 22 D. 344; *J. W. Anderson and Co's Trustee* v. *Fleming* (1871) 9 M. 718.
114. *Scarfe* v. *Morgan* (1838) 4 M. & W. 270.    115. [1915] 1 Ch. 621.
116. *Wallace* v. *Woodgate* (1824) 1 C. & P. 575. In Scotland, the lien extends to upkeep as well as improvement: see *Miller* v. *Hutcheson* (1881) 8 R. 489, 492, *per* Lord Young.
117. *Bevan* v. *Waters* (1828) 3 C. & P. 520.

covering a mare,[118] even though the charge would include the cost of keep during the rendering of the services producing the improvement. In *Re Southern Livestock Producers Ltd.*[119] it was held that a farmer housing, feeding and caring for pigs had no lien on them for sums spent on them because either: (i) routine care was not improvement; or (ii) if supervision of natural increase was improvement, it was impossible to apportion the farmer's expenditure between that and ordinary upkeep.

To acquire a lien, the person improving the goods must acquire possession of them. In a Scottish case,[120] where a ship was taken from the builders' yard to an engineers' yard to have engines put in, the shipbuilders leaving a man on board throughout, it was held that the engineers had no lien over the ship because they had never been in possession of her. In England and Wales it has been held[121] that a trainer has no lien over a racehorse, because he has no right of continuing possession, if the owner can take him away for any races he chooses and select the jockeys. Similarly a garage where a car is kept would have no lien for improvements if the owner were entitled to drive the car out as and when she pleased.[122] In *Albemarle Supply Co. Ltd.* v. *Hind & Co.*,[123] on the other hand, the Court of Appeal held that a repairer of taxicabs did not lose his lien by allowing the cabs out to ply for hire during the day on condition that they returned to his garage every night. There is, however, no doubt that if a lien has come into existence it is lost if the lienee parts with possession of the goods.[124]

**Goods taken for improvement by someone other than the owner** Problems as to liens sometimes arise when the hirer of a vehicle takes it for repair and the owner seeks to get it back from a repairer who claims a lien. It seems to be settled that, if the obligation to repair is placed on the hirer, and he is not expressly prohibited from creating a repairer's lien, the lien binds the owner. In *Green* v. *All Motors Ltd.*[125] a hire-purchase contract relating to a motor car placed the repairing obligation on the hirer; the hirer took the car

118. *Scarfe* v. *Morgan* (1838) 4 M. & W. 270.
119. [1964] 1 W.L.R. 24.
120. *Ross & Duncan* v. *David Baxter & Co.* (1885) 13 R. 185. See also *Castle-Douglas and Dumfries Railway Co.* v. *Henry Lee, Son, and Freeman* (1859) 22 D. 18, from which it seems that a building contractor in Scotland cannot have a lien to retain possession of land as security for paying his bill (here for constructing a railway line) because the owner of the land is in possession throughout.
121. *Forth* v. *Simpson* (1849) 13 Q.B. 680.
122. *Hatton* v. *Car Maintenance Co. Ltd.* [1915] 1 Ch. 621.    123. [1928] 1 K.B. 307.
124. *Pennington* v. *Reliance Motor Works Ltd.* [1923] 1 K.B. 127.
125. [1917] 1 K.B. 625. See also *Keene* v. *Thomas* [1905] 1 K.B. 136 (dog-cart).

to a garage for repair; the garage proprietor knew the person who brought it in was a hirer; during the repair work the hirer defaulted on his hire-purchase payments; and the owner tried to repossess the car. The Court of Appeal held that the garage proprietor had a lien as against the owner for the cost of the repairs. Even if the hire-purchase contract does prohibit the hirer from creating a lien over the vehicle, if the hirer has contracted to keep it in repair a lien will arise in favour of a repairer who does not know of the prohibition.[126] Equally, even if the hirer has not contracted to keep the vehicle in repair, he has implied authority to create a repairer's lien if it is reasonable to do so and it is not prohibited by the hire-purchase agreement.[127]

If the owner of goods takes them to repairer A, who sub-contracts the work to repairer B without the knowledge or authority of the owner, no lien arises in favour of B in the absence of a trade custom.[128]

**Sale**   At common law, the lienee had no right to sell the goods; he could only hold on to them until he was paid. The court could order a sale at its discretion, which it would do to save the goods (in the case of goods which would deteriorate in store) or to save the lienee expense, as in the case of a trainer's lien over a horse which was eating her head off.[129] That is still the position in Northern Ireland.

In Great Britain, the Disposal of Uncollected Goods Act 1952 gives a person who accepts goods in the course of his business for repair or other treatment a right to sell the goods if the person who brought them in does not pay or tender the charges for the work or take delivery of the goods or give directions as to their delivery. If there is a surplus on sale, the balance of the proceeds is recoverable by the person who brought the goods for repair or treatment; if there is a deficit, the balance of his charges is recoverable by the artisan.

126. *Albemarle Supply Co. Ltd.* v. *Hind & Co.* [1928] 1 K.B. 307. Scotland: see *Lamonby* v. *Authur G. Foulds Ltd.* 1927 S.C. 89.
127. *Tappenden* v. *Artus* [1964] 2 Q.B. 185.
128. *Pennington* v. *Reliance Motor Works Ltd.* [1923] 1 K.B. 127. See also *Buxton* v. *Baughan* (1834) 6 C. & P. 674; *Cassils & Co.* v. *Holden Wood Bleaching Co. Ltd.* (1914) 84 L.J.K.B. 834, p. 222 *ante*.
129. *Larner* v. *Fawcett* [1950] 2 All E.R. 727.

## Unpaid Vendor of Goods

The Sale of Goods Act 1893, which is in force throughout the United Kingdom, and which largely codifies the old case-law, confers on an unpaid seller:[130] (i) a lien, (ii) a right of stoppage in transitu, (iii) a right of resale and (iv) where the property has not passed to the purchaser, a right to withhold delivery (section 39). Section 40 gives the unpaid seller in Scotland a right, while the goods are in his hands or possession, to attach them by arrestment or poinding.[131]

In England and Wales and Northern Ireland, it has always been the law that a sale of goods passes the property to the buyer, even if the goods remain in the seller's possession, and that is the position under the Sale of Goods Act 1893. Apart from minor amendments of detail, the main change the Act introduced into the unpaid seller's security for the price was the creation of a right of resale.

In Scotland, prior to 1893, property did not pass to a buyer of goods until they were delivered to him. Accordingly, an unpaid seller refusing to deliver was exercising a right of retention of his own goods. That is now changed, and under the 1893 Act the position of the property is uniform throughout the United Kingdom.

**Unpaid Seller's Lien**   The Sale of Goods Act 1893, section 41, provides that the seller's lien is the right to retain possession of the goods he has sold, notwithstanding that he is in possession as agent or bailee or custodier for the buyer, until payment or tender of the price, where: (*a*) the goods were sold without any stipulation as to credit; or (*b*) the goods were sold on credit and the term of credit has expired; or (*c*) the buyer becomes insolvent.

Where part delivery of the goods has been made, the unpaid seller may exercise his lien over the undelivered goods unless the partial delivery was made in such circumstances as to show an agreement to waive the lien (section 42).

In accordance with section 43, the lien is lost by: (*a*) delivery to a carrier or other bailee or custodier for transmission to the buyer

---

130. Defined in s. 38. As to conflict of law problems, see Chesterman, 'Choice of Law Aspects of Liens and Similar Claims in International Sale of Goods' (1973) 22 *International and Comparative Law Quarterly*, 213.
131. Poinding rather than arrestment is the appropriate form of diligence. One can poind someone else's property, but one cannot arrest in one's own hands. See *Lochhead* v. *Graham* (1883) 11 R. 201, 204, *per* Lord Kinnear.

without reserving any right to dispose of the goods; or (*b*) the buyer or his agent lawfully obtaining possession of the goods; or (*c*) waiver. The lien is not lost by the seller obtaining judgment or a decree for the price. In *Paton's Trustee* v. *Finlayson*[132] there was a sale of a growing crop of potatoes. The potatoes were later lifted by the purchaser, but were left on the vendor's land to be pitted. The Court of Session held that the vendor was still in possession of the potatoes and so had not lost his lien by virtue of section 43(1) (*b*).

In England and Wales and Northern Ireland, an unpaid vendor of land or of incorporeal personality has an equitable lien for the price. But a vendor of goods has no such equitable lien – he has only the possessory lien under the Sale of Goods Act – at least where ordinary articles of commerce are sold under an ordinary commercial agreement.[133]

Where a main contractor contracts to do some work for a land-owner, and orders some items to be supplied by a sub-contractor, the unpaid sub-contractor has no lien on the sum payable by the landowner to the main contractor.[134] That is well settled, and *Bellamy* v. *Davey*[135] is an exceptional case. It involved the supply of some tanks by a sub-contractor. The latter had not finished making the tanks when a receiver was appointed of the main contracting company, so that the property in the unfinished tanks was still in the sub-contractor. A declaration was granted that the sub-contractor need not go on with the work without payment; and for convenience an order was made that the sub-contractor complete the work and have a first charge on the money payable therefor to the main contractor.

**Stoppage In Transitu**  The Sale of Goods Act 1893, section 44, declares that the right of stoppage in transitu is the right to resume possession of goods in course of transit to the buyer, and retain possession of them until payment or tender of the price, if the buyer becomes insolvent.

By virtue of section 45, goods are deemed to be in the course of transit from the time they are delivered to a carrier by land or water,

132. 1923 S.C. 872. England and Wales: it was held in *Howes* v. *Ball* (1827) 7 B. & C. 481 that an unpaid vendor of a coach who had delivered it under an agreement that he could retake it had no right against a transferee from the purchaser.
133. *Transport and General Credit Corp.* v. *Morgan* [1939] Ch. 531, 546, *per* Simonds J. Equitable lien: see pp. 228–31, *post.*
134. *Pritchett and Gold and Electrical Power Storage Co. Ltd.* v. *Currie* [1916] 2 Ch. 515.
135. [1891] 3 Ch. 540.

or other bailee or custodier, for transmission to the buyer, until the buyer or his agent takes delivery from that carrier, bailee or custodier. If, when the goods are at their destination, the carrier, bailee or custodier acknowledges to the buyer that he holds the goods on the buyer's behalf, and continues in possession as agent for the buyer, the transit is at an end. If the goods are rejected by the buyer, and the carrier, bailee or custodier continues in possession, the transit is not deemed to be at an end even if the seller has refused to receive the goods back. If goods are delivered to a ship chartered by the buyer, it is a question of fact whether the goods are in the possession of the master as a carrier or as agent for the buyer. If a carrier, bailee or custodier wrongfully refuses to deliver the goods to the buyer or his agent, the transit is deemed to be at an end. When the carrier has delivered part of the goods, the seller may stop the remainder in transitu unless the partial delivery was made in such circumstances as to show an agreement to waive the right to stop the rest.

Section 46 provides that the seller may stop the goods by taking actual possession of them or by giving notice of stoppage to the carrier, bailee or custodier who is in possession of the goods. On receiving notice of stoppage, the carrier, bailee or custodier must redeliver the goods to the seller, or deliver them according to his directions, at the seller's expense.

**Disposition by Buyer**   The Sale of Goods Act 1893, section 47, provides that the seller's lien and his right of stoppage in transitu are not affected by a sale or other disposition of the goods by the buyer, unless the seller has assented thereto,[136] except where documents of title have been given to the buyer and they have been transferred on sale to a person taking the documents in good faith and for valuable consideration. If the person taking the documents from the buyer does so not on sale, but by way of pledge or other disposition, the lien or right of stoppage in transitu is retained but is subject to the rights of the transferee.[137]

**Other Priority Conflicts**   The shipowner's lien for freight[138] has priority over the unpaid vendor's right of stoppage in transitu. Therefore, to get the goods back after the stoppage, the vendor must pay

---

136. As to the nature of the assent required, see *Mordaunt Bros.* v. *British Oil and Cake Mills Ltd.* [1910] 2 K.B. 502.
137. See also p. 173, *ante*.   138. See pp. 202–3, *ante*.

the freight even if someone else, such as the consignee, is contractually liable for it to the shipowner.[139]

Other carriers also have a lien for their charges. In *Mechan & Sons Ltd.* v. *North Eastern Railway Co.*[140] the Court of Session held that a claim by the railway company to a lien for a sum due to them by the consignees did not stop the goods being in transit so as to interfere with the vendor's right of stoppage.

**Effect of Lien or Stoppage on Contract**   The contract of sale is not rescinded by the exercise of the seller's lien or by stoppage in transitu (Sale of Goods Act 1893, section 48). But if the seller re-sells the goods, the new buyer gets a good title as against the original buyer. The seller may re-sell the goods if they are perishable or if he gives notice to the buyer of his intention to do so and the buyer does not pay or tender the price within a reasonable time. The seller may also claim damages if he suffers any. Where the contract of sale reserves an express right to the vendor to re-sell the goods on the purchaser's default, re-sale does rescind the contract; but without prejudice to any claim for damages.

## Equitable Liens in England and Wales and Northern Ireland

An equitable lien is not based on possession: it is analogous to a mortgage by equitable charge,[141] and is enforceable in similar ways. No such security exists in Scotland.[142]

**Unpaid Vendor's Lien**   Unpaid sellers of goods have a possessory lien under the Sale of Goods Act 1893;[143] unpaid sellers of other kinds of property have an equitable lien, on the property sold, for the price. Most of the reported cases relate to land, but there seems to be no reason why the lien should not apply to all types of incorporeal property too. It has been held that the same lien as that enjoyed by an unpaid vendor of land is available, for example, to unpaid vendors of debts,[144] beneficial interests under a trust of personalty,[145] patents[146] and shares.[147]

---

139. *Booth Steamship Co. Ltd.* v. *Cargo Fleet Iron Co. Ltd.* [1916] 2 K.B. 570.
140. 1911 S.C. 1348. Carriers' liens; see p. 221, *ante*.      141. See pp. 24–5, *ante*.
142. See, however, chapter 12, as to the hypothec of a landlord or superior.
143. See pp. 225–6, *ante*.      144. *Collins* v. *Collins* (*No. 2*) (1862) 31 Beav. 346.
145. *Davies* v. *Thomas* [1900] 2 Ch. 462; *Re Stucley* [1906] 1 Ch. 67.
146. *Dansk Rekylriffel Syndikat Aktieselskab* v. *Snell* [1908] 2 Ch. 127.
147. *Ex parte Sheppard* (1841) 2 Mont. D. & De G. 431; *Langen & Wind Ltd.* v. *Bell* [1972] Ch. 685.

This lien is to secure the price, whether a lump sum or any other variety of money payment. In *Re Mead*[148] specific performance had been ordered of a contract for the sale of land, the purchase price being payable by instalments. Some of the instalments were not yet due. It was declared that the vendor had a lien, and he was given liberty to apply as further instalments became payable. In *Dansk Rekylriffel Syndikat Aktieselskab* v. *Snell*[149] it was held that the vendor of a patent had a lien over it for minimum royalties promised as part of the consideration for the sale.

The vendor's lien arises when the contract of sale is entered into (though it is not enforceable by action before the date set for completion).[150] When it does become enforceable by action, the normal equitable remedies are available: the court may order a sale, appoint a receiver or allow the lienee into possession. In the case of a vendor of land, he may have an order for sale even if the purchaser has built on the land. In *Wing* v. *Tottenham and Hampstead Junction Railway Co.*[151] the Court of Appeal in Chancery made an order for sale despite the fact that the purchaser had built a railway on the land and was ready for traffic. The same court made a similar order in *Munns* v. *Isle of Wight Railway Co.*[152] and appointed a receiver pending the sale.

Obviously the vendor can have no lien if he is not an unpaid vendor – if he has received the consideration for the sale. In *Buckland* v. *Pocknell*[153] land was sold in consideration of a promise to pay an annuity. It was held that there was no lien for payment of the annuity because the consideration was not *payment of the annuity* but a *promise to pay the annuity*, which promise the vendor had received from the purchaser. Similarly, in *Re Albert Life Assurance Co.*,[154] where there was a sale by a society of its whole undertaking to a company in consideration of the company taking on all the liabilities of the society, the liquidator of the society was held to have no lien over assets transferred to the company merely because the company did not discharge all the liabilities of the society: the company took them on, and that was the consideration. In *Capital Finance Co. Ltd.*

148. (1880) 15 Ch. D. 651.     149. [1908] 2 Ch. 127.
150. *Re Birmingham* [1959] Ch. 523.     151. (1868) L.R. 3 Ch. App. 740.
152. (1870) L.R. 4 Ch. App. 414.
153. (1843) 13 Sim. 406. See also *Dixon* v. *Gayfere* (1857) 1 De G. & J. 655. Ireland: cf. *Richardson* v. *M'Causland* (1817) Beat. 457, where land was sold in consideration of the purchaser entering into a covenant to pay the vendor's rent and to supply her with hay and corn and where, the purchaser having so covenanted, the vendor was held to have a lien for performance.
154. (1870) L.R. 11 Eq. 1 64. See also *Mackreth* v. *Symmons* (1808) 15 Ves. 329; *Parrott* v. *Sweetland* (1835) 3 My. & K. 655; *Re Brentwood Brick and Coal Co.* (1876) 4 Ch. D. 562.

v. *Stokes*[155] the consideration for the sale of the land was a price expressed to be payable as to a quarter in cash and, as to three-quarters, to be on loan to the purchaser on security of a legal mortgage of the land sold. The legal mortgage was granted by the purchaser to the vendor, but it shortly became void for non-registration under the Companies Act 1948, section 95.[156] As an unpaid vendor's lien does not require such registration,[157] an attempt was made to fall back on that. It was unsuccessful because the vendor had got what he bargained for, even if he subsequently lost some of it.[158]

If, on the other hand, the vendor takes express security for the purchase price, that does not necessarily preclude his having an equitable lien for it too. There are three main possibilities: (i) the loan of the purchase-money on security substitutes an obligation to repay the loan for an obligation to pay the purchase price, in which case there is no lien because there is no unpaid vendor;[159] (ii) the security is for the obligation to pay the price and the circumstances are such as to show an intention to rely on the express security and abandon the lien, in which case there is no lien;[160] (iii) the security is for the obligation to pay the price but there is no intention to abandon the lien and there is no inconsistency between the lien and the express security, in which case the lien and the express security co-exist.[161]

The unpaid vendor does not lose his lien, as against a chargee, by going out of possession after creating the charge.[162]

Being an equity, a lien (unless registrable) prevails against third parties, except a bona fide purchaser of a legal or equitable estate or interest in the property without notice of the lien; and that is so even if there is a receipt for the purchase money in the conveyance or transfer.[163]

It seems from *Uziell-Hamilton* v. *Keen*[164] that the lien of an unpaid vendor of land is registrable in England and Wales as a class C (iii) land charge.[165] There is, however, nothing in the Land Charges Act

---

155. [1969] 1 Ch. 261. See also p. 99, *ante*.      156. See pp. 119–20, *ante*.
157. See p. 120, *ante*.
158. Cf. *Congresbury Motors Ltd.* v. *Anglo-Belge Finance Co. Ltd.* [1971] Ch. 81 and *Coptic Ltd.* v. *Bailey* [1972] Ch. 446, pp. 99–100, *ante*.
159. *Capital Finance Co. Ltd.* v. *Stokes* [1969] 1 Ch. 261, above.
160. *Mackreth* v. *Symmons* (1808) 15 Ves. 329. Ireland: *Re Stewart* [1925] 2 I.R. 51.
161. *Collins* v. *Collins* (*No. 2*) (1862) 31 Beav. 346. Ireland: see *Hughes* v. *Kearney* (1803) 1 Sch. & Lef. 132; *Kelaghan* v. *Daly* [1913] 2 I.R. 328.
162. *London and Cheshire Insurance Co. Ltd.* v. *Laplagrene Property Co. Ltd.* [1971] Ch. 499.
163. *Mackreth* v. *Symmons* (1808) 15 Ves. 329; *Rice* v. *Rice* (1854) 2 Drew. 73.
164. (1971) 22 P. & C.R. 655.      165. Land Charges Act 1972, s. 2(4) (iii).

to suggest that the expression 'equitable charge' is meant to include a lien. If it is, then it may also be that, in the case of registered land, the lien can be protected under the Land Registration Act 1925, section 49(1) (c), by notice; under section 54, by caution; or by registration under section 26. If the vendor is in possession, his lien is an overriding interest under section 70(1) (g).

Certainly a vendor's lien over incorporeal property is not registrable. In *Langen & Wind Ltd.* v. *Bell*[166] there was a contract for the sale of shares under which the price was not payable until after the transfer. Because the vendor's lien would be vulnerable to a person bona fide acquiring an interest in the shares from the purchaser, if he acquired it for value and without notice of the lien, it was held that the purchaser would not be granted specific performance without safeguarding the vendor. In this case the vendor was safeguarded by ordering the share certificate and transfer to be held by the purchaser's solicitor, as stake-holder, until payment of the price.

**Purchaser's Lien**   Where there is a contract for the sale of land, and completion does not in the event take place, the purchaser has a lien on the land for reimbursement of certain types of expenditure, provided that the failure to complete is not due to the purchaser's default,[167] and provided that the purchaser has not abandoned the contract.[168] The nature of the lien is exactly the same as that of the unpaid vendor's lien.[169]

The purchaser's lien will secure: (1) return of his deposit, if it has been paid to the vendor,[170] but not if it has been paid to a stake-holder because then the purchaser is not the vendor's creditor and so cannot be his secured creditor;[171] (2) return of any other part of the purchase price paid to the vendor;[172] (3) reimbursement of the cost of investigating the vendor's title;[173] (4) reimbursement of costs incurred in successfully defending an action by the vendor for specific performance where the vendor fails on the ground that a good title has not been adduced;[174] and (5) at least in some circumstances, reimbursement of expenditure on the land. This last head

166. [1972] Ch. 685.
167. See *Wythes* v. *Lee* (1855) 3 Drew. 396; *Rose* v. *Watson* (1864) 10 H.L.C. 672; *Whitbread & Co. Ltd.* v. *Watt* [1902] 1 Ch. 835.
168. *Dinn* v. *Grant* (1852) 5 De G. & Sm. 451.    169. See pp. 228–31, *ante*.
170. *Whitebread & Co. Ltd.* v. *Watt* [1902] 1 Ch. 835; *Lee-Parker* v. *Izzet* [1971] 1 W.L.R. 1688.
171. *Combe* v. *Swaythling* (*Lord*) [1947] Ch. 625.   172. *Rose* v. *Watson* (1864) 10 H.L.C. 672.
173. *Kitton* v. *Hewett* [1904] W.N. 21.    174. *Turner* v. *Marriott* (1867) L.R. 3 Eq. 744.

is illustrated by *Middleton* v. *Magnay*.[175] A person who had agreed to take a lease was there held entitled to a lien for his expenditure on the premises, when it turned out that no lease was going to be granted, it having been agreed originally that that outlay was to be repaid by the person contracting to grant the lease if completion did not take place.

## Person Preserving or Improving Someone Else's Property

An artisan who improves goods belonging to his customer has a common law possessory lien for his charges.[176] A salvor who salves a ship has a maritime lien for his charges.[177] In general, these are the only liens for improvement or preservation of someone else's property. Except in a few special cases, improvement or preservation of another person's land or incorporeal property gives rise to no equitable lien.

**The general rule** Most of the unsuccessful claims to liens have related to: (i) expenditure on improving land; or (ii) paying premiums on a life insurance policy.

The general rule that one who spends money voluntarily on someone else's land has no claim for reinbursement, by lien or otherwise, is illustrated by *Leigh* v. *Dickeson*.[178] It was there held by the Court of Appeal that one tenant in common who paid for repairs to the premises had no claim for a contribution from his co-tenant unless the land was being partitioned. This rule has recently been applied by the House of Lords to cases of husband and wife. In *Pettitt* v. *Pettitt*[179] the legal title to the matrimonial home was held by the wife. When the parties were divorced, it was held that the husband had no claim to a share in the proceeds of the house for the value of work done by him or materials supplied at his expense in modernising the premises. In *Gissing* v. *Gissing*[180] the legal title to the matrimonial home belonged to the husband. When the parties were divorced, it was held that the wife had no claim to any interest in the premises founded on her expenditure on the garden or otherwise on the home.

In relation to a life insurance policy the rule is similar: a person

---

175. (1864) 2 H. & M. 233.     176. See p. 221, *ante*.
177. See p. 197, *ante*.
178. (1884) 15 Q.B.D. 60. Ireland: *Munster and Leinster Bank Ltd.* v. *McCann* [1937] Ir. Jur. Rep. 40; *Re Kavanagh* (1953) [1952] Ir. Jur. Rep. 38.
179. [1970] A.C. 777.
180. [1971] A.C. 886. Cf. *Hargrave* v. *Newton* [1971] 1 W.L.R. 1611; *Hazell* v. *Hazell* [1972] 1 W.L.R. 301; *Cooke* v. *Head* [1972] 1 W.L.R. 518.

who pays premiums on it voluntarily does not acquire any rights over someone else's policy. In *Re Leslie*[181] a wife took out a policy on her own life. The husband paid the premiums during his life, and after his death his executors paid them out of his estate. It was held that the husband's estate had no claim upon the policy. In *Falcke* v. *Scottish Imperial Insurance Co.*[182] the Court of Appeal held that the payer of the premiums still got no lien even though he was the owner of the equity of redemption in the policy (the legal title to which was in the mortgagee). In *Re Stokes*[183] a bankrupt, unknown to his trustee in bankruptcy, took out a life insurance policy and paid the premiums till his death. It was held that the bankrupt's estate had no claim, even to the return of the premiums; all the policy moneys must go to the trustee in bankruptcy.

**Exceptional cases** In *Re Leslie*[184] Pearson J. and Fry L.J., in a single judgment, mentioned four exceptional cases where a lien was created: (i) by contract with the owner; (ii) where the payer has a lien as trustee;[185] (iii) by subrogation to the rights of trustees;[185] (iv) where the payer is a mortgagee who has a right to add the amount to his security.[186] To these cases two others should be added; (v) certain special rules in bankruptcy; (vi) where there is a mistake as to the ownership of the property or an expectation of the acquisition of an interest in it. There also appears to be in Ireland: (vii) an extended doctrine of salvage.

**Contract with the owner** This need not be an explicit contract. In *Grabiner* v. *Brew*[187] the husband paid the premiums, both during the marriage and after divorce, on a life insurance policy belonging to the wife. The Court of Appeal held that he had a lien on the policy for the amount of premiums paid after the divorce because he had done so as the wife's agent. Contracts have sometimes been held to exist between husband and wife as to expenditure on the matrimonial home.[188]

**Bankruptcy** There is no lien, but sometimes an officer of the court is ordered to observe a higher standard of conduct than other people, and pay money which is not legally recoverable. In *Re*

181. (1883) 23 Ch. D. 552. See also *Strutt* v. *Tippett* (1890) 62 L.T. 475; *Re Jones' Settlement* [1915] 1 Ch. 373. Scotland: in *Wylie's Executrix* v. *M'Jannett* (1901) 4 F. 195 it was held that a creditor who paid the premiums on his debtor's life insurance policy acquired no lien over the policy for the amount of the premiums.
182. (1886) 34 Ch. D. 234.   183. [1919] 2 K.B. 256.
184. (1883) 23 Ch. D. 552.
185. Trustee's lien: see pp. 235–6, *post*; subrogation: see pp. 236–7, *post*.
186. See p. 31, *ante*.   187. (1964) 108 S.J. 1030.
188. See *Davis* v. *Vale* [1971] 1 W.L.R. 1022; *Cracknell* v. *Cracknell* [1971] P. 356; *Cowcher* v. *Cowcher* [1972] 1 W.L.R. 425.

*Tyler*[189] the wife paid premiums on a life insurance policy belonging to the husband, which vested in the Official Receiver on the husband's bankruptcy. It was ordered that the Official Receiver, being an officer of the court, pay the amount of the premiums back to the wife. This special consideration is not given to the payer if the existence of the policy is concealed from the trustee in bankruptcy.[190]

**Mistake as to ownership or expectation of change therein**

First, if all the parties are mistaken as to the ownership of the property on which money is spent, believing it to belong to the payer, the latter will have a lien. In *Re Foster (No. 2)*[191] a father had a policy of insurance on his son's life. After the father's death, the son paid the premiums. Everyone concerned thought the policy belonged to the son. When the son died, his personal representative was held to have a lien on the policy moneys for the amount of the premiums paid by the son.

Secondly, if one person, mistakenly believing himself to be the owner, spends money on property while the true owner, knowing of the mistake, abstains from setting the other person right and leaves him to persevere in his error, the person expending money acquires an equity in the property.[192] Such cases usually concern land. The way of effectuating the equity depends on the circumstances. It may be a lien for the return of the money.

Finally, an equity may be acquired by someone who spends money on another person's property expecting to be granted some interest in that property. In *Hussey* v. *Palmer*[193] an elderly widow went to live in her daughter and son-in-law's house. She paid for the cost of building an extra bedroom on to it, for her to use. After she had lived there for about a year and a quarter, differences arose and she moved away. The Court of Appeal held (Cairns L.J. dissenting) that she had an equitable interest in the house to the value of her outlay. A lien would seem appropriate, but the majority thought there was a resulting or constructive trust of the house.

In all these cases, a lien is the appropriate equity if justice would be done by charging the property with repayment of the outlay. Other methods of effectuating this kind of equity over another

189. [1907] 1 K.B. 865. See also *Re Condon* (1874) L.R. 9 Ch. App. 609; *Re Carnac* (1885) 16 Q.B.D. 308.
190. *Tapster* v. *Ward* (1909) 101 L.T. 503; *Re Phillips* [1914] 2 K.B. 689. See also *Re Hall* [1907] 1 K.B. 875.
191. [1938] 3 All E.R. 610.    192. *Ramsden* v. *Dyson* (1866) L.R. 1 H.L. 129.
193. [1972] 1 W.L.R. 1286.

person's land include: a declaration that there is a licence (e.g., to use or leave something on someone else's land);[194] an injunction to resist being put out of someone's else's land;[195] and a trust.[196]

**Salvage in Ireland**   There was a general review of this jurisdiction in *Fetherstone* v. *Mitchell*,[197] where a judgment creditor was held entitled to a lien for expenditure on preserving the debtor's property. In *Re Power's Policies*[198] a solicitor acted for both parties in a mortgage of life insurance policies, and himself took a second mortgage of the policies. He paid the premiums on them thereafter. It was held that he had priority over the first mortgagee in respect of his lien for the amount of the premiums only in respect of payments after he had made it clear to the first mortgagee that he was not paying as the mortgagor's agent.

**Liens under Trusts and Covenants**   By the Trustee Act 1925, section 30(2),[199] restating the previous law, a trustee may reimburse himself or pay or discharge out of the trust premises all expenses incurred in or about the execution of the trusts or powers. Case law establishes that, if he pays out of his own pocket, his right to reimbursement is supported by a lien on the trust property.

**Trustee's lien for obligatory outgoings**   If a trustee has to pay such outgoings as calls on shares, or insurance premiums,[200] out of his own pocket, he has a lien on the shares or insurance policy for the amount. It seems that he has no lien if he could have paid out of trust moneys available to him and thus had no need to resort to his own money.[201]

**Trustee's lien for improving land**   He is entitled to a lien for permanent improvements to trust land he has paid for out of his own pocket.[202] In *Darke* v. *Williamson*[203] a chapel held by trustees was being repaired. The cost exceeding the trust money available, the excess was borrowed by some of the trustees, who personally engaged to repay the loan. It was held that they had a lien for an indemnity, but that the lien could not be enforced by sale or foreclosure because that would destroy the whole trust: they could have

---

194. See *Inwards* v. *Baker* [1965] 2 Q.B. 29.   195. See *Ward* v. *Kirkland* [1967] Ch. 194.
196. See *Binions* v. *Evans* [1972] Ch. 359.   197. (1848) 11 Ir. Eq. Rep. 35.
198. [1899] 1 I.R. 6.
199. Equivalent legislation: Trustee Act (Northern Ireland) 1958, s. 31(2).
200. *Re Smith's Estate* [1937] Ch. 636; *Re Roberts* [1946] Ch. 1.
201. *Clack* v. *Holland* (1854) 19 Beav. 262.
202. *Rowley* v. *Ginnever* [1897] 2 Ch. 503. Ireland: *Minnitt* v. *Lord Talbot de Malahide* (1876) 1 L.R. Ir. 143; (1881) 7 L.R. Ir. 407.
203. (1858) 25 Beav. 622. Ireland: *Bowman* v. *Hill* [1907] 1 I.R. 451.

their share if the chapel were sold otherwise than in enforcement of the lien or if the trust came to an end.

**Trustee's Lien for Purchase-Money** In *Re Pumfrey*[204] trustees with power to invest in buying real property bought real property, at the request of the beneficiaries, costing more than the fund available for investment. One trustee borrowed the balance from a bank, and deposited the title deeds to the trust land with the bank as security. It was held that: (*a*) the trustee was personally liable to the bank for the amount of the loan; (*b*) the trustee had a lien for an indemnity, over the trust land in so far as its value exceeded the amount contributed by the trust fund to its purchase, for his liability to the bank; and (*c*) the bank, as mortgagee of the trustee's lien, was subrogated to and could enforce the lien by sale.

**Trustee's lien for damages** A trustee has a lien over the trust property for reimbursement of damages he has to pay personally in the course of reasonable management of a trust business. In *Re Raybould*[205] the trustee had to pay damages for letting down the surface of neighbouring land while running a colliery. It was held that the plaintiff could enforce the judgment against the trustee personally and against the trust property by subrogation to the trustee's lien.

**Trustee's lien for costs of litigation** If trustees win an action they bring or defend to protect the trust property, they have a lien, by way of first charge on capital and income, for reimbursement of their proper costs. In *Re Holden*[206] the action in question was an unsuccessful attempt by the settlor to set the trust aside. The trustees were held to have such a lien for the costs of their successful defence when the trust later became void on account of the settlor's bankruptcy. The same applies to an action which the trustees compromise.[207] If trustees obtain the leave of the court to bring or defend an action, they will always be reimbursed their costs, including those incurred in applying for leave. If they litigate without the leave of the court, they have a lien for their costs only if they can prove it was proper to bring or defend the action. If they have lost, it may still have been proper. But if they cannot prove propriety, their lien will be limited to such amount as it would have cost to apply to the court for leave.[208]

**Beneficiary's lien by subrogation** A beneficiary has a lien

204. (1882) 22 Ch. D. 255.　　205. [1900] 1 Ch. 199.
206. (1887) 20 Q.B.D. 43.　　207. *Stott* v. *Milne* (1884) 25 Ch. D. 710.
208. *Re Beddoe* [1893] 1 Ch. 547.

over the trust property for advances made for some purpose that the trustees were liable to pay for. In *Todd* v. *Moorhouse*[209] the tenant for life, at the request of the trustees, lent them money to pay calls on trust shares. He was held to have a lien on the shares for repayment.

**Lien arising out of covenant**  A covenant between A and B that A will pay an annuity to C out of specified estates, or out of all his estates, gives C an equitable lien on the specified estate, or on all A's estates, as the case may be.[210] On the other hand, if the covenant to pay did not specify any estate on which the annuity was to be charged, it would confer no equity on C.[211]

## Tenant's Lien

It was held in *Lee-Parker* v. *Izzet*[212] that a tenant for a term of years had a lien over future rent in respect of the cost of repairs paid for by him when the landlord was in breach of covenant by not doing them. It seems that that is properly considered as a set-off, as it means the tenant can deduct the amount from the rent.

## Landlord's Lien in Scotland

Where a tenant has erected buildings which he has a right to remove at the end of the tenancy, the landlord has a right to retain possession of them until he is paid arrears of rent.[213]

In *Paton's Trustee* v. *Finlayson*[214] farmers were held to have possession of potatoes and hence the right to retain them for rent when a merchant had rented the farmers' ground to grow the potatoes and had lifted and pitted them there. (The farmers got possession either on planting or on pitting.)

## Other Liens

It would be difficult to catalogue all the liens that exist; more difficult still to catalogue everything that has been called a lien or right of retention. They sometimes arise out of partnership or suretyship transactions. Sometimes the articles of association of a

---

209. (1874) L.R. 19 Eq. 69.  210. See *Ravenshaw* v. *Hollier* (1834) 7 Sim. 3.
211. See *Ravenshaw* v. *Hollier* (1835) 4 L.J. Ch. 119.  212. [1971] 1 W.L.R. 1688.
213. *Smith* v. *Harrison & Co's Trustee* (1893) 21 R. 330. As to the landlord's hypothec, see pp. 239–43, *post*.
214. 1923 S.C. 872.

company will stipulate a lien over shares for repayment of share-holders' debts to the company. There are liens for customs and excise duties: statutory liens for tolls and other such dues. Contracts commonly stipulate for liens. For example, a building contract is quite likely to contain a term that, if the builder does not complete the work, the customer is to be entitled to retain the builder's machinery and materials on the customer's premises. The examples given in this chapter are the main liens: those which are of the greatest commercial use and which illustrate the different legal categories.

Most difficult of all would be a catalogue of liens which have been claimed and which courts have held not to exist.

# 2 hypothec in Scotland

To hypothecate property is to give it as security in some way which involves neither the dominium (legal ownership) nor the possession of it passing to the creditor. Such is the nature, for example, of the equitable mortgage of land in England and Wales and of the modern mortgage of registered land in Northern Ireland. In the law of Scotland, hypothecation was never possible by agreement until the passing of nineteenth and twentieth century legislation. The common law of Scotland demanded that a contractual security pass to the creditor either title (which carries the right to possession) or physical possession. Exceptions now created by statute are mortgages of aircraft[1] and ships,[2] agricultural charges[3] and floating charges.[4]

However, the common law of Scotland does provide a hypothec by operation of law in strictly limited circumstances. One example is the lien of a solicitor for his costs over a fund in court belonging to his client.[5] The commonest example to which the expression 'hypothec' is usually applied is the landlord's hypothec for his rent[6] over the goods which his tenant produces or grows or brings on the land.[7] This landlord's hypothec is a creature of the law, not of agreement. The law prescribes which landlords have it and when, how it is enforced and in respect of what goods. A landlord who has

1. See p. 118, *ante*.     2. See pp. 176–87, *ante*.
3. See pp. 142–4, *ante*.     4. See pp. 126–43, *ante*.
5. See pp. 211–12, *ante*.
6. The landlord has the same hypothec for royalties under a mining lease as he has for other kinds of rent: *Liquidators of the Linlithgow Oil Co. Ltd.* v. *Earl of Rosebery* (1903) 6 F. 90.
7. There is a general discussion of the landlord's hypothec by Lord President M'Neill in *Duffy* v. *Gray* (1858) 20 D. 580, 588–90.

no hypothec by operation of law cannot reserve himself one by agreement with his tenant.[8]

The purpose of the landlord's hypothec is to provide security for the payment of rent. To some extent, there is an analogy with the landlord's power, in England and Wales, to levy distress for rent and with Northern Ireland procedures for enforcing payment of rent,[9] but the hypothec in Scotland is associated with much more extensive rights in the landlord, and hence more effective security, then those which exist in other parts of the United Kingdom.

Besides the landlord, a superior has a similar hypothec over his vassal's goods as security for payment of the feuduty.[10]

**Exemptions and Qualifications**  In general, the landlord will not be able to enforce his hypothec against those few necessities of life that a bankrupt is allowed to withhold in his sequestration. Furthermore, there have been statutory reductions of the extent permitted to the landlord's hypothec at common law.

The earliest of these statutes was the Hypothec Amendment (Scotland) Act 1867 which, by section 2, applies only to farms. Section 3 of that Act exempts from the landlord's hypothec agricultural produce bona fide purchased from the tenant for its fair market value and delivered to the purchaser and removed from the farm. By section 4, there is no hypothec for rent more than three months in arrear. Section 5 provides that, if the tenant lets out fields for grazing, the hirer's animals are subject to the landlord's hypothec only for the amount the hirer has to pay the tenant for the grazing.[11] Certain exemptions for the tenant's furniture, agricultural implements, etc., are laid down by section 6. Finally, section 7 requires the maintenance of a register of sequestrations.[12]

Next, in 1880, the Hypothec Abolition (Scotland) Act – a wildly misnamed statute – introduced strict regulation of the landlord's rights with regard to the rent of land, exceeding two acres in area, let for agriculture or pasture.

The House Letting and Rating (Scotland) Act 1911, section 10, gave exemption from the landlord's hypothec to the tenant of a

8. *M'Gavin* v. *Sturrock's Trustee* (1891) 18 R. 576.
9. The Judgments (Enforcement) Act (Northern Ireland) 1969, s. 122(1), abolished distress for rent. Under ss. 32–4, orders can be made for the sale and seizure of goods.
10. In *Yuille* v. *Lawrie* (1823) 2 S. 155 it was held that the superior in an urban tenement had a hypothec over bona invecta et illata.
11. See *Steuart* v. *Ledingham* (1878) 5 R. 1024.
12. Sequestration: see p. 242, *post.*

small dwelling-house[13] for bedding, the tools of his trade and such further furniture and plenishing as the tenant might select to the value of £10.

On the other hand, the landlord's hypothec is not affected by the changes made in the law relating to the sale of goods in 1893[14] or by those made in bankruptcy law in 1913.[15]

**Making the Tenant Stock the Land**   Although the landlord's hypothec is in some respects in the nature of a floating security, as the tenant may acquire and dispose of goods, the landlord is not at the mercy of complete freedom on the tenant's part. The landlord cannot have a hypothec over goods which were never on the premises during the lease in respect of which the rent is owed,[16] but he has a right to make the tenant have some possessions on the land and thus provide security. In *Wright* v. *Wightman*,[17] where there was a lease of a house for three years at an annual rent, the tenant was ordered to plenish the house with sufficient furniture to secure the current year's rent.[18]

**Making the Tenant Keep the Land Stocked**   The landlord can detain goods on the ground, or get them back on to the land if the tenant has removed them.[19] He can also get court orders to the necessary effect if self-help proves inadequate to the occasion.

In *Henry Nelmes & Co.* v. *Ewing*[20] the tenant was the keeper of a billiard room. For years he had hired a table, cues and other equipment. When the owner removed these, it was held that the landlord could have them brought back to be subjected to the hypothec.

But when furniture has been removed from the premises, the landlord cannot normally obtain a warrant to have it brought back, so as to subject it to the hypothec, without notice to the other party.[21]

**Goods Not Belonging to the Tenant**   It seems that, if there is a mixture of the tenant's goods on the premises with goods belonging

13. Defined in s. 1 of the 1911 Act, as amended by the Valuation and Rating (Scotland) Act 1956, s. 37.
14. Sale of Goods Act 1893, s. 61(5).       15. Bankruptcy (Scotland) Act 1913, s. 115.
16. *Thomson* v. *Barclay* (1883) 10 R. 694.
17. (1875) 3 R. 68. See also *Thomson* v. *Handyside* (1833) 12 S. 557.
18. See *Whitelaw* v. *Fulton* (1871) 10 M. 27 for an order as to a shop.
19. *Crichton* v. *Earl of Queensberry* (1672) Mor. 6203. See also *Goldie* v. *Oswald's Trustees* (1839) 1 D. 426.       20. (1883) 11 R. 193.
21. *Johnston* v. *Young* (1890) 18 R. (J.) 6; *Gray* v. *Weir* (1891) 19 R. 25; *M'Laughlan* v. *Reilly* (1892) 20 R. 41; *Jack* v. *Black* 1911 S.C. 691; *Shearer* v. *Nicoll* 1935 S.L.T. 313.

to third parties, all the goods are subject to the hypothec if they are the sort of things you would expect to find on land of that kind, if they are lawfully brought there and if they do not belong to a third party who also lives there. In *D. H. Industries Ltd.* v. *R. E. Spence & Co. Ltd.*[22] an industrial machine belonging to a third party was held to be subject to the landlord's hypothec, because the machine was part of the ordinary plenishings of the premises. In *Henry Nelmes & Co.* v. *Ewing*[23] the court went to the length of allowing the landlord to have the third party's goods brought back on to the premises, after the owner had removed them, lawfully as against the tenant, so as to subject them to the hypothec. It seems from *M'Intosh* v. *Potts*[24] that a piano on hire to the tenant is subject to the hypothec if all the other furniture in the house belongs to the tenant. Goods sold by the tenant and paid for by the purchaser, but left with the tenant on his premises, are covered by the landlord's hypothec.[25]

On the other hand, the following goods belonging to a third party have been held to be free from the landlord's security for his rent: goods wrongly detained by the tenant;[26] a piano belonging to the tenant's daughter;[27] where the tenant was an agent, his principal's samples sent to him for display;[28] and a piano hired by the tenant (the only article on the premises belonging to a third party), all the other furniture on the premises being the property of the landlord.[29]

**Enforcement of the Hypothec**   When the rent is in arrear, the landlord's normal method of enforcing his security is by sequestration. This is a proceeding in the sheriff court which results in an order for an inventory being made of the goods subject to the hypothec and, if the rent is not paid, ultimate sale of enough of them to pay off what is due to the landlord.

It was held in *Donald* v. *Leitch*[30] that the landlord could sequestrate for the current year's rent and that, if good cause was required, displenishment by the tenant was good cause. In that case, the tenant of the Dalziel Arms, Motherwell, was sending the hotel furniture for auction in Glasgow.

22. 1973 S.L.T. (Sh.) 26.     23. (1883) 11 R. 193: see p. 241, *ante*.
24. (1905) 7 F. 765.     25. *Ryan* v. *Little* 1910 S.C. 219.
26. *Jaffray* v. *Carrick* (1836) 15 S. 43.
27. *Bell* v. *Andrews* (1885) 12 R. 961. The piano was given to her by a relative living elsewhere. It is obvious that a young daughter living at home must keep her property in her father's house. It would have been different if the tenant, having the piano on the premises as his own, had given it to his daughter.
28. *Pulsometer Engineering Co. Ltd.* v. *Gracie* (1887) 14 R. 316.
29. *Edinburgh Albert Buildings Co.* v. *General Guarantee Corp. Ltd.* 1917 S.C. 239.
30. (1886) 13 R. 790.

**Ranking**  Apart from the claim of a third party that he owns the goods, and that they are therefore not subject to the landlord's hypothec, few questions of priority can arise. If the goods are subject to the hypothec, the landlord will take priority over third parties' proprietary rights, whether as owners or as holders of a floating charge when the tenant is a limited liability company. A Crown debt, however, ranks against the goods in priority to the landlord's hypothec.

**Landlord's Mortgagee**  A mortgagee in possession has the landlord's hypothec against tenants to whom the mortgaged premises have been let by the mortgagor,[31] but a mortgagee has no such right in security when not in possession.[32]

---

31. *Robertson's Trustees* v. *Gardner* (1889) 16 R. 705.
32. *Railton* v. *Muirhead* (1834) 12 S. 757.

# 13 stocks and shares as security

Throughout this book, the expressions 'security' and 'rights in security' have been used to designate property segregated by a debtor from the generality of his assets so as to give his creditor, if otherwise unpaid, the right to appropriate that property to the payment of his debt. 'Security' is commonly used in other senses as well. The word sometimes means a document evidencing a right to receive a sum of money. In this sense, a debenture may be called a security, even though the company may not have secured the debt by a fixed or floating charge. Similarly, a share certificate is sometimes called a security, because it evidences the shareholder's entitlement to a proportion of the company's assets if it is wound up while solvent. A bond may thus be called a security, and bills of exchange and promissory notes are often referred to as negotiable securities. By analogy, an investment evidenced by such a document may itself be called a security. In this way, stocks and shares are called securities and, in the case of government stock, 'gilt-edged securities.'

In this chapter, 'security' means what it means elsewhere in the book. Owners of stocks and shares, like owners of land and goods, may wish to raise money on security of their property. For this purpose they may mortgage or otherwise create rights in security over their stocks and shares.

Security over the following types of property is excluded from the scope of this chapter:

(1) debentures: a debenture either evidences an unsecured debt,

in which case the security is the debt;[1] or it evidences a fixed or floating charge, in which case the security given is a sub-charge;[2]

(2) bonds: a bond is given to support an unsecured debt[1] or guarantee;[3]

(3) units in a unit trust: these are a particular kind of equitable interest under a trust.[4]

This chapter is concerned with the giving of express[5] security over stocks and shares, not with liens which arise over them, or over the documents relating to them, by operation of law, or with charging orders imposed by the court in favour of a judgment creditor. Money is commonly raised on the security of stocks and shares to provide the cost of buying them, to provide working capital for use in business, to secure an overdraft at a bank or by way of obtaining extended time for repayment from an unsecured creditor who is pressing for his money back.

## Legal Mortgages in England and Wales and Northern Ireland

As was the case with land in England and Wales before 1926, a legal mortgage of any other kind of property (except a ship) is achieved today by transferring the mortgagor's legal title to the mortgagee subject to an agreement for re-transfer on redemption. During the period of the mortgage, the mortgagor has an equitable interest in the shares, the equity of redemption.

The legal title to most shares is governed by registration. The company keeps a register of shareholders, and the legal title to a share is vested in the person whose name appears on the company's register as the owner of it. A transferee becomes the legal owner by having his name substituted on the register for that of the transferor. How he achieves that depends on the requirements of the company's articles of association. Usually, the company issues to the shareholder a document called a share certificate which states the shareholder's name and the number of shares he is registered as owning. The usual procedure for transferring shares is for the transferor to sign a document of transfer and give it, with the share certificate, to the transferee; the latter then sends both documents to the company. The company will then register the transferee as

1. Unsecured debt as security: see pp. 270–83, *post.*
2. Company charges and sub-charges: see pp. 119–20, 126–43 *ante.*
3. Suretyship and cautionry: see pp. 284–312, *post.*
4. Beneficial interests under trusts as security: see pp. 277–81, *post.*
5. Bankers' and stockbrokers' liens over stocks and shares: see pp. 213–14, *ante.*

owner of the shares (at which point the legal title has passed) and issue him a new share certificate. The company will not be aware of whether the transferee is a buyer, a donee or a mortgagee: that depends on the agreement between the transferor and the transferee.

Exceptionally, and only in the case of a public company or gilt-edged stock, ownership is not registered but the share or stock certificate is made out in the form that the bearer (unnamed) is the owner. By custom, such documents are negotiable, so that legal ownership of the shares or stock passes by delivery of the certificate to a bona fide holder without notice of any defect in his predecessor's title. Sometimes letters of allotment are issued in this form, negotiable until a name is entered; and the named person will then apply for registration.

So far as the nature of the property admits, the rules relating to legal mortgages of land[6] apply to legal mortgages of stocks and shares. For example, *Bradley* v. *Carritt*[7] is a case where the House of Lords invalidated a term of the mortgage agreement because it created a clog on the equity of redemption. There is no point in repeating the rules common to land and incorporeal property, and what follows relates to the special position of stocks and shares.

**Remedies of the mortgagee to enforce his security**  The only remedy common to shares and land in every particular is foreclosure.[8] Going into possession is clearly an inapposite concept in relation to incorporeal property, while the appointment of a receiver is an irrelevance because the mortgagee, as legal owner of the shares, will receive the dividends from the company anyway.

The mortgagee's other normal remedy, sale of the mortgaged property free from the equity of redemption, arises more readily in the cases of shares than it does in the case of land. A mortgage of shares is not normally by deed, so that there will not normally be a statutory power of sale. If the agreement between the parties does not expressly confer a power of sale on the mortgagee, he will nevertheless have such a power by implication of law, if the date for redemption has passed,[9] or if no date is specified for repayment,[10] provided the mortgagee has given the mortgagor reasonable notice (i.e. notice allowing an adequate time for redemption) requiring repayment and the mortgagor does not redeem within that time.

---

6. See chapters 2, 3, 4, and 6, *ante*.    7. [1903] A.C. 253. See p. 50, *ante*.
8. *General Credit and Discount Co.* v. *Glegg* (1883) 22 Ch. D. 549.
9. *Tucker* v. *Wilson* (1714) 1 P. Wms. 261.
10. *Deverges* v. *Sandeman, Clark & Co.* [1902] 1 Ch. 579.

On the other hand, if there is no statutory or express power of sale, and the conditions for the exercise of the implied power of sale have not been satisfied, a purchaser for value from the mortgagee of a legal interest in the shares takes subject to the equity of redemption unless he has no notice of its existence, whether the securities are negotiable or not.[11]

**Duty to re-transfer on redemption** Every mortgagee, whatever the mortgaged property, is obliged to re-transfer it to the mortgagor on redemption. In the case of shares readily available on the stock exchange, the question has arisen whether the mortgagee must re-transfer the identical shares mortgaged or whether it is enough that he transfer to the mortgagee an identical number of similar shares. The courts have always required the former. This rule applies to equitable mortgages as well.

In *Tutt* v. *Mercer*[12] there was a mortgage of a South-Sea Co. receipt for a subscription of £500, to secure a debt of £1,100. The mortgagee was also the beneficial owner of another such receipt. The mortgagee wrongly sold the mortgaged receipt for £2,700, but pretended he had sold his own. Later, the mortgagor defaulted, and the mortgagee sold his own receipt for £595. The House of Lords held that the mortgagee must account for the £2,700 not the £525. Although the receipts were in other respects identical, the mortgagee, at the time he sold the mortgaged one, had breached his duty to have it ready for re-transfer on payment of the debt. In *Ellis & Co's Trustee* v. *Dixon-Johnson*[13] the debtor deposited with his creditor debentures, bonds and share certificate, together with blank transfers of these holdings. After making a secret unauthorised sale of them, the creditor went bankrupt. The trustee in bankruptcy sued the debtor for the debt. He failed, because the House of Lords held that returning the mortgaged property was a condition of exacting payment. (By this time, the market value of the investments exceeded the amount due to the bankrupt.) In *Langton* v. *Waite*[14] mortgagees sold the mortgaged stock and later, on redemption, transferred to the mortgagor similar stock which they had bought for less than they had sold the mortgaged stock for. They were held liable to account to the mortgagor for their profit.

**Limitation of actions** In England and Wales, the Limitation

---

11. *Earl of Sheffield* v. *London Joint Stock Bank Ltd.* (1888) 13 App. Cas. 333. See also *Colonial Bank* v. *Cady* (1890) 15 App. Cas. 267. As to Scotland, see pp. 255–7, *post.*
12. (1725) 2 Bro. P.C. 563.   13. [1925] A.C. 489.
14. (1868) L.R. 6 Eq. 165, reversed on other grounds: (1869) L.R. 4 Ch. App. 402. See also *André* v. *Crauford* (1771) 1 Bro. P.C. 366.

Act 1939, section 18(1), provides that no action may be brought to recover the principal money secured on any property more than twelve years after the right to receive it accrued.[15] Section 18(2) states that no foreclosure action can be brought in respect of mortgaged personal property more than twelve years after the right to foreclose accrued, unless the mortgagee has taken possession, in which case the period does not start to run unless and until he discontinues possession.[16] By section 18(5), the right to recover interest is barred six years after it has become due, except: (*a*) where a prior incumbrancer is in possession, in which case all arrears of interest during that period of possession are recoverable if the action is brought within one year of the discontinuance of the possession; or (*b*) in certain cases of mortgages of future interests or of life insurance policies, where it is a term of the agreement that arrears of interest are to be treated as part of the principal sum secured, in which cases the period starts to run from the date when the right to recover the principal sum accrues.[17]

Since the concept of possession can only be applied to corporeal property, the provisions for a mortgagee in possession of personalty do not affect mortgagees of shares.

Redemption is an equitable remedy and, no statutory period of limitation having been enacted, is barred by laches. In *Lockwood* v. *Ewer*,[18] where there was a legal mortgage of East India stock, the right to redeem was held to be barred by the lapse of twenty years after the date for repayment (fourteen years after the mortgagee had sold the stock).

**New issues** If the company makes a bonus issue of shares, the mortgagor's right to redeem clearly extends to the additional shares. If the company offers a rights issue (i.e., new shares for which existing shareholders have the right to subscribe), presumably the mortgagee can take them as part of his security, adding the price to the principal sum secured unless the mortgagor reimburses him. Presumably the mortgagee cannot disclaim or sell the rights unless he has consulted the mortgagor and the latter has refused to pay for the new shares.[19]

**Calls** If the mortgaged shares are not fully paid up, the

15. Equivalent legislation: Statute of Limitations (Northern Ireland) 1958, s. 38(1). By s. 41, the debt is extinguished when the time has run.
16. No equivalent in Northern Ireland, where there is no foreclosure.
17. Equivalent legislation: Statute of Limitations (Northern Ireland) 1958, s. 39.
18. (1742) 9 Mod. 275.
19. That seems to be the law of Scotland: see *Waddell* v. *Hutton* 1911 S.C. 575.

company may call for all or part of the unpaid capital at any time, and the balance, if any, will have to be contributed by the shareholder if it is needed for the payment of debts on winding up. As against the company, the person liable to pay up outstanding capital is the registered owner of the shares. As between mortgagor and mortgagee the position is as follows.[20] First, the mortgagor is liable for calls made before the mortgage. If a call is made before the mortgage and unpaid when the mortgage is made, so that the company exact payment from the mortgagee, the latter is entitled to be indemnified by the mortgagor. Secondly, the mortgagee is liable, and the mortgagor is not, for calls made during the mortgage.[21] Thirdly, the mortgagor must indemnify the mortgagee in respect of calls made after the mortgagor has paid off the debt and called for a re-transfer of the shares, as the mortgagee is then a trustee of the shares for the mortgagor.

There is an unsettled question as to whether a mortgagor can insist on paying off his debt without redeeming the mortgaged property. Suppose the property to consist of worthless, partly paid-up, shares. If he could do so, it would be worth the mortgagor's while to pay the debt and refuse a re-transfer of the shares, leaving the mortgagee liable to calls. One possible answer is that the rule that the mortgagee is liable for calls at any time is wrong and that he should always be entitled to an indemnity from the mortgagor.

**Voting at company meetings** The legal owner of the shares is the person entitled to vote. In the case of a legal mortgage of shares, that is the mortgagee. If the mortgage agreement is silent on voting, the mortgagee can vote without regard to the wishes of the mortgagor.[22] In *Puddephatt* v. *Leith*[23] the legal mortgagee of shares undertook, by a letter written to the mortgagor prior to the mortgage agreement, only to vote in accordance with the mortgagor's wishes. When the mortgagee ignored her wishes, the mortgagor was granted a prohibitory injunction to restrain votes against her wishes and a mandatory injunction to compel votes in accordance with them.

## Deposit of Documents in England and Wales and Northern Ireland
Unlike the deposit of title deeds to land, it has never been settled whether a deposit of such a document as a share certificate by way of security creates an equitable mortgage of the

20. *Phené* v. *Gillan* (1845) 5 Hare 1.
21. See also *Re Patent Elastic Pavement and Kamptulicon Co.* (1850) 3 De G. & Sm. 146.
22. *Siemens Bros. & Co. Ltd.* v. *Burns* [1918] 2 Ch. 324.
23. [1916] 1 Ch. 200.

investment or a pledge of the document. On principle, such a deposit should be an equitable mortgage,[24] for otherwise it is difficult to see how the creditor can enforce his security against the investment. Nevertheless, there is a string of older cases going the other way.

In *South-Sea Co.* v. *Duncomb*[25] a deposit of a stock certificate was treated as the pawn of a chattel. That, of course, was before deposit of title deeds was recognised as an equitable mortgage of land. But long after that recognition, a deposit of debentures was treated as a pledge in *Donald* v. *Suckling*.[26] A few years later, in *Carter* v. *Wake*,[27] a depositee of company bonds was held entitled to an order for their sale, but not to an order for foreclosure (though he was given liberty to bid at the sale), on the footing that the transaction was a pledge of chattels. Then in *Colonial Bank* v. *Cady*[28] Lords Halsbury, Watson, Bramwell and Herschell all spoke of deposit of certificates as a pledge.

So far as sale is concerned, there is generally no problem for the depositee because the debtor will give him a negotiable document or a blank transfer or a power of attorney. If, however, deposit is a pledge and not a mortgage, there can be no foreclosure; and if the document pledged is a share certificate, the shares being transferable only on the books of the company, and the depositee is given no express power to sell the shares, the difference between pledge and equitable mortgage is crucial. An equitable mortgagee can apply to the court for sale or foreclosure while the pledgee cannot do either: he can sell only the piece of paper, which gives no right to the shares.

It was this problem that led to a change of attitude in *Harrold* v. *Plenty*.[29] There, a share certificate was deposited as security for a debt. The depositee was given no transfer; in fact there was no document relating to the transaction. It was held that there had been no pledge but an equitable mortgage, evidencing an agreement to make a legal mortgage as in the case of deposit of title deeds or of an insurance policy.[30] Accordingly it was further held that the depositee could get an order, on default of repayment, for transfer

24. At least, where the company's articles require production of the certificate on a transfer of the shares. As to the situation where they do not, see the Irish case of *Re Butler* [1900] 2 I.R. 153. As to deposit of title deeds to land, see pp. 25-7, *ante*.
25. (1731) 2 Stra. 919.
26. (1866) L.R. 1.Q.B. 585. See also *Halliday* v. *Holgate* (1868) L.R. 3 Ex. 299, where it was held that the assignee in the bankruptcy of the depositor could not sue the depositee for conversion by selling, without tendering the amount of the debt.
27. (1877) 4 Ch. D. 605.    28. (1890) 15 App. Cas. 267.
29. [1901] 2 Ch. 314.    30. Insurance policy: see pp. 259-60, *post*.

and foreclosure of the shares. That was a decision of first instance, but the Court of Appeal took a similar view when they held, in *Stubbs* v. *Slater*[31] that a deposit of a share certificate with a blank transfer was a mortgage, not a pledge, and that the mortgagee had the same implied power of sale as if his mortgage had been a legal one. Yet in *Ellis & Co's Trustee* v. *Dixon-Johnson*[32] the House of Lords, in arriving at their conclusion, said it was all the same whether the deposit was viewed as a mortgage or a pledge, and declined to say which it was. It is expected that the House of Lords, if one day forced to choose, will opt for deposit by way of security being an equitable mortgage. That is assumed to be the law in the rest of this chapter.

In *Stubbs* v. *Slater*,[31] where the equitable mortgagee by deposit was held to have an implied power of sale, the Court of Appeal also held that he could sell all the mortgaged shares, not just enough to pay himself off, and account to the mortgagor for the balance of the proceeds.[33]

**Sub-mortgage** Where there is a deposit by way of mortgage, the mortgagee can deposit the document by way of sub-mortgage. If the head mortgagee is also given a blank transfer of the shares he can use that to transfer his mortgage or to make a sub-mortgage, thus enabling the transferee or sub-mortgagee to get registered as the legal owner of the shares.[34] If there is a sub-mortgage in this fashion, the registered sub-mortgagee's title will only be as security for the amount due from the head mortgagor to the sub-mortgagor even if the latter borrowed more than that from the sub-mortgagee.[35]

**Fraud by depositee or agent** Deposit of share certificates with a blank transfer, and deposit of a negotiable paper, both make it easy for the depositee to abuse his position.

In *Fry* v. *Smellie*[36] share documents were handed by the owners to their agent, together with a blank transfer, with instructions to borrow £250 for the owners on the security of these shares. The

---

31. [1910] 1 Ch. 632.   32. [1925] A.C. 489. See p. 247, *ante*.
33. The rule may be different in Scotland: see pp. 255–6, *post*.
34. *Re Tahiti Cotton Co.* (1874) L.R. 17 Eq. 273.
35. *France* v. *Clark* (1886) 26 Ch. D. 257.
36. [1912] 3 K.B. 282. See also *Perry Herrick* v. *Attwood* (1857) 2 De G. & J. 21; *Brocklesby* v. *Temperance Permanent Building Soc.* [1895] A.C. 173; *Rimmer* v. *Webster* [1902] 2 Ch. 163; *Fuller* v. *Glynn, Mills, Currie & Co.* [1914] 2 K.B. 168. In *Dodds* v. *Hills* (1865) 2 H. & M. 424 it was held that a legal mortgagee who took from a trustee in breach of trust, but without notice, had priority over the beneficiaries. That would not be the case with an equitable mortgagee: *Ortigosa* v. *Brown* (1878) 47 L.J. Ch. 168; *Roots* v. *Williamson* (1888) 38 Ch. D. 485.

agent borrowed £100 on that security, and appropriated the money to his own use. The Court of Appeal held that the owners could not redeem the shares without paying the mortgagee what their agent had borrowed. That is the penalty of putting into the agent's hands the power to deal with the legal title. But in *Jameson* v. *Union Bank of Scotland*[37] the owner was held able to recover his shares from the lender without paying him what the agent had borrowed and made off with, because the circumstances of the approach to the lender by the agent had been such as to put the lender on inquiry as to the scope of the agent's authority.

In *Rumball* v. *Metropolitan Bank*[38] bearer scrip certificates for shares – negotiable by delivery by the custom of the stock exchange and of dealers – were left by their owner with his stockbroker for the purpose of paying instalments of the purchase price. The broker, in fraud of the owner, deposited the certificates with a lender as security for the loan. It was held that the original owner was not entitled to the shares as against the new owner who had lent money to the stockbroker. In *Re Burge, Woodall & Co.*[39] brokers deposited their own documents and documents they held for a client with a bank to secure their own overdraft, and subsequently went bankrupt. The bank sold the bankrupts' client's securities. It was held that the client could have the brokers' securities applied towards the balance due to him from the brokers by their trustee in bankruptcy by analogy to the marshalling of securities.[40]

## Equitable Mortgages, Otherwise than by Way of Deposit, in England and Wales and Northern Ireland

First, there can be a mortgage by equitable charge, similar to an equitable charge over land. In *Wise* v. *Lansdell*[41] there was a mortgage of shares by equitable charge, supported by a blank transfer. The mortgagee did not use the blank transfer to get himself registered as the legal owner of the shares. The mortgagor went bankrupt, and his trustee in bankruptcy disclaimed the shares. It was held that the mortgagor, as registered owner, was entitled to vote at company meetings.

37. (1913) 109 L.T. 850.
38. (1877) 2 Q.B.D. 194. *Goodwin* v. *Robarts* (1876) 1 App. Cas. 476 is a similar case involving Russian and Hungarian government stock. See also *Gorgier* v. *Mieville* (1824) 3 B. & C. 45; *Baker* v. *Nottingham and Nottinghamshire Banking Co. Ltd.* (1891) 60 L.J.Q.B. 542; *London Joint Stock Bank* v. *Simmons* [1892] A.C. 201; *Bentinck* v. *London Joint Stock Bank* [1893] 2 Ch. 120.
39. [1912] 1 K.B. 393.
40. Marshalling: see pp. 88–90, *ante*. It was an analogy, not marshalling, which is properly available to the creditor only.
41. [1921] 1 Ch. 420.

Secondly, an agreement to make a legal mortgage itself creates an equitable mortgage. In *Cumming* v. *Prescott*[42] it was held that an equitable mortgage of shares was not to be presumed from the fact of a loan by B to A when A gave B an order to the company secretary to transfer A's shares to B, the order saying nothing about it being security, and B not having used the order.

Thirdly, there may be a mortgage of an equitable interest in shares. It was held in *Slade* v. *Rigg*[43] that a mortgagee of a reversionary interest in stock in the public funds could have a foreclosure order even if the assignment to the mortgagee conferred an express power of sale.

**Priority of Equitable Mortgages in England and Wales and Northern Ireland**  An equitable mortgagee who gets the share certificate or similar document is fairly well protected. But not completely. In *Rainford* v. *James Keith & Blackman Ltd.*,[44] after he had deposited share certificates, with a blank transfer, as security, the owner sold the shares, without the knowledge of the mortgagee, to a purchaser without notice of the mortgage. The purchaser was registered as legal owner of the shares because the company accepted a silly explanation for the non-production of the certificate. When the mortgagee sued them the company were held liable because they actually received the money (in repayment of a debt owed to them by the mortgagor) with notice of the circumstances. Had the company not received the money or had notice, the mortgagee would have lost his security.

An equitable mortgagee who does not get the share certificate is in an even more vulnerable position in the face of fraud by an absconding or insolvent mortgagor. For this reason, equitable mortgagees have sought to protect themselves by giving notice of the mortgage to the company. This is an attempt to extend the rule in *Dearle* v. *Hall*[45] (that the priority of successive assignments of a beneficial interest under a trust is governed by the order in which the assignees give notice of their assignments to the trustees). It would be an extension because the company is not a trustee for its shareholders; yet in *Cumming* v. *Prescott*[46] it was held that the equitable mortgagee of shares depended for his priority on giving

---

42. (1837) 2 Y. & C. Ex. 488.
43. (1843) 3 Hare 35. See also *Wayne* v. *Hanham* (1851) 9 Hare 62.
44. [1905] 2 Ch. 147.    45. (1823) 3 Russ. 1. See pp. 84, *ante*, 278–81, *post*.
46. (1837) 2 Y. & C. Ex. 488. See also *Martin* v. *Sedgwick* (1846) 9 Beav. 333; *Binney* v. *Ince Hall Coal and Cannel Co.* (1866) 35 L.J. Ch. 363.

notice to the company secretary. That point of view seems never to have been explicitly overruled, but it was disapproved by Lord Selborne in the House of Lords in *Société Générale de Paris* v. *Walker*.[47]

In that case, A gave a share certificate and a blank transfer to B to secure a debt. Later A gave a blank transfer of the same shares to the appellants, a security for a debt he owed them, telling them that the certificate had been lost or mislaid. Neither B nor the appellants used their respective blank transfers to get registered, so both mortgages of the shares were equitable. The House of Lords held that B had priority over the appellants because he had both the earlier equity and the better one (because he had the share certificate). Lord Selborne's opinion was that *Dearle* v. *Hall* was irrelevant and that giving notice to the company was inoperative.

That opinion is probably correct, and is generally regarded as correct. The reason for that is not, as is sometimes thought, legislation now embodied, as to England and Wales, in the Companies Act 1948, section 117, which provides: 'No notice of any trust, expressed, implied or constructive, shall be entered on the register [of shareholders], or be receivable by the registrar, in the case of companies registered in England.'[48] The reason is that Lord Selborne's view represents the commercial realities. It is not part of the job of a company to maintain a register of how members deal with their property: the registrar is concerned only with who are members. Section 117 is irrelevant because an equitable mortgage is not a trust.

As between one equitable mortgagee of shares and another, the best that can be done is to serve on the company a notice in lieu of distringas.[49] Such a notice does not directly affect priorities. What it does is to compel the company to give the person who served it eight days notice before registering a transfer of the shares to which the notice in lieu of distringas relates. That gives time for the equitable mortgagee to do something before the legal title gets registered in a bona fide purchaser for value without notice; for example, apply for an injunction to prohibit registration.

Even if it has no effect as between equitable mortgagees of the same shares, ordinary notice to the company of the existence of such a mortgage can protect the mortgagee against the company. The articles of association of some companies give the company an

---

47. (1885) 11 App. Cas. 20, 30.
48. Equivalent legislation: Companies Act (Northern Ireland) 1960, s. 114.
49. England and Wales: R.S.C. 1965, O. 50, r. 11.

equitable charge (commonly called a lien) over the shares in that company as security for any debt owed to the company by the shareholder. In *Bradford Banking Co. Ltd.* v. *Henry Briggs, Son & Co. Ltd.*[50] the company's articles of association gave them a 'first and permanent lien and charge' over the shares for all debts due to the company from the shareholder. The shares were mortgaged to the bank, who gave the company notice of their equitable mortgage. The House of Lords held that, in consequence, the bank's mortgage had priority over the company's lien as to debts incurred by the shareholder to the company after the company had notice of the mortgage. The principle of *Hopkinson* v. *Rolt*[51] was applied, and it was pointed out that Lord Selborne's remarks in *Société Générale de Paris* v. *Walker*[52] were obiter dicta.

**Rights in Security in Shares in Scotland**  Such rights are constituted by the traditional methods of giving non-possessory security, viz. bond and assignation in security or an ex facie absolute assignation (usually with a back bond or back letter). By and large, the rules relating to stocks and shares as security are those governing the old equivalent forms of heritable security,[53] so far as the nature of the property allows. For example, an ex facie absolute assignation of a share in a company, with a back bond, is security for subsequent debts as well as those owing at the date of the disposition.[54]

**Duty to return identical shares**  It seems that, on redemption, the creditor must return the actual shares given in security, and not similar shares, though that duty may be excluded by express or implied contract.[55] The case of *Nelson* v. *National Bank of Scotland*[56] seems to extend that duty, in part, to realisation of the security. It was there held that an assignee in security of shares owed a duty to the debtor to sell no more of the shares than necessary to liquidate the debt (or at least to keep the over-sale within reasonable bounds), and to return the rest of the shares in specie. It was held that a second secured creditor, who knew that the first creditor had sold more shares than he needed to sell to raise what he was owed, must require the first creditor to restore the shares sold unnecessarily

---

50. (1886) 12 App. Cas. 29. Ireland: *Rearden* v. *Provincial Bank of Ireland* [1896] 1 I.R. 532.
51. (1861) 9 H.L.C. 514, p. 34, footnote 17, *ante.*
52. (1885) 11 App. Cas. 20, p. 254, *ante.*
53. See pp. 21, 35, 60, 61, 62, 65, 66, 77–80, 81, 90–1, *ante.*
54. *Russell* v. *Earl of Breadalbane* (1831) 5 W. & S. 256.
55. *Crerar* v. *Bank of Scotland* 1922 S.C. (H.L.) 137.    56. 1936 S.C. 570.

and hand the whole lot over to the second creditor. Breach of that duty, on a rising market, is visited by an award of damages, being the difference between the sale price and the higher value on the day of accounting for the proceeds.

**Intimation and ranking** In order to have a legally constituted security, the creditor must become the registered owner of the shares. It seems, however, that an equitable security is effectively created for some purposes as soon as the assignation is intimated to the company and before they have altered the register of shareholders. In *Burns* v. *Lawrie's Trustees*[57] it was held that, as from the intimation, the assignee had priority over the company's lien for debts subsequently becoming due to them from the assignor.

Secondly, the assignation seems to be enough to protect the assignee from unsecured creditors on a bankruptcy, even without intimation to the company. In *Guild* v. *Young*[58] the order of events was: (1) transfer in security executed by the debtor; (2) bankruptcy of the debtor; (3) successful application by the creditor to the company for registration. It was held that the creditor had a valid security during the period between the execution of the transfer and its registration because the debtor had done all he needed to do to pass the title and the creditor could get registered at any time. This decision would look more at home elsewhere in the United Kingdom and makes an uncomfortable bedfellow for the general lack of recognition in Scotland of secret equities. In *Redfearn* v. *Somervail*[59] the registered owner of a share in a company assigned it in security of his debt. The creditor intimated the assignation to the company (who did not alter their register). The registered owner (the debtor) was, unknown to the company, trustee of the share for himself and his partner. The House of Lords held that the creditor prevailed over both partners because no secret equity was to have effect.

**Rights issues** It seems from *Waddell* v. *Hutton*[60] that a mortgagee of shares is liable in damages to the mortgagor if he declines to take up a rights issue (i.e., an opportunity given to existing shareholders to buy more shares from the company) without communicating with the mortgagor, if the shares become worth more than the issue price.

**Other transactions** No other type of security is known to the law of Scotland. A security cannot be created by deposit of a share certificate (though a pledge might be). Even a blank transfer would

---

57. (1840) 2 D. 1348.   58. (1884) 22 S.L.R. 520.
59. (1813) 1 Dow 50.   60. 1911 S.C. 575.

seem to be of no avail, at least so long as it remains blank. The Act anent Blank Bonds and Trusts of 1696 provides that '. . . no bonds assignations dispositions or other deeds [shall] be subscrived blank in the person or persons name in whose favors they are conceived and . . . the forsaid person or persones [shall] be either insert before or at the Subscriveing or at least in presence of the same witnesses who were witnesses to the Subscribing before the delivery Certifieing that all writs otherways Subscribed and delivered blank as said is shall be declared null . . .'

# 14 security over insurance policies

Mortgages of life insurance policies are a common form of security for a loan. If the insurance is with a sound company or underwriter, the policy is a safe security, provided it is fully paid up or the debt secured is no more than the sum insured less further premiums or no more than the surrender value of the policy. The event insured against is bound to happen sooner or later. Insurance policies other than life policies may also be mortgaged, but only to go with an interest in the thing to which the risk relates. For example, a mortgage of a ship may be supported by a mortgage of the policy insuring her.[1] A life insurance policy may be mortgaged to anyone because a creditor has an insurable interest in the life of his debtor.

The circumstances in which life insurance policies are used as security are very varied, but the following three are probably the most usual: (a) to secure an overdraft at a bank; (b) to secure a loan from the insurance company which issued the policy; (c) as additional security for a building society advancing money on a mortgage of land.[2]

---

1. See *Swan* v. *Maritime Insurance Co.* [1907] 1 K.B. 116.
2. See p. 103, *ante*. When a mortgagee of land and insurance policies under one deed sells the land but not the policies, he must hand over the mortgage deed to the purchaser because he retains no land so as to make the Law of Property Act 1925, s. 45(9) (a) applicable, unless the right to retain the deed is specified in the contract of sale: *Re Williams and Duchess of Newcastle's Contract* [1897] 2 Ch. 144, decided on s. 2, r. 5, of the Vendor and Purchaser Act 1874, which is still in force in Northern Ireland.

**Legal Mortgages in England and Wales and Northern Ireland** A life insurance policy is a chose in action,[3] i.e., a legal right to recover a sum of money. With the exception of negotiable instruments, choses in action were not assignable at common law except to or by the King. On the other hand, most choses in action, including insurance policies, have for centuries been assignable in equity. Choses in action which had previously been assignable in equity became assignable at law in the 1870s,[4] but it had become possible to assign a life insurance policy, so as to give the assignee a right of action against the insurance company without joining the assignor, in the previous decade. It is now therefore possible to give a legal mortgage of such a policy by using either (a) the method of assignment for choses in action generally;[5] or (b) the Policies of Assurance Act 1867. A legal mortgage is an assignment subject to a right of redemption.[6]

The Policies of Assurance Act 1867, section 1, provides that an assignee of a policy can sue the insurance company at law for the policy monies when they have become due. By section 2, the right of action of the assignee is subject to equitable defences. Section 3 confines rights under section 1 to assignees who have given the insurance company written notice of their assignments, and lays down that, if there is more than one assignment, priorities of assignees rank in order of the dates on which the company received the notices. The Act applies only to absolute assignments, which seems to mean an assignment of the whole policy in such a fashion that the assignee's title will not determine by the effluxion of time and will not arise or determine on the fulfilment of a condition. An assignment is none the less absolute because, in certain circumstances, the assignor will have a right to a re-assignment.[7]

**Equitable Mortgages in England and Wales and Northern Ireland** An insurance policy can be mortgaged in equity by: (a) deposit of the policy; (b) written or oral equitable charge;[8] (c) agreement to make a legal mortgage.[9] Equitable mortgages are not

---

3. Choses in action: see pp. 270–83, *post.*
4. See pp. 272–3, *post.* 5. See pp. 272–6, *post.*
6. Ireland: see *Murphy* v. *Taylor* (1850) 1 Ir. Ch. Rep 92, where an assignment which was absolute in form was proved to be intended as security for a loan and hence a mortgage.
7. See the authorities on choses in action generally, p. 273, footnote 36, *post.*
8. See *Jones* v. *Consolidated Investment Assurance Co.* (1858) 26 Beav. 256 (letter charging a life insurance policy in equity).
9. See *Spencer* v. *Clarke* (1878) 9 Ch. D. 137 (agreement to execute an assignment on request and to deposit the policy, by way of security).

assignments within the Policies of Assurance Act 1867, so the mortgagee cannot sue the insurance company, when the policy moneys are due, without joining the mortgagor as a party or, if he is dead, joining his personal representatives.[10] To do so ensures that, if they pay, the insurance company will get a discharge binding the person with the legal title.

**No personal representatives**  It occasionally happens that an equitable mortgagee is placed in difficulties, when he is seeking payment from the insurance company after the mortgagor has died, because there is no personal representative of the deceased. In England and Wales, the court may dispense with a personal representative if one has not been appointed.[11] In *Curtius* v. *Caledonian Fire and Life Insurance Co*.[12] the Court of Appeal exercised that power[13] so as to allow an equitable mortgagee of a life insurance policy to sue the insurance company when the plaintiff was owed more by the deceased than the amount due on the policy and the estate was insolvent.

**Effect of depositing the policy as security**  There is no doubt that this transaction creates an equitable mortgage.[14] It binds the trustee in bankruptcy of the owner of the policy whether or not notice of the mortgage has been given to the insurance company.[15]

It was held in *Re Kerr's Policy*[16] that, in the case of an informal deposit as security for an existing loan, when nothing was said about interest, interest was payable.

## The Position of the Parties in England and Wales and Northern Ireland

So far as the nature of an insurance policy permits, the law governing mortgages of life insurance policies is the same as that relating to mortgages of land;[17] and the rights and remedies of the parties are the same as those of mortgagors and mortgagees of land.

For example the rule against clogging the equity of redemption was applied in *Davis* v. *Symons*.[18] There, a debt was secured by

10. *Crossley* v. *City of Glasgow Life Assurance Co.* (1876) 4 Ch. D. 421 (deposit); *Spencer* v. *Clark* (1878) 9 Ch. D. 137 (charge).     11. R.S.C., O. 18, r. 15.
12. (1881) 19 Ch. D. 534. See also *Webster* v. *British Empire Mutual Life Assurance Co.* (1880) 15 Ch. D. 169.     13. Then under the Chancery Improvement Act 1852, s. 44.
14. See *Glaholm* v. *Rowntree* (1837) 6 A. & E. 710; *Cook* v. *Black* (1842) 1 Hare 390; *Ferris* v. *Mullins* (1854) 2 Sm. & Giff. 378; *Dufaur* v. *Professional Life Assurance Co.* (1858) 25 Beav. 599; *White* v. *British Empire Mutual Life Assurance Co.* (1868) L.R. 7 Eq. 394.
15. *Re Wallis* [1902] 1 K.B. 719.
16. (1869) L.R. 8 Eq. 331.     17. See chapters 3, 4 and 6, *ante*.
18. [1934] Ch. 442. See also *Salt* v. *Marquess of Northampton* [1892] A.C. 1. As to the rule against clogs on the equity of redemption, see pp. 45–7, *ante*.

mortgage of land and two endowment policies (i.e., policies under which the monies were to become payable by the insurance company if the insured lived to a specified age or died younger). The term of the mortgage was twenty years. Both insurance policies were going to mature before the redemption date. The mortgage contained a provision that, if the mortgagor survived until the maturity of each policy, the policy moneys were to go to the mortgagee in reduction of the debt. It was held that, while the twenty year period was not necessarily oppressive in itself, here the policies were in substance made irredeemable, so that period was void as a clog on the equity of redemption and the policies could be redeemed earlier.

Another example of the application of the same rules as those applicable to land is in respect of the mortgagee's duty to account. A mortgagee, whether legal[19] or equitable,[20] who receives policy moneys to an amount greater than the debt secured on the policy must account to the estate of the insolvent deceased, as a trustee of the surplus, even if the deceased died owing him other, unsecured, debts. (If the estate is solvent, the mortgagee can probably set off the surplus on the policy against the unsecured debts.)[21]

There are some aspects of mortgages of insurance policies which are subject to special rules or which give rise to special problems.

**Mortgagee Paying Premiums**  Generally, when a life insurance policy is mortgaged, the mortgagor contracts to pay the premiums. If the mortgagor does not do so, the mortgagee who pays them to keep the policy alive is entitled to add the amount he so pays to the debt secured by the mortgage. There is nothing peculiar to insurance policies in the rule that a mortgagee may add to his security sums necessarily spent to preserve the mortgaged property: simply that a mortgagee of an insurance policy is more likely than most other mortgagees to find himself in this position. In *Bellamy* v. *Brickenden*[22] it was held that, on redeeming a policy, the mortgagor had to pay the mortgagee the amount of premiums paid by the latter and interest on premiums paid within the previous six years. In *Gill* v. *Downing*[23] a mortgagee who paid premiums was held

19.  *Talbot* v. *Frere* (1878) 9 Ch. D. 568. Cf. *Re Haselfoot's Estate* (1872) L.R. 13 Eq. 327. See also *Re Jeffery's Policy* (1872) 20 W.R. 857.
20.  *Beyer* v. *Adams* (1857) 3 Jur. N.S. 710.
21.  Yet another example is provided by *Beaton* v. *Boulton* [1891] W.N. 30, where the usual rules for reopening foreclosure were applied.
22.  (1861) 2 J. & H. 137. See also *Earl Fitzwilliam* v. *Price* (1858) 4 Jur. N.S. 889; *Re Weniger's Policy* [1910] 2 Ch. 291.
23.  (1874) L.R. 17 Eq. 316.

entitled to be repaid them out of the policy moneys when these became payable by the insurance company, even though he was not yet entitled to be repaid the principal debt.

**Limitation of actions** Mortgages of personal property, including insurance policies, are governed by the Limitation Act 1939, section 18.[24] By subsection (3), the mortgagee's right to recover the money or to foreclose is not 'deemed to accrue as long as that property comprises any further interest or any life insurance policy which has not matured or been determined.'

**Priorities** The general principles of equity[25] apply, but only in so far as they have not been modified by section 3 of the Policies of Assurance Act 1867.[26]

In *Spencer* v. *Clarke*[27] A first mortgaged his policy by depositing it with B, and then gave a second mortgage to C by agreeing to assign the policy to him on request, and to deposit it with him. It was held that B had priority over C because he had the prior equity. C had given the insurance company notice before B had, but that was irrelevant because: (*a*) the Act applied only to assignments; (*b*) C had constructive notice of B's mortgage because C should have made proper inquiries as to the whereabouts of the policy (instead of being fobbed off, as he was, by A's silly lie).

North J. expressed the opinion obiter in *Newman* v. *Newman*[28] that section 3 of the Act of 1867 affected only the company, not the priorities, inter se of the assignees; so that one who took an assignment, with notice of a prior assignment, of which no notice had been given to the company, and himself gave notice of the second assignment to the company, did not thereby gain priority over the prior assignee.

In *Re Weniger's Policy*[29] A gave B a first mortgage by charge, then gave C a second mortgage by charge, and finally gave B a third mortgage. C gave notice to the company before B gave notice of his first mortgage and before B took the third mortgage. However, C did not make inquiries as to the whereabouts of the policy, when taking the second mortgage, so he acquired constructive notice of B's first mortgage. Parker J. held that the mortgages ranked in the order of their creation. Although the second was notified to the company before the first, the learned judge said[30] that a mortgagee

---

24. See p. 247, *ante*. Equivalent legislation: Statute of Limitations (Northern Ireland) 1958, ss. 38 and 41.
25. See pp. 84–6, *ante*.    26. See p. 259, *ante*.
27. (1878) 9 Ch. D. 137.    28. (1885) 28 Ch. D. 674, 680–1.
29. [1910] 2 Ch. 291.    30. [1910] 2 Ch. 295.

could not gain priority, by giving notice, over a prior incumbrance of which he had actual or constructive notice at the time of making the advance. The third mortgage ranked after the second because the second mortgage was notified to the company before the third advance was made.

On the other hand, a second mortgage taken without notice of the first will acquire priority over the first if the second mortgagee notifies the insurance company at a time when the first mortgagee has not done so. In *Re Lake*[31] the debtor executed an equitable mortgage of an insurance policy in favour of one creditor, but told no one about it. Later, the debtor made another equitable mortgage of the same policy, to a trustee for another creditor, and told him but did not disclose the existence of the first mortgage. The second mortgagee gave the insurance company notice. The debtor died, and then the first mortgage was discovered. The first mortgagee then gave the insurance company notice. It was held that the second mortgagee had priority, because he gave notice first, on the lines of the rule in *Dearle* v. *Hall*.[32]

**Insurance Policy Taken Out by Creditor in England and Wales and Northern Ireland** A creditor may insure his debtor's life and, if the creditor pays the premiums, the policy belongs to the creditor. If the amount of the insurance is more than the amount of the debt, the creditor, as owner of the policy, is entitled to the whole of the policy monies when they become payable by the insurance company. If, on the other hand, though the creditor takes out the policy the debtor pays the premiums, the transaction is treated as if the debtor had taken out the policy and mortgaged it to the creditor.

**Example 1** Christopher insures the life of Derek, who owes him £500, for £1,000. Christopher pays the premiums to the insurance company, but Derek reimburses him the amounts. Later, Derek pays off his debt of £500 to Christopher. Derek dies, so that the insurance company become liable to pay £1,000 to Christopher. The court will hold that Derek's estate is entitled in equity to the £1,000.[33]

**Example 2** Charles insures the life of Donald, who owes him £750, for £1,000. Charles pays the premiums to the insurance company, but Donald reimburses him the amounts. Later,

31. [1903] 1 K.B. 151.  32. (1823) 3 Russ. 1; (1828) 3 Russ. 48. See pp. 278–81, *post*.
33. See *Holland* v. *Smith* (1806) 6 Esp. 11.

Donald pays off his debt of £750 to Charles. Donald subsequently goes bankrupt. The court will hold that the equitable ownership of the policy has vested in Donald's trustee in bankruptcy, so that he will become entitled to the £1,000 when Donald dies. [34]

The same reasoning applies where the debtor does not actually reimburse the creditor for the premiums, if he undertakes liability to do so. In *Morland* v. *Isaac* [35] the creditor charged the debtor with the premiums and the debtor accepted liability to pay them, though he did not reimburse the creditor the amount of the premiums or repay the principal debt. After the debtor's death, it was held that his estate was entitled to the balance of the policy monies after allowing the creditor his debt and reimbursement of the premiums. So clearly is such a case treated as if it were a mortgage of the policy, that, in *Salt* v. *Marquess of Northampton*, [36] an agreement that the policy was to belong to the creditor absolutely if the debtor died without paying the debt was held void by the House of Lords as a clog on the equity of redemption.

On the other hand, if the creditor pays the premiums, and debits the debtor with the amount in his books, but the debtor does not agree to pay them, the policy belongs to the creditor and he can keep the whole of the policy monies, even if the debtor knew of the existence of the policy. [37]

In *Courtenay* v. *Wright* [38] the transaction was treated as a mortgage where the creditor paid the ordinary premiums, not debiting the debtor with the amounts, the only contribution of the debtor being to pay extra premiums charged during a period he spent abroad. When he paid the debt, the debtor was held entitled to an assignment of the policy. Other such cases, [39] however, have gone the other way.

**Insurance Policy as Security in Scotland**  An insurance policy may be used to secure a creditor by giving him a bond and assignation in security or by making in his favour an ex facie absolute assignation. As with other property, the former will secure only

---

34. See *Re Storie's Will Trusts* (1859) 1 Giff. 94.
35. (1855) 20 Beav. 389. See also *Lea* v. *Hinton* (1854) 5 De G.M. & G. 823; *Salt* v. *Marquess of Northampton* [1892] A.C. 1.
36. [1892] A.C. 1.
37. *Bruce* v. *Garden* (1869) L.R. 5 Ch. App. 32, where the debtor did not even know the creditor was debiting him with the premiums. (The debtor will usually know that a policy is being taken out because of having to furnish information to the insurance company.)
38. (1860) 2 Giff. 337.
39. *Gottlieb* v. *Cranch* (1853) 4 De G.M. & G. 440; *Knox* v. *Turner* (1870) L.R. 5 Ch. App. 515; *Preston* v. *Neele* (1879) 12 Ch. D. 760.

money then lent,[40] while the latter secures all advances made on the faith of it.[41] The Policies of Assurance Act 1867[42] applies throughout the United Kingdom.

**Importance of Intimation** Notwithstanding the terms of section 3 of the Act of 1867,[42] it was held in *Caledonian Insurance Co.* v. *Beattie*[43] that an assignation in security was complete when the debtor had done everything that had to be done by him. Such an assignation was held to be valid against other creditors even though the assignee did not intimate it to the insurance company until after the debtor had died insolvent. On the other hand, arrestment takes priority over an assignation in security that has not been intimated to the company.[44]

**General Principles** So far as the nature of an insurance policy is consistent with the rules relating to the old types of heritable security, those rules apply to security over such policies. An example is provided by *Murray* v. *Smith*.[45] There the creditor secured on a life insurance policy sold it by auction, at which he was the highest bidder. Six years later, when the creditor still had the policy, the debtor discovered what had happened. It was held that the sale was void, so that the debtor could still redeem the policy.

**Deposit of the policy** Deposit of a policy, at least if the depositee is not the company that issued it, gives the creditor no right in security.[46]

---

40. *National Bank of Scotland* v. *Forbes* (1858) 21 D. 79.
41. See *Robertson's Trustee* v. *Riddell* 1911 S.C. 14.
42. See p. 259, *ante*.
43. (1898) 5 S.L.T. 349.   44. *Strachan* v. *M'Dougle* (1835) 13 S. 954.
45. (1899) 6 S.L.T. 357.   46. *Wylie's Executrix* v. *M'Jannet* (1901) 4 F. 195.

# 15 security over other incorporeal property

Apart from stocks and shares and insurance policies, there are other commercially valuable species of incorporeal personal property (incorporeal moveables). Practically all property which is saleable is in practice used to give as security. The types of property considered in this chapter are: (i) goodwill of a business; (ii) copyrights; (iii) patents; (iv) trade marks; (v) debts; (vi) beneficial interests under trusts; (vii) expectations of becoming entitled to money in the future.

**Goodwill of a Business**  Goodwill is of two kinds. First, there is the expectation of continued custom on specific premises, which is the variety commonly associated with shops and hotels, for example. Secondly, there is the expectation of continued custom for a person or firm, irrespective of where they operate, based on the special skill or service offered by that person or firm. For the sake of simplicity, these will be referred to as premises goodwill and personal goodwill respectively. Neither variety of goodwill has any existence separately from the business which has the expectation of future custom; hence it is inconceivable that goodwill could be mortgaged or otherwise assigned except as part of a mortgage or assignment of the business.

   **Personal goodwill**  Security over a business undertaking (not including any premises), if given by a limited liability company, is a floating charge.[1] An individual businessman or partnership (other

1. See pp. 126–43, *ante*.

than a friendly society or, in England and Wales, a farmer) apparently has no capacity to create floating charges, so it would seem that what could be offered by way of security in respect of a business would be debts,[2] future book debts[3] and goodwill. (Stock-in-trade would have to be excluded, as a bill of sale[4] or transfer of possession would stop the business operating as a going concern.) Now the personal goodwill may be inseparably attached to an individual or it may be attached to his name. In the latter case, the creditor, if he has to foreclose, will get the goodwill if he gets the name. The former case is more difficult, because one cannot foreclose on a person. The best the creditor can do is to contract that, after foreclosure, the debtor will either continue in the business as an employee or, if he does not, will not compete with the business which has passed to the creditor on foreclosure or been sold by him to realise his security.

**Premises goodwill** Security over a business undertaking including premises, if not by way of floating charge, generally takes the form of a mortgage of the premises (i.e. a mortgage of land or, in Scotland, a standard security). Since goodwill attached to premises is simply one aspect of the value of the premises (like its site, view, condition and fittings), a mortgage of business premises should, and normally will, carry the goodwill to the mortgagee as part of his security.

In *Chissum* v. *Dewes*[5] it was held that a mortgage of business premises included goodwill attached to the premises, so that an equitable mortgagee was entitled, on sale of the premises and goodwill, to the whole of the proceeds. On the same footing, it was held in *Palmer* v. *Barclays Bank Ltd.*[6] that a mortgagee selling the premises owed no duty to the mortgagor to make express reference, in his advertisement, to the goodwill – that just went to the value of the premises unless these were something additional, e.g., a covenant by the mortgagor not to compete with the business after sale. Application of this principle also leads to the conclusion that, if mortgaged business premises are the subject of compensation on compulsory acquisition, and the compensation includes an element for goodwill, the whole sum goes to the mortgagee;[7] and that (under English law) a mortgagee of business premises can get a receiver and

2. See pp. 270–83, *post.*    3. See pp. 281–3, *post.*
4. See pp. 114–16, *ante.*    5. (1828) 5 Russ. 29.
6. (1971) 23 P. & C.R. 30.
7. *King* v. *Midland Railway Co.* (1868) 17 W.R. 113; *Pile* v. *Pile* (1876) 3 Ch. D. 36.

manager appointed to protect his security,[8] not just a receiver as where premises are mortgaged without a business.[9]

In *Re Bennett*[10] A, the fee simple owner, granted a lease for thirty-one years of his public house to B; and B sublet it to A. Later, A mortgaged the fee to C. It was held that C's mortgage did not include the goodwill because the current ownership of it was in A as underlessee, not as freeholder, and express words would be necessary to pass a reversionary interest in goodwill.

Of course, a mortgage of business premises will not carry personal goodwill because that is nothing to do with the value of the premises. In *Cooper* v. *Metropolitan Board of Works*[11] the Court of Appeal held that a tailor, who had mortgaged his premises, which were later compulsorily acquired, could keep the compensation for loss of his goodwill.

**Copyrights**  Copyright relates to original literary work and other artistic creations such as music, pictures and sculpture. It belongs to the creator or, if he is a servant employed to create such works, to his employer. Copyright, which comes into existence when the work has been created, consists of the right to reproduce the work, to license other people to reproduce it, and to stop, or claim the profits of, unauthorised reproduction.

A copyright may be assigned, partly or totally, by an instrument in writing,[12] as may a future copyright.[13] A legal mortgage is made in England and Wales and Northern Ireland by assignment subject to a proviso for redemption; and in Scotland by assignation in security or ex facie absolute assignation. Equitable mortgages in England and Wales and Northern Ireland are by equitable charge or by agreement for a legal mortgage. So far as the nature of the property admits, mortgages of copyright are governed by the same principles as those which apply to mortgages of land.[14]

If the owner of the copyright wishes to contract for publication of copies of his work, he may either assign the copyright to the publisher or keep the copyright and grant the publisher a licence to publish. A publisher cannot, in general, give rights in security over a licence to publish because enforcement of the security by sale

8. *County of Gloucester Bank* v. *Rudry Merthyr Steam and House Coal Colliery Co.* [1895] 1 Ch. 629 (mortgage of a colliery).
9. See *Whitley* v. *Challis* [1892] 1 Ch. 64, where the Court of Appeal decision that a mortgage of hotel premises did not include the business conducted there seems perverse.
10. [1899] 1 Ch. 316.   11. (1883) 25 Ch. D. 472.
12. Copyright Act 1956, s. 36 (3).   13. Copyright Act 1956, s. 37(1).
14. See chapters 3, 4 and 6.

would be inconsistent with the interest the owner of the copyright has in the publisher's style, form, standards and manner of doing business.[15]

Copyright also exists in registered designs. Under the Registered Designs Act 1949, section 19, mortgages of these are dealt with in the same way as mortgages of patents.[16]

**Patents**  A patent gives the inventor and his assigns the same rights over an invention as a copyright gives an author over his work. In the case of an invention, however, the rights do not arise out of the act of inventing but out of the governmental grant and registration of the patent.

Changes in entitlement to a patent are effected by entry on the register. Section 74(1) of the Patents Act 1949 states that a mortgagee of a patent or a share therein must apply to the comptroller for registration of notice of his interest, though section 74(2) also says that the mortgagor may apply. Registration would seem to minimise the difference between one type of mortgage and another so that, in England and Wales and Northern Ireland, there will be little practical difference between a legal and an equitable mortgage.

A legal mortgage in England and Wales and Northern Ireland is created by assigning the patent to the mortgagee subject to a proviso for redemption. A legal assignment must probably be by deed[17] and, if it is not clear from the instrument that the assignment is by way of security, the assignee will be registered as proprietor. If it is clear that the transaction is a mortgage, it is quite in order for the comptroller to register the assignee 'as mortgagee.'[18] In whichever way the mortgagee is registered, the mortgagor, as owner of the equity of redemption,[19] can sue a third party for infringement without joining the mortgagee.[18]

No formality is required for an equitable assignment of a patent,[20] except that the comptroller must be satisfied that an assignment has occurred (which in practice means a document whether or not

---

15. *Griffith* v. *Tower Publishing Co. Ltd.* [1897] 1 Ch. 21.
16. See below.     17. See *Re Casey's Patents* [1892] 1 Ch. 104.
18. *Van Gelder, Apsimon & Co.* v. *Sowerby Bridge United District Flour Soc.* (1890) 44 Ch.D. 374.
19. See pp. 45–50, *ante.*
20. See *Re Casey's Patents* [1892] 1 Ch. 104 for a case of registration of an equitable assignment of a one-third share in a patent.

under seal), so presumably an equitable mortgage may be created by charge or agreement for a legal mortgage.[21]

In Scotland, mortgages of patents would be by assignation in security or ex facie absolute assignation.

So far as the nature of the property allows, mortgages of patents are governed by the same principles as those which apply to mortgages of land.[22]

**Trade Marks**  Mortgages of trade marks are similar to those of patents.[23] The Trade Marks Act 1938, section 22(1), provides that a registered trade mark is assignable, with or separately from the goodwill of the business in which it is used. Subsection (3) enacts that an unregistered mark trade used in the same business is assignable with a registered mark. By section 25(1), an assignee of a registered trade mark must get registered.

**Debts: England and Wales and Northern Ireland**  If A owes B an unsecured debt, and B borrows from C, B may give C the debt owed by A as security. The commercial effect is rather similar to that of A standing as surety for B's debt to C, but the legal structure is quite different.[24] At common law, debts were not assignable, except to or by the King, unless they were in the form of negotiable instruments. Hence, apart from these two exceptional cases, there could not be a legal mortgage of a debt until the statutory introduction of legal assignments.

**Negotiable instruments**  A documentary promise to pay a sum of money, or a documentary authority to collect a sum of money from someone else, is a negotiable instrument if it is so treated by the custom of those who habitually deal with the type of document in question. The quality of being negotiable imparts two features: (i) that the title to the debt is transmissible by delivery of the instrument (if the money is expressed to be payable to the bearer or it is made out in blank) or by endorsement and delivery (if the payee is named in the instrument);[25] (ii) that a transferee who takes the instrument in good faith and for value, without notice of any defect in the title of the transferor, obtains a good title to the

21. By the Patents Act 1949, s. 73(4), no notice of any trust, express, implied or constructive, is to be entered on the register, and the comptroller is not affected by any such notice. That does not affect an equitable mortgagee, for his rights do not arise from a trust.
22. See chapters 3, 4 and 6.     23. See pp. 269–70, *ante*.
24. As to suretyship, see pp. 284–312, *post.*
25. By custom some instruments are only negotiable if made out to bearer.

debt even if his mediate or immediate predecessor had a defective title or none. Such a transferee of a bill of exchange or promissory note is known as a holder in due course if the bill is complete and regular on the face of it, and the transfer is taken before the bill or note is overdue and without notice of dishonour.[26] Customs change, and new types of instrument may come to be accepted as negotiable. The examples most commonly encountered today are cheques, other bills of exchange and promissory notes. Other, less common, negotiable instruments include bearer debentures, stocks and bonds.[27] An instrument which belongs to a negotiable class may itself not be negotiable because the drawer or a holder writes a restriction on it. For example, a cheque may be crossed 'not negotiable' by the drawer or by an endorsee. In such a case, the cheque remains transferable, but ceases to be negotiable.

A negotiable instrument is not a suitable type of property to be mortgaged, partly because the mortgagor has scant protection against an unscrupulous mortgagee who negotiates it when he should not. But that is not the only reason. Lord Cranworth L.C., in *Hills* v. *Parker*,[28] said: 'I do not say that there might not be such a thing as a mortgage of bills of exchange, but it has not happened to me in the course of a pretty long familiarity with legal proceedings even to have heard of such a case.' It would be rare, if it ever did happen, he said, because, when the bill becomes due, it cannot be treated any longer as a mere mortgage security, for the holder must get the acceptor to pay the amount due on it and apply that in part or full discharge of the debt. In that case, a debtor gave his creditor bills of exchange expressed to be redeemable. The House of Lords held that that was not a mortgage, so that the bills were redeemable on paying the holder their face value, not the whole debt owed to him. (It is more sensible to use a bill of exchange to pay the debt or, if the bill is for more than the debt, to have the bill discounted by a bank and pay the debt out of the proceeds.)

Despite the risks, negotiable instruments are deposited – presumably that is a pledge – as security for short-term loans. Some of the cases involve such deposits by a wrongdoer.

In *Collins* v. *Martin*[29] the plaintiff had deposited bills of exchange with his bank to collect the money when due, having endorsed the bills in blank for that purpose. The bank deposited them with the

---

26. Bills of Exchange Act 1882, s. 29.
27. As to bearer scrip as security, see pp. 246, 251–2, *ante*.
28. (1866) 14 L.T. 107, 108–9.
29. (1797) 1 Bos. & P. 648. See also *Foster* v. *Pearson* (1835) 1 C.M. & R. 849.

defendant as security for a loan. The bank having gone bankrupt, it was held that the defendant was entitled to the bills as against the plaintiff. A similar decision was given in *Wookey* v. *Pole*,[30] where the plaintiff sent a bearer Exchequer bill to his stockbroker for sale, and the stockbroker, instead of selling it, deposited the bill with the defendant banker as security for a loan to the stockbroker. Likewise in *Bechuanaland Exploration Co.* v. *London Trading Bank Ltd.*,[31] where a thief deposited a negotiable debenture as security, the depositee was held entitled as against the person from whom the debenture was stolen. In all these cases, the depositee received the negotiable instrument in good faith and for value, without notice of the depositor's want of title.

On the other hand, in *Treuttel* v. *Barandon*,[32] a bill of exchange payable to A's order was endorsed by A; 'Pay to B, or order, for account of C' (the plaintiff). B deposited the bill with D (the defendant) as security for a loan by D to B. It was held that (it being a case of deposit, not discount), as the endorsement gave D notice that B had the bill for account of C, C could get the bill from D without paying what D had lent B on the security of it.

**Other debts**   By the Law of Property Act 1925, section 136,[33] replacing provisions first contained in the Supreme Court of Judicature Act 1873, section 25(6):

(1) Any absolute assignment by writing under the hand of the assignor (not purporting to be by way of charge only) of any debt or other legal thing in action,[34] of which express notice in writing has been given to the debtor, trustee or other person from whom the assignor would have been entitled to claim such debt or thing in action, is effectual in law (subject to equities having priority over the right of the assignee) to pass and transfer from the date of such notice—

(a)  the legal right to such debt or thing in action;

(b)  all legal and other remedies for the same; and

(c)  the power to give a good discharge for the same without the concurrence of the assignor:

Provided that, if the debtor, trustee or other person liable in respect of such debt or thing in action has notice—

---

30. (1820) 4 B. & Ald. 1.    31. [1898] 2 Q.B. 658.
32. (1817) 8 Taunt. 100. See also *Haynes* v. *Foster* (1833) 2 Cr. & M. 237.
33. Northern Ireland: Supreme Court of Judicature Act (Ireland) 1877, s. 28(6).
34. There are no other legal things in action besides debts, unless sums of money due under contracts are not counted as debts.

(*a*) that the assignment is disputed by the assignor or any person claiming under him; or

(*b*) of any other opposing or conflicting claims to such debt or thing in action;

he may, if he thinks fit, either call upon the persons making claim thereto to interplead concerning the same, or pay the debt or other thing in action into court under the provisions of the Trustee Act 1925.

(2) This section does not affect the provisions of the Policies of Assurance Act 1867.[35]

A legal mortgage of a debt is made by assigning it, in accordance with the statute, to the creditor, subject to a proviso for redemption. It has been settled by plentiful authority[36] that an assignment is none the less absolute on account of the possibility that the assignee may become subject to a duty to re-transfer the debt to the transferor.[37] The mortgagee, in accordance with the statute, takes subject to prior equities such as a right of set-off arising out of a transaction between the mortgagor and his debtor which was in train when the mortgage was made.[38] So far as the nature of the property permits, the principles governing mortgages of debts are the same as those applicable to mortgages of land.[39]

An equitable mortgage of a debt may be made by charge or by agreement for a legal mortgage. Equitable assignments of debts have always been possible, and they remain so after the statutory introduction of legal assignments.[40] Any clear intention to mortgage a debt, unless it is intended as a legal mortgage and complies with the statutory requirements, will take effect as an equitable mortgage. An equitable mortgage is subject to the equities of third parties against the mortgagor, existing at the time of the mortgage. For example, if there is an equitable mortgage of a bond voidable for fraud, it is voidable as against the mortgagee too.[41] In *Christie* v. *Taunton, Delmard, Lane & Co.*[42] an equitable mortgage was held to

---

35. See p. 259, *ante.*
36. *Burlinson* v. *Hall* (1884) 12 Q.B.D. 347; *Ibberson* v. *Neck* (1886) 2 T.L.R. 427; *Tancred* v. *Delagoa Bay and East Africa Railway Co.* (1889) 23 Q.B.D. 239; *Cronk* v. *M'Manus* (1892) 8 T.L.R. 449; *Hughes* v. *Pump House Hotel Co. Ltd.* [1902] 2 K.B. 190. See also *Bank of Liverpool and Martins Ltd.* v. *Holland* (1926) 43 T.L.R. 29.
37. For the similar view on mortgages of life insurance policies, see p. 259, *ante.*
38. *Re Knapman* (1881) 18 Ch. D. 300. See also *Re Jones* [1897] 2 Ch. 190. Ireland: *Re Gwelo (Matabeleland) Exploration and Development Co. Ltd.* [1901] 1 I.R. 38.
39. See chapters 3, 4 and 6.
40. See further, Marshall, *The Assignment of Choses in Action*; Keeton and Sheridan, *Equity*, pp. 292–328.
41. *Turton* v. *Benson* (1719) 1 P. Wms. 496.    42. [1893] 2 Ch. 175.

be subject to the mortgagor's debtor's right to set off debts becoming due to him from the mortgagor before the mortgagee gave notice of the mortgage to the mortgagor's debtor, but not in respect of those becoming due after that.

There must be consideration for an equitable mortgage of a debt. Consideration will normally consist of the mortgagee making the mortgagor an advance. However, an equitable mortgage to support an existing loan is suspect: past consideration will not do, so there must be something additional such as the mortgage giving the mortgagor more time to pay. The courts are fairly ready to imply that such forbearance is the consideration from the mere making of the mortgage.[43] Provided there is consideration and the intention is clear, said the Court of Appeal in *Gorringe* v. *Irwell India Rubber and Gutta Percha Works*,[44] no special form is required for an equitable mortgage of a debt, nor is notice by the mortgagee to the mortgagor's debtor necessary. In that case, A Co. wrote to B: '. . . we . . . hold at your disposal the sum of about £425 due to use from Messrs *Cayzer, Irvine & Co.* for goods delivered by us to them up to the 31st of December, 1884, until balance of our acceptance of a [bill of exchange for] £660 14s 11d in your favour, and which fell due on the 11th inst., and is retired by you, has been paid.' That was held to constitute a valid equitable mortgage, so that when winding up of the A Co. began, B's security was fully established notwithstanding that notice was not given to Cayzer, Irvine & Co. until later.

Although notice is not necessary, it is prudent for the mortgagee to give notice to the mortgagor's debtor for two reasons: (*a*) so that that debtor will know whom to pay; and (*b*) so as to avoid being affected by subsequent equities arising in favour of that debtor against the mortgagor.[45] Reason (*a*) is exemplified by *Stocks* v. *Dobson*:[46] A owed money to B; B sold the debt to C, making an equitable assignment; C mortgaged the debt to D; C gave notice to A of his assignment but D did not give a notice of his mortgage; A paid C. It was held that D had no rights against A.

Provided there is consideration and the intention is clear, a purported legal mortgage of a debt will take effect as an equitable mortgage if any of the statutory requirements for a legal mortgage is lacking.

First, a legal mortgage must be by vesting the legal title to sue the

43. Compare the need for consideration in suretyship contracts, pp. 289–90, *post*.
44. (1886) 34 Ch. D. 128. See also *Ex parte Steward* (1843) 3 Mont. D. & De G. 265.
45. See *Christie* v. *Taunton, Delmard, Lane & Co.* [1893] 2 Ch. 175, p. 273–4, *ante*.
46. (1853) 4 De G. M. & G. 11.

mortgagor's debtor absolutely in the mortgagee, subject only to an equity of redemption. Giving a determinable interest is not an absolute assignment. In *Durham Bros.* v. *Robertson*[47] A owed B a debt which B assigned to C until B paid off his debt to C. The Court of Appeal held that the assignment was not absolute: it involved automatic reverter of the property to B on paying C whereas an ordinary mortgage requires re-transfer of the property on redemption. Therefore C's mortgage was equitable and so he could not sue A without joining B as a party. Whether assignment of part of a debt can be an absolute assignment has never been authoritatively determined; but the current of authority favours a negative answer. The Court of Appeal left it as a query in *Hughes* v. *Pump House Hotel Co. Ltd.*;[48] Darling J. held, in *Skipper & Tucker* v. *Holloway*,[49] that there could be an absolute assignment of part of a debt, but the Court of Appeal reversed his decision without considering that point; in *Forster* v. *Baker*[50] Bray J. held that an assignment of part of a debt could not be absolute, but the Court of Appeal affirmed his decision on another ground, expressly leaving that one open; in *Re Steel Wing Co. Ltd.*[51] P. O. Lawrence J. held an assignment of part of a debt by way of security to be an equitable charge; in *Williams* v. *Atlantic Assurance Co. Ltd.*,[52] in the Court of Appeal, Greer L.J. held (Scrutton and Slesser L.JJ. expressing no opinion on the matter) that an assignment of part of a debt (not by way of mortgage) was not within section 136 of the Law of Property Act 1925; while, finally, in *Walter & Sullivan Ltd.* v. *J. Murphy & Sons Ltd.*[53] the Court of Appeal held that there was an equitable charge, so that the chargor could not sue the debtor for any part of the debt without joining the chargee as a party, where the creditor had given the debtor authority to pay part of the debt to the creditor's creditor.

Secondly, an assignment by way of charge cannot be a legal mortgage. Where there is a charge, i.e., the mortgagee is entitled to claim only what is due to him as opposed to the whole debt standing as security, the mortgagee cannot sue his mortgagor's debtor without joining the mortgagor as a party.[54]

---

47. [1898] 1 Q.B. 765. See also *Gorringe* v. *Irwell India Rubber and Gutta Percha Works* (1886) 34 Ch. D. 128, p. 274, *ante*.
48. [1902] 2 K.B. 190.  49. [1910] 2 K.B. 630.
50. [1910] 2 K.B. 636.  51. [1921] 1 Ch. 349.
52. [1933] 1 K.B. 81. Ireland: to the same effect is the decision of Gibson J. in *Conlan* v. *Carlow C.C.* [1912] 2 I.R. 535, also not a mortgage case.
53. [1955] 2 Q.B. 584.
54. See *Mercantile Bank of London Ltd.* v. *Evans* [1899] 2 Q.B. 613; *Jones* v. *Humphreys* [1902] 1 K.B. 10; *Hughes* v. *Pump House Hotel Co. Ltd.* [1902] 2 K.B. 190.

Thirdly, if there is any other want in the statutory formalities for a legal assignment (the mortgage is not in writing, or is not under the hand of the assignor, or is not notified to the mortgagor's debtor), the security must be equitable.

The importance of distinguishing between legal and equitable mortgages is threefold: (i) an equitable mortgage is invalid unless there is consideration, but a legal mortgage is valid without consideration: this is related to the next distinction; (ii) an equitable mortgagee must join the mortgagor, as co-plaintiff, if he is willing, or as co-defendant, in an action to enforce payment of the debt, while a legal mortgagee, as legal owner of the debt, can sue the debtor without such joinder; and (iii) as to priorities. There can only be one legal mortgage of a debt because the legal mortgagee gets the whole legal title – any subsequent mortgage, being a mortgage of the equity of redemption, must be equitable.[55] If an equitable mortgage is made first, and then a legal mortgage, the legal mortgagee will take free from the equitable mortgage if he takes for value and without notice of the prior mortgage.[56] If there are two or more equitable mortgages, and the equities are equal, they presumably rank in order of the dates of their creation. A later equitable mortgagee without notice of an earlier one may have priority, as having the better equity, if he gives notice to the mortgagor's debtor before the earlier mortgagee does – indeed, if his equitable mortgage was by absolute assignment, in writing, under the hand of the assignor, the later mortgagee will convert his equitable mortgage into a legal one if he gives the debtor notice in writing.

**Debts: Scotland**  As with other types of property, debts may be given in security of other debts, by bond and assignation in security or by ex facie absolute assignation. In the case of negotiable instruments, the law is uniform throughout the United Kingdom. In other cases of debt, '. . . by the law of Scotland the *jus crediti* in debts may be made the subject of an effectual security, provided the debt be assigned and the assignation completed according to the method recognised as proper for the completion of such rights. But to make it effectual the assignee must have a right which he can enforce against the debtor in his own name, because it is indispensable for

55. See *Cronk* v. *M'Manus* (1892) 8 T.L.R. 449.
56. As to these equitable principles see pp. 84–6, *ante*.

the efficacy of a security that the secured creditor should have *jus in re*.'[57] Hence, an agreement to mortgage a debt creates no security. In *W. R. Graham & Co.* v. *Raeburn & Verel*[58] there was an agreement to repay a debt by paying £2,000 a year out of the profits of operating a ship. When the debtor company went into liquidation without having paid off the whole debt, it was held that that promise gave the creditor to whom it was made no preference, over the other creditors, in respect of the profits from the ship. It was a case of contract, not security. It would have been otherwise if a trust had been established.

The security is not established until the assignation of the debt has been intimated to the person who is liable to pay it. For that reason, it was held in *Liquidator of the Union Club Ltd.* v. *Edinburgh Life Assurance Co.*[59] that a company could not give security over its uncalled capital without intimation to every shareholder.

Security over a debt is subject to all pleas competent against the author when the assignation was made; but a claim emerging subsequently is not competent to be pleaded against the assignee.

**Beneficial Interests Under Trusts** In Scotland, there is no reason to distinguish between these, as security, and debts, but in England and Wales and Northern Ireland, because of the separate nature of equitable principles from those of the common law, separate rules apply to certain aspects of the mortgage transaction.

**England and Wales and Northern Ireland** Since a beneficial interest under a trust is itself equitable, any security over it must be an equitable mortgage. Such a mortgage can be created by assignment subject to a right of redemption or by any acts showing an intention to charge the equitable interest with the payment. Writing is not required, unless the trust is of land, but prudence would suggest documentary evidence of this kind of transaction. Notice to the trustees is not necessary in order to constitute the security, but is desirable for several reasons: in particular, (*a*) so that the trustees will know whom to pay; and (*b*) to preserve priority.[60]

On the whole, mortgages of equitable interests under trusts are

57. *Per* Lord Kinnear, *Bank of Scotland* v. *Liquidators of Hutchison, Main & Co. Ltd.* 1914 S.C. (H.L.) 1, 4.
58. (1895) 23 R. 84.
59. (1906) 8 F. 1143.
60. See pp. 278–81, *post*.

governed by the principles which apply to equitable mortgages of other types of property.[61]

Where the trust is of an absolute interest in a sum of money, and the mortgagor is absolutely entitled to a share, it seems that a mortgage by assignment will be equated to a charge, as it would be strange to allow realisation of a large sum of money in satisfaction of an obligation to pay a smaller sum. In *Re Bell*[62] a one-eighth share in a reversionary interest in £8,000 was assigned by way of mortgage to secure a debt of £400. The trustees also had notice of subsequent incumbrances on this share. The mortgagee's assignee claimed the whole £1,000 when the reversion fell in, but the trustees were only prepared to pay him what was due on the mortgage. The Court of Appeal held that the trustees were right.

**Priorities**  If there are two or more mortgages of an equitable interest under a trust, the general rule in England and Wales is that the mortgages rank in the order in which notice in writing of them was received by the trustees.[63] It is habitually called the rule in *Dearle* v. *Hall*. In Northern Ireland, that rule applies only to priorities of successive assignments of an equitable interest under a trust of personalty, including a trust for sale of land, and there is no requirement that the notice be in writing (priorities of mortgages of an interest under a trust of land are governed there by the principles that equal equities rank in order of creation and that better equities prevail over worse ones).[64]

The rule in *Dearle* v. *Hall* is to some extent an inroad on the principle that no one can transfer what he does not own. For example, if A is the beneficiary under a trust and he first assigns his interest absolutely to B, who does not give notice of the assignment to the trustees, and later A mortgages the interest to C who, being unaware that B is the owner, takes in good faith and gives notice to the trustees, C has priority over B. That means that C, who took

---

61. See *Smith* v. *Smith* [1891] 3 Ch. 550 (mortgagee of reversionary interest in fund in court, who had not demanded payment, held entitled to six months notice of redemption or six months interest in lieu); *Campbell* v. *Holyland* (1877) 7 Ch. D. 166 (rules for foreclosure of mortgage of remainder under trust of personalty the same as those for foreclosure of mortgage of land); *Stamford, Spalding and Boston Banking Co.* v. *Ball* (1862) 4 De G.F. & J. 310 (mortgage, by way of trust, of revisionary interest in stock: no foreclosure or sale inconsistent with terms of trust).

62. [1896] 1 Ch. 1. See also *Hockey* v. *Western* [1898] 1 Ch. 350.

63. *Dearle* v. *Hall* (1823) 3 Russ. 1, (1828) 3 Russ. 48; *Foster* v. *Cockerell* (1835) 3 Cl. & Fin. 456; Law of Property Act 1925, s. 137. See also the Land Registration Act 1925, s. 102. By s. 138 of the Law of Property Act 1925, the trust instrument, the trustees or the court may nominate a trust corporation (not being a trustee of the trust concerned) to receive notices of dealings with equitable interests.

64. See pp. 84–8, *ante*.

from someone who had parted with all his interest in the property, acquires a valid mortgage and that B is thereby reduced to owning an equity of redemption. But the rule in *Dearle* v. *Hall* does not apply where the person making the assignment never had an interest under the trust, even if he and the assignee thought he had.[65] Nor does it apply to the beneficiaries of a sub-trust. In *Hill* v. *Peters*[66] a solicitor lent clients' money on a mortgage of an equitable interest under a trust and gave notice to the trustees of the existence of the mortgage. The solicitor then executed a declaration of trust of the mortgage in favour of his clients. Later still, in breach of that trust, the solicitor purported to sub-mortgage the head equitable interest to the plaintiff, who, unlike the solicitor's clients, gave notice to the head trustees. It was held that the rule in *Dearle* v. *Hall* was inapplicable: a beneficiary had no need to give notice of his beneficial interest. The beneficiaries (the clients) under the sub-trust had no right to enforce payment by the head trustees: only their trustee (the solicitor) could do that, and their rights were against him. Accordingly, the clients, having the prior equity, ranked before the sub-mortgagee, whose interest was consequently reduced to that of an unsecured creditor of the solicitor.

Where the rule in *Dearle* v. *Hall* does apply, the important consideration is that notice be given, not why it is given. In *Smith* v. *Smith*[67] the trustee, who was the mortgagee's relative, was told in order to reassure him. In *Lloyd* v. *Banks*[68] the trustee, a solicitor, acted on reading about the transaction in a newspaper. In both these cases there was held to be effective notice for the purpose of priority.

If the mortgagee is a trustee, there is no need for further notice (so long, in England and Wales, as the mortgage itself is in writing). In *Willes* v. *Greenhill*[69] a trustee-beneficiary mortgaged his equitable interest to another trustee. The mortgagee–trustee served notice on the mortgagor-trustee. The Court of Appeal in Chancery held that effective notice had been given. In the light of *Lloyd's Bank* v. *Pearson*,[70] it must have been the notice to the mortgagee-trustee, consisting of the assignment, and not the subsequent notice to the mortgagor-trustee, that counted. Notice to the mortgagor-trustee alone, if he is not the sole trustee, will not be enough. In *Lloyd's Bank* v. *Pearson*[70] A, B and C were the trustees, and A was also a

65. *B.S. Lyle Ltd.* v. *Rosher* [1959] 1 W.L.R. 8.
66. [1918] 2 Ch. 273.    67. (1833) 2 Cr. & M. 231.
68. (1868) L.R. 3 Ch. App. 488. See also *Meux* v. *Bell* (1841) 1 Hare 73.
69. (1861) 4 De G.F. & J. 147.    70. [1901] 1 Ch. 865.

beneficiary. A mortgaged his equitable interest to D, and no notice was given to B or C. After that, A mortgaged his interest to E, who had previously inquired of B and C and been told they knew of no incumbrances, and who gave B and C notice of his mortgage. It was held that E prevailed over D.

These last few cases raise the more general issue of when protection is obtained, for the purpose of the rule in *Dearle* v. *Hall*, by giving notice to only one of several trustees. One trustee who receives notice should tell his co-trustees and either annex the notice to the trust instrument or file it with the trustees' papers and endorse a note on the trust instrument. But he may not: he may be inefficient; or he may be a trustee-beneficiary bent on fraud. On the other hand, the system is not foolproof even if notice is given to all the trustees. They may neglect to pass the information on to their successors; they may even forget themselves.

**Example 1** Thomas and Ursula are the trustees and Cyril is a beneficiary. Cyril mortgages his interest to Abigail, who gives notice to Thomas and Ursula. Thomas and Ursula die, Vera and William being appointed trustees in their place. Cyril then mortgages his interest to Bernard, who has been told by Vera and William that they know of no incumbrance on Cyril's interest, and who gives notice of his mortgage to Vera and William. The court will hold that Abigail has priority over Bernard.[71]

**Example 2** Sheila and Terence are the trustees and Charles is a beneficiary. Charles mortgages his interest to Angela, who gives notice to Sheila and Terence. Later Charles offers to mortgage his interest to Benjamin, who makes inquiries of Sheila and Terence. Sheila and Terence have forgotten about Angela, and disclose no incumbrances to Benjamin. Charles mortgages his interest to Benjamin, who gives notice to Sheila and Terence. The court will hold that Angela has priority over Benjamin. If Benjamin sues Sheila and Terence for damages, the court will hold them not liable.[72]

Giving notice to all trustees gives a better chance that everything

---

71. See *Re Wasdale* [1899] 1 Ch. 163.
72. See *Low* v. *Bouverie* [1891] 3 Ch. 82. Despite the establishment, in *Hedley Byrne & Co. Ltd.* v. *Heller & Partners Ltd.* [1964] A.C. 465, of limited non-contractual liability for negligent misrepresentation, *Low* v. *Bouverie* has recently been approved by the Privy Council in *Mutual Life and Citizens' Assurance Co. Ltd.* v. *Evatt* [1971] A.C. 793 and the House of Lords in *Woodhouse A. C. Israel Cocoa Ltd. S.A.* v. *Nigerian Produce Marketing Co. Ltd.* [1972] A.C. 741.

thereafter will happen in due course, but notice to one trustee will generally be enough to preserve priority under the rule in *Dearle* v. *Hall*.

The state of the authorities seems to be this: notice to one trustee, provided he is not also the mortgagor-beneficiary,[73] will protect the mortgagee, but the notice will cease to have effect if the one trustee who has had notice ceases to be a trustee without having passed the information on to his co-trustees or his successor. The efficacy of notice to one of several trustees is illustrated by the House of Lords decision in *Ward* v. *Duncombe*.[74] A and B were the trustees. C, a beneficiary, made a settlement of his equitable interest. Notice of the settlement was given to A, but not to B. Later, C offered D a mortgage of the same equitable interest. When D inquired about incumbrances, A was evasive while B said he knew of none. D took the mortgage and gave notice of it to A and B. A died and E was appointed trustee in his place. The House held that the settlement had priority over the mortgage. According to *Timson* v. *Ramsbottom*,[75] had A died and been replaced by E before D made inquiries, B and E not having learned of the settlement, the mortgage would have had priority. The authority of *Timson* v. *Ramsbottom* was at one time thought to have been shaken by *Ward* v. *Duncombe*, but it was later applied[76] to govern priorities (though not of mortgages) and has never been expressly overruled.

**Expectancies**   People raise money not only on the security of the property they own, but also on the security of property they hope to own one day (provided their hopes are well founded, otherwise a willing lender will not be forthcoming). One may offer as security the legacy one hopes to get under the will of a testator who is still alive, or the share one hopes to get on intestacy of someone who is still alive, or the damages one hopes to get from a defendant in a trial which has yet to take place. A businessman frequently raises a loan on the security of his future book debts (commonly sums that will become payable by customers for goods he will sell them in the future). In Scotland, there is no such security: if the lender deals on the faith of the borrower's expectations, all he gets is a contract as an

---

73. *Browne* v. *Savage* (1859) 4 Drew. 635; *Lloyd's Bank* v. *Pearson* [1901] 1 Ch. 865.
74. [1893] A.C. 369. See also *Smith* v. *Smith* (1833) 2 Cr. & M. 231; *Meux* v. *Bell* (1841) 1 Hare 73; *Browne* v. *Savage* (1859) 4 Drew. 635; *Willes* v. *Greenhill* (1861) 4 De G.F. & J. 147.
75. (1837) 2 Keen 35.
76. *Re Phillips' Trusts* [1903] 1 Ch. 183. Ireland: *Re Hall* (1880) 7 L.R. Ir. 180 (also not a security case).

unsecured creditor; but in England and Wales and Northern Ireland, equity gives effect to a mortgage of an expectancy.

No formality is required: merely some clear intention to make the expectancy security for the advance. As the transaction is to be enforced in equity, there must be consideration. An existing debt is not consideration, but forbearance to enforce payment of it is, even if there is no express agreement for further time, as the law readily implies an agreement to that effect from the fact of forbearance.[77] It was on that basis, in *Glegg* v. *Bromley*,[78] that the Court of Appeal held that there was a valid mortgage of damages to be recovered in a pending action for slander.

So long as the expectancy remains an expectancy, the creditor has merely the benefit of a contract; but when the expected property falls in, in favour of the debtor, the creditor automatically has an equitable mortgage of it, without any further act on the part of the debtor. In *Tailby* v. *Official Receiver*[79] there was an assignment of future book debts by way of security, the assignee in turn re-assigning to someone else. This latter person gave notice to a subsequent book debtor of the assignor to pay him, not the assignor, and the book debtor complied. The assignor's trustee in bankruptcy sued the payee for the amount and failed. That shows that the payee was a secured creditor. The same advantage in bankruptcy is shown by *Re Lind*.[80] There, A mortgaged to B the share A expected to get of his mother's estate when she (alive at the date of the mortgage) died intestate. Later, while his mother was still alive, A mortgaged the same spes successionis to C. Then A went bankrupt. Neither B nor C proved for their debts in A's bankruptcy. After A got his discharge, he mortgaged the same expectancy to D. After that, A's mother died intestate. The Court of Appeal held that the priority of A's creditors was: B, C, D. They pointed out that an assignment of a spes was not a mere contract; as soon as A's mother died, A became a trustee of his share of her estate for the assignees. B and C had therefore properly elected to rely on their security and had not lost their debts by not proving in the bankruptcy.

In *Re Kent and Sussex Sawmills Ltd.*[81] the company, being indebted to their bank, wrote to a customer authorising the customer to remit sums due to the company direct to their bank. That was held to be

77. Compare the need for consideration in suretyship contracts, pp. 289–90, *post.*
78. [1912] 3 K.B. 474.
79. (1888) 13 App. Cas. 523. As to bills of sale, see pp. 114–16, *ante.*
80. [1915] 2 Ch. 345. See also *Re Gillott's Settlement* [1934] Ch. 97.
81. [1947] Ch. 177.

a charge on future book debts and therefore void as against the liquidator of the company for non-registration under the Companies Act:[82] it was an equitable assignment by way of security.

Priorities of successive mortgages of an expectancy are governed by the rule in *Dearle* v. *Hall*,[83] notice being given to the mortgagor's debtor when he becomes that. This is an unhappy rule, as the mortgagees have to keep their eyes open for the mortgagor's expectations to be fulfilled and then engage in a scramble to give notice first. Its arbitrariness is well illustrated by *Re Dallas*.[84] In that case there was a mortgage to A of a legacy under the will of a person who was still alive, followed by another mortgage of the same legacy to B. Then the testator died, having appointed the legatee as his executor. The executor renounced, and C was appointed administratrix. Next day, B gave notice of his mortgage to C. A few days later, as soon as he had heard of C's appointment, A gave her notice. The Court of Appeal held that B came before A; B had given notice first, and the rule as to priority depending on notice was not related to the conduct, such as negligence, of the earlier mortgagee.

**Equitable Mortgages Generally**    Equitable mortgages of debts, of beneficial interests under trusts and of expectancies are governed , subject to the special rules already mentioned and subject to the nature of the property, by the same rules as those which apply to equitable mortgages of land.[85] For example, in *Williams* v. *Price*[86] it was held that the equitable mortgagee of a judgment debt who enforced the judgment was liable to account to the mortgagor not only for the amount he recovered but also for what, but for his wilful default or neglect, he would have got.

Running of time against the mortgagee is provided for by the Limitation Act 1939, section 18 (England and Wales),[87] and the Statute of Limitations (Northern Ireland) 1958, sections 38 and 41.

---

82. Registration of company charges: see pp. 119–20, *ante*.
83. See pp. 278–81, *ante*.
84. [1904] 2 Ch. 385. See also *Johnstone* v. *Cox* (1881) 19 Ch. D. 17.
85. See pp. 84–6, *ante*.    86. (1824) 1 Sim. & St. 581.
87. See pp. 247–8, *ante*.

# 16 personal security

All types of security dealt with in the earlier chapters of this book involve rights over some, or all, property belonging to the debtor. A loan may also be made on the strength of the borrower finding a third party who is willing to pay the debt if the debtor does not pay it himself. The creditor may wish to protect himself in this way whether or not the debtor gives proprietary security for the debt, and the third party may or may not be required to give proprietary security.

Basically, there are two types of contract in which the loan is said to be on personal security: (1) (the more usual) where the third party promises the creditor to pay if the principal debtor does not; (2) where the third party binds himself to the creditor as co-principal debtor, but contracts with the borrower that, as between themselves, the third party is only bound to pay if the borrower does not. The contract is called one of guarantee or suretyship (or, in Scotland, one creating a cautionary obligation), and the third party is known as a gurantor, surety or, in Scotland, cautioner.[1] The word 'guarantee' must be approached with circumspection because it is used in several other senses, and sometimes with no meaning at all. Sometimes it just means a warranty; sometimes it signifies a retailer's willingness to do free repairs, for a stated period, to goods he has sold; and sometimes it is a contract under which the buyer of goods

1. The most recent general book on the subject is Rowlatt, *Law of Principal and Surety*, 3rd ed. (1936). In Scotland, contract (1), above is sometimes known as 'proper cautionry' and contract (2) as 'improper cautionry': see Gloag and Irvine, *Law of Rights in security*, pp. 673–4.

is conferred rights against the manufacturer in return for giving up his rights against the seller under the Sale of Goods Act 1893.[2] This chapter is concerned only with a guarantee in one of the two senses set out at the beginning of this paragraph, i.e., with sureties and cautioners.

Such contracts of guarantee must be distinguished from similar arrangements which import quite different rules. First, if the borrower and the third party bind themselves as co-principal debtors, without any contract between themselves that the third party is only liable to pay if the borrower defaults, there is no relationship of principal and surety. Secondly, indemnity to the creditor may be in one category or the other. It all depends on whether it amounts to a promise to pay the creditor if the principal debtor does not. One variety of indemnity contract is an insurance policy. On the whole, insurance is not a suretyship or cautionary obligation, and there are legal differences from the negotiation state onwards (e.g., a person proposing insurance to an insurer must make full disclosure as to the nature of the risk, but a creditor owes a much less onerous duty to a prospective guarantor). Yet an insurance policy may be a guarantee, and be subject to the rules regulating both types of contract, if the risk insured against is the failure of one of the insured's debtors to pay his debt.

There may be more than one surety or cautioner for the same debt, and if there are several they may each guarantee part of the debt or the whole debt. There are therefore legal problems arising: (*a*) between principal and surety; (*b*) between creditor and surety; and (*c*) between co-sureties. Except for one or two minor differences in detail as between Scotland, on the one hand, and England and Wales and Northern Ireland, on the other hand, the law as to suretyship and cautionary obligations is uniform throughout the United Kingdom.

Guarantees are most commonly given when money is borrowed – a guarantee of an overdraft at a bank is a commonplace example. They are also given in respect of other money obligations under contracts, e.g., a guarantee for a buyer's obligation to pay for goods, or for a commercial traveller's obligation to account to his employer for money he collects from customers. Sometimes a surety or cautioner, in effect, guarantees good behaviour on the part of an office-holder whose duties include handling money which

2. No longer possible in the case of a consumer sale, under the Supply of Goods (Implied Terms) Act 1973, s. 4.

does not belong to him, e.g., a guarantee that an administrator will duly administer the estate of someone who has died. All these obligations are governed by similar rules of law, as is the suretyship or cautionary obligation which descends upon someone who endorses a bill of exchange or promissory note. But there are other varieties of surety or cautioner who are outside the scope of this chapter because, although they make themselves liable to pay money, they contract to do so on the occasion of a default in some non-monetary obligation. One example, which occurs throughout the United Kingdom, is the surety or cautioner for bail – supporting an obligation of an accused person to appear at a stipulated time before a criminal court. Another example, occurring only in Scotland, is cautio judicio sisti – whereby the cautioner makes himself liable to pay if a defender fails to appear before a civil court.[3]

### The Extent of a Guarantee

Exactly what the surety or cautioner has guaranteed, and therefore what his liability is, depends in the first instance on the terms of the agreement between him and the creditor.

For example, when a guarantor dies, the question may arise whether his estate is liable for debts incurred by the principal debtor after the death or only for the amount owed to the creditor at the date of the death. In *Lloyd's* v. *Harper*,[4] the surety gave the plaintiffs a guarantee of all X's underwriting liabilities, in consideration of which guarantee Lloyd's admitted X to membership. The surety having died, X defaulted on his liabilities. The Court of Appeal held that, the surety having given Lloyd's an apparently unlimited guarantee of X's liabilities, and Lloyd's having given consideration once for all, and there being nothing in the contract allowing the surety to determine the guarantee in his lifetime, the guarantee was not ended by the surety's death, or by notice to Lloyd's of the death. Here, one of the determining factors was that Lloyd's could not determine X's membership, once having granted it on the faith of the guarantee; so they could not stop X incurring further underwriting obligations after the surety's death. If the guarantee had

3. See *Lindsay* v. *Fairfoull* (1633) Mor. 2031; *Telfer* v. *Muir* (1774) Mor. 2054; *Charles and James Brown & Co.* v. *Wilson* (1790) Mor. 2059; *Cowan* v. *Aitchison* (1797) Mor. 2061; *Tasker* v. *Mercer* (1802) Mor. App. (Cautio Judicio Sisti) 8; *Muir* v. *Collett* (1866) 5 M. 47.
4. (1880) 16 Ch. D. 290. See also *Bradbury* v. *Morgan* (1862) 1 H. & C. 249. In the circumstances of *Coulthart* v. *Clementson* (1879) 5 Q.B.D. 42, on the other hand, the guarantee was held revoked by the surety's death, or at least on receipt by the creditor of notice of the death.

been, say, of X's overdraft at a bank, the bank could (in the absence of contract to the contrary), on receiving notice of the surety's death, refuse to allow X to increase his debit balance.

In Scotland, the same principle applies, that the effect of death depends on the terms of the contract.[5]

There is no limit to the questions of interpretation that can arise on a contract, and a contract for personal security is no exception. The law reports are full of such cases, and one more contrast will serve to illustrate the point.

**Example 1**  Albert owes Belinda £50,000 of which payment is due. Albert asks for further time and Belinda agrees that he may pay by ten monthly instalments of £5,000 if Christopher will guarantee performance. Christopher agrees to guarantee performance of Albert's contract. Albert defaults on payment of the first instalment, which default Belinda treats as repudiation of the contract, and she accepts that repudiation. The court will hold that the whole £50,000 becomes due immediately as damages for breach of the contract to pay by instalments and that Christopher is liable to pay that sum to Belinda. Christopher had guaranteed the whole of Albert's contract, which included an obligation to pay damages on breach.[6]

**Example 2**  Albert owes Belinda £50,000, payment of which is due. Albert asks for further time, and Belinda agrees that he may pay by ten monthly instalments of £5,000 if Christopher will guarantee performance. Christopher agrees to guarantee payment of each instalment not duly paid by Albert. Albert defaults on payment of the first instalment. Belinda cannot claim more than £5,000 from Christopher until the second instalment is overdue, because Christopher has not guaranteed the whole contract but only payment of each instalment.[7] (If Belinda treats Albert's default as repudiation and accepts that repudiation, she can sue Albert for £50,000, but she will probably not be able to make Christopher liable for anything at all because the obligation guaranteed by Christopher has ceased to exist.)

---

5. In *University of Glasgow* v. *Miller* (1790) Mor. 2106 and *British Linen Co.* v. *Monteith* (1858) 20 D. 557 it was held that a cautioner who contracted for himself and his successors bound his estate.
6. See *Moschi* v. *Lep Air Services Ltd.* [1973] A.C. 331.
7. See *Re Hawkins* [1972] Ch. 714.

## Validity of Guarantees

**Principal Debtor's Undertaking Not Legally Enforceable**   It would be reasonable to suppose that, if the person claiming to be creditor had no legally enforceable claim against the alleged principal debtor, there would also be no claim against the guarantor of the payment that the alleged principal debtor may have promised to make. That was certainly the court's view of the law in *Coutts & Co.* v. *Browne-Lecky*,[8] where Oliver J. held that a purported guarantee of an infant's overdraft at a bank was void. There was no principal debt because the infant's promise to repay had no legal effect. Straightforward though that may be, this decision of first instance stands as the sole authority for such a clear-cut proposition.

Support is available for the view that there can be no valid guarantee if the principal debtor's undertaking is prohibited and penalised by statute (such as an undertaking by a company to buy its own shares). That seemed to have been decided by the House of Lords in the Scottish case of *Swan* v. *Bank of Scotland.*[9] However, in *Coutts & Co.* v. *Browne-Lecky*[8] Oliver J. thought that *Swan* v. *Bank of Scotland* was decided not on the penalty but on the voidness. That is probably incorrect, for, in Scotland, as Gloag and Irvine said:[10]

The rule that, in order to the validity of an accessory contract of guarantee, there must exist a liability, actual or prospective, on the part of a principal debtor, is modified to this extent, that it is not necessary that the principal debt should be exigible against the principal debtor by process of law. For our law, following the Roman law, regards it as a sufficient foundation for the contract of cautionry that the principal debtor should be bound by a natural obligation – bound morally, though not legally. In other words, the creditor may have a good title to sue the cautioner, though he has no action to enforce payment from the principal debtor.

At the other end of the scale is *Garrard* v. *James.*[11] In that case there was no prohibition by statute, let alone penalty. A company entered into a purported contract which was void because it was

---

8. [1947] K.B. 104. As to Scotland, see below.
9. (1836) 10 Bligh N.S. 627. See also *Heald* v. *O'Connor* [1971] 1 W.L.R. 497.
10. *Law of Rights in Security*, pp. 649–50.
11. [1925] Ch. 616. See also *Yorkshire Railway Wagon Co.* v. *Maclure* (1881) 19 Ch. D. 478, affirmed by the Court of Appeal on other grounds: (1882) 21 Ch. D. 309. Ireland: *Munster and Leinster Bank Ltd.* v. *Barry* [1931] I.R. 671.

ultra vires. Two of its directors guaranteed performance by the company. All the parties believed in good faith that the company's contract was valid. It was held that the agreement was enforceable against the surety despite the fact that it could not be enforced against the company. In *Coutts & Co.* v. *Browne-Lecky*,[12] Oliver J. thought this line of authority anomalous and could see no reason for it. In *Heald* v. *O'Connor*,[13] Fisher J. thought the distinction between the various lines of authority to be one of construction. He asked:

> Did the guarantor undertake to pay only those sums which the principal debtor could lawfully be called upon to pay but had not duly paid, or did he promise to pay those sums which the principal debtor had promised to pay but had not paid whether the principal debtor could lawfully be called upon to pay them or not?

But the learned judge expressed no opinion whether that approach would hold good where the principal agreement was void because prohibited by statute.

**Guarantees of Hire-Purchase and Similar Contracts**  Restrictions on the enforcement of guarantees relating to hire-purchase, credit-sale and conditional sale agreements are contained in legislation throughout the United Kingdom.[14]

**Requirement of Consideration**  Guarantee being a contract, in England and Wales and Northern Ireland there must be consideration for the surety's promise (unless it is made by deed).[15] In the case of a loan, the consideration for a guarantee of repayment is usually the making of the loan or, where the debt exists before the guarantee is given, postponement of the date for repayment. Past consideration being no consideration, the mere existence of a debt will not support a guarantee. But without express undertakings by the creditor, the courts will readily imply that he has given, as consideration for a guarantee of an existing debt, further time for payment if he does in fact forbear to sue for his money on the strength of the personal security.[16] *Provincial Bank of Ireland Ltd.* v. *Donnell*[17] is a rare case in

12. [1947] K.B. 104.     13. [1971], 1 W.L.R. 497, 506.
14. England and Wales: Hire-Purchase Act 1965, ss. 5(2) (*a*), (*b*), 22, 23, 30(1) (*b*); Hire-Purchase (Scotland) Act 1965, ss. 5(2) (*a*), (*b*), 22 (unlike the other Acts, requiring, inter alia, the guarantee to be signed before two witnesses unless the court dispenses with that requirement in any action on the guarantee), 23, 30; Hire purchase Act (Northern Ireland) 1966, ss. 5, 22, 23, 30.
15. Scotland: see *Grant* v. *Campbell* (1818) 6 Dow 239.
16. A similar attitude is taken in respect of equitable mortgages of debts to secure existing loans; see p. 274, *ante*.     17. [1934] N.I. 33.

which no such implication could be made. A husband had mortgaged his life insurance policy to the plaintiffs; later, the wife, in consideration of past and future advances by the plaintiffs to the husband, guaranteed the payment of the premiums. The Court of Appeal of Northern Ireland held the wife's guarantee void for lack of consideration. On the evidence, so far as the past advances were concerned, the plaintiffs were forbearing to sue anyway, without the guarantee, and had no intention of suing if the guarantee were not given. With regard to future advances, the plaintiffs did not promise to make any, and had no intention of doing so.

In Scotland, the law as to consideration does not apply, and, provided that there is a writ of the cautioner to support the obligation, the cautioner will be bound by it.

## Requirement of Writing
**England and Wales and Northern Ireland**   In England and Wales, by the Statute of Frauds 1677, section 4:

> No action shall be brought whereby to charge the defendant upon any special promise to answer for the debt default or miscarriage of another person unless the agreement upon which such action shall be brought or some memorandum or note thereof shall be in writing and signed by the party to be charged therewith or some other person thereunto by him lawfully authorized.[18]

The Mercantile Law Amendment Act 1856, section 3, provides that, if section 4 of the Statute of Frauds is otherwise complied with, the promise is not invalid 'by reason only that the consideration for such promise does not appear in writing, or by necessary inference from a written document.'[19]

Since the beginning of the eighteenth century, it has been clearly settled that the requirement of writing applies only to guarantees and not to cases where the defendant has made himself the principal debtor in a transaction in which, but for the defendant's intervention, someone else would have appeared to be the principal debtor. The distinction was stated pithily by the Court of King's Bench in *Birkmyr* v. *Darnell*:[20]

> If two come to a shop, and one buys, and the other, to gain him credit, promises the seller, *if he does not pay you, I will;* this is a

---

18. Northern Ireland: like provision is made by the Statute of Frauds (Ireland) 1695, s. 2.
19. Northern Ireland: the Act of 1856 applies.
20. (1704) 1 Salk. 27, 28.

collateral undertaking, and void without writing, by the Statute of Frauds: but if he says, *Let him have the goods, I will be your paymaster*, or *I will see you paid*,[21] this is an undertaking as for himself, and he shall be intended to be the very buyer, and the other to act but as his servant.

In *Sutton & Co.* v. *Grey*[22] the Court of Appeal pointed out that section 4 of the Statute of Frauds applies only where the person who makes the promise is, but for the liability which attaches to him by reason of the promise (of guarantee), totally unconnected with the transaction. Hence, they held it did not apply to a term, constituting part of the terms of employment of an agent, that the agent would reimburse the principal for losses incurred by dealings with a third party. Later the same year, the Court of Appeal held[23] that a contract of indemnity was not within the section.

Controversy was caused in 1789 by the decision, in *Pasley* v. *Freeman*,[24] that, while writing was required for a guarantee, A could sue B in tort if A was induced to contract with C by B's fraudulent oral misrepresentation that C's credit was good. That controversy was settled by the Statute of Frauds Amendment Act 1828, section 6, a section which has been criticised[25] as a reform, and which is ungrammatical in expression. It provides:

No action shall be brought whereby to charge any person upon or by reason of any representation or assurance made or given concerning or relating to the character, conduct, credit, ability, trade, or dealings of any other person, to the intent or purpose that such other person may obtain credit, money, or goods upon,[26] unless such representation or assurance be made in writing, signed by the party to be charged therewith.[27]

In *Banbury* v. *Bank of Montreal*[28] the House of Lords decided that that section applied to fraudulent representations only, not to negligent or innocent misrepresentations. In 1918, there was no action in tort for misrepresentation which was not fraudulent unless it was contained in a company prospectus, so that any action for damages founded on a negligent or innocent misrepresentation would have had to sound in breach of contract or breach of fiduciary duty. *Hedley Byrne & Co. Ltd.* v. *Heller & Partners Ltd.*[29] introduced a

21. See also *Lakeman* v. *Mountstephen* (1874) L.R. 7 H.L. 17.
22. [1894] 1 Q.B. 285.    23. *Guild & Co.* v. *Conrad* [1894] 2 Q.B. 885.
24. 3 T.R. 51. See also Sheridan, *Fraud in Equity*, pp. 12–13, 20–1, 28–31.
25. See *Fraud in Equity*, pp. 13–14.    26. *Sic*.
27. Northern Ireland: this Act applies.
28. [1918] A.C. 626.    29. [1964] A.C. 465.

limited liability in tort for negligent misrepresentation, but in *W. B. Anderson & Sons Ltd.* v. *Rhodes (Liverpool) Ltd.*[30] Cairns J. reiterated that the Act of 1828 was confined to fraud. That is presumably still the case, although the Misrepresentation Act 1967, section 2, has introduced a limited liability in tort for innocent misrepresentation.[31]

**Scotland** It seems that, as a result of the Mercantile Law Amendment Act, Scotland 1856, section 6, the law is the same as that of England and Wales.

Seventeenth century Scottish statutes required attested writ for contracts, but it was clear that that did not extend, even before 1856, to a guarantee granted *in re mercatoria* (in the course of trade), when a writing signed by the cautioner was sufficient. It was doubtful whether guarantees in respect of private and non-commercial obligations required attestation and, if so, what kinds of guarantee fell into that category.[32] The dispute was quieted by the 1856 Act.

Section 6 of the Act of 1856 provides:

> . . . all Guarantees, Securities, or Cautionary Obligations made or granted by any Person for any other Person, and all Representations and Assurances as to the Character, Conduct, Credit, Ability, Trade, or Dealings of any Person, made or granted to the Effect or for the Purpose of enabling such Person to obtain Credit, Money, Goods, or Postponement of Payment of Debt, or of any other Obligation demandable from him,[33] shall be in Writing, and shall be subscribed by the Person undertaking such Guarantee, Security, or Cautionary Obligation, or making such Representations or Assurances, or by some Person duly authorised by him or them, otherwise the same shall have no Effect.

In *National Bank of Scotland* v. *Campbell*[34] it was held that no formalities were needed beyond those required by the section: therefore all guarantees in writing were valid without testing; and in *Gibson* v. *Alston's Trustees*[35] it was said that the section had made the law of Scotland the same as that under the legislation applying in England and Wales.

It was held in *Crosbie* v. *Brown*[36] that section 6 of the Act of 1856

---

30. [1967] 2 All E.R. 850, 862–5.
31. Equivalent: Misrepresentation Act (Northern Ireland) 1967, s. 2.
32. See *Wright* v. *Paterson* (1814) 6 Pat. App. 38.
33. As to such representations and assurances, see *Clydesdale Bank Ltd.* v. *Paton* (1896) 23 R. (H.L.) 22.
34. (1892) 19 R. 885. See also *Church of England Life and Fire Assurance Trusts and Annuity Co.* v. *Wink* (1857) 19 D. 1079.
35. (1893) 1 S.L.T. 62.
36. (1900) 3 F. 83. See also *Walker's Trustees* v. *M'Kinlay* (1880) 7 R. (H.L.) 85.

did not stop a cautioner who had paid the debt getting a contribution from a second cautioner[37] without writ, at least in the case of a bill of exchange, so the pursuer was allowed to prove orally that the obligation was a cautionary one.

### Guarantee by Fewer Persons than Anticipated

If two or more sureties are expected to join in making a guarantee, and one or more sign it but, without the approval of the signatories, one or more of the other persons does not join in guaranteeing the obligation, the one or more who do sign are not bound.[38]

### Revocation of the Guarantee Before it is Acted Upon

Where the guarantee is of repayment of advances to be made in the future, it may be withdrawn, without liability, before it is acted on,[39] i.e., before any debt is created.

### Non-Disclosure of Material Facts During Negotiations

There is no reason to believe that guarantees differ from the general run of contracts with regard to what is proper during negotiations. That is to say, a contract may be set aside if one party induced the other to enter into it by making material misrepresentations (and the party misled may, in certain circumstances, sue for any damage he has suffered); but there is no duty to disclose material facts. In other words, if one speaks, one must tell the truth, but one is under no obligation to speak at all.

The view has sometimes been expressed that guarantees are analogous to insurance contracts in this respect. A person making a proposal to an insurance company must disclose all material facts, or the policy will be liable to be set aside, because the details of the risk to be insured against are peculiarly within the knowledge of the proposer. Applying this principal by analogy, a creditor would be under a duty to disclose to the prospective guarantor all he knew about the risk of the principal debtor defaulting. There is no judicial support for such an analogy, and it might be supposed that the guarantor would know the principal debtor's business as well as

---

37. As to rights of contribution between guarantors, see pp. 300–2, *post.*
38. *Hansard* v. *Lethbridge* (1892) 8 T.L.R. 346. See also *Evans* v. *Brembridge* (1856) 8 De G.M. & G. 100, where a sole surety was held not bound because he thought he was one of two; *National Provincial Bank of England* v. *Brackenbury* (1906) 22 T.L.R. 797, where three sureties were held not bound because they thought they were three of four. Scotland: *Blair* v. *Taylor* (1836) 14 S. 1069; *Paterson* v. *Bonar* (1844) 6 D. 987.
39. *Offord* v. *Davies* (1862) 12 C.B.N.S. 748. See also *Grant* v. *Campbell* (1818) 6 Dow 239 (Scotland).

the creditor, or would ask relevant questions before binding himself.

The authorities in England and Wales are mildly equivocal. In *Owen* v. *Homan*[40] Lord Truro L.C. said, obiter:

> ... the creditor must make a full and fair and honest communication of every circumstance calculated to influence the discretion of the surety in entering into the required obligation.

That dictum must be read in context: Lord Truro was dealing only with the standard required of a communication voluntarily made by the creditor: he did not decide that there was a duty to communicate. He probably meant no more than this: if a creditor makes a statement to a prospective surety, the statement amounts to a misrepresentation, if relevant knowledge is omitted, if the reasonable listener would believe he was being told all.

Authority in Scotland is clear, and the law is probably uniform on this matter throughout the United Kingdom. In *Hamilton* v. *Watson*[41] the House of Lords held that a creditor had no duty to the prospective cautioner to disclose the purpose for which money was being lent, and that failure to do so did not vitiate the cautionary obligation. Subsequent decisions of the Court of Session[42] have established that the creditor has no duty of disclosure to the cautioner during negotiations for a guarantee.

As with any other contract, a guarantee will be set aside for fraud.[43] This may lead, in some circumstances, to a sort of duty of disclosure. First, a partial statement may comprise a representation that everything is being divulged. Secondly, non-verbal conduct may be fraudulent unless accompanied by an explanation. In *French* v. *Cameron*[44] a cautionary obligation was reduced on that ground. The conduct was keeping on a servant (known to be dishonest) if he obtained security; in the absence of explanation, that amounted to holding out the servant as being trustworthy. A similar case was *Railton* v. *Matthews*,[45] where Lord Campbell said[46] in the House of Lords: 'If the defenders had facts within their knowledge which it

---

40. (1851) 3 Mac. & G. 378, 396. See also *Pidcock* v. *Bishop* (1825) 3 B. & C. 605.
41. (1845) 4 Bell's App. 67.
42. *Young* v. *Clydesdale Bank Ltd.* (1889) 17 R. 231; *Royal Bank of Scotland* v. *Greenshields* 1914 S.C. 259.
43. In *Stone* v. *Compton* (1838) 5 Bing N.C. 142 a guarantee was rescinded for fraud. See also *Pidcock* v. *Bishop* (1825) 3 B. & C. 605. Scotland: in *Wallace's Factor* v. *M'Kissock* (1898) 25 R. 642 and *Sutherland* v. *W. M. Low & Co. Ltd.* (1901) 3 F. 972 a cautionary obligation was reduced for fraud. See also *Spence* v. *Brownlee* (1834) 13 S. 199.
44. (1893) 20 R. 966.
45. (1844) 3 Bell's App. 56. See also *Smith* v. *Bank of Scotland* (1829) 7 S. 244; *Royal Bank of Scotland* v. *Ranken* (1844) 6 D. 1418.
46. 3 Bell's App. 67.

was material the surety should be acquainted with, and which the defenders did not disclose, in my opinion the concealment of those facts – the undue concealment of those facts – discharges the surety . . .' These decisions are not based squarely on fraud, nor are they simple cases of concealment. Lord Campbell referred to 'undue concealment.' The concealment was undue because the guarantees were fidelity guarantees, and in these cases the law of Scotland imposes a duty of disclosure of all material facts.

## Rights of the Creditor

When the contractual date for payment has arrived or, if there is no such date, when payment has been duly demanded, if the principal debtor does not pay, the creditor can sue him or the guarantor or both together. If there is more than one guarantor, the creditor can sue one or more or all of them for the whole debt (unless, of course, the guarantee is of less than that). There is no obligation on the creditor (unless the contract says so) to try and make the principal debtor pay before proceeding against a guarantor.[47] A guarantor who is made to pay may have consequential rights against the creditor,[48] the principal debtor[49] or other guarantors.[50]

In Scotland, at common law, in some not very clearly defined cases, a cautioner could not be sued unless it had been established that the principal debtor could not pay.[51] The law was brought into line with that of England and Wales by the Mercantile Law Amendment Act, Scotland 1856, section 8, which provides:[52]

> Where any Person shall . . . become bound as Cautioner for any Principal Debtor, it shall not be necessary for the Creditor to whom such Cautionary Obligation shall be granted, before calling on the Cautioner for Payment of the Debt to which such Cautionary Obligation refers, to discuss or do Diligence against the Principal Debtor, as now required by Law; but it shall be competent to such Creditor to proceed against the Principal Debtor and the said Cautioner, or against either of them, and to use all Action or Diligence against both or either of them which

47. See *Wright* v. *Simpson* (1802) 6 Ves. 714. Scotland: see below.
48. See pp. 296–7, *post.*    49. See pp. 297–300, *post.*
50. See pp. 300–3, *post.*
51. See the discussion by the House of Lords in *Wishart* v. *Wishart* (1837) 2 S. & M'L. 564.
52. See also *Sheldon & Ackhoff* v. *Milligan* (1907) 14 S.L.T. 703.

is competent according to the Law of Scotland: Provided always, that nothing herein contained shall prevent any Cautioner from stipulating in the Instrument of Caution that the Creditor shall be bound before proceeding against him to discuss and do Diligence against the Principal Debtor.[53]

The right of the cautioner, to insist that the principal debtor be discussed before the cautioner is held liable, thus now depends upon his stipulating expressly for that right in the cautionary obligation.

## Rights of the Guarantor Against the Creditor

**Transfer of Securities** The principal right, against the creditor, of a guarantor who has paid the debt, is to a transfer of any securities for payment which the principal debtor may have given to the creditor. In England and Wales and Northern Ireland that right was made statutory by the Mercantile Law Amendment Act 1856, section 5, which provides[54] that a surety who pays is entitled to have assigned to him, or to a trustee for him, any security held by the creditor, and to enforce the security against the principal debtor or a co-surety, standing in place of the creditor. Since nothing is said about knowledge, the Act presumably gives the right to the surety whether or not he knew of the existence of the security when giving the guarantee.[55]

It has been held in Scotland[56] that the rule that a cautioner who pays the whole debt is entitled to take over and enforce securities held by the creditor does not apply to securities given to the creditor by someone other than the principal debtor or a fellow cautioner (in effect, then, given by a cautioner for the cautioner). Presumably English law is the same, for section 5 of the Act of 1856 only envisages enforcing the security against the principal debtor or a co-surety.

A cautioner who has paid only part of the debt has no right to a transfer of securities from the creditor,[57] who, of course, still needs

53. See also *Ewart* v. *Latta* (1865) 3 M. (H.L.) 36, 40, *per* Lord Westbury L.C.
54. See also *Re Jeffery's Policy* (1872) 20 W.R. 857.
55. See *Duncan, Fox & Co.* v. *North and South Wales Bank* (1880) 6 App. Cas. 1.
56. *Thow's Trustee* v. *Young* 1910 S.C. 588.
57. Scotland: *Ewart* v. *Latta* (1865) 3 M. (H.L.) 36. See also *Sligo* v. *Menzies* (1840) 2 D. 1478.

them himself. So, if the surety who has paid is a surety for the whole debt, but with a limit,[58] and he has paid up to his limit, but there is still outstanding debt, he has no right to get securities from the creditor.[59]

It follows from a guarantor's limited right to a transfer of securities on payment that there must be limits on the creditor's power to release securities to the principal debtor or another guarantor before payment. The rule is settled that, if the principal debtor gives the creditor security at the time of the suretyship agreement, release of the security before payment discharges the surety from his liability even if the surety was unaware of the existence of the security when he undertook the obligation.[60] That is but an example of the general principle that a guarantor is discharged by any agreement, subsequent to the contract of guarantee, between creditor and principal debtor that could affect detrimentally the position of the guarantor.[61] But in *Newton* v. *Chorlton*[62] it was held that a surety was not discharged by the creditor releasing to the principal debtor a security entered into after the making of the suretyship agreement.

**Marshalling**  In *Heyman* v. *Dubois*[63] A mortgaged two life insurance policies to the insurance company. In respect of one mortgage, B was surety for repayment of the loan. A went bankrupt, and B was made to pay the debt for which he was surety. After A had died, B was held entitled to marshal so as to be reimbursed out of the proceeds of the several policies.

## Guarantor's Right to be Indemnified by the Principal Debtor

**After Payment of Debt**  Unless it is excluded by the contract of the parties,[64] a guarantor who has paid all or part of the debt has a right to be indemnified by the principal debtor. The guarantor is entitled to sue the principal debtor for reimbursement.[65]

58. This generally happens when A guarantee's B's overdraft, but with a stated limit, and the bank lend B more than A's limit.
59. Ireland: *Huggard* v. *Representative Church Body* [1916] 1 I.R. 1.
60. *Pearl* v. *Deacon* (1857) 1 De G. & J. 461. Cf. *Chatterton* v. *Maclean* [1951] 1 All E.R. 761. Ireland: see *Northern Banking Co. Ltd.* v. *Newman* [1927] I.R. 520.
61. See pp. 303–5, *post*.     62. (1853) 10 Hare 646.
63. (1871) L.R. 13 Eq. 158.
64. Scotland: *Williamson* v. *Foulds* [1927] S.N. 164. See also *Owen* v. *Brysson* (1833) 12 S. 130.
65. *Re A Debtor* [1937] Ch. 156; *Re Salisbury-Jones* [1938] 3 All E.R. 459; *Anson* v. *Anson* [1953] 1 Q.B. 636.

Pearson J. examined the basis of the right in *Anson* v. *Anson*,[66] saying:

> . . . the right can be placed on that basis of presumed contract or implied contract or, I am tempted to say, actual contract . . .
>
> . . . a possible alternative basis of the right of reimbursement . . . is that the debt is the debt of the principal debtor and so remains, and therefore when the surety is called upon to pay the position has to be put right between the parties so that the liability comes once more to be the liability of the principal debtor.

**Quia Timet Relief** Unless the contract says so, a guarantor who has not paid the creditor has no right to indemnity against the principal debtor if the creditor has not given the principal debtor further time for payment, the date for payment has not yet arrived and the surety has been neither damnified nor put in danger.[67] Nevertheless, a surety or cautioner who has not yet been made to pay anything has, in some circumstances, rights against the principal debtor. The normal right[68] is to an order that the debt be paid by the principal debtor and that, upon such payment, the guarantor be discharged from liability. The circumstances in which the guarantor can obtain such an order are: (1) that the date for payment has arrived and the guarantor has been asked to pay; or (2) that the date for payment has arrived and the creditor has notified his intention to realise some security for payment given by the guarantor; or (3) that there is no specified date for payment, but the debt is payable on demand or notice, and the guarantor's liability has continued as long as can reasonably be expected.

The guarantor cannot sue the principal debtor for a discharge before the date on which the creditor could sue the principal debtor for payment.[69] Nor can there be quia timet proceedings leading to an order inconsistent with the contract of the parties.[70]

**Quia timet relief when the guarantor has been asked to pay** In such a case, the surety can sue the principal debtor[71] or someone else who has contracted to give an indemnity. In *Wooldridge* v. *Norris*[72] it was held that a surety who had been asked to pay

66. [1953] 1 Q.B. 636, 641, 643.    67. *Dale* v. *Perry* (1808) 2 Bro. C.C. 582 n.
68. As to a different right, see *Re Anderson-Berry* [1928] Ch. 290, p. 300, *post*.
69. *Dale* v. *Perry* (1808) 2 Bro. C.C. 582 n.; *Padwick* v. *Stanley* (1852) 9 Hare 627.
70. *Morrison* v. *Barking Chemicals Co. Ltd.* [1919] 2 Ch. 325. See also *Bradford* v. *Gammon* [1925] Ch. 132.
71. See *Earl of Ranelagh* v. *Hayes* (1683) 1 Vern. 189; *Nisbet* v. *Smith* (1789) 2 Bro. C.C. 579; *Tate* v. *Crewdson* [1938] Ch. 869.
72. (1868) L.R. 6 Eq. 410.

(though he had not paid or been sued for payment) could sue the estate of a person who had contracted to indemnify him, and who had died leaving property on trust to pay the principal debtor's debt. He could sue the executors for administration, payment of the debt, and indemnity.

**Quia timet relief when the creditor intends to enforce the guarantor's security**   In *Watt* v. *Mortlock*[73] the principal debtor had an overdraft at a bank. The plaintiff, in relation to the bank, made himself co-principal debtor and, in relation to the principal debtor, surety. The surety gave the bank proprietary security. Later, when the bank gave the surety notice that they would realise the security, it was held that the plaintiff could get a quia timet order against the principal debtor for payment and discharge.

**Quia timet relief to remove the cloud**   When the guarantee is of a debt of indefinite duration, the guarantor is not obliged to wait all his life under a possible liability (or even to pass it on to his estate). He is only obliged to remain under the cloud for a reasonable time. After that, even if he has not been asked to pay, he is entitled to have his contingent liability removed by an order for payment by the principal debtor. The principle was considered by Goff J. in *Thomas* v. *Nottingham Incorporated Football Club Ltd.*[74] There, the guarantee was of an overdraft. Liability was to arise on demand and be binding until the surety served notice of discontinuance on the bank (after which he would not be liable for further advances). The surety served notice of discontinuance on the bank (although the bank made no demand) and claimed against the principal debtor a declaration that he, the surety, was exonerated and an order that the principal debtor pay. Both were granted: the fact that liability depended on demand, and no demand had been made, was no bar to the relief. Goff J. applied *Ascherson* v. *Tredegar Dry Dock and Wharf Co. Ltd.*[75] and said that *Bradford* v. *Gammon*[76] was either wrong or a case of a particular contract. The learned judge said:[77]

> The principle is that the surety is entitled to remove the cloud which is hanging over him. It would be strange indeed, as it seems to me, if he can do that where no demand is required, notwithstanding there is no present likelihood of any attempt to recover against him, and yet when his liability arises as between

73. [1964] Ch. 84.
74. [1972] Ch. 596. Ireland: *Matthews* v. *Saurin* (1893) 31 L.R. Ir. 181. Scotland: see *Kinloch* v. *M'Intosh* (1822) 1 S. 457; *Doig* v. *Lawrie* (1903) 5 F. 295.
75. [1909] 2 Ch. 401: see p. 300, *post.*
76. [1925] Ch. 132, p. 298, footnote 70, *ante.*     77. [1972] Ch. 606.

himself and the creditor only upon demand, he cannot seek to remove the cloud until it has started to rain, especially as the provision in the contract of suretyship that the creditor must make a demand upon the surety is clearly a provision for the benefit of the surety. It would be odd, I think, if that provision served as between himself and the principal debtor to put himself in a much worse position than that in which he would stand if it was not there.

In *Ascherson* v. *Tredegar Dry Dock and Wharf Co. Ltd.*[78] five directors guaranteed their company's overdraft up to £20,000. One of the directors died, whereupon the bank closed the account with just under £17,220 owing. The court granted the dead surety's executors a declaration that they were entitled to be discharged by the company paying the bank the amount owing when the account was closed, or the less amount owing if some had since been paid off, and interest.

**Quia timet restraining order**  In *Re Anderson-Berry*[79] the sureties to a bond for the administration of an intestate's estate brought a quia timet action against the administrator, who proposed to distribute assets, ignoring a contingent liability of which he had been informed. The Court of Appeal granted them an order restraining him from doing so.

**Scotland**  The cloud is usually removed automatically by the operation of statutory prescription.[80]

## Rights of One of Several Guarantors Against the Other or Others

**Contribution**  Where there are two or more co-sureties for the same debt, and one of them pays it in full, that one can recover a contribution of a rateable share from the other co-surety or the others.[81] The same rule applies in Scotland when there are two or more cautioners.[82]

---

78. [1909] 2 Ch. 401.
79. [1928] Ch. 290. Ireland: *Hibernian Fire and General Insurance Co. Ltd.* v. *Dorgan* [1941] I.R. 514.
80. See pp. 307–10, *post*, for the present law and recently enacted changes.
81. *Dering* v. *Earl of Winchelsea* (1787) 1 Cox C.C. 318; *Mayhew* v. *Crickett* (1818) 2 Swanst. 185; *Reynolds* v. *Wheeler* (1861) 10 C.B.N.S. 561.
82. *Maxwell's Creditors* v. *Heron's Trustees* (1794) Mor. 2136; *Anderson* v. *Dayton* (1884) 21 S.L.R. 787 (where it was held that, even though the cautioner who paid had taken an assignment of the debt from the creditor, he could only sue each of the other cautioners for his proportion); *James Marshall & Co.* v. *Pennycook* 1908 S.C. 276.

It was decided in *Dering* v. *Earl of Winchelsea*[83] that the right of contribution among co-sureties existed even if each surety had contracted by a separate instrument. On the other hand, one surety cannot force a contribution from another surety if they are not co-sureties, but the one who has paid was surety for the principal debtor and the other surety.[84]

The Court of Appeal, in *Ex parte Snowdon*,[85] held that a surety could not sue his co-surety for a contribution until he had paid more than his rateable share. For example, with three sureties for a debt of £9,000, one surety could not enforce any contribution from the others until he had paid more than £3,000 to the creditor. If he had paid, say, £6,000, it would seem that he could recover £1,500 from each of the co-sureties, assuming they were all sureties for the whole debt (but it is possible that the correct view is that he could recover £2,000 from each of them).

Actually, the surety need not delay seeking a contribution until he has laid out money: the right to sue the co-surety arises on an order to pay the creditor. That, at least, was the view of Wright J. in *Wolmershausen* v. *Gullick*,[86] where one surety had been ordered by the court to pay the whole debt. The learned judge held that the judgment debtor could sue her co-surety for a contribution before paying. The creditor not being a party to the latter suit, the learned judge said[87] that the plaintiff (the surety who had been ordered to pay the debt) could have a declaration of the liability of the defendant co-surety and:

> a prospective order under which, whenever she has paid any sum beyond her share, she can get it back, and I therefore declare the Plaintiff's right to contribution, and direct that, upon the Plaintiff paying her own share, the Defendant . . . is to indemnify her against further payment or liability, and is, by payment to her or to the principal creditor or otherwise, to exonerate the Plaintiff from liability beyond the extent of her own share.

If there are several sureties for different amounts, adding up to the total debt, and they are called on to pay less than the total, it seems that, inter se, the sureties are liable to contribute the same fractions of the payment called for as their limits of liability are fractions of the total debt.

83. (1787) 1 Cox C.C. 318.    84. *Re Denton's Estate* [1904] 2 Ch. 178.
85. (1881) 17 Ch. D. 44.    86. [1893] 2 Ch. 514.
87. [1893] 2 Ch. 529, where Wright J. also said, on limitation of actions: '. . . even if the statute can begin to run before the surety has paid more than his proportion, at any rate it does not run until his liability is ascertained . . .'

**Example** Philip owes Olive £150. Philip has four sureties. Norman guarantees £50, Marion £50, Leslie £25 and Keith £25. The sureties are called upon to pay Olive £48. Among themselves, the co-sureties are liable to contribute as follows: Norman £16, Marion £16, Leslie £8, Keith £8. The guarantors of one-third of the debt must contribute one-third of the payment and the guarantors of one-sixth of the debt must contribute one-sixth of the payment.[88]

The right to contribution may be affected, by reduction in the amount to be contributed, if the surety who paid is subsequently reimbursed in part by a third party.

**Example** George owes Henrietta £2,000, Ian and Jacob being co-sureties for the whole debt. Ian pays Henrietta the £2,000, whereupon Henrietta assigns to Ian a policy under which George's life is insured for £750. George dies, by which time Ian has paid £50 in premiums on the life insurance policy. Ian receives £750 from the insurance company. Jacob has gone bankrupt. Ian can prove in Jacob's bankruptcy for a contribution, but only, it would seem, for one of £300. (£2,000 – the debt paid by Ian – and £50 – the premiums – less £1,000 – the amount of Ian's liability, half the debt – less £750 – the policy moneys Ian received.)[89]

Where there are three or more guarantors, the amount the solvent ones must contribute is apparently increased if one or more of them should be insolvent. The authority is not very impressive. In England and Wales, in the seventeenth century, it was held[90] that, if A, B and C were co-sureties, and A paid the whole debt, A could recover half, not one-third, from B if C were insolvent. That seems a reasonable way of casting the total or partial loss of C's contribution equally upon A and B instead of leaving A the victim of having been the one who paid it: it removes the adjustment of A's and B's rights inter se from the influence of the creditor's decision whom to sue.

This view has also commended itself in Scotland. It seems from *Buchanan* v. *Main*[91] that, if there are five cautioners, A, B, C, D and E, and the whole debt is settled by A and B paying one-half of it each, and it is doubtful whether C and D are solvent but E is, then A and B can each recover one-sixth of the debt (not only one-tenth) from E.

88. See *Ellesmere Brewery Co.* v. *Cooper* [1896] 1 Q.B. 75.
89. See *Re Arcedeckne* (1883) 24 Ch. D. 709.
90. *Peter* v. *Rich* (1630) 1 Ch. Rep. 34; *Hole* v. *Harrison* (1675) 1 Ch. Cas. 246. Cf. *Swain* v. *Wall* (1642) 1 Ch. Rep. 149.
91. (1900) 3 F. 215.

## Sharing (Communication) of Securities

**England and Wales and Northern Ireland** In *Steel* v. *Dixon*[92] Fry J. decided that two sureties (out of a total of four) who had been granted a mortgage of a house and furniture by the principal debtor, must share the benefit of that security with their two co-sureties. All four having contributed equally to paying the debt when the principal debtor defaulted, the two mortgagees realised their security. The learned judge held that the two unsecured sureties could recover a quarter each of the net proceeds of sale. He said that the principle applied whether the debtor gave the security at the time of the suretyship contract, in performance of a contractual obligation to do so, or voluntarily thereafter; and whether the other sureties knew of the giving of the security, or not. But, like the right of contribution itself, the right to share the benefit of a security, being equitable, was (he said) subject to the usual equitable defences and susceptible of exclusion by the contract of the parties.

**Scotland** A cautioner who has been given security by the principal debtor is under a duty to communicate the benefit of it to his unsecured fellow cautioner. As stated in *Fisher* v. *Campbell*,[93] the duty is not to share it equally, but to pass on any residue that is left after the secured cautioner has reimbursed himself. The duty of communication is displaced by a contrary contract between the cautioners,[94] and does not arise in respect of a security given to one of several cautioners by someone other than the principal debtor.[95]

## Discharge of the Guarantor Otherwise than by Payment of the Debt

### Agreement Between Creditor and Principal Debtor

**The general principle** After a guarantor has undertaken his obligation, if the creditor arrives at an agreement with the principal debtor, and that agreement does or might affect prejudicially the guarantor's obligations, and the guarantor does not agree to the change, the guarantor is discharged.[96] The Court of Appeal, in

---

92. (1881) 17 Ch. D. 825.
93. *Creditors of Angus Fisher* v. *Creditors of Patrick Campbell* (1778) Mor. 2134. See also *Humble* v. *Lyon* (1792) Hume 83; *Milligan* v. *Glen* (1802) Mor. 2140 and Mor. App. (Cautioner) 4; *Finlayson* v. *Smith* (1827) 6 S. 264.
94. *William Hamilton & Co.* v. *Freeth* (1889) 16 R. 1022.
95. *Scott* v. *Young* 1909, 1.S.L.T. 47 (security given by debtor's wife).
96. England and Wales: see *Pidcock* v. *Bishop* (1825) 3 B. & C. 605; p. 294, *ante* (discharge of surety by creditor releasing security). Scotland: *Stirling* v. *Forrester* (1821) 3 Bligh 575; *Speirs* v. *Houston's Executors* (1829) 3 W. & S. 392; *Bonar* v. *McDonald* (1850) 7 Bell's App. 379; *Allan, Buckley Allan & Milne* v. *Pattison* (1893) 21 R. 195; *N. G. Napier*

*Holme* v. *Brunskill*,[97] put it in this way: if it is not self-evident that the change in the relations between the creditor and the principal debtor is immaterial to the surety, whether the surety is or may be prejudiced by the change is not a question of fact but a question for the judgment of the surety, who will be discharged if the change is made without consulting him.

An illustration of how the principle operates is provided by *Aitken's Trustees* v. *Bank of Scotland*.[98] The creditor bank gave the principal debtor an unconditional discharge when he paid off his overdraft except for £500 (which was the limit up to which the cautioner had guaranteed repayment of the overdraft). The cautioner had not agreed to the discharge of the principal debtor. The Court of Session held that the agreement between the bank and their customer discharged the cautioner, who could then recover from the bank £500 he had deposited with them in support of his cautionary obligation.

Alteration of the arrangements between the creditor and the principal debtor, without the guarantor agreeing or even being consulted, does not discharge the guarantor if he could not be prejudiced by the alteration.[99]

In Scotland, by statute, the cautioner is not discharged by certain agreements by the creditor on the principal debtor's bankruptcy, or relating to the debtor's composition or deed of arrangement. By the Bankruptcy (Scotland) Act 1913, section 52:[100]

> When a creditor has an obligant bound to him along with the bankrupt for the whole or part of the debt, such obligant shall not be freed from his liability for such debt in respect of any vote given or dividend drawn by the creditor, or of his assenting to the discharge of the bankrupt, or to any composition or deed of arrangement; but such obligant may require and obtain, at his own expense, from such creditor, as assignation to the debt, on payment of the amount thereof, and in virtue thereof enter a claim on the said estate, and vote and draw dividends, if otherwise legally entitled to do so.

Ltd. v. *Crosbie* 1964 S.C. 129. See also *Cooper* v. *Richard Blakemore & Co.* (1834) 12 S. 834 (creditor declining payment tendered by principal debtor); *Lawson* v. *Coldstream* (1837) 15 S. 930.

97. (1877) 3 Q.B.D. 495.    98. 1944 S.C. 270

99. Scotland: *Waugh* v. *Clark* (1876) 14 S.L.R. 125; *James Marshall & Co.* v. *Pennycook* 1908 S.C. 276; *Hamilton's Executor* v. *Bank of Scotland* 1913 S.C. 743.

100. See also ss. 51 (as to a cautioner for the payment of an annuity) and 140–1 (as to cautioners for compositions).

## Creditor giving principal debtor more time for payment

In cases where the debt is repayable on a specified date, if the creditor allows extra time for payment that is one variety of agreement which may prejudice the guarantor. It is an example which has been before the courts frequently. Such an agreement has been held, in England and Wales,[101] Ireland[102] and Scotland[103] to operate as a release to the surety or cautioner. Further, in *Mayhew* v. *Crickett*[104] it was held that the surety was discharged when the creditor, having obtained judgment against the principal debtor, withdrew execution. In *Forsyth* v. *Wishart*[105] it was held that the cautioner was discharged when the creditor bound himself, by contract with a third party, to give the debtor extra time for payment.

Mere inactivity on the part of the creditor – mere forbearance to sue the principal debtor for the money if it has not been paid on the due date – does not discharge the guarantor if the forbearance is unilateral, not in pursuance of an agreement to give the debtor more time to pay.[106]

Extension of time for payment can operate as a discharge to the guarantor only if the contract between the creditor and the principal debtor provided for payment on a specific date or within a specified period. If payment is due on notice being given, or on demand, and the guarantee is without time limit, the guarantor's obligations are not rendered more onerous by the creditor agreeing not to exact payment for a while.[107]

## Creditor Careless of the Guarantor's Interests
### Failure to supervise the principal debtor
In general, the creditor owes the guarantor no duty to supervise the debtor in such

101. *Nisbet* v. *Smith* (1789) 2 Bro. C.C. 579; *Rees* v. *Berrington* (1795) 2 Ves. Jun. 540; *Samuell* v. *Howarth* (1817) 3 Mer. 272; *Oakeley* v. *Pasheller* (1836) 10 Bligh N.S. 548; *Davies* v. *Stainbank* (1855) 6 De G.M. & G. 679; *Overend, Gurney & Co.* v. *Oriental Financial Corp.* (1874) L.R. 7 H.L. 348; *Midland Counties Motor Finance Co. Ltd.* v. *Slade* [1951] 1 K.B. 346. See also *Owen* v. *Homan* (1851) 3 Mac & G. 378.
102. *Maingay* v. *Lewis* (1870) I.R. 5 C.L. 229; *Provincial Bank of Ireland* v. *Fisher* [1919] 2 I.R. 249.
103. *Stirling* v. *Forrester* (1821) 3 Bligh 575; *Richardson* v. *Harvey* (1853) 15 D. 628; *Caledonian Banking Co.* v. *Kennedy's Trustees* (1870) 8 M. 862; *C. & A. Johnstone* v. *Duthie* (1892) 19 R. 624. Cf. *Aikman* v. *Fisher* (1835) 14 S. 56.
104. (1818) 2 Swanst. 185.     105. (1859) 21 D. 449.
106. England and Wales: *Eyre* v. *Everett* (1826) 2 Russ. 381. Scotland: *Fleming* v. *Wilson* (1823) 2 S. 296; *Hay & Kyd* v. *Powrie* (1886) 13 R. 777.
107. England and Wales: see *Twopenny* v. *Young* (1824) 3 B. & C. 208, where it was held, with this type of guarantee, that the creditor's taking further security from the debtor was not an extension of time which discharged the surety. Scotland: see *C. & A. Johnstone* v. *Duthie* (1892) 19 R. 624.

a way as to deter or prevent him from any action diminishing his own capacity to pay. If any watchdog activities are called for, the most appropriate source of surveillance is the guarantor himself. Sometimes, however, the creditor is in a supervisory position anyway. For example, the creditor may be the debtor's employer and the guarantee may be of the employee's integrity in handling the employer's money. In such a case the employer has duties to the guarantor in matters affecting the employment but not as to the other conduct of the employee. The employer is not expected to be at the employee's leisure-time elbow, urging him to church when his inclination is towards the casino; but the guarantor would be discharged if the employer connived at the employee's embezzlement or laid down a system of work which made embezzlement easy, tempting and difficult to detect. In *Snaddon* v. *London, Edinburgh and Glasgow Assurance Co. Ltd.*[108] it was held that the cautioner was released by the creditor delaying in informing the cautioner of embezzlement, known to the creditor, by the principal debtor.

**Failure to preserve priority**  In *Fleming* v. *Thomson*[109] the House of Lords held the cautioner to be discharged by the negligence of the creditor in allowing a third party to obtain priority in respect of security for the debt.

## Agreement Between Creditor and One of Several Guarantors

After the guarantors have undertaken their obligations, if the creditor arrives at an agreement with one of them, and that agreement does, or might, affect prejudicially the obligations of the other or others, and that other or those others do not agree to the change, there is a discharge of the guarantor or guarantors not agreeing,[110] on the same basis as discharge by an agreement between the creditor and the principal debtor.[111]

In particular, if the creditor releases one of the guarantors,

108. (1902) 5 F. 182. See also the following other Scottish cases: *Leith Bank* v. *Bell* (1831) 5 W. & S. 703; *Mactaggart* v. *Watson* (1835) 3 Cl. & Fin. 525; *Creighton* v. *Rankin* (1840) 7 Cl. & Fin. 325; *Falconer* v. *Lothian* (1843) 5 D. 866; *Biggar* v. *Wright* (1846) 9 D. 78; *Waugh* v. *Clark* (1876) 14 S.L.R. 125; *Dundee and Newcastle Steam Shipping Co. Ltd.* v. *National Guarantee and Suretyship Assoc. Ltd.* (1881) 18 S.L.R. 685; *Bonthrone* v. *Patterson* (1898) 25 R. 391; *Britannia Steamship Insurance Assoc. Ltd.* v. *Duff* 1909 S.C. 1261; *Bank of Scotland* v. *Morrison* 1911 S.C. 593. Ireland: *Madden* v. *M'Mullen* (1860) 13 I.C.L.R. 305; *Donegal C.C.* v. *Life and Health Assurance Assoc.* [1909] 2 I.R. 700; *Fraher* v. *Waterford C.C.* [1926] I.R. 505; *Wicklow C.C.* v. *Hibernian Fire and General Insurance Co.* [1932] I.R. 581.
109. (1826) 2 W. & S. 277. See also *Wright's Trustees* v. *Hamilton's Trustees* (1835) 13 S. 380; *Drummond* v. *Rannie* (1836) 14 S. 437.
110. Scotland: *Stirling* v. *Forrester* (1821) 3 Bligh 575.
111. See pp. 303–5, *ante*.

without the consent of the others, that operates to release all of them.[112] That rule has been made statutory in Scotland by the Mercantile Law Amendment Act, Scotland 1856, section 9, which provides:[113]

> ... where Two or more Parties shall become bound as Cautioners for any Debtor, any Discharge granted by the Creditor in such Debt or Obligation to any One of such Cautioners without the Consent of the other Cautioners shall be deemed and taken to be a Discharge granted to all the Cautioners; but nothing herein contained shall be deemed to extend to the Case of a Cautioner consenting to the Discharge of a Co-cautioner who may have become bankrupt.

**Partners as Creditors or Principal Debtors** If the guarantee is given to a partnership, or is in respect of partnership debts, the position of the guarantor is affected by the departure, replacement or addition of a partner. Such events are provided for in section 18 of the Partnership Act 1890, which applies throughout the United Kingdom:

> A continuing guaranty or cautionary obligation given either to a firm or to a third person in respect of the transactions of a firm is, in the absence of agreement to the contrary, revoked as to future transactions by any change in the constitution of the firm to which, or of the firm in respect of the transactions of which, the guaranty or obligation was given.

**Limitation of Actions in England and Wales and Northern Ireland** Guarantee is a contract and governed by the rules of limitation applying to contracts generally. The only special point is that time starts to run in favour of a surety only when a demand is made of him, not from the date when the principal debt is due for payment.[114]

**Prescription in Scotland** By the Cautioners Act 1695, the Parliament of Scotland provided:

> ... no man binding and engaging ... for and with another

---

112. As to the position where not all the prospective guarantors sign in the first place, see p. 293, *ante*.
113. See also *Church of England Life and Fire Assurance Trusts and Annuity Co.* v. *Wink* (1857) 19 D. 1079; *Morgan* v. *Smart* (1872) 10 M. 610.
114. *Re J. Brown's Estate* [1893] 2 Ch. 300; *Bradford Old Bank Ltd.* v. *Sutcliffe* [1918] 2 K.B. 833.

conjunctly and severally in any bond or Contract for soumes of money shall be bound for the said soumes for longer than seven years after the date of the bond bot that from and after the said siven years the said Cautioner shall be eo ipso free of his Caution And . . . whoever is bound for another either as express Cautioner or as Principal or Co-principal shall be understood to be a Cautioner to have the benefit of this Act providing that he have either clause of relief in the bond or a bond of relief a part intimat personally to the Creditor at his receiving of the bond . . .

This colourfully but unsystematically drafted statute left many problems of interpretation to be settled by the judgment of the courts. It is repealed by the Prescription and Limitation (Scotland) Act 1973, which brings cautionary obligations within the general law of negative prescription. However, there will, for a few years, be cautionary obligations affected by the Act of 1695.

**Transactions to which the Act did not apply**  Where the Act did not apply, the general law of prescription operated in favour of the party under a liability. It has been held that the 1695 Act did not apply to: (1) a cautionary obligation for an unliquidated sum;[115] (2) a bill of exchange;[116] (3) a bond of corroboration;[117] (4) a cautionary obligation supporting a composition.[118] There may be a fifth exception. It seems from *Molleson* v. *Hutchison*,[119] an unsatisfactory decision arrived at by a majority of four judges to three, that if a bond provided for payment of interest on the principal debt during the period for which that debt remains unpaid after the date on which payment was due, cautioners for the interest were not protected by the expiry of seven years after the debt was due for payment because each instalment of interest was a new debt when that instalment became due. The majority seem to have given insufficient weight to the proposition in the Act that after seven years from the date of the bond the cautioner shall be eo ipso free of his caution.

**The need for a clause or bond of relief**  In respect of transactions to which the Act of 1695 did apply, its terms are obscure as to the instances in which it applied. The Act begins with a universal reference to persons undertaking conjointly and severally

---

115. *Ewart* v. *Lothian* (1762) Mor. 11027; *Bremner* v. *Campbell* (1842) 1 Bell's App. 280.
116. *Sharp* v. *Hervey* (1808) Mor. App. (Bill of Exchange) 28.
117. *Scot* v. *Rutherford* (1715) Mor. 11012; *Lady Henrietta Gordon* v. *Tyrie* (1748) Mor. 11025; *Wallace* v. *Campbell* (1749) Mor. 11026.
118. *Cuthbertson* v. *Lyon* (1823) 2 S. 291. See also *Anderson* v. *Wood* (1821) 1 S. 31.
119. (1892) 19 R. 581.

with another person for a debt (apt to include co-principals as well as cautioners); then says that after seven years the 'said' cautioner (not apt to include a co-principal) is 'eo ipso' relieved of his obligation; and ends by saying that cautioners and co-principals alike are to have the benefit of the Act only if there is a clause or bond of relief notified to the creditor. Out of this tangle, the courts have produced a set of workable principles, based on a common-sense approach to the need to legislate, as it is manifestly impossible to interpret a self-contradictory statute in a self-consistent way.

First, a person who undertook a cautionary obligation by contracting as express cautioner (i.e., 'proper cautionry') in the same contract as that by which the principal debtor undertook to pay his debt was entitled to relief under the Act without the necessity of including in the contract any clause of relief.[120]

Secondly, a person who undertook a cautionary obligation in respect of an existing debt was not entitled to relief under the Act unless the contract of caution contained a relieving clause or a bond of relief was made and communicated to the creditor at the time of entering into the cautionary obligation.[121]

Thirdly, in the case of a co-principal debtor, the same principle applied, i.e., no relief without a clause or bond to that effect.[122] This applied where the case was one of a genuine co-principal and also in the case of improper cautionry, e.g., in the case of an ex facie co-principal debtor who was informally understood to be only a cautioner.[123]

**Contracting out** Where a guarantor who was ex facie a cautioner expressly renounced the benefit of the Act of 1695, it was held in *Norie* v. *Porterfield*[124] that the renunciation was ineffective and that therefore the cautioner remained protected by prescription.

In *M'Gregor's Executors* v. *Anderson's Trustees*,[125] when the debt was more than five years overdue, the creditors called for payment. The cautioner asked them for the indulgence of more time, which was granted. Eventually, the creditors sued the cautioner when the

---

120. *Ross* v. *Craigie* (1729) Mor. 11014; *Douglas, Heron & Co.* v. *Riddick* (1792) Mor. 11032; *Scott* v. *Yuille* (1831) 5 W. & S. 436; *Wilson* v. *Tait* (1840) 1 Rob. App. 137, 149, *per* Lord Cottenham L.C.; *Monteith* v. *Pattison* (1841) 4 D. 161; *Stocks* v. *M'Lagan* (1890) 17 R. 1122.
121. *Caves* v. *Spence* (1742) Mor. 11020; *Hogg & Co.* v. *Holden* (1765) Mor. 11029; *Howison* v. *Howison* (1784) Mor. 11030; *Wilson* v. *Tait* (1840) 1 Rob. App. 137.
122. *Ewart* v. *Lothian* (1762) Mor. 11027; *Drysdale* v. *Johnstone* (1839) 1 D. 409.
123. *Smyth* v. *Ogilvies* (1825) 1 W. & S. 315.
124. (1724) Mor. 11013.    125. (1893) 21 R. 7.

debt was more than ten years overdue. They were held to fail on the ground that the defender was protected by the Act of 1695.

**General Law of Prescription** This is now contained, with effect from 25th July 1976, in the Prescription and Limitation (Scotland) Act 1973, section 6 and schedule 1, paragraph 1(g) of which provides for a general five-year period for actions to enforce 'any obligation arising from, or by reason of any breach of, a contract or promise,' subject to exceptions not material to cautionary obligations. There are allowances made for cases of fraud, error or disability, but, by section 7, these do not apply after the lapse of twenty years. The periods of five and twenty years apply to cautionary obligations whether or not they are constituted or evidenced by probative writ (see schedule 1, paragraph 2(c)).

Paragraph 3 of schedule 1 states:

(1) Subject to sub-paragraph (2) below, where by virtue of a probative writ two or more persons (in this paragraph referred to as 'the co-obligants') are bound jointly and severally by an obligation to pay money to another party the obligation shall, as respects the liability of the co-obligants, be regarded for the purposes of sub-paragraph (c) of the last foregoing paragraph as if it were a cautionary obligation.

(2) Nothing in the foregoing sub-paragraph shall affect any such obligation as respects the liability of any of the co-obligants with respect to whom the creditor establishes –

(a) that the co-obligant is truly a principal debtor, or

(b) if that co-obligant is not truly a principal debtor, that the original creditor was not aware of that fact at the time when the writ was delivered to him.

**Assignment of the Debt** If the creditor assigns the debt, that does not release a surety, who remains a guarantor in favour of the assignee.[126]

**Proof in Bankruptcy**

**Bankruptcy of Principal Debtor** If there is a guarantor for the whole debt, the creditor may either prove for it in the principal debtor's bankruptcy (in which case, if he is not paid in full, he may sue the guarantor for the balance) or recover the whole sum from

126. *Wheatley* v. *Bastow* (1855) 7 De G.M. & G. 261; *Bradford Old Bank Ltd.* v. *Sutcliffe* [1918] 2 K.B. 833.

the guarantor (in which case the guarantor may prove for the amount in the principal debtor's bankruptcy).

The position is more complicated if the creditor recovers part of the debt from the guarantor, even though the guarantee is of the whole debt. That may occur because there is a limit on the guarantee, as where the guarantor undertakes liability for an overdraft, up to a stated limit, and the customer goes bankrupt owing the bank more than that. If the creditor recovers the debt from the guarantor up to the amount of the latter's limit, the general rule is that the payment by the guarantor does not reduce the debt of the principal debtor, so that the creditor can prove for the whole debt in the principal debtor's bankruptcy, and the guarantor can prove for nothing.[127] The creditor may do that even if the guarantor has only produced his payment by realising a security given to him by the principal debtor.[128] Although the creditor may so prove for the whole debt, he may not recover more than the difference between the whole debt and what the guarantor paid him.[128]

**Example 1** Peter owes his bank £500. He wants to borrow more. The bank agree provided a surety is found. Olive agrees to act as surety for the repayment of the overdraft, with a limit of £2,000. Later, Peter goes bankrupt, his overdraft then being £3,000. Olive pays the bank £2,000. The bank prove in Peter's bankruptcy for £3,000. Peter's trustee in bankruptcy pays proving creditors a dividend of 10p in the pound. The bank will get £300 from the trustee.

**Example 2** The facts are as in example 1, above, except that Peter's trustee in bankruptcy pays proving creditors a dividend of 50p in the pound. The bank get £1,000 (not £1,500, because they have already had £2,000 of the £3,000 debt from Olive).

In *Mackinnon's Trustee* v. *Bank of Scotland*[129] a somewhat different conclusion was reached, but the circumstances were unusual. It was a case of an overdraft, and of a cautioner with a limit. When the principal debtor was solvent, the cautioner obtained a release from the bank by paying off part of the overdraft (the cautioner's limit). Later, when the principal debtor went bankrupt, it was held that

127. England and Wales: *Ex parte National Provincial Bank of England* (1881) 17 Ch. D. 98; *Re Sass* [1896] 2 Q.B. 12. Northern Ireland: *Ulster Bank Ltd.* v. *Lambe* [1966] N.I. 161; *Re An Arranging Debtor No. A. 1076* [1971] N.I. 96. Scotland: *Harvie's Trustees* v. *Bank of Scotland* (1885) 12 R. 1141. As to the rule against double ranking in bankruptcy in Scotland see, further, Gloag and Irvine, *Law of Rights in Security*, pp. 317-18.
128. *Midland Banking Co.* v. *Chambers* (1869) L.R. 4 Ch. App. 398.
129. 1915 S.C. 411.

the bank could prove only for the amount of the overdraft at that time, not the whole debt.

**Bankruptcy of Guarantor** It was held in *Re Houlder*[131] that, in the bankruptcy of one of several co-sureties, the creditor could prove for the whole debt. He need give no credit for payments made by other sureties after the date of the bankruptcy (so long as the creditor did not recover more altogether than the amount of the debt).

131. [1929] I Ch. 205.

# Index

# index